THE RIGHTS OF THE ACCUSED UNDER THE SIXTH AMENDMENT

Trials, Presentation of Evidence, and Confrontation

THIRD EDITION

Paul Marcus, David K. Duncan,
Tommy Miller, and Joëlle Anne Moreno

ABA AMERICAN BAR ASSOCIATION
Criminal Justice Section

Cover design by Jill Tedhams/ABA Design

Printed in the United States of America.

25 24 23 22 21   5 4 3 2 1

A catalog record for this book is available from the Library of Congress.

Discounts are available for books ordered in bulk. Special consideration is given to state bars, CLE programs, and other bar-related organizations. Inquire at Book Publishing, ABA Publishing, American Bar Association, 321 N. Clark Street, Chicago, Illinois 60654-7598.

www.ShopABA.org

CONTENTS

ABOUT THE AUTHORS

Paul Marcus (co-author and editor) is the Haynes Professor of Law at the College of William and Mary. Formerly the law dean at the University of Arizona, his teaching and research interests are in criminal justice and comparative law. He has spoken to numerous judicial, bar, and university groups in the United States and has taught and lectured in several other nations. He is a graduate of the UCLA School of Law. Prior to going into teaching, Professor Marcus clerked on the United States Court of Appeals for the District of Columbia and practiced law in Los Angeles. He is the author of several books in the criminal justice area and has written numerous articles in the field as well.

David K. Duncan (co-author) retired in 2018 as a United States Magistrate Judge sitting in Phoenix. He is a former chair of the Ninth Circuit Magistrate Judges Executive Board and served on that circuit's Information Technology Committee. Prior to joining the District Court in 2001, he was an Assistant United States Attorney. Before government service, he was a partner in the Phoenix firms of Osborn Maledon, P.A., and Meyer, Hendricks, Victor, Osborn & Maledon, P.C. He attended Brown University and the University of Arizona. He obtained his JD, with high distinction, from the University of Arizona, where he was an editor of the *Arizona Law Review* and a member of The Order of the Coif. He served as a law clerk to the Hon. William D. Browning, U.S. District Judge in Tucson.

Tommy Miller (co-author) served as a United States Magistrate Judge for the Eastern District of Virginia from 1987 to 2015. He is also an adjunct professor of law at the College of William and Mary, teaching both criminal and civil courses. Judge Miller served on the Advisory Committee on Criminal Rules and participated in the restyling of the Federal Rules of Criminal Procedure. He has spoken to many judicial and bar groups and was a member of the Federal Judicial Center's Magistrate Judge Education Committee. Prior to becoming a judge, he was the Deputy Chief of the Criminal Division for the U.S. Attorney's Office in the Eastern District of Virginia. He graduated from the College of William and Mary Law School.

Joëlle Anne Moreno (co-author) is a professor of law at Florida International University. A former federal prosecutor at the United States Department of Justice, her work focuses on the constitutional constraints on the police (including the future of the Confrontation Clause) and the misuse of pseudoscientific evidence by courts (including childhood vaccine claims and specious defenses to child abuse cases). She has presented her work to judges, academics, and practitioners at numerous legal, medical, and scientific conferences around the world. Professor Moreno is a graduate of the University of Pennsylvania Law School and Swarthmore College, and perhaps most importantly to a native New Yorker, Stuyvesant High School.

ACKNOWLEDGMENTS

The authors wish to express their deep appreciation to Felicia Burton, Director of the Faculty and Academic Support Center, William & Mary Law School. Her outstanding support made this book possible.

With thanks to the excellent law students at the College of William and Mary for their fine research support.

—Paul Marcus

I am most grateful for the support of my co-authors and for the keen assistance of Laura Clymer when she was a student at the Sandra Day O'Connor Arizona State University College of Law.

—David Duncan

To my students at the College of William and Mary Law School who have taught me more than they know. I especially wish to thank those students and my law clerks that assisted me with this project.

—Tommy Miller

And, especially . . . in memory of Professor Francisco José Moreno, a lifelong intellectual who managed to never take himself too seriously. With love from his daughter Joëlle.

—Joëlle Moreno

PREFACE

The Sixth Amendment to the United States Constitution deserves a book devoted to those key provisions that impact mightily on defendants in criminal prosecutions.[1] This was the conclusion of the ABA board members and editors who approached the four of us to write this book. We come from different backgrounds (private practice of law, former prosecutors, academics, jurists) and from different parts of the nation. The four of us, however, were in agreement that such a book was necessary and could provide a genuine service to judges, academics, and lawyers working in the field. In the almost two years needed to complete the first edition of this work, we became increasingly convinced of the value of our project as we explored the wide range of essential criminal justice topics that fall within the scope of the Sixth Amendment:

The Right to a Speedy Trial requires the practitioner to look at history—both colonial and English—to comprehend the significance and evolution of this right throughout our time as an independent nation. To fully understand the scope and application of the speedy trial right, one must also examine the overlapping state and federal statutory schemes, the reach of the constitutional provision, and the state and federal rules of criminal procedure. The United States Supreme Court has weighed in on the defendant's right to a speedy trial in a number of major decisions, including the leading case of *Barker v. Wingo*. While the justices have focused primarily on the language and meaning of the Sixth Amendment, analyses from other courts include consideration of the Due Process Clause as well as a number of statutes of limitation.

1. A book about the Sixth Amendment will almost immediately conjure up visions of the right to counsel, and *Gideon v. Wainwright*. Quite properly so, as the counsel right is a vital component of the amendment and has occupied lawyers and judges for over five decades. As any criminal justice professional knows, however, it is not the only essential protection provided to the accused by the Sixth Amendment. The right to counsel has such a rich and complex history that it merits its own book and, therefore, this book does not include *Gideon* and the right to counsel.

The Right to a Public Trial occupies a central role in our longstanding effort to ensure fairness in the criminal justice system and the process of charging and trying a criminal defendant. If the government wishes to convict any citizen of a crime, it must do so in the open, allowing all to view the process of the prosecution. Yet, for much of our history it was not clear who held this right. Did it belong to the public, to the media, or to the accused? Chapter 2 of the book answers those questions. It also addresses the complicated issues surrounding the closure of trial proceedings and the related determination of which rules govern the closure of pretrial proceedings.

The Right to a Jury Trial has significant historical roots both in our country and in England. We have always viewed the right to be tried before one's peers as essential to our system of criminal justice. Still, numerous questions have arisen as to the application of this right. The distinction between petty and nonpetty offenses remains important today, as do issues surrounding the deadlocked jury, the size and composition of juries, and the application of the right to nontraditional criminal matters such as juvenile proceedings and deportation actions. *Apprendi v. New Jersey* and its successor decisions have recognized the right in new areas, such as sentencing. In the context of jury composition, the Supreme Court's *Batson* decision has led to a wealth of litigation designed to eliminate the use of peremptory challenges for forbidden, discriminatory purposes.

The Place of Prosecution provision is the only section specifically mentioned twice in the Constitution. On its face, the right might seem fairly obvious. The defendant can only be tried where she lives, or where she committed her offense. In practice, however, the problems created by this provision—and their myriad solutions—are far from obvious. A variety of issues may arise when the government seeks to establish venue, or when the defendant attempts to change venue. The Supreme Court has also decided a number of important cases involving change of venue claims based on undue pretrial publicity including the famous decision in *Sheppard v. Maxwell*. Practice matters that complicate the constitutional analysis include the application of the Federal Rules of Criminal Procedure, waiver by the defendant, and determinations involving multiple jurisdiction crimes.

The Right to Be Informed of the Nature and Cause of the Accusations encompasses a range of significant and complex practical and constitutional concerns. The prosecutor must initially determine which accusatory instrument is required and appropriate. Does he move forward with an indictment, an information, or a complaint? Especially in state prosecutions, the answer may not be obvious, as numerous state statutes and state constitutional provisions may be applicable. Serious questions also can be raised with the involvement of the grand jury. Moreover, numerous practice issues are implicated including waiver of rights, sufficiency of the indictment, claims of duplicity or multiplicity, and requests for bills of particulars.

The Confrontation Clause has been an important component of criminal trials throughout our legal history, but the United States Supreme Court paid little attention to it until fairly recently. Over the past five decades, the Court has incorporated the right against the states, emphasized the importance of effective cross-examination by the accused, and explored the complexities of multi-defendant trials and co-defendant confessions. However, only very recently have the justices focused on the language and history of the provision to determine the admissibility of out-of-court statements made by prosecution-sponsored witnesses including expert and child witnesses or the forfeiture of the right. The Confrontation Clause has been the most robust area of new Sixth Amendment jurisprudence. Recent developments articulated by the Court in *Williams v. Illinois, Bullcoming v. New Mexico, Michigan v. Bryant, Giles v. California, Melendez-Diaz v. Massachusetts, Davis v. Washington, Crawford v. Washington,* and *Ohio v. Clark* are all discussed in depth.

The Compulsory Process Clause guarantees the defendant's right to obtain witnesses on his behalf. The history of compulsory process reveals a dramatic shift in the way this provision has been viewed over the centuries, resulting in far greater protections for the accused. Still, the most important action of the Supreme Court remains the decisive opinion written 200 years ago by Chief Justice John Marshall in the prosecution of Aaron Burr. Modern disputes generally focus on interference with the right by the prosecution, the application of the right as to confidential informants, and the role of use immunity.

CHAPTER 1

The Right to a Speedy Trial

I. Historical Basis

The right to a speedy trial developed from English law. The colonies adopted the speedy trial right in their charters and other fundamental documents.[1] In *Klopfer v. North Carolina*, Chief Justice Warren succinctly traced the maturity of the right[2] from the Assize of Clarendon (1166) through the Magna Carta (1215).[3] Using Sir Edward Coke's analysis of the English speedy trial right, he equated the delay of a trial to a denial of justice.[4] "The history of the right to a speedy trial and its reception in this country clearly establish that it is one of the most basic rights preserved by our Constitution."[5]

By the time the Supreme Court decided *Klopfer* in 1967, all fifty states provided speedy trial protection for their citizens.[6] Thus, the *Klopfer* Court held that the Sixth Amendment[7] right to a speedy trial was incorporated through the Fourteenth Amendment,[8] and applied in full force to the states.[9] Since the vast majority of criminal cases are

1. Klopfer v. North Carolina, 386 U.S. 213, 225–26 & nn.15–21 (1967).

2. *Id.* at 226.

3. "We will sell to no man, we will not deny or defer to any man either justice or right." *Id.* at 223 (quoting the Magna Carta).

4. *Id.* at 224.

5. *Id. at 226.*

6. *Id.*

7. "In all criminal prosecutions, the accused shall enjoy the right to a speedy and public trial, by an impartial jury of the State and district wherein the crime shall have been committed[.]" U.S. Const. amend. VI.

8. "[N]or shall any state deprive any person of life, liberty, or property, without due process of law[.]" U.S. Const. amend. XIV, § 1.

9. *Klopfer*, 386 U.S. at 222–23. In earlier cases, the Court held that the other provisions of the Sixth Amendment—the right to counsel and the right of confrontation—were incorporated through the Fourteenth Amendment. Seeing the right to a speedy trial just

prosecuted in the state systems, speedy trial violations will most likely occur in state, not federal, court.[10]

II. Constitutional Speedy Trial Issues

The Sixth Amendment provides that "[i]n all criminal prosecutions, the accused shall enjoy the right to a speedy and public trial, by an impartial jury of the State and district wherein the crime shall have been committed."[11] The Supreme Court has applied the constitutional requirement of a "speedy trial" differently depending on the stage of the proceedings when the delay occurred.

A. Delay in Charging or Arresting the Defendant

1. Process Applies

In 1971, shortly after the speedy trial right was incorporated to apply to the states, in *United States v. Marion*[12] the Court determined that the Sixth Amendment right to a speedy trial did not apply before a defendant was charged or arrested.[13] The defendants in *Marion* filed motions to dismiss the indictment because a delay of three years between the government's discovery of the crime and the indictment violated their Sixth Amendment speedy trial right and Fifth Amendment[14] due process rights.[15] The district court dismissed the indictment based on the government's failure to speedily prosecute.[16]

The Court focused on the speedy trial language of the Sixth Amendment and determined that, on its face, the clause protects only a defendant who is "accused" and exists only when a prosecution has

---

as "fundamental" as the other two rights, Chief Justice Warren concluded that the right to a speedy trial should likewise be incorporated. *See* SUSAN N. HERMAN, THE RIGHT TO A SPEEDY AND PUBLIC TRIAL: A REFERENCE GUIDE TO THE UNITED STATES CONSTITUTION 175 (2006).

10. U.S. DEP'T OF JUSTICE, BUREAU OF JUSTICE STATISTICS, FELONY SENTENCES IN STATE COURTS, 2006 STATISTICAL TABLES (rev. Nov. 22, 2010), tbl. 11.6 (noting that in 2006, there were 1,132,290 state felony convictions, in contrast with 72,983 federal felony convictions).

11. U.S. CONST. amend. VI.

12. United States v. Marion, 404 U.S. 307 (1971).

13. *Id.* at 313.

14. "No person shall be held to answer for a capital, or otherwise infamous crime, . . . nor be deprived of life, liberty, or property, without due process of law." U.S. CONST. amend V.

15. HERMAN, *supra* note 9, at 187; ROBERT L. MISNER, SPEEDY TRIAL: FEDERAL AND STATE PRACTICE 13 (1983).

16. *Marion*, 404 U.S. at 310.

begun.[17] The Court found no support in the English common law for Marion's argument that the Sixth Amendment right applied prior to the arrest of a defendant.[18] The Court also examined Federal Rule of Criminal Procedure 48(b) and determined that the criminal rules permitted dismissal only after a defendant was arrested.[19]

Marion affirmed that the statutes of limitation, and not the defendant's right to a speedy trial, protect against the prosecution of overly stale criminal charges.[20] The justices noted that the statutes of limitation provide a fixed period of time after the criminal act in which a criminal case may be prosecuted.[21] This limitation protects individuals from defending themselves against, and being punished for, charges based on acts committed long ago.[22] The Court suggested that the statutes of limitation may also encourage law enforcement to promptly investigate criminal activity.[23]

Marion also claimed that potential prejudice and the passage of time violated his due process rights.[24] The government conceded that if preindictment delay caused substantial prejudice to the defendant and the delay was intended by the government to gain a tactical advantage over the defendant, the Due Process Clause of the Fifth Amendment required dismissal of the indictment.[25] The Court found that Marion did not prove this type of violation because he had not offered evidence of actual prejudice caused by the preindictment delay or an intentional delay by the government designed to gain an unfair advantage.[26]

Four years later, in *Dillingham v. United States*, the Supreme Court, in a per curiam opinion, clarified that speedy trial rights attach before

---

17. *Id.* at 313 ("[T]he Sixth Amendment speedy trial provision has no application until the putative defendant in some way becomes an 'accused.'").

18. *Id.* at 314–15 & n.6. The Court stated that cases cited by Marion "fail[ed] to establish a definite rule that the Founders sought to constitutionalize," and found the Government's argument regarding the history of the Sixth Amendment to be "more persuasive." *Id.* at 314 n.6.

19. *Id.* at 319. Current Rule 48(b) provides that "[t]he court may dismiss an indictment, information, or complaint if unnecessary delay occurs in: (1) presenting a charge to a grand jury; (2) filing an information against a defendant; or (3) bringing a defendant to trial." FED. R. CRIM. P. 48(b).

20. *Marion*, 404 U.S. at 322.

21. *Id.* at 323 (quoting Toussie v. United States, 397 U.S. 112, 114–15 (1970)).

22. *Id.*

23. *Id.*

24. *Id.* at 324.

25. *Id.*; *see also* HERMAN, *supra* note 9, at 187–88.

26. *Marion*, 404 U.S. at 325–26.

indictment (or issuance of other formal charges) at the time of arrest.[27] The decision in *Dillingham* is notable because the Court's conclusion is inconsistent with prior determination that other Sixth Amendment rights, such as right to counsel, apply only at the time of commencement of formal judicial proceedings and not at arrest.[28] Although the *Dillingham* Court failed to address the doctrinal distinction, one commentator has opined that the speedy trial right applies regardless of whether there is a trial, but other Sixth Amendment rights apply during judicial proceedings.[29]

The Court was presented with a preindictment due process claim based on a delay of indictment in *United States v. Lovasco*.[30] The criminal offenses occurred between July 25 and August 31, 1973. Within a month, postal inspectors presented a report to the U.S. Attorney's Office, but the U.S. Attorney did not initiate a prosecution for seventeen months.[31] The government stipulated that little additional information was developed in the seventeen months after receiving the report[32] and the defendant testified at the district court hearing that his case was prejudiced by the deaths of two material witnesses, one who sold guns to the defendant and the other who witnessed the sales of all of the guns.[33] The defendant, however, failed to explain how these witnesses would have helped his case.[34] The government offered no explanation for the delay, but disagreed that the investigation had ended at the time of the completion of the postal inspector's report.[35]

The Court adopted a rule, hinted at in *Marion*, that a motion to dismiss based on a violation of due process caused by preindictment or prearrest delay involves a two-prong test, requiring an examination of (1) proof of prejudice to the defendant and (2) any explanation

---

27. Dillingham v. United States, 423 U.S. 64, 65 (1975).

28. United States v. Gouveia, 467 U.S. 180, 190 (1984) (holding that the speedy trial right protects an accused's liberty interest, minimizes pretrial incarcerations and restrictions on liberty while on bail, and shortens the disruption of life caused by arrest and pending charges, while the right to counsel protects a defendant during trial-like proceedings.). *See also* HERMAN, *supra* note 9, at 189.

29. As stated in *Brewer v. Williams*, 430 U.S. 387, 398 (1977), the right to counsel begins "at or after the time that judicial proceedings have been initiated." *See also* Massiah v. United States, 377 U.S. 201, 205 (1964) (holding that a defendant has a right to counsel in connection with police interrogation as soon as he is arraigned).

30. United States v. Lovasco, 431 U.S. 783 (1977).

31. *Id.* at 784–85; *see also* HERMAN, *supra* note 9, at 189.

32. *Lovasco*, 431 U.S. at 785.

33. *Id.*

34. *Id.* at 786.

35. *Id.*

for the delay.[36] The opinion focused on the government's explanation for the delay. According to the Court, a defendant's due process rights are not violated when the government establishes that the reason for the delay was that it was continuing the case for further investigation. Even though the defendant was somewhat prejudiced by the lapse of time, his due process rights were not violated.[37]

The *Lovasco* Court also noted that prosecutors are not required to seek an indictment as soon as probable cause exists.[38] They may develop the case to a point where they are satisfied that they have evidence to prove the case beyond a reasonable doubt.[39] Neither law enforcement nor defendants nor the courts are well served if there is a mandate to charge as soon as probable cause is found.[40] Requiring a prosecutor to charge a defendant as soon as proof beyond a reasonable doubt is established against a defendant on one charge would disrupt the normal investigative process.[41] Otherwise, a defendant may be indicted before charges against others are mature, or before evidence of other illegal acts by the defendant are ready for prosecution.[42] Such a rule, moreover, could prevent the prosecutor from giving full consideration to not prosecuting in a particular case.[43]

No due process violation was found by the Court on the facts presented in *Lovasco*.[44] Because so few cases had been decided in the lower courts, these courts had not had the opportunity to sufficiently examine the constitutional reasons for delay.[45] The lower courts are left with the task of applying the particular facts to "the settled principles of due process," according to *Lovasco*.[46]

---

36. *Id.* at 790; *see also* HERMAN, *supra* note 9, at 189–90 (detailing the two-prong test).

37. *Lovasco*, 431 U.S. at 796 (holding that an "investigative delay" undertaken by the government is "fundamentally unlike delay undertaken 'to gain tactical advantage over the accused,'" which was prohibited by the Court in *Marion*); *see also* HERMAN, *supra* note 9, at 190.

38. *Lovasco*, 431 U.S. at 791.

39. *Id.*

40. *Id.* at 791–92; *see* HERMAN, *supra* note 9, at 190 (encouraging premature prosecution would require courts to expend scarce resources on "insubstantial or incomplete" prosecutions).

41. *Lovasco*, 431 U.S. at 792.

42. *Id.* at 792–93; see also United States v. Lively, 852 F.3d 549, 567 (6th Cir. 2017) (the defendant failed to present evidence that the government intentionally delayed indictment in this multiple-jurisdiction and multiple-defendant case).

43. *Id.* at 794.

44. *Id.* at 796.

45. *Id.* at 796–97.

46. *Id.* at 797.

2. *Statutes of Limitation*

Statutes of limitation are creations of both the federal and state legislatures, and vary among the jurisdictions. For example, the general statute of limitations for violent felonies ranges from seven years to fifteen years depending on the state,[47] while the statute of limitations is five years for noncapital federal crimes.[48]

On rare occasions, the circumstances of the crime can extend the statutory period. For example, acts of terrorism usually have an eight-year statute of limitations, but the period is increased if the offense results in, or creates a foreseeable risk of, death or serious bodily injury.[49] And, in most jurisdictions, there is no time limit for the prosecution of a capital offense.[50]

Statutes of limitation are located in the codebooks of the various jurisdictions. The previous examples demonstrate that care must be taken to consider all potentially applicable statutes to ensure that an exception does not apply to a particular crime.

B. Postcharge or Postarrest Delay

The Supreme Court held in *Barker v. Wingo*[51] that four main factors should be considered when analyzing a speedy trial issue raised by one who has been accused of a crime: (1) the length of the delay, (2) the reason for the delay, (3) the demand of the right to a speedy trial by the defendant, and (4) whether the delay has resulted in prejudice to the defendant.[52] These four factors, the Court held, should be applied to the fact-specific circumstances of each allegation of a speedy trial violation.[53]

1. *Length of Delay*

The actual length of the delay of a trial is the threshold factor in determining whether a case should be reviewed in light of the speedy trial clause.[54] Substantial delay, amounting to a presumptively

---

47. *See, e.g.*, ARIZ. REV. STAT. § 13–107 (seven years); GA. CRIM. CODE § 17–3-1 (fifteen years).
48. 18 U.S.C. § 3282(a).
49. 18 U.S.C. § 3286 (2006).
50. *See, e.g.*, 18 U.S.C. § 328; FLA. STAT. § 775.15; OKLA. STAT. ANN. tit. 22, §§ 151–153.
51. Barker v. Wingo, 407 U.S. 514 (1972).
52. *Id.* at 530.
53. *Id.*
54. *Id.*

prejudicial effect upon the defendant, must be shown in order for the balancing test to continue beyond this first step.[55] The Supreme Court noted that the lower courts have found postaccusation delay "presumptively prejudicial" as the length of the delay approaches one year.[56]

2. Reason for Delay

If there has been a substantial delay, the prosecution's reason for the delay becomes important.[57] Any deliberate attempt to delay the trial should weigh greatly against the prosecution.[58] If the government's negligence is the reason for the delay, the delay is weighed less heavily but still held against the government.[59] However, where the prosecution has a legitimate reason for delaying the trial, such as the illness of a witness, the delay is justified, and the case will not be dismissed on speedy trial grounds.[60]

3. Demand by Defendant

The third factor incorporates the defendant's responsibility to promptly assert his Sixth Amendment right.[61] That is, if a defendant fails to object to a delay on the grounds of a speedy trial violation, it is assumed that the defendant is not seeking a speedy trial.[62] Such a situation typically arises when a defendant attempts to strategically

---

55. *Id.* A number of states have sought to define clearly the application of this principle. Ohio is a prominent example. *See, e.g.*, State v. Selvage, 687 N.E.2d 433 (Ohio 1997).

56. Doggett v. United States, 505 U.S. 647, 652 n.1 (1992); *see also* United States v. Irizarry-Colon, 848 F.3d 61, 70 (1st Cir. 2017) (when there are superseding indictments, the length of delay is calculated from the first indictment for speedy trial clause purposes).

57. *Wingo*, 407 U.S. 514, 531 (1972).

58. *Id.* The Supreme Court of Louisiana found that '[t]he majority of the seven-year delay was caused by the 'lack of funding.'" State v. Boyer, 56 So.3d 1119, 1142 (2011). The United States Supreme granted certiorari to consider whether such a delay should weigh against the State. Boyer v. State, 133 S. Ct. 420 (2012). After argument the Court dismissed the writ of certiorari as improvidently granted. 133 S. Ct. 1702 (2013). Four justices would have decided the case to determine whether a state's failure to fund a defense should weigh against the State. *Id.* at 1704. In times of tight state budgets, this issue may be ripe for further litigation.

59. *Id.; see also* United States v. Ferreira, 665 F.3d 701, 707–08 (6th Cir. 2011).

60. *Barker*, 407 U.S. at 517. "A court must weigh whether the government needed time to collect witnesses, file pretrial motions, track down the accused, and otherwise prepare for trial." State v. Sears, 849 N.E.2d 1060, 1063 (Ohio 2005).

61. *Barker*, 407 U.S. at 528.

62. *Id.* at 531–32; *see also* State v. Rachie, 427 N.W.2d 253, 257 (Minn. Ct. App. 1988).

delay the trial—even though such a delay may actually result in less-convincing witness testimony or a dissipation of evidence prior to the start of the trial—and later raises a speedy trial claim.[63] On the other hand, if a defendant repeatedly and vigorously demands a speedy trial, the government is alerted that a speedy trial issue will be present throughout the case.[64]

4. Prejudice to the Defendant

The final, and likely most significant,[65] factor considers whether the defendant has been prejudiced. Here, the court should assess three potential sources of prejudice: (1) oppressive pretrial incarceration, (2) unnecessary anxiety and concern of the accused, and (3) the possibility that the defense will be impaired by the delay.[66] If the defendant has suffered little or no real prejudice, there is no speedy trial violation.[67]

After engaging in this balancing test, the *Barker* Court affirmed the defendant's conviction, finding that the defendant had not been denied his Sixth Amendment right to a speedy trial.[68]

C. Delay in Sentencing and Supervised Release Violations

In 2016, the Supreme Court decided that the time period between conviction and sentence was not subject to the protection of the speedy trial clause.[69] The Court ruled that the speedy trial clause applied only to the time between arrest or indictment through conviction.[70] Instead of the speedy trial clause, the Due Process Clauses of the Fifth and Fourteenth Amendments provide constitutional protection against excessive delays.[71]

---

63. *Barker*, 407 U.S. at 527 n.25; *see also* United States v. Black, 830 F.3d 1099, 1122–1223 (10th Cir. 2016) (defendant did not forcefully demand a speedy trial and contributed to much of the delay by filing motions unrelated to the main charge).

64. United States v. Tigano, 880 F.3d 602, 617 (2d Cir. 2018).

65. State v. Recor, 549 A.2d 1382, 1385 (Vt. 1988) (noting that prejudice is "the most important consideration").

66. *Barker*, 407 U.S. at 532.

67. *Id.* at 534.

68. *Id.* at 536; Wilson v. State, ___ So. 3d ___, 2020 WL 7382048 (Ala. Crim. App. 2020), is an example of an appellate court approving 94- and 97-month speedy trial delays.

69. Betterman v. Montana, 578 U.S. ____, 136 S. Ct. 1609, 1613 (2016).

70. *Id.*

71. *Id.* at 1617.

Predating but in agreement with the reasoning in Betterman, the Ninth Circuit held that the speedy trial clause does not apply to supervised release violation hearings, since the hearings were not a separate criminal prosecution or an extension of the original trial.[72]

D. Delay in Appeals

The Supreme Court has not addressed the application of the Sixth Amendment to delays in deciding appeals. Most courts have relied upon the Due Process Clauses of the Fifth and Fourteenth Amendments to determine whether a defendant's rights have been violated by a delayed appeal.[73]

Using the due process test, the defendant must show actual prejudice to support a motion to dismiss for appellate delay; once again, the court will consider the length of the delay, reasons for the delay, whether the reasons justified the delay, and whether the defendant asserted his right to a timely appeal.[74] If the defendant loses the appeal, then any presumption of prejudice caused by a delay is rebutted, and no due process violation can be found.[75] The remedy for a delayed appeal is ordinarily not dismissal of the indictment, but directing the appeal to be heard.[76]

E. Sanctions for a Constitutional Violation of the Speedy Trial Right

One year after *Barker*, the question of the proper remedy for a violation of a defendant's speedy trial right was presented. In *United States v. Strunk*,[77] the appeals court wrote that the traditional remedy for a violation of the Sixth Amendment speedy trial right was dismissal of the indictment.[78] However, the judges decided to create a different remedy for the defendant. His conviction was affirmed, but the court ordered that the time period from indictment to arraignment be subtracted from his federal sentence.[79]

---

72. United States v. Gavilanes-Ocaranza, 772 F.3d 624, 628 (9th Cir. 2014).

73. United States v. Smith, 94 F.3d 204 (6th Cir. 1996) (holding that the Sixth Amendment speedy trial right applies only in trial court); United States v. Hawkins, 78 F.3d 348 (8th Cir. 1996).

74. United States v. Wiktor, 146 F.3d 815, 819 (10th Cir. 1998).

75. *Id.*

76. *Id.* at 815.

77. 467 F.2d 969 (7th Cir. 1973).

78. *Id.* at 972.

79. *Id.* at 973.

The Supreme Court granted the petition for certiorari to consider whether, where a court finds a speedy trial violation, the only remedy is dismissal of the indictment.[80] The Supreme Court rejected the flexible remedy approach adopted by the intermediate court, holding that the dismissal of charges with prejudice was the only remedy that could support the policies behind the right to a speedy trial.[81] The opinion explained:

> [S]uch denial is unlike some of the other guarantees of the Sixth Amendment. For example, failure to afford a public trial, an impartial jury, notice of charges, or compulsory service can ordinarily be cured by providing those guaranteed rights in a new trial. The speedy trial guarantee recognizes that a prolonged delay may subject the accused to an emotional stress that can be presumed to result in the ordinary person from uncertainties in the prospect of facing public trial or of receiving a sentence longer than, or consecutive to, the one he is presently serving—uncertainties that a prompt trial removes. . . . The remedy chosen by the Court of Appeals does not deal with these difficulties.[82]
>
> The Government's reliance on *Barker* to support the remedy fashioned by the Court of Appeals is further undermined when we examine the Court's opinion in that case as a whole. It is true that *Barker* described dismissal of an indictment for denial of a speedy trial as an "unsatisfactorily severe remedy."[83] Indeed, in practice, "it means that a defendant who may be guilty of a serious crime will go free, without having been tried."[84] But such severe remedies are not unique in the application of constitutional standards.
>
> In light of the policies which underlie the right to a speedy trial, dismissal must remain, as *Barker* noted, "the only possible remedy."[85]

---

80. Strunk v. United States, 412 U.S. 434, 436 (1973).
81. *Id.* at 439–40.
82. *Id.*
83. *Id.* at 439.
84. *Id.*
85. *Id.* at 440.

III. Dismissals Pursuant to Federal Rule of Criminal Procedure 48

A. History of Rule

Federal Rule of Criminal Procedure 48 was adopted in 1944, predating *Barker v. Wingo* and the Speedy Trial Act by almost thirty years.[86] When adopted, Rule 48(a) required the government to receive leave of court before the dismissal of a criminal charge and prohibited the government from dismissing the prosecution during the trial without the defendant's consent.[87] Rule 48(b) applied to delays in the prosecution of a defendant.

B. Dismissal under Federal Rule of Criminal Procedure 48(b)

The language of Rule 48(b),[88] as well as the Supreme Court's comment on the rule in *Marion*, establishes that the rule is applicable only to postarrest situations.[89] The purpose of Rule 48(b) is to enforce the Sixth Amendment right to a speedy trial.[90] Rule 48(b) lost much of its utility after the Supreme Court decided *Barker* and once the Speedy Trial Act became fully effective in 1980.[91] Most of the cases decided under this rule predate the Speedy Trial Act.[92]

After the *Barker* decision and the implementation of the Speedy Trial Act, one appellate court decided that if the district court found that a defendant's speedy trial right was not violated by the delay between indictment and trial, then the district court need not review a motion for dismissal under Rule 48(b) for unnecessary delay.[93] If Rule 48(b) is relied upon to dismiss an indictment for unnecessary delay, but that delay does not amount to a constitutional violation, the dismissal is without prejudice, unless the court specifically states that the dismissal is with prejudice.[94] Some courts have held that a

---

86. Fed. R. Crim. P. 48 Advisory Committee Notes (1944).

87. *Id.*

88. "The Court may dismiss an indictment, information, or complaint if unnecessary delay occurs in: (1) presenting a charge to a grand jury; [or] (2) filing an information against a defendant; [or] (3) bringing a defendant to trial." *Id.* 48(b).

89. *Marion*, 404 U.S. 307, 319 (1971).

90. *Pollard*, 352 U.S. 354, 361 (1957).

91. Wright, King & Klein, Federal Practice and Procedure: Criminal 814 (3d ed. 2004).

92. *Id.*

93. United States v. Dunn, 345 F.3d 1285, 1297 (11th Cir. 2003).

94. United States v. Stoker, 522 F.2d 576, 580 (10th Cir. 1975).

dismissal under Rule 48(b) cannot be made with prejudice, unless the government had been warned of this severe consequence.[95]

Defense counsel filing a motion to dismiss under the Sixth Amendment speedy trial provisions of the Speedy Trial Act should consider including a motion to dismiss under Rule 48(b) for unnecessary delay. Some courts have held that Rule 48(b) imposes a stricter standard of tolerable delay than does the Sixth Amendment.[96] Further, the power to dismiss under Rule 48(b) must be more expansive than under the Sixth Amendment, or otherwise the power would be superfluous.[97]

IV. Federal Speedy Trial Act

Two years after *Barker v. Wingo* was decided, the Speedy Trial Act of 1974 was passed by Congress to put teeth in the defendant's speedy trial rights, and out of dissatisfaction with speedy trial jurisprudence.[98] Senator Sam Ervin, the Act's chief sponsor, explained the policy behind the Act as follows: "[T]he courts, undermanned, starved for funds, and utilizing 18th century management techniques, simply cannot cope with burgeoning caseloads. The consequence is delay and '[t]he solution is to create initiative within the system to utilize modern management techniques.'"[99]

The Act established temporary time limitations to give the courts an opportunity to prepare for the severe time limits, which went into effect in July 1980.[100] As originally enacted, from July 1, 1975, to July 1, 1979, trials of all defendants detained solely because they were awaiting trial would commence no later than ninety days following the beginning of continuous detention.[101] However, on August 2, 1979, the effective date of the Act was postponed to July 1, 1980, extending the temporary time limitations by one year.[102] After July 1, 1980, the Act required that criminal defendants be tried within 100 days after arrest or service of summons, with the exclusion of certain limited periods of delay.[103] Despite the requirements

---

95. United States v. Loud Hawk, 628 F.2d 1139, 1149–51 (9th Cir. 1979).

96. *See, e.g.*, United States v. Zabady, 546 F. Supp. 35, 38 (M.D. Pa. 1982); United States v. Rowbotham, 430 F. Supp. 1254, 1256 (D. Mass. 1977).

97. United States v. McLemore, 447 F. Supp. 1229, 1237 (E.D. Mich. 1978).

98. *See* United States v. Mehrmanesh, 652 F.2d 766, 769 (9th Cir. 1981).

99. *See* Herman, *supra* note 9, at 205.

100. 18 U.S.C. § 3163(c) (2012).

101. Misner, *supra* note 15, at 208 (citing 18 U.S.C. § 3164(b) (supp. IV 1974)).

102. Pub. L. No. 96–43, § 6, 93 Stat. 328 (1979).

103. Misner, *supra* note 15, at 208 (citing 18 U.S.C. § 3161 (supp. IV 1974)); Pub. L. No. 96–43, § 6, 93 Stat. 328 (1979) (postponing enactment from July 1, 1979 to July 1, 1980).

of the Speedy Trial Act, there is a wide variance among the district courts in the time to dispose of criminal cases. For example, for the twelve-month period ending March 30, 2020, the median time for disposition of criminal cases ranged from 1.3 months in New Mexico to 20.6 months in the Eastern District of New York.[104] Lastly, the Act created experimental pretrial service agencies in ten selected districts to provide support and supervisory services to noncustodial defendants awaiting trial.[105]

A. General Time Limitations

The current Speedy Trial Act has the goal of trying individuals within 100 days after their arrest.[106] The Act delineates several general time limitations. The Act commands that indictments be filed within thirty days of arrest or summons, allowing for a thirty-day extension if there has been no grand jury in session in the first thirty-day period.[107] Further, trial must begin within seventy days from the date the indictment was filed, or from when the date the defendant "has appeared before a judicial officer of the court," whichever is later.[108] In addition, unless the defendant consents to the contrary, trial may not begin within

---

104. It appears that the culture of the legal community contributes greatly to the variance, since a study of the statistics shows little relationship between the caseload of the district and the speed of disposition. *See* UNITED STATES COURTS, FEDERAL COURT MANAGEMENT STATISTICS, http://www.uscourts.gov/Statistics/FederalCourtManagement Statistics/FederalCourtManagementStatistics_Archive.aspx (last visited Aug. 22, 2020).

105. MISNER, *supra* note 15, at 208 (citing 18 U.S.C. §§ 3152–3155 (supp. IV 1974)).

106. *Id.* at 209.

107. 18 U.S.C. § 3161(b) (2006) (effective Oct. 13, 2008) ("Any information or indictment charging an individual with the commission of an offense shall be filed within thirty days from the date on which such individual was arrested or served with a summons in connection with such charges. If an individual has been charged with a felony in a district in which no grand jury has been in session during such thirty-day period, the period of time for filing the indictment shall be extended an additional thirty days."); *see also* 18 U.S.C. § 3172(2) ("'offense' means any Federal criminal offense which is a violation of any Act of Congress and is triable by any court established by Act of Congress (other than a Class B or C misdemeanor or an infraction, or an offense triable by court-martial, military commission, provost court, or other military tribunal).").

108. *Id.* § 3161(c)(1) ("In any case in which a plea of not guilty is entered, the trial of a defendant charged in an information or indictment with the commission of an offense shall commence within seventy days from the filing date (and making public) of the information or indictment, or from the date the defendant has appeared before a judicial officer of the court in which such charge is pending, whichever date last occurs. If a defendant consents in writing to be tried before a magistrate judge on a complaint, the trial shall commence within seventy days from the date of such consent.").

thirty days of the defendant's first appearance.[109] The Act also requires that a court set the case for trial "at the earliest practicable time" after consulting both sides, so that, when possible, trial is scheduled more quickly than statutory deadlines require.[110]

These time restrictions apply equally to cases where an initial indictment is refiled after having been dismissed or dropped.[111] Case law has interpreted this to mean that a new thirty-day deadline is set from the time of refiling, unlike the judicial interpretation of similar provisions in state codes.[112]

B. Exceptions and Tolling Provisions

Subsection (h) of the Speedy Trial Act provides a nonexclusive list of events that will toll the time periods set out in the previous section.[113] The list includes delays resulting from mental competency and/or physical capacity determinations,[114] incompetence or incapacitation of the defendant,[115] pretrial motions (from filing through disposition),[116]

---

109. *Id.* § 3161(c)(2) ("Unless the defendant consents in writing to the contrary, the trial shall not commence less than thirty days from the date on which the defendant first appears through counsel or expressly waives counsel and elects to proceed pro se."); *see* United States v. Rojas-Contreras, 474 U.S. 231, 236 (1985) (holding that a new thirty-day trial preparation period does not begin from the filing of a superseding indictment).

110. 18 U.S.C. § 3161(a) ("In any case involving a defendant charged with an offense, the appropriate judicial officer, at the earliest practicable time, shall, after consultation with the counsel for the defendant and the attorney for the Government, set the case for trial on a day certain, or list it for trial on a weekly or other short-term trial calendar at a place within the judicial district, so as to assure a speedy trial.").

111. *Id.* § 3161(d)(1) ("If any indictment or information is dismissed upon motion of the defendant, or any charge contained in a complaint filed against an individual is dismissed or otherwise dropped, and thereafter a complaint is filed against such defendant or individual charging him with the same offense or offense based on the same conduct or arising from the same criminal episode, . . . the provisions of subsection (b) and (c) of this section shall be applicable with respect to such subsequent complaint, indictment, or information, as the case may be.").

112. *See, e.g.*, United States v. Myers, 666 F.3d 402 (6th Cir. 2012); United States v. DeJohn, 368 F.3d 533, 539 (6th Cir. 2004).

113. 18 U.S.C. § 3161(h) (2006).

114. *Id.* § 3161(h)(1)(A) ("[D]elay resulting from any proceeding, including any examinations, to determine the mental competency or physical capacity of the defendant [shall be excluded.]").

115. *Id.* § 3161(h)(4) ("Any period of delay resulting from the fact that the defendant is mentally incompetent or physically unable to stand trial [shall be excluded.]"); *see also* United States v. Romero, 833 F.3d 1151, 1155 (9th Cir. 2016) (the Speedy Trial Act requires the exclusion of all time during which a defendant is incompetent to stand trial).

116. *Id.* § 3161(h)(1)(D) ("[D]elay resulting from any pretrial motion, from the filing of the motion through the conclusion of the hearing on, or other prompt disposition of, such

trial on other charges,[117] interlocutory appeal,[118] and consideration of plea agreements.[119]

The clock is tolled for a period of delay resulting from the absence or unavailability of the defendant or a witness.[120] Delay "relating to the transfer of a case or removal of any defendant" from another district is likewise exempted from the calculation of the relevant time period.[121] The Act also tolls the clock in the event that

---

motion [shall be excluded.]"); *see* United States v. Tinklenberg, 131 S. Ct. 2007, 2012–17 (2011) (18 U.S.C. § 3161(h)(1)(D) stops the speedy trial clock automatically upon the filing of a motion regardless of whether the motion has any impact on the trial date).

117. 18 U.S.C. § 3161(h)(1)(B) ("[D]elay resulting from trial with respect to other charges against the defendant [shall be excluded].").

118. *Id.* § 3161(h)(1)(C) ("[D]elay resulting from any interlocutory appeal [shall be excluded.]").

119. *Id.* § 3161(h)(1)(G) ("[D]elay resulting from consideration by the court of a proposed plea agreement to be entered into by the defendant and the attorney for the Government [shall be excluded.]"); *see also* United States v. Sutton, 862 F.3d 547, 554 (6th Cir. 2017) (for speedy trial purposes, the day the defendant withdraws his guilty plea becomes the day of his indictment).

120. *Id.* § 3161(h)(3):

> (A) Any period of delay resulting from the absence or unavailability of the defendant or an essential witness [shall be excluded.].
> (B) For purposes of subparagraph (A) of this paragraph, a defendant or an essential witness shall be considered absent when his whereabouts are unknown and, in addition, he is attempting to avoid apprehension or prosecution or his whereabouts cannot be determined by due diligence. For purposes of such subparagraph, a defendant or an essential witness shall be considered unavailable whenever his whereabouts are known but his presence for trial cannot be obtained by due diligence or he resists appearing at or being returned for trial.

See also id. § 3161(k):

> (1) If the defendant is absent (as defined by subsection (h)(3)) on the day set for trial, and the defendant's subsequent appearance before the court on a bench warrant or other process or surrender to the court occurs more than 21 days after the day set for trial, the defendant shall be deemed to have first appeared before a judicial officer of the court in which the information or indictment is pending within the meaning of subsection (c) on the date of the defendant's subsequent appearance before the court.
> (2) If the defendant is absent (as defined by subsection (h)(3)) on the day set for trial, and the defendant's subsequent appearance before the court on a bench warrant or other process or surrender to the court occurs not more than 21 days after the day set for trial, the time limit required by subsection (c), as extended by subsection (h), shall be further extended by 21 days.

121. *Id.* § 3161(h)(1)(E) ("[D]elay resulting from any proceeding relating to the transfer of a case or the removal of any defendant from another district under the Federal Rules of Criminal Procedure [shall be excluded.]").

prosecution has been deferred to permit the defendant to demonstrate good conduct.[122]

Some delays that are part of the tolling provisions are subject to reasonability requirements or caps. Delays resulting from joinder of a defendant to a codefendant whose clock has not yet run must be "reasonable" to toll the Act's requirements.[123] Delays resulting from transportation of any defendant from another district, or to and from places of examination or hospitalization, are discounted from the relevant time period, but delays over ten days are "presumed to be unreasonable."[124] A catchall provision exempting periods when the court has "any proceeding concerning the defendant" under advisement is subject to a thirty-day cap after the issue is joined.[125] However, an administrative motion which does not require a response or hearing is under advisement at the time the motion is filed and only tolls the speedy trial clock for thirty days.[126] Also, where a finding has been made by a preponderance of the evidence under 18 U.S.C. § 3292 that the evidence of an offense is located in a foreign country, any period of court-ordered delay, not to exceed one year, shall be excluded from the general time limitations.[127]

Finally, under certain limited circumstances, the Act can be tolled when a judge grants a continuance on her own motion, or at the

122. *Id.* § 3161(h)(2) ("Any period of delay during which prosecution is deferred by the attorney for the Government pursuant to written agreement with the defendant, with the approval of the court, for the purpose of allowing the defendant to demonstrate his good conduct [shall be excluded.]").

123. *Id.* § 3161(h)(6) ("A reasonable period of delay when the defendant is joined for trial with a codefendant as to whom the time for trial has not run and no motion for severance has been granted [shall be excluded.]").

124. *Id.* § 3161(h)(1)(F) ("[D]elay resulting from transportation of any defendant from another district, or to and from places of examination or hospitalization [shall be excluded], except that any time consumed in excess of ten days from the date an order of removal or an order directing such transportation, and the defendant's arrival at the destination shall be presumed to be unreasonable."); *see* United States v. Tinklenberg, 131 S. Ct. 2007, 2017 (2011) (the ten-day period in § 3161(h)(1)(F) includes holidays and weekends).

125. *Id.* § 3161(h)(1)(H) ("[D]elay reasonably attributable to any period, not to exceed thirty days, during which any proceeding concerning the defendant is actually under advisement by the court [shall be excluded.]").

126. United States v. Hicks, 779 F.3d 1163, 1172 (10th Cir. 2015).

127. *Id.* § 3161(h)(8) ("Any period of delay, not to exceed one year, ordered by a district court upon an application of a party and a finding by a preponderance of the evidence that an official request, as defined in section 3292 of this title, has been made for evidence of any such offense and that it reasonably appears, or reasonably appeared at the time the request was made, that such evidence is, or was, in such foreign country.").

request of the government or a defendant.[128] For the Act to be tolled, the judge must find that "the ends of justice served by the granting of such continuance outweigh the best interest of the public and the defendant in a speedy trial."[129] The judge must set forth in the record of the case (orally or in writing) the reasoning as to why the balance weighs in favor of the continuance.[130] The Act outlines certain factors that must be considered in determining whether to grant a continuance.[131] These factors include whether failure to continue the case would result in a miscarriage of justice;[132] whether the case is so unusual or so complex that it is unreasonable to expect adequate preparation for pretrial proceedings or trial within the time limits;[133] whether there was delay in filing an indictment following arrest;[134] and whether failure to continue the case would deny the defendant reasonable time to obtain counsel, would deny either party continuity

128. *Id.* § 3161(h)(7)(A) ("Any period of delay resulting from a continuance granted by any judge on his own motion or at the request of the defendant or his counselor at the request of the attorney for the Government, if the judge granted such continuance on the basis of his findings that the ends of justice served by taking such action outweigh the best interest of the public and the defendant in a speedy trial. No such period of delay resulting from a continuance granted by the court in accordance with this paragraph shall be excludable under this subsection unless the court sets forth, in the record of the case, either orally or in writing, its reasons for finding that the ends of justice served by the granting of such continuance outweigh the best interests of the public and the defendant in a speedy trial."); *see* Zedner v. United States, 547 U.S. 489 (2006) (holding that a defendant may not prospectively waive rights under the Speedy Trial Act and a district judge must make an express finding about the ends of justice balance in granting a continuance).

129. 18 U.S.C. § 3161(h)(7)(A).

130. *Id.; see also* United States v. Koerber, 813 F.3d 1262, 1278 (10th Cir. 2016) (if the district court fails to set out its reasons for an ends-of-justice exclusion of a time period, then that time is not excluded from the speedy trial time calculation even if there were sufficient facts and reasons in the record).

131. *Id.* § 3161(h)(7)(B).

132. *Id.* § 3161(h)(7)(B)(i) ("Whether the failure to grant such a continuance in the proceeding would be likely to make a continuation of such proceeding impossible, or result in a miscarriage of justice.").

133. *Id.* § 3161(h)(7)(B)(ii) ("Whether the case is so unusual or so complex, due to the number of defendants, the nature of the prosecution, or the existence of novel questions of fact or law, that it is unreasonable to expect adequate preparation for pretrial proceedings or for the trial itself within the time limits established by this section.").

134. *Id.* § 3161(h)(7)(B)(iii) ("Whether, in a case in which arrest precedes indictment, delay in the filing of the indictment is caused because the arrest occurs at a time such that it is unreasonable to expect return and filing of the indictment within the period specified in section 3161(b), or because the facts upon which the grand jury must base its determination are unusual or complex.").

of counsel, or would deny counsel the reasonable time necessary for effective preparation.[135]

Moreover, for the Act to be tolled, the continuance cannot be granted "because of general congestion of the court's calendar, or lack of diligent preparation or failure to obtain available witnesses on the part of the attorney for the Government."[136]

Finally, subsection (h)(5) of the Speedy Trial Act reiterates that the interval between an indictment's dismissal and refiling is not simply tolled. Instead, the clock begins anew.[137] Similarly, subsection (i) provides that if trial did not commence within the general time limitations outlined in 18 U.S.C. § 3161 because the defendant withdrew a plea of guilty or *nolo contendere*, the defendant shall be deemed indicted, for purposes of the time limitations, on the day the withdrawal of the plea is final.[138]

---

135. *Id.* § 3161(h)(7)(B)(iv) ("Whether the failure to grant such a continuance in a case which, taken as a whole, is not so unusual or so complex as to fall within clause (ii), would deny the defendant reasonable time to obtain counsel, would unreasonably deny the defendant or the Government continuity of counsel, or would deny counsel for the defendant or the attorney for the Government the reasonable time necessary for effective preparation, taking into account the exercise of due diligence."); *see also* United States v. Gonzales-Martinez, 825 F.3d 51, 58 (1st Cir. 2016) (the defendant was not denied counsel when the court conditioned the admission of new counsel on being prepared for the trial as scheduled, particularly since the defendant had two other attorneys at trial who had represented the defendant since the beginning of the case).

136. *Id.* § 3161(h)(7)(C) ("No continuance under subparagraph (A) of this paragraph shall be granted because of general congestion of the court's calendar, or lack of diligent preparation or failure to obtain available witnesses on the part of the attorney for the Government.").

137. *Id.* § 3161(h)(5) ("If the information or indictment is dismissed upon motion of the attorney for the Government and thereafter a charge is filed against the defendant for the same offense, or any offense required to be joined with that offense, any period of delay from the date the charge was dismissed to the date the time limitation would commence to run as to the subsequent charge had there been no previous charge.").

138. *Id.* § 3161(i) ("If trial did not commence within the time limitation specified in section 3161 because the defendant had entered a plea of guilty or nolo contendere subsequently withdrawn to any or all charges in an indictment or information, the defendant shall be deemed indicted with respect to all charges therein contained within the meaning of section 3161, on the day the order permitting withdrawal of the plea becomes final."); *see also* United States v. Sutton, F.3d 547, 554 (6th Cir. 2017) (the day the defendant withdraws his guilty plea becomes the day of his indictment).

C. Sanctions for Violating the Statute

A violation of the Speedy Trial Act results in the dismissal of the complaint.[139] The Act provides that the judge may dismiss the case with or without prejudice.[140] In making that decision, a court must consider three factors: "the seriousness of the offense; the facts and circumstances of the case which led to the dismissal; and the impact of a reprosecution on the administration of . . . justice."[141]

It must be noted that the defendant bears the burden of proof on a motion to dismiss for failure to commence trial within the time limits set out in section 3161(c).[142] However, the government has the burden of going forward with evidence that delay due to the absence or unavailability of the defendant or an essential witness should be excluded from the time computation.[143] Moreover, if the defendant fails to move for dismissal on speedy trial grounds prior to trial or the

---

139. *Id.* § 3162(a):

> (1) If, in the case of any individual against whom a complaint is filed charging such individual with an offense, no indictment or information is filed within the time limit required by section 3161(b) as extended by section 3161(h) of this chapter, such charge against that individual contained in such complaint shall be dismissed or otherwise dropped. In determining whether to dismiss the case with or without prejudice, the court shall consider, among others, each of the following factors: the seriousness of the offense; the facts and circumstances of the case which led to the dismissal; and the impact of a reprosecution on the administration of this chapter and on the administration of justice.
>
> (2) If a defendant is not brought to trial within the time limit required by section 3161(c) as extended by section 3161(h), the information or indictment shall be dismissed on motion of the defendant. The defendant shall have the burden of proof of supporting such motion but the Government shall have the burden of going forward with the evidence in connection with any exclusion of time under subparagraph 3161(h) (3). In determining whether to dismiss the case with or without prejudice, the court shall consider, among others, each of the following factors: the seriousness of the offense; the facts and circumstances of the case which led to the dismissal; and the impact of a reprosecution on the administration of this chapter and on the administration of justice. Failure of the defendant to move for dismissal prior to trial or entry of a plea of guilty or nolo contendere shall constitute a waiver of the right to dismissal under this section.

See generally Martha L. Wood, Note, *Determination of Dismissal Sanctions Under the Speedy Trial Act of 1974*, 56 FORDHAM L. REV. 509 (1987).

140. 18 U.S.C. § 3162(a)(1); *see also* United States v. Stevenson, 832 F.3d 412, 420 (3d Cir. 2016) (heroin and firearm offenses are serious crimes, so it was proper for the district court to find that the first factor should favor dismissal without prejudice).

141. 18 U.S.C. § 3162(a)(1).

142. *Id.* § 3162(a)(2).

143. *Id.*

entry of a plea of guilty or *nolo contendere*, the defendant waives the right to dismiss on these grounds.[144]

The Act also suggests sanctions for attorney misconduct that causes delay,[145] specifically where counsel:

> (1) knowingly allows the case to be set for trial without disclosing the fact that a necessary witness would be unavailable for trial; (2) files a motion solely for the purpose of delay which he knows is totally frivolous and without merit; (3) makes a statement for the purpose of obtaining a continuance which he knows to be false and which is material to the granting of a continuance; or (4) otherwise willfully fails to proceed to trial without justification consistent with section 3161 of this chapter.[146]

While suggesting specific sanctions, the Act provides that the courts retain all other authority to punish misconduct[147] and directs the courts to follow procedures set out in the Federal Rules of Criminal Procedure when punishing counsel for the federal government.[148]

The Act contains provisions related to detainer procedures, where the attorney for the federal government knows a person charged with an offense is already serving a term of imprisonment.[149] These procedures are beyond the scope of this chapter, but see section VI for a discussion of speedy trial requirements in the interstate agreement on detainers.

---

144. *Id.*

145. *Id.* § 3162(b).

146. "[T]he court may punish any such counsel or attorney, as follows: (A) in the case of an appointed defense counsel, by reducing the amount of compensation that otherwise would have been paid to such counsel pursuant to section 3006A of this title in an amount not to exceed 25 per centum thereof; (B) in the case of a counsel retained in connection with the defense of a defendant, by imposing on such counsel a fine of not to exceed 25 per centum of the compensation to which he is entitled in connection with his defense of such defendant; (C) by imposing on any attorney for the Government a fine of not to exceed $250; (D) by denying any such counsel or attorney for the Government the right to practice before the court considering such case for a period of not to exceed ninety days; or (E) by filing a report with an appropriate disciplinary committee. The authority to punish provided for by this subsection shall be in addition to any other authority or power available to such court." *Id.*

147. *Id.*

148. *Id.* § 3162(c) ("The court shall follow procedures established in the Federal Rules of Criminal Procedure in punishing any counsel or attorney for the Government pursuant to this section.").

149. *Id.* § 3161(j).

V. State Speedy Trial Provisions

In the state courts, the right to a speedy trial is protected at several levels. The Sixth Amendment still protects the right, as do most state constitutions.[150] Similar to the federal system, statutes of limitation function to combat unduly long delays in bringing charges.[151] In addition, state rules and state statutes often provide bright line rules to guarantee defendants a speedy trial. These multiple sources often overlap in their protection of the right to speedy trial, creating coextensive rights and protections that will be analyzed the same way. However, in some jurisdictions the protections offered by the state constitutional clause may differ from that of the U.S. Constitution or the state statute, necessitating a separate method of determining violations of the right.[152]

A. State Constitutional Provisions

All states are bound to incorporate the Sixth Amendment's protection of the right to a speedy trial.[153] The seminal case, as mentioned earlier, is *Klopfer v. North Carolina*, where the Supreme Court recognized the right to a speedy trial as a fundamental right.[154] The *Klopfer* Court was heavily influenced by the presence of the right throughout history[155] and, in particular, its importance at the founding of the nation.[156] The decision made reference to the existence of speedy trial protection in all fifty states.[157]

However, in most states, an accused need not rely on the Due Process Clause of the Fourteenth Amendment for protection of the right to speedy trial, as almost every state has written a speedy trial clause into its own state constitution.[158] With the exceptions of Nevada and New York, all state constitutions articulate some protection for the right to a speedy trial,[159] though the specificity of that language

---

150. *See generally* Francis C. Amendola et al., 22A C.J.S. Criminal Law § 851.

151. *See* part III, A.2.

152. *Constitution—State Constitutions, in* 2 Crim. Prac. Manual § 31:38 (Mar. 2012).

153. Klopfer v. North Carolina, 386 U.S. 213, 222 (1967).

154. *Id.* at 223.

155. *See id.* at 223–25 (tracing the right to as far back as the middle 1100s).

156. *Id.* at 225 (noting the mention of a right to speedy trial in several early United States documents).

157. *Id.* at 226.

158. Nat'l Inst. of Law Enforcement & Criminal Justice, Speedy Trial 59–158 (1978).

159. *Id.* (identifying Nevada and New York as lacking a speedy trial clause in their state constitutions).

varies from state to state. Some statutes are more vague than others, offering only a general rule that all cases should be heard without delay.[160] The vast majority of other states' clauses parallel the language of the Sixth Amendment,[161] often including a variation on the phrase "speedy trial."[162]

In addition to their similar wording, many state constitution speedy trial protections are coextensive with the application of, and the rights offered by, the Sixth Amendment. Consequently, there is no advantage to invoking one constitution's speedy trial clause over the other.[163] To promote clarity and predictability, many jurisdictions have stated that any alleged constitutional violation of the speedy trial right will be analyzed in accordance with federal standards.[164] Practically speaking, this results in most states applying the four-factor *Barker* test in the same way as federal courts, in order to determine whether a state constitutional right has been violated.[165]

Yet exceptions do exist. First, not all states follow *Barker* perfectly. For example, New York applies its own test, modeled after *Barker*, but with an additional fifth factor considering the nature of the crime committed.[166] A Montana opinion infused several bright line rules into factors of the *Barker* test.[167] Idaho also added a caveat to the *Barker* test, mandating that defendants be tried within the term following

---

160. *E.g.*, MASS. CONST. pt. 1, art. 11; N.C. CONST. art. 1, §§ 18, 21; N.H. CONST. pt. 1, art. 14; W. VA. CONST. art. 3, § 14 (adding "unreasonable" before delay).

161. *See* Gregory P.N. Joseph, *Speedy Trial Rights in Application*, 49 FORDHAM L. REV. 611, 613, n.16 (1981).

162. *E.g.*, ARK. CONST. art. 2, § 10 ("In all criminal prosecutions, the accused shall enjoy the right to a speedy and public trial."); TEX. CONST. art. 1, § 10 ("In all criminal prosecutions the accused shall have a speedy public trial by an impartial jury."); VA. CONST. art. 1, § 8 ("[I]n criminal prosecutions the accused shall have the right . . . to have a speedy public trial.").

163. *See, e.g.*, *State and U.S. Constitutional Right to a Speedy Trial*, *in* 5A MICHIGAN COURT RULES PRACTICE § 6004.1 (2d ed.).

164. *Constitutional Right to Speedy Trial, Generally*, *in* 26 STANDARD PENNSYLVANIA PRACTICE 2D § 132:279 (Pennsylvania courts assess speedy trial violations of either constitution under the federal guidelines because the two constitutional protections are seen as coextensive); *Interaction with State Speedy Trial Rule*, *in* 15 FLA. JUR. 2D *Criminal Law-Procedure* § 1718.

165. *See* Section V. For a partial list of states applying *Barker*, *see* Joseph, *supra* note 162, at n.18.

166. 7 NEW YORK PRACTICE, NEW YORK PRETRIAL CRIMINAL PROCEDURE § 9:10.

167. State v. Ariegwe, 167 P.3d 815 (Mont. 2007) (setting 200 days as the cutoff for presumptive prejudice requiring a full *Barker* analysis, relieving the defendant of the burden to prove prejudice if the prosecution causes 275 days of delay or more, and automatically fulfilling the assertion requirement of *Barker* if a demand was made or a motion for dismissal on speedy trial grounds was made).

their indictment.[168] Second, there are states, such as California, that view their state constitution's speedy trial clause as providing a right different from that of the Sixth Amendment.[169] In these states, the state constitutional right may attach at a different time than the Sixth Amendment right, or a different showing may be required to establish a violation.[170] Ultimately, dissatisfaction with the case-by-case approach of *Barker* and the lack of firm, clear timetables in constitutional protection led to legislative actions.[171] The federal legislature passed the Speedy Trial Act of 1974,[172] and many state legislatures passed similar statutory provisions setting specific time limits to protect the right to a speedy trial.[173]

B. State Speedy Trial Statutes

To further protect and clarify the speedy trial rights of the Sixth Amendment and most state constitutions, all states have enacted statutes that offer bright line rules to help identify violations of the right.[174] These bright line rules are usually in the form of time limits within which a defendant must be brought to trial to avoid violating the statutory speedy trial right. Because of these time limits, statutes tend to be narrower and more definite than state constitutional provisions. The timetables of these statutes vary from state to state, but it is common to require trial within 180 days of the filing of an indictment or information.[175] Timetables range from as short as sixty days in several states[176] to as long as a year in Arkansas.[177]

---

168. *Constitution—State Constitutions, in* 2 CRIM. PRAC. MANUAL § 31:38 (Mar. 2012).

169. *Relationship Between State and Federal Guarantees, in* 19A CAL. JUR. 3D *Criminal Law: Rights of the Accused* § 181.

170. People v. Benhoor, 99 Cal. Rptr. 827 (Cal. Ct. App. 2009) (describing the differences between the Sixth Amendment and the California Constitution's speedy trial clauses).

171. FAIR TRIAL RIGHTS OF THE ACCUSED 187 (Ronald Banaszak ed., 2002).

172. *Id.; see* 18 U.S.C.A. § 3161 (West).

173. *See infra* section V.B.

174. NAT'L INST. OF LAW ENFORCEMENT & CRIMINAL JUSTICE, SPEEDY TRIAL 59–158 (1978), *available at* https://www.ncjrs.gov/pdffiles1/Digitization/48110NCJRS.pdf. Although not all states have constitutional provisions protecting the right to a speedy trial, every state has some statutory protection in place.

175. MISNER, *supra* note 15, at 330–35. States that apply a 180-day time limit include Colorado, Florida, Indiana, Kansas, Maryland, Missouri, New York, Pennsylvania, and West Virginia.

176. *E.g.*, CAL. PENAL CODE § 1382; MINN. R. CRIM. P. 11.10; NEV. REV. STAT. § 178.556; WASH. R. CRIM. P. 3.3; WIS. STAT. ANN. § 971.1.

177. ARK. R. CRIM. P. 28.1.

However, states apply various exceptions and special rules to their statutes. For example, some states may have separate timetables depending on whether the defendant is incarcerated,[178] or whether the trial is for a felony or a misdemeanor.[179] Some states expedite the trial time limit if the defendant makes a specific demand for speedy trial.[180] Yet, in virtually all jurisdictions, failing to make a demand for speedy trial will weigh against, or eliminate, the defendant's claim that his right was violated.[181] To be sure, "repeated requests for a speedy trial weigh heavily in favor of the accused."[182] Texas courts even assert that the longer a defendant waits to make a demand for speedy trial, the more the defendant's inaction will weigh against finding a violation.[183]

State statutes diverge on the remedy for a violation of the statutory right to a speedy trial. Statutes in some states mandate that upon violation of the right, the charge be dismissed with prejudice so the same charges cannot be refiled.[184] In contrast, many states do not require dismissal with prejudice but leave it to the courts' discretion whether the same charges should be allowed to be brought against the defendant again, while some others mandate dismissal without prejudice.[185] Dismissals without prejudice may give the prosecution the opportunity to violate the speedy trial right of the defendant and simply refile to start a new clock on the time limit.

Of course, just because the defendant's trial does not start within the time limit does not mean his right has been violated. There are three reasons trials may begin after the statutory period and still not violate the statutory speedy trial right. First, defendants can waive

178. MISNER, *supra* note 15, at 362 (listing nine months as the limit for defendants in county jail, but twelve months for those presently incarcerated in state prison); *cf. id.* at 693 (noting that in Virginia the time limit to bring a defendant to trial is five months if the defendant is in custody but nine months if the defendant is not in custody).

179. *E.g.*, OHIO REV. CODE ANN. § 2945.71 (2011) (setting a 45-day limit on third- and fourth-degree misdemeanors but a 270-day limit for a felony trial).

180. *E.g.*, FLA. R. CRIM. P. 3.191(a)(2) (allowing a defendant to shorten the period from 180 days down to 60 days if he makes a speedy trial demand on the court).

181. *See, e.g.*, 725 ILL. COMP. STAT. 5/103–5(f); Kelley v. State, 568 So. 2d 405 (Ala. Crim. App. 1990); Durdin v. State, 955 S.W.2d 912 (Ark. Ct. App. 1997).

182. Roberson v. State, 864 So. 2d 379, 394 (Ala. Crim. App. 2002).

183. Bryan v. State, 2007 WL 1133216, at *3 (Tex. Crim. App. 2007).

184. MISNER, *supra* note 15, at 330–35. Examples include Alaska, Idaho, New Mexico, Ohio, and Washington.

185. *Id.* Connecticut's, Oregon's, and Virginia's statutes state that dismissal is without prejudice. Many of the other states allow courts to order that the charges be dismissed with or without prejudice.

their right to speedy trial.[186] Like other fundamental rights, waiver of the right to a speedy trial must be made intentionally either in writing or in court.[187] The right is also waived if not timely asserted.[188] A trial will be allowed even if the statutory time limit has passed if the defendant caused the delay by his own action.[189] For example, the time from which a defendant files a motion until the time the court rules on that motion does not count toward the statutory time limit in which he must be brought to trial.[190] Second, these motions include motions to dismiss, to suppress evidence, and to change venue.[191] Nor may a defendant use his own unavailability to reach the statutory time limit.[192] Finally, delays caused by the defendant are not the only delays that toll the statute of limitation. If the court finds there was good cause to justify the delay, it will not be held to violate the defendant's right to speedy trial.[193] Without extreme circumstances, congestion in the courts is no excuse for a delay that violates the statutory time limit.[194] Similarly, if defendant's counsel is unavailable due to other cases, any delay caused by continuances will not be counted toward the speedy trial time limit.[195] However, if the prosecution requests a continuance because material evidence is unavailable,[196] or because a prosecution witness is unavailable,[197] the delay caused by the continuance will not be counted in the speedy trial time limit.

---

186. *See* State v. Blackburn, 887 N.E.2d 319 (Ohio 2008).

187. *Id.*

188. *See, e.g.*, Patrick Furman, *The Ins and Outs, Stops and Starts of Speedy Trial Rights in Colorado—Part I*, 31 Colo. Law. 115, 117 (2002) (noting that failure to make a motion for dismissal on speedy trial grounds and going to trial without having objected on speedy trial grounds also constitute waiver of the right).

189. *E.g.*, 725 Ill. Comp. Stat. 5/103–5 (denying the right to trial within 120 days if delay was attributable to the defendant).

190. As stated by one state court: "Indeed the general rule can be stated that the accused is not entitled to a dismissal for delay in bringing him to trial when such delay has been caused by proceedings or motions instituted by him, such as motions for a change of venue." Cody v. Justice Court, 47 Cal. Rptr. 716 (Cal. Ct. App. 1965).

191. *Id.; see also* Carr v. State, 934 N.E.2d 1096, 1101 (Ind. 2010).

192. *E.g.*, Leonard v. State, 685 S.W.2d 786, 787–88 (Tex. Ct. App. 1985).

193. State v. Griffin, 760 N.W.2d 336, 340 (Minn. Ct. App. 2009).

194. *Id.*

195. People v. Sutton, 227 P.3d 437 (Cal. 2010), *reh'g denied* (May 20, 2010), *modified* (May 20, 2010).

196. State v. Turner, 564 N.W.2d 231 (Neb. 1997).

197. Jensen v. Superior Court, 72 Cal. Rptr. 3d 594, 596 (Cal. Ct. App. 2008) (holding that if the prosecution does its due diligence by issuing subpoenas and the witness does not show, there is good cause to continue).

VI. Speedy Trial Requirements in the Interstate Agreement on Detainers

A. Introduction

The United States, the District of Columbia, and forty-eight states have adopted the Interstate Agreement on Detainers.[198] Louisiana and Mississippi are the only states not parties to the Agreement.[199] The Agreement applies only to prisoners who are serving a sentence and who have charges pending in another state, the District of Columbia, or a federal court.[200] Further, the Speedy Trial Act incorporates detainer procedures, separate from the Interstate Agreement on Detainers, which apply to the federal government.[201]

B. Provision for Speedy Trial on Request of the Prosecutor

The prosecutor in a state where charges are pending who has lodged a detainer against the prisoner may file a written request for temporary custody with the state or federal prison where the prisoner is serving the sentence.[202] Article V of the Agreement provides the procedures for temporarily obtaining the prisoner for trial on all charges

---

198. 18 U.S.C. app. 2 § 2.

199. The notes included in 18 U.S.C. app. 2 § 1 list the fifty federal and state members of the Agreement. Louisiana and Mississippi are omitted. A search of the statutes of Louisiana and Mississippi did not produce a reference to the Agreement.

200. *Id.* § 2 arts. III(a), IV(a).

201. *See* 18 U.S.C. § 3161(j):

> (1) If the attorney for the Government knows that a person charged with an offense is serving a term of imprisonment in any penal institution, he shall promptly—
> (A) undertake to obtain the presence of the prisoner for trial; or
> (B) cause a detainer to be filed with the person having custody of the prisoner and request him to so advise the prisoner and to advise the prisoner of his right to demand trial.
> (2) If the person having custody of such prisoner receives a detainer, he shall promptly advise the prisoner of the charge and of the prisoner's right to demand trial. If at any time thereafter the prisoner informs the person having custody that he does demand trial, such person shall cause notice to that effect to be sent promptly to the attorney for the Government who caused the detainer to be filed.
> (3) Upon receipt of such notice, the attorney for the Government shall promptly seek to obtain the presence of the prisoner for trial.
> (4) When the person having custody of the prisoner receives from the attorney for the Government a properly supported request for temporary custody of such prisoner for trial, the prisoner shall be made available to that attorney for the Government (subject, in cases of interjurisdictional transfer, to any right of the prisoner to contest the legality of his delivery).

202. 18 U.S.C. app. 2 § 2 art. IV.

that were contained in the detainer.[203] The trial of the prisoner must begin within 120 days of her arrival in the prosecuting state.[204] Absent continuances for good cause, the charge will be dismissed with prejudice if the defendant is not tried within the 120-day limitation.[205]

C. Provisions for Speedy Trial on Notice by Prisoner

A prisoner serving a sentence in one state with a detainer filed against her in another state may request disposition of all of the charges pending in the detainer.[206] The defendant must be brought to trial within 180 days of the prosecutor's receiving the prisoner's request.[207] Failure to comply with this deadline will result in dismissal with prejudice of the charges.[208]

D. Sanctions

The sanction of dismissal with prejudice for time limit violations set out in sections A and B are modified as to the United States. The district court may dismiss with or without prejudice after considering the seriousness of the offense, the facts that led to the dismissal, and the impact of a reprosecution on the Agreement and the administration of justice.[209]

Beyond the scope of this chapter are other provisions of the Agreement that may lead to dismissal of the charges contained in the detainer. These provisions include the antishuttling provisions[210] and the use of a writ of *habeas corpus ad prosequendum* to produce a prisoner against whom a detainer has already been filed.[211] Since the sanctions for a violation of the Agreement are severe, both prosecutors and counsel for the defendant should closely examine the facts to make certain the proceedings comply with the Agreement.

---

203. *Id.* art. V.
204. *Id.* art. IV(c).
205. *Id.* art. III(a).
206. *Id.* art. III(d).
207. *Id.* art. III(a).
208. *Id.* art. III(d).
209. 18 U.S.C. app. 2 § 9(1).
210. *Id.* § 2 arts. III(d), IV(e).
211. United States v. Mauro, 436 U.S. 340 (1978).

VII. Speedy Trial Issues in a Pandemic

Coronavirus disease 2019 (COVID-19) swept through the United States beginning in the winter and spring of 2020. Governors issued stay-at-home orders, limited the size of gatherings, required mask wearing, and instituted other limitations that prevented criminal trials in the nation's courts.[212]

Federal and state courts closed to comply with local mandates issued to reduce the spread of the virus.[213] These closures left criminal defendants in jail or on bond awaiting a trial that may have been months off.[214] Federal and state courts entered orders changing trial procedures, including scheduling of trials, and the orders were repeatedly modified as the positive test rate for COVID-19 waxed and waned in the jurisdiction.[215]

The Eastern District of Virginia's approach to COVID-19 matters is illustrative. The Chief Judge issued a series of General Orders that addressed the changing conditions of the COVID-19 pandemic.[216] General Order 2020-2,[217] which addresses continuances of misdemeanor and infraction cases, and General Order 2020-3,[218] which addresses felony continuances as well as grand jury scheduling, are the first of many that address continuances of criminal trials. Each order makes an explicit finding of facts that justifies the continuances to protect public safety by restraining the spread of COVID-19 and finds that it is in the public interest to exclude the period of the continuance from the time limits of the Speedy Trial Act.[219]

There was a brief period in September 2020 to October 2020 where some jury trials were conducted in the Eastern District of Virginia. A trial order in *United States v. Green* is an excellent example of a trial judge striving to accommodate a speedy trial demand by a pro se defendant amid the complications caused by COVID-19.[220] The

---

212. Boutros et al., *Collision of the Speedy Trial Clock with the Coronavirus's Slowdown Realities*, 35 Crim. Just. 49 (2020).

213. *Id.* at 52.

214. *Id.*

215. *Id.* at 52–53.

216. Coronavirus (COVID-19) Guidance, https://www.vaed.uscourts.gov/covid-19 (last updated Mar. 18, 2021).

217. General Order 2020-2 (Mar. 13, 2020), https://www.vaed.uscourts.gov/sites/vaed/files/General%20Order%202020-02.pdf.

218. General Order 2020-3 (Mar. 16, 2020), https://www.vaed.uscourts.gov/sites/vaed/files/General%20Order%202020-03.pdf.

219. General Order 2020-2, *supra* note 217, ¶ 2.

220. United States v. Green, 2020 WL 5877893 (E.D. Va. 2020).

complications that prevented a speedy trial included a COVID-19 outbreak in the defendant's jail that prevented him from being transported to the courthouse; COVID-19-caused delays in reviewing pretrial discovery by the pro se defendant; COVID-19 health rules that required the court to use three courtrooms to conduct each felony jury trial; and the backlog of jury trial cases that accumulated between March 2020 and September 2020 that filled the trial dates for the few courtrooms available.[221] The court concluded that these factors as well as those set forth in the General Orders of the Court required a continuance.[222]

A district court dismissed an indictment with prejudice finding that the defendant's Speedy Trial Act[223] rights were violated because the Central District of California suspended criminal jury trials during the Covid-19 pandemic.[224] The Ninth Circuit found that the emergency orders temporarily suspending criminal jury trials were proper because of the unique circumstances caused by the pandemic which made jury trials unsafe.[225]

The court concluded that the lower court erred by denying the government's motion to continue based on the ends of justice provision of the Act[226] when it ruled that criminal jury trials were physically possible within the district. Therefore the defendant was entitled to a jury trial within the time limits of the Speedy Trial Act.[227] The district court read the word "impossible" from 18 U.S.C. § 3161(h)(7)(B)(i) in isolation and that a full reading of the Speedy Trial Act does not limit granting an ends of justice continuances only in cases where it is physically impossible to hold a jury trial.[228] The district court was also criticized for failing to consider both statutory[229] and non-statutory factors[230] when it denied the government's motion for continuance based on the ends of justice provision of the Act.[231]

The district court's decision to dismiss the case with prejudice was also reversed because it failed to consider all the factors required

---

221. *Id.* at 2–4.
222. *Id.* at 4–5.
223. *See* Section IV.
224. United States v. Olsen, 494 F. Supp. 3d 722 (C.D. Ca. 2020).
225. United States v. Olsen, --- F.3d ---(9th Cir. 2021), 2021 WL 1589359 (April 23, 2021).
226. 18 U.S.C. §3161(h)(7)(A), *see* ftn.134.
227. Olsen at *4–6.
228. *Id.* at *6.
229. *Id.*
230. *Id.* 18 U.S.C. § 3161(h)(7)(B).
231. Olsen at *7.

for such an action,[232] and because the "district court primarily based its decision on the perceived need to deter the Central District from continuing its jury trial suspension."[233]

State courts with their much higher volume of cases also faced tough decisions to attempt to address speedy trial issues. For example, on April 1, 2020, the Supreme Judicial Court of Massachusetts continued all criminal trials in Massachusetts until May 4, 2020.[234] Subsequent orders kept extending the prohibition on trials. In each order, the court made findings that the "continuances serve the ends of justice and outweigh the best interests of the public and the criminal defendant in a speedy [trial and that], therefore, the time periods of such continuances shall be excluded from speedy trial competitions" under Massachusetts law.[235]

Constitutional speedy trial considerations also apply to COVID-19 continuances. The *Barker v. Wingo*[236] four-part analysis set out in section II.B guides the courts in deciding whether the lengthy COVID-19 continuances are constitutional. Recall also that the Supreme Court observed that the lower courts found that delays approaching one year are "presumptively prejudicial."[237]

A lawyer presented with speedy trial issues during the pandemic must examine general orders and case-specific orders to understand the COVID-19 trial delays in that jurisdiction. The National Center for State Courts has helpful links on its website to individual state COVID-19 information.[238]

A defense attorney should discuss the speedy trial problems with her client. If the defendant wishes to argue for a speedy trial based on either statutory or constitutional grounds, counsel should file a motion demanding a speedy trial. Counsel and the defendant should consider waiving constitutional rights such as the right to trial by jury and the right to confront some witnesses in person and perhaps stipulate to uncontested facts. If these waivers do not damage the defendant's case, they may provide for a quicker trial before a judge.

---

232. *Id.* at *8.

233. *See* Section IV. Id. at *7.

234. Order Regarding Court Operations under the Exigent Circumstances Created by the CoronAvirus (Covid-19) Pandemic (Apr. 1, 2020), https://www.mass.gov/doc/supreme-judicial-court-order-regarding-court-operationsunder-the-exigent-circumstances-created/download.

235. *Id.* ¶ 9.

236. Barker v. Wingo, 407 U.S. 514, 530 (1972).

237. Doggett v. United States, 505 U.S. 647, 652 n.1 (1992).

238. *Coronavirus and the Courts*, NCSC, https://www.ncsc.org/newsroom/public-health-emergency (last visited Mar. 30, 2021).

CHAPTER 2

The Right to a Public Trial

I. Historical Origin of the Right

"The trial is always public."[1] This remark from Joseph Story's *1833 Commentaries on the Constitution* suggests that he is stating the obvious. Indeed, the interest in public trials is twice recognized in the Bill of Rights. This chapter focuses on the accused's right to a public trial under the Sixth Amendment and reviews the potential overlay with, and distinction from, the First Amendment right.

The Founders' interest in public trials was likely a reflection of the English Common Law and several state constitutions that recognized a right to a public trial.[2] "[O]ne of the most conspicuous features of English justice, that all judicial trials are held in open court, to which the public have free access, . . . appears to have been the rule in England from time immemorial."[3]

The public trial right can trace its origins in England to before the Norman Conquest when freemen of the community were expected to attend public meetings and sit in judgment in criminal matters.[4] Sir Thomas Smith recorded in 1565 that criminal proceedings are "doone openlie in the presence of the Judges, the Justices, the enquest, the prisoner, and so manie as will or can come so neare as to heare it, and all depositions and witnesses given aloude, that all men may heare from the mouth of the depositors and witnesses what is saide."[5] As the trial process evolved, its public nature was never questioned.[6] It

1. 3 Story, Commentaries on the Constitution of the United States 662 (1833).
2. Richmond Newspapers, Inc. v. Virginia, 448 U.S. 555, 590–91 (1980) (Brennan, J., concurring).
3. *Id.* at 566–67 (quoting Jenks, The Book of English Law 73–74 (6th ed. 1967)).
4. Pollock, The Expansion of the Common Law 140 (1904).
5. Smith, De Republica Anglorum 101 (Alston ed. 1972).
6. *See generally* Note, *Legal History: Origins of the Public Trial*, 35 Ind. L.J. 251 (1960).

is no surprise then that colonial Americans transplanted this key feature of their ancestors' legal tradition. Early records report that the Virginia Assembly took care in the mid-1600s to protect the public's right to attend trial, as did the Pennsylvania Frame of Government of 1682, which provided "[t]hat all courts shall be open."[7] After the ratification in 1791 of the Sixth Amendment with its public trial right, most of the states included a public trial right in their constitutions. All but two states would eventually recognize the right to a public trial as a command of their constitution, statute, or common law.[8]

This tradition of public trials is so grounded in the firmament and practice of America's judicial system that when the Supreme Court first addressed the public trial right in *In re Oliver* in 1948, it observed that "we have been unable to find a single instance of a criminal trial conducted in camera in any federal, state or municipal court during the history of this country."[9] Nevertheless, as discussed later in the

---

7. 1 SCHWARTZ, THE BILL OF RIGHTS: A DOCUMENTARY HISTORY 129, 140 (1971); *see also* HERMAN, THE RIGHT TO A SPEEDY AND PUBLIC TRIAL (2006), for a comprehensive review of the historical development of the right to a public trial.

8. Forty-eight of the fifty states protected the right to a public trial. Forty-five have constitutional provisions specifically guaranteeing the right: ALA. CONST., art. 1, § 6; ALASKA CONST., art. 1, § 11; ARIZ. CONST., art. 2, §§ 11, 24; ARK. CONST., art. 2, § 10; CAL. CONST., art. 1, § 15; COLO. CONST., art. 2, § 16; CONN. CONST., art. 1, § 8; DEL. CONST., art. 1, §§ 7, 9; FLA. CONST., art. 1, § 16; GA. CONST., art. 1, §§ 1, 11; HAW. CONST., art. 1, § 11; IDAHO CONST., art. 1, § 13; ILL. CONST., art. 1, § 8; IND. CONST., art. 1, §§ 12, 13; IOWA CONST., art. 1, § 10; KAN. CONST., Bill of Rights, § 10; KY. CONST., Bill of Rights, §§ 11, 14; LA. CONST., art. 1, §§ 16, 22; ME. CONST., art. 1, § 6; MICH. CONST., art. 1, § 20; MINN. CONST., art. 1, § 6; MISS. CONST., art. 3, §§ 24, 26; MO. CONST., art. 1, § 18(a); MONT. CONST., art. 2, § 24; NEB. CONST., art. 1, § 11; N.J. CONST., arts. 1, 10; N.M. CONST., art. 2, § 14; N.C. CONST., art. 1, §§ 18, 24; N.D. CONST. art. 1, §§ 13, 22; OHIO CONST., art. 1, §§ 10, 16; OKLA. CONST., art. 2, § 20; OR. CONST., art. 1, § 11; PA. CONST., art. 1, §§ 9, 11; R.I. CONST., art. 1, § 10; S.C. CONST., art. 1, §§ 9, 14; S.D. CONST., art. 6, §§ 7, 20; TENN. CONST., art. 1, §§ 9, 17; TEX. CONST., art. 1, § 10; UTAH CONST., art. 1, §§ 11, 12; VT. CONST., ch. 1, art. 10; VA. CONST., art. 1, § 8; WASH. CONST., art. 1, §§ 10, 22; W. VA. CONST., art. 3, §§ 14, 17; WIS. CONST., art. 1, § 7; WYO. CONST., art. 1, § 8. In addition, New Hampshire has held that the due process clause of its constitution, pt. 1, art. 15, requires that criminal trials be held in public. Martineau v. Helgemoe, 379 A.2d 1040, 1041 (N.H. 1977). Maryland by judicial decision requires open proceedings. Dutton v. State, 91 A. 417, 422–423 (Md. 1914). New York by statute provides for open trials. N.Y. CIV. RIGHTS LAW, art. 2, § 12 (McKinney 1976). Only Massachusetts and Nevada appear to have no state provision for public trials. *But see* Commonwealth v. Marshall, 253 N.E.2d 333 (Mass. 1969) (relying on *In re Oliver* to find exclusion from the courtroom to be violative both of the U.S. Constitution and of state law on closure at trial for sex offense where victim is a minor).

9. *In re Oliver*, 333 U.S. 257, 266 (1948). The Court recognized in a footnote that juvenile cases and cases within the jurisdiction of courts martial could be taken as understandable exceptions. *Id.* at n.12. *Oliver* arose from petitioner's 60-day sentence after a judge sitting as a one-man grand jury (as permitted under Michigan law) found him guilty of

chapter, the right is not absolute and may be overcome by a proper showing of an overriding interest.

II. Whose Right Is It?

A. Right of the Accused

The text of the amendment provides that "the accused shall enjoy the right to a speedy and public trial," which would suggest that the defendant controls the assertion of the right. Sweeping and often-cited language in the Supreme Court's opinion in *Gannett Co. v. DePasquale*[10] supports this interpretation. "Our cases have uniformly recognized the public-trial right guarantee as one created for the benefit of the defendant."[11] However, focusing on the defendant's perspective fails to embrace the reality that interests beyond the defendant's drive judicial decision making in this area. While it is the declared right of the "accused" in the text of the Sixth Amendment, the public's interest in a public trial is widely recognized. "It has never been suggested that by phrasing the public-trial guarantee right as a right of the accused, the Framers intended to reject the

---

contempt for providing evasive and contradictory answers to his questions—all of which occurred in the secrecy of the grand jury chamber. *Id.* at 258. The Supreme Court held that this secret trial deprived petitioner of his due process rights under the Fourteenth Amendment. *Id.* at 276. *Oliver* did not present a question under the Sixth Amendment because "[p]rocedural safeguards for criminal contempts do not derive from the Sixth Amendment. Criminal contempt proceedings are not within 'all criminal prosecutions' to which the Amendment applies." Levine v. United States, 362 U.S. 610, 616 (1960); Richmond Newspapers, Inc. v. Virginia, 448 U.S. 555, 591 n.16 (1980) (Brennan, J. concurring).

10. Gannett Co. v. DePasquale, 443 U.S. 368 (1979).

11. *Id.* at 380. The *Gannett* opinion directs considerable attention and many pages to the point that this Sixth Amendment right enures to the benefit of the defendant alone. This is explained by the fact *Gannett* presented the question of whether the public had a right to attend a pretrial suppression hearing and four justices did not believe such a right existed under the Sixth or First Amendments. The fifth justice voting with the majority in *Gannett,* Justice Powell, found that the press had a First Amendment right to attend trial but that, in this particular case, the defendant's right to fair trial free of harmful pretrial publicity trumped the press's First Amendment right. The four dissenters in *Gannett* believed the First Amendment did confer a public trial right. With the right case they could expect Justice Powell to join them and so hold. Exactly one year later in *Richmond Newspapers,* the Supreme Court by a 7–1 vote found a First Amendment right for the public to attend trial. The Court has never deemed it necessary to explicitly reverse *Gannett* because *Richmond Newspapers* addressed the public's right to attend trial under the First Amendment and *Gannett* found no right of the public to attend a suppression hearing under the Sixth Amendment. Courts have since recognized the public's First Amendment right to attend suppression hearings. United States v. Brooklier, 685 F.2d 1162, 1170 (9th Cir. 1982).

common-law rule of open proceedings."[12] This wider view is explained by a shared sense that the public trial is axiomatic in a democracy[13] and by the overlay of First Amendment considerations.

B. Right of the Public under the First Amendment

Remarkably, it was only in 1980 that the Supreme Court first addressed whether there existed a First Amendment right to attend a trial. In *Richmond Newspapers, Inc. v. Virginia*,[14] the Court found the public's and press's right to attend criminal trials to be implicit in the guarantees of the First Amendment.[15] While admitting that neither the Constitution nor the Bill of Rights contains an explicit guarantee of the public's right to attend trial,[16] the Court found that "without the freedom to attend such trials, which people have exercised for centuries, important aspects of freedom of speech and 'of the press could be eviscerated.'"[17] Since the ruling in *Richmond Newspapers*, any broadening of the public trial right under a First Amendment analysis has generally been linked to the defendant's Sixth Amendment right as "there can be little doubt that the explicit Sixth Amendment right of the accused is no less protective of a public trial than the implicit First Amendment right of the press and public."[18]

C. Incorporation of the Sixth Amendment Public Trial Right

No Supreme Court case explicitly incorporates the Sixth Amendment right to a public trial into the Fourteenth Amendment due process rights applicable to the states. However, there can be no doubt about its tacit incorporation. First, in *Washington v. Texas*[19] and in *Duncan v.*

---

12. *Gannett*, 443 U.S. at 385.

13. The public trial right "reflects the tradition of our system of criminal justice that a trial is a 'public event' and that '[w]hat transpires in the court room is public property.'" *Id.* at 412 (Blackmun, J., concurring in part, dissenting in part) (quoting Craig v. Harney, 331 U.S. 367, 374 (1947)).

14. *Richmond Newspapers*, 448 U.S. 555 (1980).

15. *Id.* at 580.

16. *Id.* at 575.

17. *Id.* at 580 (quoting Branzburg v. Hayes, 408 U.S. 665, 681 (1972)).

18. Waller v. Georgia, 467 U.S. 39, 46 (1984). But note that the most recent Supreme Court case to address the public trial right, *Presley v. Georgia*, 558 U.S. 209 (2010), deemed "[t]he extent to which the First and Sixth Amendment public trial rights are coextensive" to be "an open question." *Presley*, 558 U.S. at 213.

19. Washington v. Texas, 388 U.S. 14, 18 n.11 (1967).

Louisiana,[20] the Court listed the Sixth Amendment public trial right as one already incorporated and cited *In re Oliver*.[21] Second, in *Waller v. Georgia*, the Supreme Court applied the Sixth Amendment right to a state court suppression hearing.[22]

III. Interests Served by the Public Trial Right

Whether the public trial right is addressed under the First or Sixth Amendments, courts frequently cite four interests that are served by a public trial. Public trials (1) help ensure a fair trial; (2) remind the prosecutor and the judge of their responsibility to the accused and the importance of their functions; (3) encourage witnesses to come forward; and (4) discourage perjury.[23] The public trial is a "safeguard against any attempt to employ our courts as instruments of persecution. The knowledge that every criminal trial is subject to contemporaneous review in the forum of public opinion is an effective restraint on possible abuse of judicial power."[24] Providing a public trial to the accused assures that "the public may see he is fairly dealt with and not unjustly condemned and that the presence of interested spectators may keep his triers keenly alive to their responsibility and to the importance of their function."[25]

People function more effectively when others are watching and their performance is the subject of public scrutiny. So it is that the judge, prosecutor, defender, and expert witness will all perform their responsibilities better if they are subject to the review and the comment of the public and perhaps their peers in particular. The public spotlight will also discourage corrupt collusion between or among any of the trial's participants. Perjury and false testimony will seem less likely if what is said in open court is tested by what is said and known in the community.[26] Moreover, witnesses who have not been called to testify may step forward to correct the record if what is said at trial is publicly known.

---

20. Duncan v. Louisiana, 391 U.S. 145, 148 n.10 (1968).

21. Notwithstanding that *In re Oliver* was founded on the Due Process Clause of the Fourteenth Amendment and not the Sixth Amendment as explained above.

22. *Waller*, 467 U.S. 39, 40–41 (1984).

23. *Id.* at 46–47; Peterson v. Williams, 85 F.3d 39, 43 (2d Cir. 1996).

24. *In re Oliver*, 333 U.S. 257, 270 (1948).

25. *Id.* at 271 n.25 (quoting 1 Cooley, Constitutional Limitations 647 (8th ed. 1927)).

26. As Blackstone observed, "a witness may frequently depose that in private, which he will be ashamed to testify in a public and solemn tribunal." 3 Blackstone, Commentaries *373 (1866).

In addition, courts have recognized a more therapeutic societal benefit of having crimes presented in a forum that involves the community in the resolution.[27] "[N]o community catharsis can occur if justice is done" behind closed doors.[28]

IV. When May a Trial Be Closed?

These compelling rationales in favor of a public trial create a strong presumption in favor of open proceedings that may be overcome only if the following standards are met:

- The party seeking to close the proceeding must advance an overriding interest that is likely to be prejudiced.
- Closure must be no broader than necessary to protect that interest.
- Trial court must consider reasonable alternatives to closing the proceedings.
- Trial court must make findings adequate to support the closure.[29]

Although the presumption is strong, the right is not absolute. It "may give way in certain cases to other rights or interests, principally the defendant's right to a fair trial or the government's interest in inhibiting disclosure of sensitive information."[30]

---

27. When a shocking crime occurs, a community reaction of outrage and public protest often follows. *See* H. Weihofen, The Urge to Punish 130–31 (1956). Thereafter the open processes of justice serve an important prophylactic purpose, providing an outlet for community concern, hostility, and emotion. Without an awareness that society's responses to criminal conduct are underway, natural human reactions of outrage and protest are frustrated and may manifest themselves in some form of vengeful "self-help," as indeed they did regularly in the activities of vigilante "committees" on our frontiers.

> The accusation and conviction or acquittal, as much perhaps as the execution of punishment, operat[e] to restore the imbalance which was created by the offense or public charge, to reaffirm the temporarily lost feeling of security and, perhaps, to satisfy that latent "urge to punish."

Richmond Newspapers, 448 U.S. 555, 571 (1980) (quoting Mueller, *Problems Posed by Publicity to Crime and Criminal Proceedings*, 110 U. Pa. L. Rev. 1, 6 (1961)).

28. *Id.*

29. Presley v. Georgia, 558 U.S. 209, 213 (2010).

30. *Waller*, 467 U.S. 39, 45 (1984).

A. Overriding Interest That Is Likely to Be Prejudiced

While not common, courts have allowed for closures where witnesses, in particular children, would be intimidated by the presence of the public.[31] Barring the press from a pretrial bail-reduction hearing was approved in one case where the defendant met his burden of showing likely prejudice from pretrial publicity.[32] The court may adapt procedures to conceal the identity of informants or undercover police officers,[33] to protect law enforcement measures that would be compromised if disclosed,[34] or to deal with the special challenges presented with child victims.[35] Also, judges have broad discretion to exclude or restrict spectators to preserve order and safety in their courtrooms.[36] However, a court should not accept "a bald assertion of intimidation" and must undertake an independent inquiry to verify

---

31. Federal law is quite explicit on this point. *See* 18 U.S.C. § 3509(b)(1)(B):

> The court may order that the testimony of the child be taken by closed-circuit television . . . if the court finds that the child is unable to testify in open court in the presence of the defendant, for any of the following reasons:
>
> (i) The child is unable to testify because of fear.
>
> (ii) There is a substantial likelihood, established by expert testimony, that the child would suffer emotional trauma from testifying.
>
> (iii) The child suffers a mental or other infirmity.
>
> (iv) Conduct by defendant or defense counsel causes the child to be unable to continue testifying.

Numerous states have similar requirements. *See, e.g.*, N.Y. Crim. Proc. Law § 65.10; Va. Code § 18.2-67.9; W. Va. Code § 62-6B-4.

32. United States v. Chagra, 701 F.2d 354, 365 (5th Cir. 1983).

33. United States v. Lucas, 932 F.2d 1210, 1216–17 (8th Cir. 1991) (approving use of a screen to shield identity of undercover agent); People v. Mickens, 917 N.Y.S.2d 630, 630–31 (N.Y. App. Div. 2011) (limited closure that allowed family members to attend was supported by adequate findings that officer continued his undercover work in the vicinity of the charged crimes, that he had been threatened in other undercover investigations, and that he took precautions to protect his identity).

34. United States v. Bell, 464 F.2d 667 (2d Cir. 1972) *cert. denied*, 409 U.S. 991 (1972) (exclusion of public and defendant from suppression hearing permissible to protect government's "skyjacker profile"). *But see* United States v. Clark, 475 F.2d 240, 246 (2d Cir. 1973) (error to close entire suppression hearing where only "minute portion" addressed hijacker profile).

35. For discussion of the confrontation clause cases that permit child victims to testify behind screens or on closed circuit television, see chapter 6.

36. United States *ex rel.* Orlando v. Fay, 350 F.2d 967 (2d Cir. 1965) (exclusion justified after outburst by defendant and his mother); Williams v. Indiana, 690 N.E.2d 162, 166–70 (Ind. 1997) (courtroom safety procedures requiring spectators to sign in and produce identification did not constitute closure). *See generally* United States v. Scott, 564 F.3d 34, 37–38 (1st Cir. 2009); Bell v. Evatt, 72 F.3d 421, 432–33 (4th Cir. 1995).

the necessity for a closure.[37] It is not improper to lock the doors to limit the distraction of the public's coming and going during the jury's charge, trial testimony, or closing argument.[38] Some courts have applied the constitutional test to courtroom screening that requires spectators to sign in and show identification, while others have determined that these measures do not constitute a closure.[39] State and federal statutes authorize exclusion of the public from particular proceedings such as those involving juveniles.[40] But rules providing for blanket closures in all cases involving juvenile victims have not passed constitutional muster.[41] Courts have approved closures necessary to protect matters of national security.[42]

---

37. Commonwealth v. Penn, 562 A.2d 833, 838–39 (Pa. Super. 1989); *see infra* note 52.

38. People v. Colon, 521 N.E.2d 1075, 1079–80 (N.Y. 1988) (jury charge); Commonwealth v. Dykens, 784 N.E.2d 1107, 1115 (Mass. 2003) (same); Roberts v. State, 103 A.3d 1031, 1042–43 (Me. 2014) (testimony), *overruled on other grounds in* Fortune v. State, 158 A.3d 512 (Me. 2017); People v. Woodward, 841 P.2d 954, 960 (Cal. 1992) (closing argument).

39. *See* Commonwealth v. Maldonado, 2 N.E.3d 145, 150–55 (Mass. 2014) and cases discussed therein.

40. 18 U.S.C. § 5038(e) ("Unless a juvenile who is taken into custody is prosecuted as an adult neither the name nor picture of any juvenile shall be made public in connection with a juvenile delinquency proceeding."). Some courts seal the entire case but others protect the juvenile's identity by redacting the name and sealing other identifying information. Substantial discretion is given to the judge under 18 U.S.C. § 3509(e):

> Closing the courtroom.—When a child testifies the court may order the exclusion from the courtroom of all persons, including members of the press, who do not have a direct interest in the case. Such an order may be made if the court determines on the record that requiring the child to testify in open court would cause substantial psychological harm to the child or would result in the child's inability to effectively communicate. Such an order shall be narrowly tailored to serve the Government's specific compelling interest.

41. Globe Newspaper Co. v. Superior Court, 457 U.S. 596, 607–08 (1982); Davis v. Reynolds, 890 F.2d 1105, 1110 (10th Cir. 1989) (requiring trial courts to focus on "a careful case-by-case analysis of each individual situation. . . . [A] victim's age and the nature of the offense . . . do not justify an automatic, general exclusion of the public in every case[.]"). In United States v. Yazzie, 743 F.3d 1278 (9th Cir. 2014), the appellate court approved the closing of the courtroom during the juvenile victims' testimony which occurred after the trial court reviewed video recordings of the victims' interviews and made findings that testimony in open court would harm the witnesses and make it more difficult to obtain their testimony. This opinion is also noteworthy because it recognizes efforts at trial to conceal from the jury the fact that the courtroom had been sealed. Defense counsel argued this was necessary to avoid prejudice to the defendant. *Id.* at 1284.

42. United States v. Rosen, 520 F. Supp. 2d 786, 797–800 (E.D. Va. 2007) (discussion of interplay of Classified Information Procedures Act and public trial right); United States v. Abu Marzook, 412 F. Supp. 2d 913, 919 (N.D. Ill. 2006) (closing testimony of Israeli agents involving classified information); *In re* Terrorist Bombings of U.S. Embassies in E. Afr. 552 F.3d 93, 128 (2d Cir. 2006) (addressing withholding of sensitive national security information from defendant).

B. Closure Must Be No Broader Than Necessary

The closure must be limited to no more than what is necessary to protect the overriding interest. In *Press-Enterprise Co. v. Superior Court of California*,[43] the Supreme Court found incredulous the need to seal all but three days of a six-week voir dire. "Those parts of the transcript reasonably entitled to privacy could have been sealed without such a sweeping order."[44] In a more recent sexual assault case involving teenage witnesses, the prosecution requested that the courtroom be closed to all persons.[45] The trial court adopted an alternative to exclusion that restricted ingress and egress during the juveniles' testimony so as to improve their focus and limit distraction.[46]

C. Trial Court Must Consider Reasonable Alternatives

The court must consider alternatives to closure even if the parties offer none.[47] It is ultimately the obligation of the trial court "to take every reasonable measure to accommodate public attendance at criminal trials."[48] The Court in *Presley v. Georgia* reversed the Georgia conviction squarely on this failure to consider alternatives to excluding the public from voir dire because of limited seating in the courtroom.[49] The *Presley* per curiam decision observed that some alternatives to closure could have been to "reserv[e] one or more rows for the public; dividing the jury venire panel to reduce courtroom congestion; or instructing prospective jurors not to engage or interact with audience members."[50] If trial publicity poses a threat to a fair trial, the court should consider a change of venue as opposed to barring the press.[51] Cases have advocated a hearing to develop the record of an overriding interest and for the consideration of alternatives.[52]

---

43. Press-Enterprise Co. v. Superior Court of California, 464 U.S. 501 (1984).
44. *Id.* at 513.
45. People v. Whitman, 205 P.3d 371, 380 (Colo. App. 2007).
46. *Id.*
47. *Presley*, 558 U.S. 209, 213 (2010).
48. *Id.* at 215.
49. *Id.* at 216 ("[E]ven assuming, arguendo, that the trial court had an overriding interest in closing voir dire, it was still incumbent upon it to consider all reasonable alternatives to closure.").
50. *Id.* at 215.
51. *Chagra*, 701 F.2d 354, 365 (5th Cir. 1983).
52. Guzman v. Scully, 80 F.3d 772, 775 (2d Cir. 1996) (trial court's partial closure of the courtroom violated the defendant's right to a public trial where "the trial court relied on the unsubstantiated statements of the prosecutor, rather than conducting an inquiry of

D. Findings Adequate to Support the Closure

The trial court's findings must be specific enough so as to allow a reviewing court to determine whether the standards for closure were met.[53] The Court in *Presley* recited an admonition from a First Amendment case that "'the right of access cannot be overcome by the conclusory assertion that publicity might deprive the defendant of' the right to a fair trial."[54]

V. Partial Closures

An open question after *Presley* is whether partial closures could ever be sustained on a showing of less than an overriding interest. Some jurisdictions had applied a lesser standard of a "substantial reason" for a partial closure.[55] The Sixth Circuit recently observed that "there are reasonable arguments that Waller does not apply to partial-closure

---

the prosecution witness on whose behalf the closure request was made"); *cf.* United States v. Hernandez, 608 F.2d 741, 748 (9th Cir. 1979) (upholding closure based on affidavit describing witness's fear of harm, but "mak[ing] it absolutely clear that the better course would have been for the trial judge to conduct an evidentiary hearing into the matter").

53. *Presley*, 558 U.S. at 215.

54. *Id.* at 216 (quoting Press-Enter. Co. v. Superior Court, 478 U.S. 1, 15 (1986)). In *Mitchell v. State*, 567 S.W.3d 838 (Ark. 2019), the trial judge ordered the courtroom closed during the testimony of a key state witness. The prosecuting attorney claimed that there was "credible evidence that certain members of the defendant's family have reached out in an effort to intimidate [the witness] to prevent her from testifying . . . ." *Id.* at 839. No further evidence was offered to support the claim. Held, the defendant's constitutional rights had been violated, as "no record was developed that [the witness] was actually intimidated or threatened, or by whom." *Id.* at 842.

55. *See, e.g.*, United States v. Hendricks, 950 F.3d 348, 355 (6th Cir. 2020); *Ex parte* Easterwood, 980 So. 2d 367, 376 (Ala. 2007); State v. Drummond, 854 N.E.2d 1038, 1054 (Ohio 2006); Feazell v. State, 906 P.2d 727, 729 (Nev. 1995); United States v. Osborne, 68 F.3d 94, 98–99 (5th Cir. 1995); United States v. Thompson, 713 F.3d 388, 395 (8th Cir. 2013); Woods v. Kuhlmann, 977 F.2d 74, 76–77 (2d Cir. 1992); United States v. Sherlock, 962 F.2d 1349, 1356–57 (9th Cir. 1992); Nieto v. Sullivan, 879 F.2d 743, 753 (10th Cir. 1989); Douglas v. Wainwright, 739 F.2d 531, 532–33 (11th Cir. 1984). "All federal courts of appeals that have distinguished between partial closures and total closures modify the *Waller* test so that the 'overriding interest' requirement is replaced by requiring a showing of a 'substantial reason' for partial closure, but the other three factors remain the same." United States v. Simmons, 797 F.3d 409, 414 (6th Cir. 2015); *but see* People v. Jones, 750 N.E.2d 524, 529 (N.Y. 2001) ("When the procedure requested impacts on a defendant's right to a public trial, nothing less than an overriding interest can satisfy constitutional scrutiny."). For broad discussions of the issue as pertaining to closing of the courtroom during jury selection, compare the majority and dissenting opinions in *United States v. Williams*, 974 F.3d 320 (3d Cir. 2020).

cases in the wholesale manner" applicable to complete closures.[56] Amid this unsettled state of the law, one state high court has recognized that in light of *Presley*, the question of whether the closure was total or partial was immaterial.[57] In *Longus v. State*, the courtroom remained open to all but three spectators (including the defendant's father) who were excluded on the basis that they had allegedly tried to intimidate a witness.[58] The trial court did not apply the Supreme Court's overriding interest standard and the intermediate court of appeals found that the judge had met the "substantial reason" standard required for a partial closure.[59] The Maryland Court of Appeals determined that the substantial reason test was inadequate to protect the defendant's interest because "[t]he *Waller* test, in requiring an overriding interest, demands by definition that the State's interest in closure outweigh the burden on the defendant's right to a public trial."[60] The New Mexico Supreme Court came to a similar conclusion deciding that an overriding interest must be shown for any type of courtroom closure reasoning that the *Waller* standard must also apply to partial closures for the simple reason that *Waller* requires all closures to be no broader than necessary.[61]

VI. Application to Different Phases of the Proceedings

The Sixth Amendment right to a public trial applies not only to the trial itself but also to all significant aspects of the proceedings. It covers jury selection[62] and suppression hearings[63] but not sidebar conferences addressing sensitive matters.[64] It has been held to apply to

---

56. Drummond v. Houk, 797 F.3d 400, 404 (6th Cir. 2015) (quotation omitted).

57. Longus v. State, 7 A.3d 64 (Md. App. 2010).

58. *Id.* at 69–70.

59. *Id.* at 69–71.

60. *Id.* at 76.

61. State v. Turrietta, 308 P.3d 964, 970–71 (N.M. 2013).

62. *Presley*, 558 U.S. 209 (2010); United States v. Negron-Sostre, 790 F.3d 295, 300 (1st Cir. 2015) (vacating convictions from a three-month trial which was "doomed before it started" by Puerto Rico's "longstanding practice of excluding the public from jury selection"), *but compare* State v. Russell, 357 P.3d 38, 42–43 (Wa. 2015) (off-the-record work session in a jury room for the purpose of reviewing jury questionnaires for hardship did not implicate the right).

63. *Waller*, 104 U.S. 39 (1984); United States v. Waters, 627 F.3d 345, 360–61 (9th Cir. 2010) (trial court must satisfy *Waller* test to close "omnibus" pretrial hearing that addressed administrative matters, motions in limine, and a motion to dismiss for prosecutorial misconduct).

64. Keck v. State, 2015 WL 1880587, *5 (Nev. April 21, 2015) (unpublished); Morris Publishing Group, LLC v. State, 136 So.3d 770, 782–83 (Fla. Dist. Ct. App. 2014); Rovinsky

competency hearings,[65] but one federal court found that the Sixth Amendment right does not include material witness proceedings.[66] Another court determined that there was no offense to a defendant's Sixth Amendment right where the trial judge questioned jurors in a closed proceeding about whether they felt threatened by certain spectators in the courtroom.[67] Moving voir dire to an unlocked magistrate's office because of a bomb threat in the courthouse did not violate the accused's public trial right even though no members of the public attended.[68] Mailing the verdict after a bench trial was held to be a violation. Still, the remedy was not a new trial but was to reconvene the trial and announce the verdict in open court.[69]

The names of jurors are sometimes kept secret to protect them from intimidation and to protect juror privacy. Among courts that have addressed the issue, some have found the requisite overriding interest and others have not. The matter is discussed in Chapter 3, section IX.

Historically, in the United States, many states granted the defendant the power to exclude the public from preliminary hearings.[70] The purpose was to limit adverse publicity both for those for whom no probable cause is found and for those who will face trial.[71] Because of the recognition of the public's First Amendment right to attend trial proceedings, states have since revised such rules. An order closing a preliminary hearing is permitted only where the constitutional tests for closure are met.[72]

---

v. McKaskle, 722 F.2d 197, 201 (5th Cir. 1984); People v. Virgil, 253 P.3d 553, 578 (Cal. 2011); *see also* Richmond Newspapers, 488 U.S. at 598 n.23 (Brennan, J., concurring) ("when engaging in interchanges at the bench, the trial judge is not required to allow public or press intrusion upon the huddle").

65. *In re* Times-World Corp., 488 S.E.2d 677, 681 (Va. Ct. App. 1997); Soc'y of Prof'l Journalists v. Bullock, 743 P.2d 1166, 1178 (Utah 1987).

66. United States v. Brice, 649 F.3d 793, 797 (D.C. Cir. 2011) (No plain error to exclude public from material witness proceedings as these were not "trial" proceedings. Brice had sought to unseal court records relating to witnesses who were detained under the federal material witness statute.).

67. United States v. Ivester, 316 F.3d 955, 960 (9th Cir. 2003) (public trial values are not implicated by closure due to "routine jury administrative matters that have no bearing on [a defendant's] ultimate guilt or innocence").

68. Commonwealth v. Briggs, 12 A.3d 291, 334 (Pa. 2011).

69. United States v. Canady, 126 F.3d 352, 362–65 (2d Cir. 1997).

70. *Gannett*, 443 U.S. 368, 386 (1979).

71. *Id.*

72. Eversole v. Superior Court, 195 Cal. Rptr. 816, 821 (Cal. Ct. App. 1983) (recognizing legislative revision). Reflecting this trend, the American Bar Association Standards for Criminal Justice provide: "In any criminal case, all judicial proceedings and related

In a nationally televised murder trial, the trial judge granted defendant Jodi Arias' motion to exclude the public during her death penalty mitigation phase upon the defendant's assertion that she would not testify if the public was present.[73] She argued that she had received death threats and "would not be 'able to fully communicate what she wants to say, communicate her remorse and go through all the mitigating factors and get them out there in front of the jury with the public here.'"[74] The trial court applied *Waller* and found a basis for sealing the proceedings. Upon an interlocutory appeal, the appellate court rejected this contention and unsealed her testimony.[75]

VII. Assertion of the Right

Where the defendant seeks to assert the right, a contemporaneous objection should be offered.[76] The defendant must only show that the closure affects the public in general, not a particular person. Moreover, the accused need not show any particular prejudice arising from the closure. Prejudice is presumed upon a showing of an improper closure.[77]

VIII. Remedy for a Violation

The remedy for a violation of the right is a new trial if the violation occurred at trial and was not a trivial or *de minimis* violation, as explained in the next section. "[T]he remedy should be appropriate to

---

documents and exhibits, and any record made thereof, not otherwise required to remain confidential, should be accessible to the public. . . ." ABA STANDARDS FOR CRIMINAL JUSTICE: FAIR TRIAL AND FREE PRESS, Standard 8-3.2 (3d ed. 1992).

73. KPNX-TV Channel 12 v. Stephens, 340 P.3d 1075, 1077 (Ariz. App. 2014).

74. *Id.* at 1079.

75. *Id.* at 1079–80. The appellate court did not apply a constitutional analysis because it found that Arias had not even met the standard of a state rule of criminal procedure which required a showing that an open proceeding would present "a clear and present danger to the defendant's right to a fair trial by an impartial jury." *Id.* at 1078 (*citing* Ariz. R. Crim. P. 9.3(b)).

76. Some courts have held, even after *Presley*, that "[a] defendant may, by his own acts or acquiescence, waive his right to a public trial and thereby preclude any subsequent challenge by him of an order excluding the public." People v. Virgil, 253 P.3d 553, 578 (Cal. 2011). For cases addressing waiver, see *Commonwealth v. Morganti*, 4 N.E.2d 241, 246–47 (Mass. 2014).

77. United States v. Gonzalez-Lopez, 548 U.S. 140, 149 n.4 (2006); Owens v. United States, 483 F.3d 48, 64–65 (1st Cir. 2007), *overruled on other grounds*, Weaver v. Massachusetts, 137 S. Ct. 1899 (2017).

the violation."[78] It is deemed a structural error that does not require a demonstration of prejudice, and is thus per se reversible.[79] If the violation occurs at a pretrial proceeding, such as a suppression hearing, the remedy is a new proceeding.[80] Where the trial court violated *Waller* by not considering alternatives to closure, one court has held that the appropriate remedy is a new trial and not a remand to allow the trial court to set forth any alternatives it might have considered.[81] "Prior to abridging a defendant's Sixth Amendment rights, trial courts are under an absolute duty to consider alternatives to complete courtroom closure."[82]

IX. Trivial or *De Minimis* Closures

Some closures seem trivial beyond cavil and have not warranted a new trial, such as exclusion of the public from "cumulative" testimony that composed less than six pages of a trial transcript of over 900 pages,[83] or where the closure was limited and inadvertent.[84]

---

78. *Waller*, 467 U.S. 39, 50 (1984).

79. As explained by Chief Justice Rehnquist, concurring in *Arizona v. Fulminante*, 499 U.S. 279, 310 (1991) (including public trial violation among list of constitutional errors not subject to harmless error analysis).

80. *Waller*, 467 U.S. at 50.

81. Okonkwo v. Lacy, 104 F.3d 21, 26 (2d Cir. 1997). *But see* United States v. Williams, 974 F.2d 320 (3rd Cir. 2020), where the trial judge closed the courtroom during jury selection. The majority refused to send the case back to the trial court:

> [W]e decline to exercise our discretion in this instance. The importance of the "searchlight" of the public trial is "deeply rooted" in the history of our federal constitutional order and system of justice; and it has long been a feature of our Court's jurisprudence. Nevertheless, on this record, we cannot say that the values underlying the Defendants' right to a public trial were sufficiently compromised that the costs to the fairness, integrity, and public reputation of judicial proceedings that would result from letting the District Court's error stand outweigh those that would alternatively result from reversing the Defendants' convictions and remanding for a new trial. We cannot, in sum, say that the District Court's closure of jury selection to the public "seriously affect[ed] the fairness, integrity, or public reputation of judicial proceedings."

Id. at 348. The dissenter vigorously disagreed and would have ordered a new trial. He noted that a public trial has "deep roots" in our criminal justice system and is of "critical importance to the functioning of our criminal justice system." *Id.* at 380.

82. *Id.*

83. Brown v. Kuhlmann, 142 F.3d 529, 531 (2d Cir. 1998).

84. Peterson v. Williams, 85 F.3d 39, 41 (2d Cir. 1996) (inadvertent closure for twenty minutes did not violate Sixth Amendment).

While some courts have recognized a triviality exception,[85] the breadth of this exception is likely narrow.[86]

X. Public Trial Implications for Cooperating Defendants

The public trial right confers no right to a private trial.[87] Yet at times the defendant has a strong interest in avoiding public proceedings, such as where the defendant seeks a benefit from cooperating with the government and resolves the case by a plea agreement. The government and the public's interest in effective law enforcement often benefit from such cooperation.[88] It is true that courts may agree to the

85. *Id.* at 42; United States v. Perry, 479 F.3d. 885, 890 (D.C. Cir. 2007) (exclusion of defendant's wife and 8-year-old son did not implicate interests recognized in *Waller)*; United States v. Greene, 431 Fed. Appx. 191, 194–5 (3d Cir. 2011) (court security officer's exclusion of defendant's brother from voir dire without judge's knowledge deemed "an unfortunate but de minimus breach"); Braun v. Powell, 227 F.3d 908, 918–19 (7th Cir. 2000) (exclusion of single member of excused venire was trivial and not a violation); United States v. Ivester, 316 F.3d 955, 959–60 (9th Cir. 2003) (exclusion of public during mid-trial questioning of jury to ask if they were concerned about their safety did not violate the Sixth Amendment).

86. United States v. Rivera, 682 F.3d 1223, 1229 (9th Cir. 2012) (rejecting the government's contention that the exclusion of only the defendant's family from sentencing was trivial); United States v. Gupta, 699 F.3d 682, 689 (2d. Cir. 2012) (new trial required where no *Waller* analysis was undertaken before court officer excluded defendant's family members from voir dire).

87. *See* Singer v. United States, 380 U.S. 24, 35 (1965) ("[A]though a defendant can, under certain circumstances, waive his constitutional right to a public trial, he has no absolute right to compel a private trial."). One might think that not since *Waller* could it be said that a defendant held the keys to locking the courtroom door. *Presley*, it would seem, made this clearer: "Trial courts are obligated to take every reasonable measure to accommodate public attendance at criminal trials." 558 U.S. at 213. Washington's highest court, however, recently approved a defendant's "knowing, voluntary, and intelligent waiver" of public voir dire without any consideration of the Sixth Amendment's requirements. Washington's Supreme Court, the trial judge (which had advised the defendant that whether potential jurors are questioned in private is "pretty much up to you"), the prosecutor, and the defendant's lawyer assumed that the defendant could, by waiving his public trial right, allow juror questioning to occur in private. State v. Herron, 356 P.3d 709, 743–44 (Wash. 2015). The analysis from a federal trial court suggests how the Washington practice might pass constitutional muster. In applying the very deferential standard for federal habeas review, the court determined that *Waller* "does not clearly establish that a trial court must make the *Waller* inquiry and Required Findings when the defendant does not object to closure." Pouncy v. Palmer, 2015 WL 4429547, *7 (E.D. Mich. July 20, 2015).

88. It is worth noting here that the values the Framers sought to protect in the Sixth Amendment's public trial right may well suffer where there are comparatively few trials. The framers could hardly have envisioned the reality of the twenty-first-century criminal case docket where most criminal case convictions are the result not of a trial but of a plea of guilty. The Pew Research Center reports that of the nearly 80,000 federal

sealing of cooperating plea agreements to protect the defendant and the defendant's family from potential reprisals arising from their cooperation. If all defendants plead guilty, such plea agreements may never be unsealed at any trial. Nevertheless, some judges are troubled by withholding from the community the basis for their sentencing decisions, and there is authority recognizing a qualified right of access to plea agreements and change of plea hearings.[89] On the one hand,

---

prosecutions in 2018, just two percent went to trial. More than 97 percent of federal criminal convictions are obtained through plea bargains, and most states have similar numbers. *See* PEW RESEARCH CTR., *Trials Are Rare in the Federal Criminal Justice System, and When They Happen, Most End in Convictions* (June 10 2019), https://nam11.safe-links.protection.outlook.com/?url=https%3A%2F%2Fwww.pewresearch.org%2Ffact-tank%2F2019%2F06%2F11%2Fonly-2-of-federal-criminal-defendants-go-to-trial-and-most-who-do-are-found-guilty%2Fft_19-06-11_trialsandguiltypleas-pie-2%2F&data=04%7C01%7Cfaburt%40wm.edu%7C219b2b006d964326872808d8a3902d1d%7Cb93cbc3e661d40588693a897b924b8d7%7C0%7C0%7C637439186926933296%7CUnknown%7CTWFpbGZsb3d8eyJWIjoiMC4wLjAwMDAiLCJQIjoiV2luMzIiLCJBTiI6Ik1haWwiLCJXVCI6Mn0%3D%7C1000&sdata=NQch3VoLyBT0vn5koY6kFJ3bfq2SuED45ha4SvIHkyc%3D&reserved=0. Justice Scalia's comments in *Lafler v. Cooper*, 566 U.S. 156, 185 (2012) (Scalia, J., dissenting) are worthy of note:

> In Europe, many countries adhere to what they aptly call the "legality principle" by requiring prosecutors to charge all prosecutable offenses, which is typically incompatible with the practice of charge-bargaining. Such a system reflects an admirable belief that the law is the law, and those who break it should pay the penalty provided.
>
> In the United States, we have plea bargaining a plenty, but until today it has been regarded as a necessary evil. It presents grave risks of prosecutorial overcharging that effectively compels an innocent defendant to avoid massive risk by pleading guilty to a lesser offense; and for guilty defendants it often—perhaps usually—results in a sentence well below what the law prescribes for the actual crime. But even so, we accept plea bargaining because many believe that without it our long and expensive process of criminal trial could not sustain the burden imposed on it, and our system of criminal justice would grind to a halt.

(citation omitted).

89. United States v. DeJournett, 817 F.3d 479, 485 (6th Cir. 2016) ("[J]ust as the public's presence at judicial proceedings plays a significant role in ensuring fairness in our criminal trials, its access to plea agreements negotiated by the government and an accused plays a significant role in monitoring the administration of justice by plea."). *See also* Wash. Post v. Robinson, 935 F.2d 282, 292 (D.C. Cir. 1991) ("Under the First Amendment, plea agreements are presumptively open to the public and the press."). *But see* United States v. Thomas, 905 F.3d 276, 282 (3rd Cir. 2018) ("[W]e hold that the First Amendment right of access applies to documents filed in connection with plea hearings . . . , as well as to the hearings themselves . . . . This right of access, though, is presumptive and not absolute, and it can be overcome where there is 'cause shown that outweighs the value of openness.' A district court sealing a criminal record must make 'particularized findings . . . on the record in each case, (1) establishing the existence of a compelling governmental

a good argument can be made that the four interests served by public trials apply equally to sentencing decisions and that the public has an interest in and a right to know how the prosecutor, the defendant, and the accepting court have agreed to resolve the case. On the other hand, there is also little doubt that the threat of recriminations against the cooperating defendant is real, whether on the prison yard or in the community.[90]

XI. The Impact of Pandemic Concerns on the Right

The COVID-19 pandemic has created new opportunities for courts and commentators[91] to consider the essential nature and characteristics of the public trial. Although we are writing and editing at the end of 2020 as the global pandemic death toll approaches 2 million with no end in sight, we believe that the lessons of COVID-19 will impact our fundamental understanding of the criminal trial process long after medical science has overcome the current public health crisis.

In early 2020, as the world first became aware of the new disease and its potential severity, federal courts began to address legal challenges based on confinement contagion concerns. These legal challenges initially included well-publicized requests for early release from celebrity inmates like Michael Cohen,[92] Bill Cosby,[93] and R. Kelly,[94]

---

interest, and (2) demonstrating that absent limited restrictions upon the right of access, that other interest would be substantially impaired.'"

90. The problem of protecting the cooperating defendant is made even worse by the fact that more courts now make their dockets available online. Before the Internet, even if a cooperator's plea agreement was not sealed, it would be one document among many documents that could be accessed only by traveling to the office of the clerk of court and requesting to review the case file—an action that itself was somewhat burdensome and public. Now, any person in any location can locate and examine within seconds a defendant's case file and determine whether that defendant has cooperated. Moreover, it is easy enough via the Internet to sift among thousands of cases files to search for such cooperators and brand them, also on the Internet, as snitches.

91. *See generally* Stephen E. Smith, *The Right to a Public Trial in the Time of COVID-19*, 77 Wash. & Lee L. Rev. Online 1 (2020).

92. *See generally* United States v. Cohen, No. 1:18-cr-00602-WHP (S.D.N.Y. filed Mar. 24, 2020).

93. Jessica Napoli, *Bill Cosby's Lawyers Requesting His Release from Prison over Coronavirus Concerns, Says Spokesperson*, Fox News (Mar. 25, 2020), https://www.foxnews.com/entertainment/bill-cosby-lawyers-request-prison-released-coronavirus-health-risk.

94. James Hill & Bill Hutchinson, *Judge Rejects R. Kelly's Request to Be Released from Jail over Coronavirus Fears*, ABC News (Apr. 7, 2020, 5:08 PM), https://abcnews.go.com/Health/judge-rejects-kellys-request-released-jail-coronavirus-fears/story?id=70025508.

along with new COVID-19-related bail requests[95] and speedy trial motions.[96]

Starting in the early summer, as infection rates grew across the country, courts confronted a wider range of more complicated trial-related questions requiring judges to balance public trial rights against unprecedented public health concerns. In July 2020, for example, a federal district court in Alabama decided to "partially close" trial proceedings by admitting only the defendant's family members into the courtroom, while providing a live video stream in another courtroom and on the court's website.[97] This decision, although not a complete closure, recognized the discretion permitted by the U.S. Supreme Court in *Waller v. Georgia*, which had required that

> [1] the party seeking to close the [proceeding] must advance an overriding interest that is likely to be prejudiced, [2] the closure must be no broader than necessary to protect that interest, [3] the trial court must consider reasonable alternatives to closing the proceeding, and [4] it must make findings adequate to support the closure.[98]

During the same month, a Montana federal district court addressed the additional pandemic-related problems of securing adequate juror

---

95. United States v. Crowder, No. 4:17-CR-00291-1, 2020 WL 1891878, at *5 (M.D. Pa. Apr. 16, 2020) (defendant's pandemic-related request for bail denied based in part on the fact that 31-year-old defendant had alleged no specific health concerns and, at the time, there were no COVID-19 cases in his detention facility).

96. United States v. Stephenson, No. 17-CR-199-A, 2020 WL 3263445, at *8 (W.D.N.Y. June 17, 2020) (rejecting defendant's appeal of his detention order based on speedy trial concerns and concerns over a COVID-19 outbrreak in his correctional facility based in part on the fact that 30-year-old defendant was in good physical health and defense counsel could communicate with defendant by electronic means). *See also* United States v. Velez, No. 3:19-CR-30059-MGM, 2020 WL 5440626, at *3 (D. Mass. Sept. 10, 2020) (rejecting defendant's Speedy Trial Act motion based in part on the court's broad finding that until the COVID-19 "risk can be satisfactorily managed so as to reasonably provide for the public health considerations for all participants, including the defendant and his counsel, continuances necessitated by the pandemic are in the interest of justice and are excludable under the Speedy Trial Act").

97. United States v. Fortson, No. 2:18-CR-416-WKW, 2020 WL 4589710, at *2 (M.D. Ala. Aug. 10, 2020).

98. *Id.* (citing Waller v. Georgia, 467 U.S. 39, 48 (1984)). *See also* United States v. Richards, No. 2:19-CR-353-RAH, 2020 WL 5219537, at *2 (M.D. Ala. Sept. 1, 2020).

participation and accommodating inevitable and necessary quarantine-related recesses.[99]

In three subsequent cases, the New York federal district courts considered myriad pandemic-related trial issues including (1) the impact of new and shifting travel and quarantine regulations on lawyers' and witnesses' courtroom appearances;[100] (2) whether a defendant's request for a bench trial (based on contagion risks) should be granted despite the absence of government consent;[101] and (3) the need to accommodate a defendant's right to have family members "present at trial," the impact of jurors' face masks, witnesses' potential reluctance to meet with defense investigators, and the inherent uncertainty of all pandemic-related postponement requests.[102]

Unsurprisingly, law professors and legal commentators also debated the question of how much of a criminal trial could be held using video teleconferencing technology.[103] One Virginia federal district court converted a pretrial status conference to a video teleconference, despite defense objection, after learning of multiple COVID-19 cases at the jail where the defendant was being held. By October, a Utah federal district court, in a decision that included charts reflecting domestic and global COVID-19 infection rates, conceded that the pandemic was fundamentally reshaping the criminal justice system.[104]

> So long as this pandemic continues at this pace, there is no feasible way for a criminal defendant to exercise the constitutional right to jury trial. The courts cannot compel citizens to appear for jury

---

99. United States v. Preston Coversup, No. CR 19-15-BLG-SPW, 2020 WL 4260519 (D. Mont. July 24, 2020).

100. United States v. Donziger, No. 11-CV-691 (LAK), 2020 WL 4747532 (S.D.N.Y. Aug. 17, 2020), reconsideration denied, No. 11-CV-691 (LAK), 2020 WL 5077074 (S.D.N.Y. Aug. 26, 2020).

101. United States v. Cohn, 481 F. Supp. 3d 122, 123 (E.D.N.Y. 2020).

102. United States v. Trimarco, No. 17-CR-583 (JMA), 2020 WL 5211051, at *1 (E.D.N.Y. Sept. 1, 2020).

103. *See* Jessica A. Roth, *The Constitution Is on Pause in America's Courtrooms*, The Atlantic (Oct. 10, 2020), https://www.theatlantic.com/ideas/archive/2020/10/constitution-pause-americas-courtrooms/616633/; Ann E. Marimow & Justin Jouvenal, *Courts Dramatically Rethink the Jury Trial in the Era of Coronavirus*, Wash. Post (July 31, 2020, 8:54 AM), https://www.washingtonpost.com/local/legal-issues/jury-trials-coronavirus/2020/07/31/8c1fd784-c604-11ea-8ffe-372be8d82298_story.html.

104. *See generally* United States v. Green, No. 4:20CR1, 2020 WL 5877893 (E.D. Va. Oct. 2, 2020).

> service – and attorneys, witnesses and others – if assembly is unsafe. And the government and public are not acting in ways to create safety. . . . The pandemic's effect on criminal justice is unparalleled, and denies citizens the fundamental constitutional right to trial, even though many preliminary criminal matters are permitted to occur by video under the Coronavirus Aid, Relief, and Economic Security Act ("CARES Act").[105]

Acknowledging the limits of any technological fix, because "[v]ideo and audio conferencing, used for hearings, are not available for criminal trials," the Utah court also presaged the futility of defense challenges to COVID-19-related delays by stating that, for the duration of the pandemic, public health needs would continue to outweigh the rights of the defendant to a speedy trial.[106]

Finally, as the pandemic continued into the fall and winter, courts also addressed the more practical concerns of retrofitting courthouses and changing protocols to reduce future contagion risks. For example, in Utah, the federal courts have

> made diligent preparations for resumption of in person proceedings including jury trials. Plexiglass barriers for in person hearings have been installed in all courtrooms, and two courtrooms in Salt Lake City and one in St. George are fully outfitted with barriers for jury trials. Signage has been installed, and restrictions on courthouse entry are in place. A mock jury orientation, selection, and trial was conducted so that the court and personnel are ready – when the pandemic danger subsides enough to permit jury trial.[107]

---

105. United States v. Castaneda, No. 4:20-cr-00094-DN, 2020 WL6290482, at *2 (D. Utah Oct. 27, 2020). In November 2020, the Utah federal district courts granted a series of continuance motions without setting new trial dates and denied defendants' Speedy Trial Act motions citing (in similar or identical language) unprecedented pandemic-related public health concerns. *See generally* United States v. Goodman, No. 4:20-cr-00013-DN-DPB-1, 2020 WL 6429013 (D. Utah Nov. 2, 2020); United States v. Aguerre, No. 4:19-cr-00075-DN-PK, 2020 WL 6487776 (D. Utah Nov. 4, 2020); United States v. Lopez-Jimenez, No. 4:20-cr-00008-DN-PK, 2020 WL 6487523 (D. Utah Nov. 4, 2020); United States v. Nikolyan, No. 20-CR-00038-DN-PK, 2020 WL 6487522 (D. Utah Nov. 4, 2020); United States v. Crapo, No. 4:19-CR-00135-DN-PK, 2020 WL 6546600 (D. Utah Nov. 6, 2020).

106. *Crapo*, 2020 WL 6546600 at *1–2; *see also* United States v. Jones, No. 5:20CR171, 2020 WL 6361916 (N.D. Ohio Oct. 29, 2020).

107. *See generally* United States v. Apodaca, No. 2:20 CR 123 TC, 2020 WL 6582657 (D. Utah Nov. 10, 2020).

Across the country, federal judges have been engaging in similar efforts to rethink courtroom designs and procedures to reduce contagion risks. These include the reconfiguration of courtrooms and jury deliberation rooms, the use of masks and transparent barriers, and the expansion of the vetting for potential jurors to include exposure and related health risks.[108] State courts, with the leadership of the National Center for State Courts' Pandemic Rapid Response Team, have also been addressing these same public health issues and concerns.[109]

108. *Federal Judges Reinventing the Jury Trial During Pandemic*, U.S. Cts. (Aug. 27, 2020), https://www.uscourts.gov/news/2020/08/27/federal-judges-reinventing-jury-trial-during-pandemic.

109. *See Coronavirus and the Courts*, NCSC, https://www.ncsc.org/newsroom/public-health-emergency (last visited Mar. 30, 2021).

CHAPTER 3

The Right to a Jury Trial

I. Historical Basis and Constitutional Language

In the English common law, the right to a jury trial in criminal cases developed in response to the law's need to abandon the old trials by ordeal.[1] To the Americans, the jury trial represented a liberty inherited from their English roots and a means of mitigating the power of a distant and mistrusted sovereign.[2] This helps to explain why our Founders protected this right in the body of the U.S. Constitution, in state constitutions, and in the Bill of Rights. The events that affected the development of the right to trial by jury took hundreds of years to form the modern understanding in place today.

A. Development in England

Trial by jury can be understood as a consequence of the accusatorial nature of criminal and civil justice through English history. At the time of the Norman Conquest, the county court served as the court of general jurisdiction and heard cases that affected the freeholders of the county. Twelve jurors were selected from the men of the county,

---

1. One commentator explains the concept: "For 400 years the most sophisticated persons in Europe decided difficult criminal cases by asking the defendant to thrust his arm into a cauldron of boiling water and fish out a ring. If his arm was unharmed, he was exonerated. If not, he was convicted. Alternatively, a priest dunked the defendant in a pool. Sinking proved his innocence. Floating proved his guilt. People called these trials ordeals." Leeson, *Ordeals,* 55 J. L. & Econ. 691 (2012).

2. For excellent treatments of the historical developments, see Appleman, Defending the Jury: Crime, Community, and the Constitution (2015); Carrington, *Trial by Jury, in* 6 Encyclopedia of the American Constitution 2724 (2d ed. 2000); Proffatt, A Treatise on Trial by Jury (1986); Levy, The Palladium of Justice: Origins of Trial by Jury (1999); Heller, The Sixth Amendment to the Constitution of the United States (1969).

but, at the time, jurors were expected to share their personal knowledge of the dispute at hand. Because the twelve jurors were from the same county as the parties, they presumably had knowledge of which party held the greater right in the dispute. This early practice embodied the idea that jurors must also have been witnesses. Rather than hearing evidence and declaring a verdict, the jurors simply ruled according to what they knew firsthand. The function of the early juries thus was markedly different than that of juries today. Jurors were charged with investigating the facts of the case, sifting through information, and using their own knowledge to declare a verdict.

The key event that would have the greatest influence on the trial process in England, and later in the United States, occurred eight centuries ago. In the Magna Carta of 1215, freemen were given the right to a trial by their peers before there could be a loss of person or property.[3] Although these freemen were guaranteed a type of jury trial far from that known today, the Magna Carta embodied a principle of jury trial that would greatly influence the perceived rights and liberties of the English people.

Over the years, this principle would evolve to provide defendants with the option of submitting themselves to the verdict of jurors, and to permit judges to seek verdicts from separate juries: one jury to present an accusation and another to confirm a guilty verdict.[4] Still later, the law allowed for the court to persuade the accused to consent to "putting himself upon his country."[5]

B. American Colonial Experience

The American Colonists brought the concept of the right to a jury trial with them from England. The earliest settlements in the Americas provided for trial by "the verdict of twelve honest men, to be impaneled by authority, in form of a jury upon their oaths."[6] Nearly all of the colonial charters specified that no one could lose life, liberty, or property unless convicted by a jury of twelve men.[7]

Because trial by jury was a common right in the colonies, actions by the British Parliament to restrict the use of juries in the colonies were met with vehement protest. In response to the Stamp Act, which allowed the extension of admiralty courts to circumvent trial by jury,

---

3. *Id.*
4. LEVY, *supra* note 2, at 18.
5. *Id.* at 20.
6. HELLER, *supra* note 2, at 16.
7. *Id.* at 73.

the legislature in Massachusetts wrote that "the essential Rights of British subjects were representation and trial by jury" and that "the extension of the powers of the Court of Admiralty within this province is a most violent infraction of the right of trials by juries—a right which this House, upon the principles of their British ancestors, hold most dear and sacred, it being the only security of the lives, liberties, and properties of his Majesty's subjects here."[8]

The Townshend and Coercive Acts of 1767 and 1774 infuriated Americans because these Acts allowed the Crown to try offenses in England, where juries were less likely to be sympathetic to American concerns, or in the admiralty courts with no jury at all.[9] These Acts were widely criticized, and when Congress declared the *Causes and Necessity of Taking up Arms* in 1775, it denounced statutes "extending the jurisdiction of courts of admiralty and vice-admiralty beyond their ancient limits, for depriving us of the accustomed and inestimable privilege of trial by jury, in cases affecting both life and property."[10] The Declaration of Independence also indicates that "depriving us, in many cases, of the benefit of trial by jury" was a major factor for the separation of the colonies from the Crown.[11]

Because the right to jury trial was a fundamental reason the colonists were displeased with the English government, it is not surprising that the U.S. Constitution commanded, Article III, Section 2, that "[t]he Trial of all Crimes, except in Cases of Impeachment, shall be by Jury; and such Trial shall be held in the State where the said Crimes shall have been committed." The right was further protected in the Sixth Amendment, which states that "[i]n all criminal prosecutions, the accused shall enjoy the right to a speedy and public trial, by an impartial jury of the State and district wherein the crime shall have been committed."[12] The sanctity of the jury trial was made clear, yet again, in the Supreme Court's recent decision in *Warger v. Shauers*, a unanimous ruling that jurors may not be called to disclose events

---

8. *Id.* at 86.
9. *Id.* at 86–88.
10. *Id.*
11. *Id.* at 89.
12. For a good overview, see Burns, The Death of the American Trial (2009). The author laments the decline in the number of jury trials. One commentator nicely explains why the decline continues. *See* Taslitz, *In Praise of the Jury Trial: A Review of Robert P. Burns'* The Death of the American Trial, 8(1) Int. Comm. on Evidence (2010). *See also* discussion in Chapter 2.

during deliberations, even when allegations of dishonesty in the selection process are present.[13]

II. Petty versus Nonpetty Offenses

A. Background

The Sixth Amendment and Article III of the U.S. Constitution guarantee a criminal defendant the right to trial by jury. However, the scope of this right has always been limited. The common law delineated a class of trials for "petty offenses" that were not subject to jury trial protection. The Supreme Court recognized this common law distinction in narrowing the seemingly inclusive language of the Sixth Amendment's guarantee of trial by jury to the states.[14] The theory that petty offenses are exempt from the constitutional right to trial by jury is grounded in the notion that judicial resources need not be expended for matters that are trivial in nature.[15]

To determine whether an offense was petty, early decisions relied heavily on common law practices.[16] If the offense did not require a jury at common law, it was generally viewed as petty and therefore not subject to the Sixth Amendment's jury protection.[17] In certain cases, judges considered related principles such as the moral relevance of the offense[18] and whether the offense was *malum in se* or *malum prohibitum*.[19] Later decisions qualified this approach by

---

13. Warger v. Shauers, 574 U.S. 40 (2014). The Court in *Pena-Rodriguez v. Colorado*, 137 S. Ct. 855 (2017), held that judges must make an exception to the usual rule that jury deliberations are secret when evidence is offered to show that those discussions involved racial or ethnic bias. "Racial bias . . . implicates unique historical, constitutional and institutional concerns." *Id.* at 859. For an excellent discussion of the difficulties seen with the right to a jury trial during the COVID-19 pandemic, see Melanie D. Wilson, *The Pandemic Juror*, 77 WASH. & LEE REV. ONLINE 102 (2020).

14. "So-called petty offenses were tried without juries both in England and in the Colonies and have always been held to be exempt from the otherwise comprehensive language of the Sixth Amendment's jury trial provisions. There is no substantial evidence that the Framers intended to depart from this established common-law practice. . . ." Duncan v. Louisiana, 391 U.S. 145, 160 (1968).

15. *Id.*

16. The Court in *Callan v. Wilson*, 127 U.S. 540, 549 (1888), decided that petty offenses include those exempted from trial by jury at common law. The Court observed that common law distinctions between petty and nonpetty offenses predated the Constitution, despite the language in the Constitution guaranteeing the right for "all crimes, except in cases of impeachment."

17. District of Columbia v. Colts, 282 U.S. 63, 72–73 (1930).

18. Schick v. United States, 195 U.S. 65, 67–68 (1904).

19. *Colts*, 282 U.S. at 73.

analyzing the maximum statutory penalty for the charged crime. In these cases, the focus shifted to whether the risk that the court would impose the maximum sentence made the trial serious enough to fall within the Sixth Amendment's purview respecting the jury guarantee, even though the crime would have been considered petty at common law.[20]

Over time, the Supreme Court abandoned common law precedent in deciding whether an offense was serious or petty. *Duncan v. Louisiana* held that the maximum penalty imposed is, without more, enough to signal the seriousness of the offense for jury trial purposes.[21] The Supreme Court then established that a maximum penalty imposing imprisonment time of more than six months was sufficiently severe to define the offense as nonpetty and require a jury trial.[22] Not surprisingly, the Court also held that crimes with a penalty of maximum imprisonment time of six months or less would be viewed as presumptively petty, and therefore defendants facing these shorter sentences were not entitled to be tried before a jury.[23]

B. Unresolved Applications

Although problems of interpreting and applying the right to a jury remain,[24] the most pressing concerns can often be seen in a trial for multiple petty offenses. Courts have used a number of techniques to determine how the possibility of convictions for multiple petty

---

20. District of Columbia v. Clawans, 300 U.S. 617, 625 (1937): A penalty's severity is "an element to be considered in determining whether a statutory offense, in other respects trivial and not a crime at common law, must be deemed so serious as to be comparable with common law crimes, and thus to entitle the accused to the benefit of a jury trial prescribed by the Constitution."

21. *Duncan*, 391 U.S. at 159.

22. Baldwin v. New York, 399 U.S. 66, 68–69 (1970).

23. Blanton v. City of N. Las Vegas, 489 U.S. 538, 543 (1989). This presumption is "very strong," as explained in United States v. Stanfill El, 714 F.3d 1150, 1153 (9th Cir. 2013). But see *Andersen v. Eighth Jud. Dist. Ct. in and for Cnty. of Clark*, 448 P.3d 1120 (Nev. 2019), where the defendant was charged with the offense of misdemeanor battery constituting domestic violence. The maximum authorized period of incarceration for the crime is six months. Nevertheless, a jury was required, as state law limits the right to bear arms for an individual who has been convicted of misdemeanor battery constituting domestic violence. Thus, "the Legislature has determined that the offense is a serious one."

24. These problems involve, among others, contempt proceedings and fines. *See* Muniz v. Hoffman, 422 U.S. 454, 476–77 (1975) (contempt fine of $10,000 was not enough to require the right to trial by jury as "imprisonment and fines are intrinsically different"); Int'l Union v. Bagwell, 512 U.S. 821, 839 (1994) (contempt fine of $52 million was severe enough to invoke the right).

offenses relates to jury entitlement. As recently as twenty-five years ago, there was a pervasive lack of uniformity among the courts.

The matter was not resolved until 1996 in *Lewis v. United States*,[25] when the Supreme Court held that judges should consider the severity of *each* underlying offense.[26] The justices refused to aggregate the offenses, finding that multiple petty offenses did not become severe simply by virtue of their penalties when added together.[27] The Court construed the presence of multiple petty offenses as insufficient to rise to the level of seriousness contemplated for jury entitlement. Thus, an individual sentenced to an aggregate incarceration in excess of six months, on more than one petty offense, is not normally constitutionally entitled to a jury trial.

The Supreme Court in *Duncan* incorporated the Sixth Amendment right of jury entitlement for nonpetty offenses to the states.[28] This authority set a constitutional floor, leaving discretion to the states to expand the right beyond the constitutionality requirement. The result has led to a variety of regimes across the states for defining the right to trial by jury. The broadest interpretation of the right can be found in the states that do not draw distinctions between petty and nonpetty offenses, but provide jury trials in all criminal cases upon defense demand;[29] some provide jury trial on demand where incarceration is a potential penalty.[30] The most restrictive essentially mirror the federal standard.[31]

Some states consider the nature of the offense, with reference to the constitutional standard, in deciding whether it is petty or serious. In Florida, for example, while a sentence greater than six months makes that crime serious, a sentence of less than six months does not necessarily render the crime petty.[32] A number of indicators will be

---

25. Lewis v. United States, 518 U.S. 322, 326 (1996).

26. *Id.* at 326.

27. *Id.* at 330.

28. *Duncan*, 391 U.S. at 149 (1968).

29. *E.g.*, Wisc. Const. Art. 1, § 7.

30. *E.g.*, Minn. R. Crim. P. 26.01.

31. *See* State v. Denelsbeck, 137 A.3d 462 (N.J. 2016) (ruling that defendants did not have the right to a jury trial for third or subsequent DUI offense). The legislature added significant penalties—including fines, assessments, surcharges, long-term driving suspension, and in-ignition interlock device requirement—and the court found that these additional penalties were not serious enough to trigger the right to a jury trial, as the statute only provided for 180 days in jail.

32. Reed v. State, 470 So. 2d 1382, 1384 (Fla. 1985) ("Although the severity of the maximum authorized penalty is the most obvious criterion in determining whether a crime is a serious crime, there are other criteria which, if met, will mandate that the accused be granted the right to a jury trial.").

considered in an assessment of seriousness.[33] Hawaii employs a three-factor test to resolve the question, looking to the offense's gravity, its treatment at common law, and the authorized penalty.[34]

States are split in their treatment of cases involving multiple petty offenses. Some state judges focus their attention on the duration of imprisonment for a particular crime, but others weigh aggregation where the potential incarceration time exceeds six months and the offenses arise out of the same transaction or occurrence.[35]

III. Application of the Right

The Supreme Court has consistently held that the jury trial in criminal cases is "fundamental to the American scheme of justice."[36] It is designed to protect against oppression by the government, specifically that of the "corrupt or overzealous prosecutor and . . . the compliant, biased, or eccentric judge."[37] Historically, a key question was whether this fundamental right would be extended beyond the standard criminal trial setting.

A. Contempt Actions

The clear rule in contempt actions for over half a century has been that the right to a jury trial applies if the punishment exceeds six months' imprisonment.[38] Sentences—even for contempt—"exceeding six months may not be imposed by federal courts absent a jury trial or waiver thereof."[39] As in the criminal setting, though, the justices have never been willing to apply the jury right to contempt proceedings involving petty matters.[40]

---

33. These include viewing "crimes that were indictable at common law; crimes that involve moral turpitude; crimes that are *malum in se*, or inherently evil at common law; and crimes that carry a maximum penalty of more than six months in prison." *Id.* at 1384.

34. State v. Basabe, 97 P.3d 418, 423 (Haw. App. 2004); *see also* Benitez v. Dunevant, 7 P.3d 99, 103–04 (Ariz. 2000) (recognizing the severity of maximum penalty imposed as the most significant—but not the only—factor).

35. State v. Bell, 899 P.2d 1000, 1004 (Kan. 1995) (defendant was not denied a right to jury when charged with multiple petty offenses tried under the same complaint, but arising out of a different transaction or occurrence); *see also* State v. Sanchez, 786 P.2d 42 (N.M. 1990).

36. Duncan v. Louisiana, 391 U.S. 145, 149 (1968).

37. *Id.* at 156.

38. Cheff v. Schnackenberg, 384 U.S. 373, 380 (1966).

39. *Id.* at 380.

40. [W]e are constrained to view the proceedings here as equivalent to a procedure to prosecute a petty offense, which under our decisions does not require a jury

B. Juvenile Proceedings

Juvenile court delinquency proceedings do not implicate the Sixth Amendment jury trial provision, as no "criminal prosecution" exists.[41] While the right to counsel applies in the juvenile setting,[42] the justices were unwilling to transform the basic process historically used with underage offenders.[43]

C. Deportation Matters

Deportation proceedings, like juvenile delinquency matters, are not considered criminal trials within the meaning of the Sixth Amendment, as deportation is not viewed as punishment for a crime.[44] The deportation matter can certainly be exceedingly significant,[45] yet a jury trial is not mandated.

> trial. Over 75 years ago . . . this Court stated that "in that class or grade of offences called 'petty offences,' which, according to the common law, may be proceeded against summarily in any tribunal legally constituted for that purpose," a jury trial is not required.

Id. See supra section II.

41. To say that juvenile courts have failed to achieve their goals is to say no more than what is true of criminal courts in the United States. But failure is most striking when hopes are highest.

    Despite all these disappointments, all these failures, and all these shortcomings, we conclude that trial by jury in the juvenile court's adjudicative stage is not a constitutional requirement. We so conclude for a number of reasons:

    > 1. The court has refrained, in the cases heretofore decided, from taking the easy way with a flat holding that all rights constitutionally assured for the adult accused are to be imposed upon the state juvenile proceeding. . . .
    > 2. There is a possibility, at least, that the jury trial, if required as a matter of constitutional precept, will remake the juvenile proceeding into a fully adversary process and will put an effective end to what has been the idealistic prospect of an intimate, informal protective proceeding.

McKeiver v. Pennsylvania, 403 U.S. 528, 545 (1971).

42. *In re* Gault, 387 U.S. 1 (1967).
43. The imposition of the jury trial on the juvenile court system would not strengthen greatly, if at all, the factfinding function, and would, contrarily, provide an attrition of the juvenile court's assumed ability to function in a unique manner. It would not remedy the defects of the system. Meager as has been the hoped-for advance in the juvenile field, the alternative would be regressive, would lose what has been gained, and would tend once again to place the juvenile squarely in the routine of the criminal process.

McKeiver, 403 U.S. at 547.

44. *See* Zakonaite v. Wolf, 226 U.S. 272, 275 (1912).
45. Padilla v. Kentucky, 559 U.S. 356 (2010) (in guilty plea negotiation, competent counsel must advise the accused of the serious "collateral consequence" of deportation).

D. Sentencing

The Sixth Amendment does not require that jurors determine the sentence to be imposed in a criminal jury trial.[46] This statement, while surely correct, raises two important issues.

1. Direct Involvement in Some States

Although under the Sixth Amendment the jury need not determine the sentence, states can choose to delegate this responsibility to the jury nonetheless. Accordingly, a few states involve juries in the basic sentencing decision.[47]

2. The Changing Mandate: Required Jury Fact Finding

The more difficult issue has arisen in situations in which a fact must be found in order to increase the maximum allowable penalty under a specific sentencing statute. The key case here is *Apprendi v. New Jersey*,[48] which involved a state hate-crime statute prohibiting possession of certain restricted weapons. The state law allowed a judge to increase the sentence beyond the maximum established in the sentencing guidelines if she found that the defendant's purpose in possessing the prohibited weapon was to intimidate on the basis of particular characteristics of the victim.[49] The Supreme Court focused not on the form of the rule (part of the sentencing guidelines) but on its effect, which was of a "clear 'elemental' nature."[50] As the rule required a determination of the defendant's "degree of criminal culpability," the judicially imposed enhanced sentence deprived the defendant of his right to have the jury determine a major fact.[51] The *Apprendi* Court's focus on *effects* meant that if the prosecutor must prove certain facts that increase the maximum allowable penalty and are essentially elements of the crime, a jury (not a judge) must decide

46. Spaziano v. Florida, 468 U.S. 447, 460 (1984).

47. *See* ARK. CODE ANN. § 5-4-103 (West 1997); MO. ANN. STAT. § 557.036 (West 1999); OKLA. STAT. ANN. tit. 22, §§ 926.1, 927.1 (West Supp. 2003); TEX. CRIM. PROC. CODE ANN. art. 37.07(2)(b) (Vernon 1981); VA. CODE ANN. § 19.2-295 (West 1981). For discussions of the rationale here, see King & Noble, *Felony Jury Sentencing in Practice: A Three-State Study*, 57 VAND. L. REV. 885 (2004); Hoffman, *The Case for Jury Sentencing*, 52 DUKE L.J. 951 (2003).

48. 530 U.S. 466 (2000).

49. *Id.* at 491.

50. *Id.* at 494.

51. *Id.* at 494–95 (quoting Mullaney v. Wilbur, 421 U.S. 684, 698 (1975)).

whether facts that serve as predicates to sentencing decisions have been proved beyond a reasonable doubt.[52]

The post-*Apprendi* litigation has become increasingly complex, with a number of decisions seeking to clarify the effects-based doctrine. According to the Supreme Court, judges can decide facts that increase the mandatory *minimum* sentence and do not go to an element of the crime.[53] The justices also held that there is no Sixth Amendment violation if the jury has already decided the essential fact beyond a reasonable doubt at trial,[54] if the defendant admits the fact,[55] or if the evidence of the fact is "overwhelming" and "essentially uncontroverted."[56]

The *Apprendi* rule has transformed our federal and state criminal courts. One of the most notable post-*Apprendi* decisions is *Blakely v. Washington.*[57] The issue in *Blakely* was whether a jury determination that the crime was committed with "deliberate cruelty" was a necessary factual predicate to an "exceptional" sentence under state sentencing guidelines. The state argued that because the sentence imposed was within the statutory maximum under the guidelines, the judicial finding of "deliberate cruelty" did not actually change the maximum. The justices disagreed, clarifying that the statutory maximum, for *Apprendi* purposes, was the "maximum sentence a judge may impose *solely on the basis of the facts reflected in the jury verdict or admitted by the defendant.*"[58] In *Blakely*, the statutory maximum *was*

---

52. *Id.*

53. Harris v. United States, 536 U.S. 545 (2002).

54. United States v. Booker, 543 U.S. 220, 244 (2005).

55. *Id.*

56. United States v. Cotton, 535 U.S. 625, 633 (2002). Two recent decisions of the Supreme Court are especially worthy of note. In *United States v. Haymond*, 139 S. Ct. 2369 (2019), the Supreme Court found unconstitutional a statute that mandated that a judge must sentence a defendant to an additional prison term of five years if a judge finds by a preponderance of the evidence that a defendant on supervised release possessed child pornography. While the jury initially convicted the defendant of a crime with a range of one to ten years of imprisonment, the imposition of the mandatory five years was based only on facts found by a judge by a preponderance of evidence. As such, the finding "expose[d] the defendant to a greater punishment than that authorized by the jury's guilty verdict[.]" *Id.* at 2377.

In *Hurst v. Florida*, 577 U.S. 92 (2016), the Supreme Court struck down the Florida death penalty procedures relying heavily on *Apprendi*. Under Florida law, a defendant can be sentenced to death only if certain aggravating circumstances are found by the judge. The jury could only recommend the death penalty. As such, the judge increased the maximum punishment based on her own fact-finding and violated *Apprendi*. "The Sixth Amendment requires a jury, not a judge, to find each fact necessary to impose a sentence of death." *Id.* at 94.

57. Blakely v. Washington, 542 U.S. 296 (2004).

58. *Id.* at 303.

increased by the judge's finding of fact, which violated the Sixth Amendment and invalidated the enhanced sentence.[59] Just one year later, in *United States v. Booker*, the Court would use this same rationale to declare the Federal Sentencing Guidelines nonmandatory.[60]

IV. Size of Juries in Criminal Cases

A. Historical Basis for Twelve Jurors

As noted earlier, the Sixth Amendment provides in part that "in all criminal prosecutions, the accused shall enjoy the right to a speedy and public trial, by an impartial jury." The Constitution, however, does not explicitly provide any further information regarding the size of the jury. Since the 14th century, common law has fixed the size of the jury at twelve, yet the number twelve seems to have been a "historical accident, unrelated to the great purposes which gave rise to the jury in the first place."[61] There is nothing to suggest that the Framers intended that the constitutional requirement of the jury size be the same as common law.[62] As such, the Supreme Court found the key question was not about the history of the jury's size but, rather, about the function and purposes of the jury trial.

B. Fewer Than Twelve Jurors

The Supreme Court first considered the constitutional adequacy of a six-member jury in a criminal trial in 1970 in *Williams v. Florida*.[63] The *Williams* Court concluded that the Sixth Amendment was not violated. According to the justices, a jury trial is to prevent oppression by

---

59. *Id.* at 305.

60. Finally, the [Federal Sentencing Guidelines] Act without its "mandatory" provision and related language remains consistent with Congress' initial and basic sentencing intent. Congress sought to "provide certainty and fairness in meeting the purposes of sentencing, [while] avoiding unwarranted sentencing disparities . . . [and] maintaining sufficient flexibility to permit individualized sentences when warranted." The system remaining after excision, while lacking the mandatory features that Congress enacted, retains other features that help to further these objectives.

Booker, 543 U.S. at 264.

61. Williams v. Florida, 399 U.S. 78, 89–90 (1970). Explanations of the "historical accident" include "the number 12 . . . was the number of the presentment jury from the hundred, from which the petit jury developed," and "Lord Coke's explanation that the 'number twelve is much respected in holy writ, as 12 apostles, 12 stones, 12 tribes, etc.'" *Id.* at 88–89.

62. *See id.* at 99.

63. *Id.* at 103.

the government through community participation and "the interposition between the accused and his accuser of the commonsense judgment of a group of laymen."[64] In the *Williams* Court's view, a twelve-person jury is neither more advantageous to a defendant nor more reliable than a six-person jury.[65] Indeed, some studies apparently concluded that a smaller jury could, in fact, be more advantageous to a defendant than a larger jury.[66]

In 1978, the Supreme Court placed a limit on how small a jury may be to remain constitutional. In *Ballew v. Georgia*, the Court decided that a five-person jury violates the Sixth Amendment.[67] Thus, at a minimum, the jury must be composed of six people despite the fact that the justices "admit[ted] that [they did] not pretend to discern a clear line between six members and five."[68] Still, they decided that the purposes and functions of the jury could not be fulfilled with less than six jurors, as a jury composed of less than six members is the breaking point of accuracy, reliability, and consistency, and is of "constitutional significance."[69]

C. Federal Juries

Even though the Supreme Court has decided that the Constitution does not mandate a twelve-person jury, a twelve-person jury remains a requirement for federal criminal cases under the Federal Rules of Criminal Procedure.[70] Several exceptions to the twelve-person jury requirement are worth noting. A defendant may agree to a jury of fewer than twelve at any time before the verdict is rendered.[71] A defendant may also consent to a jury of fewer than twelve returning a verdict if one or more jurors must be excused for good cause.[72] In

---

64. *Id.* at 100.

65. *Id.* at 100–02. A six-person jury is "large enough to promote group deliberation, free from outside attempts at intimidation, and to provide a fair possibility for obtaining a representative cross-section of the community." *Id.* at 100–01.

66. *Id.* at 101 n.49.

67. Ballew v. Georgia, 435 U.S. 223 (1978).

68. *Id.* at 239.

69. *Id.*

70. FED. R. CRIM. P. 23(b)(1).

71. FED. R. CRIM. P. 23(b)(2). A defendant may waive the right to a jury trial, so by the same logic, a defendant may waive the twelve-person jury requirement. *See generally* Patton v. United States, 281 U.S. 276, 299 (1930).

72. FED. R. CRIM. P. 23(b)(2)(B).

addition, the court may permit a jury of eleven "without stipulation by the parties, if the court finds good cause to excuse a juror."[73]

D. State Juries

About half the states follow the federal rule and require twelve-person juries in criminal cases.[74] The other states permit juries of fewer than twelve.[75] Of those states, only six states permit felony prosecutions to be heard by juries smaller than twelve.[76] However, even in these states, juries of twelve are still required in capital cases.[77] Twenty-three states permit juries of fewer than twelve members for misdemeanor trials.[78]

---

73. Fed. R. Crim. P. 23(b)(3); *see also* United States v. Stratton, 779 F.2d 820, 832–33 (2d Cir. 1985), *cert. denied*, 476 U.S. 1162 (1986) (upholding the constitutionality of the rule). In *United States v. Brown*, 784 F.3d 1301 (9th Cir. 2015), after a five-day trial, while the jury was deliberating, one of the jurors became ill and was excused. Defense counsel requested that the trial judge seat an alternate juror rather than proceed with eleven jurors. The court denied Brown's request, and soon thereafter the eleven-person jury returned a guilty verdict. The court on appeal noted that Rule 23(b)(3) provides "courts three options after excusing a juror for good cause during deliberations: (1) declare a mistrial; (2) proceed with 11 jurors; or (3) seat an alternate." *Id.* at 1304. The appeals judges decided that the trial could go forward with eleven jurors even when alternates are available. Moreover, the matter is left to the discretion of the trial judge.

> Here, the jury had deliberated for over a day in a complex case involving 14 counts. Significantly, the jury had asked and received answers to five substantive questions. Substituting an alternate likely would have imposed substantial additional work on the jury, the parties and the court. It also would have required the jurors to attempt to clear their minds of any conclusions they had reached. The court weighed these considerations and concluded that "justice would best be served by proceeding with a jury of 11 individuals." Under these circumstances, the district court did not abuse its discretion.

Id. at 1307.

74. Arizona, Colorado, Connecticut, Florida, Georgia, Hawaii, Idaho, Indiana, Iowa, Kansas, Louisiana, Mississippi, Missouri, New Hampshire, New Jersey, North Dakota, Ohio, Oklahoma, Oregon, Texas, Utah, Virginia, Wisconsin, and Wyoming. *See* David B. Rottman et al., State Court Organization 2004, at 233, tbl. 42 (2004), *available at* www.bjs.gov/content/pub/pdf/sco04.pdf. For an unusual problem involving the size of the jury, *see* Woodward v. Curtin, 2014 WL 5847588 (E.D. Mich. 2014) where a thirteen-person jury returned a guilty verdict (alternate juror was allowed to participate in deliberation and judgment.) Held, no error as defendant agreed to the process and there is "no clearly established federal law [which] prohibits a jury composed of 13 members."

75. Rottman et al., *supra* note 74, at 233, tbl. 42. There are also several states not listed that allow exceptions where the parties stipulate to fewer than twelve jurors.

76. *Id.*

77. *Id.*

78. *Id.*

E. Unanimity

The Supreme Court wrote in *Williams v. Florida* that a six-person jury is constitutional "particularly if the requirement of unanimity is retained."[79] The Court later addressed the issue squarely in *Burch v. Louisiana*, holding that a six-person jury must be unanimous to be constitutional.[80] The Federal Rules of Criminal Procedure provide that the verdict in all criminal cases must be unanimous.[81] The Supreme Court recently held that jury unanimity is required in state criminal trials, too.[82]

V. Unanimity in Criminal Proceedings

A. Constitutional Principles

A criminal defendant in a federal court has both statutory and constitutional rights to a unanimous jury verdict, as noted earlier.[83] Forty years ago, the Supreme Court explained that "in an unbroken line of cases reaching back into the late 1880s, the justices have recognized, virtually without dissent, that unanimity is one of the indispensable features of a federal jury trial."[84] The Court declined, however, to extend the Sixth Amendment's guarantee of a unanimous jury verdict to criminal defendants in state courts. In *Apodaca v. Oregon*, three separate Oregon juries had convicted defendants based on nonunanimous verdicts.[85] The verdicts were allowed, with the view that nonunanimous jury verdicts were sufficient for defendants' criminal convictions in state, though not federal, courts.

> [T]he purpose of trial by jury is to prevent oppression by the government by providing a "safeguard against the corrupt or overzealous prosecutor and against the compliant, biased, or eccentric judge." "Given this purpose, the essential feature of a jury obviously lies in the interposition between the accused and his accuser of the common

---

79. Williams v. Florida, 399 U.S. 78, 100 (1970).

80. Burch v. Louisiana, 441 U.S. 130 (1979) (The Court struck down a provision that misdemeanors punishable by more than six months "shall be tried before a jury of six persons, five of whom must concur to render a verdict.").

81. Fed. R. Crim. P. 31(a). *See* further discussion *infra* section V.

82. Ramos v. Louisiana, 140 S. Ct. 1390 (2020), discussed below.

83. Fed. R. Crim. P. 31(a); *Johnson*, 406 U.S. at 356; *Apodaca*, 406 U.S. at 404.

84. *Johnson*, 406 U.S. at 369. "[I]n accord both with history and precedent, that the Sixth Amendment requires a unanimous jury verdict to convict in a federal criminal trial." *Id.* at 371 (Powell, J., concurring).

85. *Apodaca*, 406 U.S. at 405–06. The verdicts were rendered 11–1 and 10–2.

> sense judgment of a group of laymen. . . ." A requirement of unanimity, however, does not materially contribute to the exercise of this common sense judgment. [A] jury will come to such a judgment as long as it consists of a group of laymen representative of a cross section of the community who have the duty and the opportunity to deliberate, free from outside attempts at intimidation, on the question of a defendant's guilt. In terms of this function we perceive no difference between juries required to act unanimously and those permitted to convict or acquit by votes of ten to two or eleven to one.[86]

The Supreme Court changed this view in *Ramos v. Louisiana*:[87]

> There can be no question either that the Sixth Amendment's unanimity requirement applies to state and federal criminal trials equally. This Court has long explained that the Sixth Amendment right to a jury trial is "fundamental to the American scheme of justice" and incorporated against the States under the Fourteenth Amendment. This Court has long explained, too, that incorporated provisions of the Bill of Rights bear the same content when asserted against States as they do when asserted against the federal government. So if the Sixth Amendment's right to a jury trial requires a unanimous verdict to support a conviction in federal court, it requires no less in state court.[88]

B. Waiver

Most federal courts do not allow criminal defendants to waive the unanimity requirement. In 1992, Justice Kennedy, then sitting as a circuit judge, wrote, "the requirement of a unanimous verdict is firmly established in the federal system."[89] Federal Rule of Criminal Procedure 31(a) explicitly requires that "[t]he verdict shall be unanimous."[90] The Second, Third, Fifth, Sixth, Ninth, and Tenth Circuits have also explicitly refused to allow a defense waiver of the unanimity requirement.[91] Only the Eleventh Circuit has allowed a waiver of the

86. *Id.* at 410–11.

87. Ramos v. Louisiana, 140 S. Ct. 1390 (2020).

88. *Id.* at 1397.

89. United States v. Lopez, 581 F.2d 1338, 1340–42 (9th Cir. 1992).

90. *Id.* at 1341.

91. *See* United States v. Pachay, 711 F.2d 488, 490–93 (2d Cir. 1983) (extensively reviewing the text, history, and purpose of Rule 31(a)). As explained in *United States v. Smedes*, 760 F.2d 109, 113 (6th Cir. 1985), "the right to a unanimous verdict is so important that it is one of the few rights of a criminal defendant that cannot, under any circumstances, be waived." *See* United States v. Morris, 612 F.2d 483, 488–89 (10th Cir. 1979) ("a right so

unanimity requirement, though only "in exceptional circumstances." In *Sanchez v. United States*,[92] the Eleventh Circuit provided the standard for such exceptional circumstances:

> Before allowing the defendant to waive the right, the following criteria should be met: (1) the waiver should be initiated by the defendant, not the judge or the prosecutor; (2) the jury must have had a reasonable time to deliberate and should have told the court only that it could not reach a decision, but not how it stood numerically, (3) the judge should carefully explain to the defendant the right to a unanimous verdict and the consequences of a waiver of that right; and (4) the judge should question the defendant directly to determine whether the waiver is being made knowingly and voluntarily.[93]

In some states, a criminal defendant may waive the right to a unanimous verdict. For example, Maryland permits a waiver of its unanimity requirement when the criminal defendant's decision is made intelligently and competently, so long as the court and prosecution consent to the waiver.[94] A criminal defendant in Michigan may also waive, but no additional consent is necessary. A valid waiver there requires only "(1) a specific knowledge of the constitutional right and (2) an intentional decision to abandon the protection of the constitutional right."[95]

C. Deadlocked Juries and the *Allen* Charge

If the jury cannot agree on a verdict on one or more counts, the court may declare a mistrial on those counts.[96] The government may retry any defendant on any count on which the jury could not agree.[97] In

fundamental it may not be waived"); United States v. Scalzitti, 578 F.2d 507, 511–12 (3d Cir. 1978) (the "unequivocal command" of Rule 31(a) cannot be waived); Sincox v. United States, 571 F.2d 876, 878 (5th Cir. 1978) ("this right may not be waived"). *See also* United States v. Cunningham 679 F. 3d 355, 386 (6th ed. 2012); United States v. Ullah, 976 F.2d 509, 512–13 (9th Cir. 1992).

92. Sanchez v. United States, 782 F.2d 928 (11th Cir. 1986).

93. *Id.* at 934.

94. Claybourne v. State, 61 A.3d 841, 853 (Md. App. 2013) ("A defendant's right to a unanimous verdict—although a fundamental right—may be duly waived by the express consent of the defendant, the State, and the court.").

95. People v. Miller, 329 N.W.2d 460, 465–66 (Mich. Ct. App. 1982).

96. Fed. R. Crim. P. 31(b)(3); Renico v. Lett, 559 U.S. 766, 774 (2010) ("A mistrial premised upon the trial judge's belief that the jury is unable to reach a verdict [has been] long considered the classic basis for a proper mistrial[.]").

97. The issue arises often, as in the prosecution of the former Illinois governor. *See* Sweeney et al., *Many Blagojevich Jurors Disappointed*, Chi. Trib. (Aug. 18, 2010), https://

declaring a mistrial, "[t]he trial judge's decision to declare a mistrial when he considers the jury deadlocked is . . . accorded great deference by a reviewing court."[98]

This view was reaffirmed in *Renico v. Lett.*[99] There the jury deliberated for a total of four hours before reporting it was deadlocked. The trial judge then declared a mistrial. The justices concluded that even with the limited period of juror deliberations, the trial judge should be given deference in declaring a deadlock and mistrial. "We have expressly declined to require 'mechanical application' of any 'rigid formula' when trial judges decide whether jury deadlock warrants a mistrial."[100]

If a deadlock is occurring, the trial court may choose to direct the jury to deliberate further.[101] The language, timing, and circumstances surrounding the judge's directions to the jury—commonly referred to as an "*Allen* charge" or "dynamite instruction"—have come under numerous courts' scrutiny. In *Allen*, decided more than a century ago, the Supreme Court approved a trial judge's direction that the jury

---

www.chicagotribune.com/news/ct-xpm-2010-08-18-ct-met-blagojevich-verdict-jury-20100818-story.html (jury deliberated for fourteen days before reaching verdict on only one of many charges).

98. Washington v. Arizona, 434 U.S. 497, 509–10 (1978).

99. 559 U.S. 766 (2010).

100. *Id.* at 767.

101. Fed. R. Crim. P. 31(d). The trial judge in attempting to have the jury reach a verdict must be careful not to act in a coercive manner. *United States v. Banks*, 982 F.3d 1098 (7th Cir. Dec. 18, 2020), illustrates the point. There, while the jury was being polled as to the unanimous guilty verdict, one juror stated he was "forced into" voting to convict. The judge then directed the jurors to continue deliberating and sent them back to the jury room for further discussion. Soon thereafter, a unanimous guilty verdict was reported. Held, the judge's action violated the defendant's right to have the verdict delivered in a noncoercive manner.

> [J]uror coercion, if it occurs, is a grave error . . . . When the judge asked [the holdout juror] if the guilty verdict against Banks was, in fact, his verdict, he replied with two striking words: "Forced into." This was far more than a simple "no." Indeed, the words "forced into" amount to Juror 32 telling the court that he was coerced into the verdict. To be clear, we do not hold that this response alone necessitated a mistrial. The rules of procedure give the trial judge the discretion to either mistry the case or order further deliberation when the jury poll reveals a lack of unanimity. . . . But Juror 32's response was alarming enough that an immediate sidebar with counsel was warranted. Instead, the judge asked several follow-up questions that only pressed Juror 32 further. Those questions and answers did little to lessen the pressure at the time, and they do nothing to assuage our concerns now. After Juror 32 said, "Forced into," the judge again asked him, "Is this your verdict?" And he responded, "I suppose so."

Id. at 1103.

continue its deliberations.[102] The justices' most recent opinion on the *Allen* charge was in 1988 in *Lowenfield v. Phelps*,[103] where the Court allowed the instruction, noting: "All of the Federal Courts of Appeals have upheld some form of a supplemental jury charge."[104]

D. States and the *Allen* Charge

Numerous state courts have disapproved of such *Allen* charges, in whole or in part.[105] The broadest condemnation was given by an Arizona court:

---

102. United States v. Allen, 164 U.S. 492, 501–02 (1896). The trial judge in *Allen* told the jurors they should "consider that the case must at some time be decided . . . and there is no reason to suppose that the case will ever be submitted to twelve men more intelligent, more impartial, or more competent to decide it, or that more or clearer evidence will be produced on the one side or the other." *See generally* Marcus, *The* Allen *Instruction in Criminal Cases: Is the Dynamite Charge About to Be Permanently Defused?*, 43 Mo. L. Rev. 613, 615–17 (1978). The judge in delivering the charge must generally also give "the admonition [to deadlocked jurors] not to give up conscientiously held beliefs." United States v. Haynes, 729 F.3d 178, 194 (2d Cir. 2013). Another technique used by some courts is to permit the lawyers to make supplement arguments to the deadlocked jury. If the judge is too involved in the process, allowing such argument may be viewed as error, as in *United States v. Evanston*, 651 F.3d 1080 (9th Cir. 2011). *But see* United States v. Della Porta, 653 F.3d 1043 (9th Cir. 2011) (practice seen as within the trial judge's discretion). There the jury requested further argument, and the judge did not direct the substance of the argument.

103. Lowenfield v. Phelps, 484 U.S. 231, 236 (1988).

104. *Id.*, n.1. This was the instruction allowed by the Court:

> Ladies and Gentlemen, as I instructed you earlier if the jury is unable to unanimously agree on a recommendation the Court shall impose the sentence of Life Imprisonment without benefit of Probation, Parole, or Suspension of Sentence.
> When you enter the jury room it is your duty to consult with one another to consider each other's views and to discuss the evidence with the objective of reaching a just verdict if you can do so without violence to that individual judgment.
> Each of you must decide the case for yourself but only after discussion and impartial consideration of the case with your fellow jurors. You are not advocates for one side or the other. Do not hesitate to reexamine your own views and to change your opinion if you are convinced you are wrong but do not surrender your honest belief as to the weight and effect of evidence solely because of the opinion of your fellow jurors or for the mere purpose of returning a verdict.

Id. at 235. *See generally* Fortune v. United States, 65 A.3d 75 (D.C. App. 2013); Bateman, *Blast It All:* Allen *Charges and the Dangers of Playing with Dynamite*, 32 U. Haw. L. Rev. 323, 342 (2010) (qupting ABA, Principles for Juries & Jury Trials 21, Principle 4(A) (2005)).

105. People v. Gainer, 566 P.2d 997 (Cal. 1977) (listing a sampling of state cases in which the courts struck down the use of *Allen* instructions); *see* Cavallaro, *Pride and Prejudice and Proof: Quotidian Factfinding and Rules of Evidence*, 55 Hastings L.J. 697 (2004). In *Hooks v. Workman*, 606 F.3d 715, 732 (10th Cir. 2010), the appellate judges rejected an

> It now appears that [the *Allen* charge's] continued use will result in an endless chain of decisions, each link thereof tempered and forged with varying facts and circumstances and welded with ever-changing personalities of the appellate court. This is not in keeping with sound justice and the preservation of human liberties and security. We are convinced that the evils far outweigh the benefits, and decree that its use shall no longer be tolerated and approved by this court.[106]

Still, in other states, such jury instructions have been allowed. In one Missouri case, the defendant claimed that the language of the trial judge's charge fell outside the scope of acceptable direction. The trial judge had instructed the jury:

> I mean there is a lot at stake here. I know that emotions among the parties and the alleged victims and the defendant are running high. The case has been pending for a long time. Thousands of hours of effort to prepare the case, present it to the jury have been put into this by both sides; lots of cost to taxpayers and I don't want to give up and throw in the towel until you all are absolutely convinced that you have given it every possible shot.[107]

The appellate court found that the trial court did not err in giving this instruction because the language was not coercive.[108] The trial judge there "did not unequivocally tell the jury that a verdict must be

---

Allen instruction given during the penalty phase of a death eligible case for being coercive ("[E]ven in death-penalty proceedings, trial courts are entitled to direct juries to deliberate for a reasonable time before declaring a mistrial. . . . Nevertheless, '[a]ny criminal defendant, and especially any capital defendant, being tried by a jury is entitled to the uncoerced verdict of that body.' Accordingly, a trial court must be vigilant to instruct the jury in a way that, given all the surrounding circumstances, does not coerce the jury into returning a death verdict."). In *Hooks*, the jury informed the court that it was split 11–1 in favor of a death sentence. Soon thereafter the jurors sent the judge a note indicating they would like to return home for an evening break. The court then instructed them to continue deliberating. *Id.*

106. State v. Thomas, 342 P.2d 197, 200 (Ariz. 1959). However, a similar jury instruction given in *State v. Williams*, 639 P.2d 1036, 1038–39 (Ariz. 1982), was upheld. The key question for the later court was whether "a reading of the instruction as a whole compels the conclusion that it fairly informs the jurors of their responsibility. . . . [Here the charge was not likely] to compel the jury to act cohesively to find appellant guilty." *Id.*

107. State v. Griffith, 312 S.W.3d 413, 420 (Mo. Ct. App. 2010).

108. *Id.* at 421. *See also* State v. Taylor, 829 S.E.2d 723, 729 (S.C. 2019): "The charge here also overemphasized the cost and expense of a retrial. While it is not error to tell the jury that a retrial will be costly, such statements are disfavored and should not be overbearing. . . . Also, telling the jury the case will 'have' to be retried is misleading. A hung jury often acts as an alarm bell to all but the unthinking, awakening one side (sometimes both) to weaknesses in their case, which can lead to a plea deal rather than a retrial."

reached. Asking jurors to 'give it every possible shot' is not the same as ordering them to return a verdict."[109]

VI. Waiver of Jury Right

All courts allow jury waiver, but most courts have limitations and requirements that must be met before a defendant can waive this right. Generally, a defendant is permitted to waive the right to a jury

---

109. *Id.* at 421–22 (Standard of review is abuse of discretion by the trial court. Abuse only occurs if the trial judge's instruction is coercive.). The extreme situation occurred in *Brewster v. Hetzel*, 913 F.3d 1042 (11th Cir. 2019), where the jury deadlocked three and a half hours into deliberation and sent the judge a note. The jurors deliberated for another hour and a half and sent another note stating that they were deadlocked. The judge asked the foreman if he thought they could come to a unanimous decision. The foreman testified no. The judge gave a standard *Allen* charge. The jury continued to deliberate into the next day with a new judge presiding. The jurors sent a third, fourth, and fifth note stating that they were still deadlocked and that one juror was the holdout. The judge instructed that they should continue deliberating and additionally gave an instruction mentioning their "oath" nine separate times. A final sixth note was sent that stated the lone holdout refused to talk to the others but was instead doing crossword puzzles. The judge ordered the bailiff to remove all reading material. The jury returned a unanimous guilty verdict less than twenty minutes later. Held, that the cumulative effect of the *Allen* charge and the other instructions was coercive. *See also* Workman v. State, 771 S.E.2d 636 (S.C. 2015). After about four hours of deliberation, the jury there reported that it was deadlocked. The judge gave an *Allen* charge directed to those holding the minority view. He stated that "[i]f a majority of you are for one particular form of a verdict, the minority ought to seriously ask themselves whether they can reasonably doubt the correctness of the judgment of the majority." The South Carolina Supreme Court found that the *Allen* charge was unconstitutionally coercive, as it was impermissibly directed at minority jurors. In *Avalos v. Lewis*, 2014 WL 5035941 (E.D. Cal. 2014), a state criminal defendant in his federal habeas corpus petition asserted that the trial judge's modified *Allen* charge was unconstitutional. In finding no error, the reviewing court laid out the three key factors in deciding if such a supplemental instruction violates due process:

> [First is] the form of the instruction. . . While the instruction informed the jurors that they should not hesitate to change their views, it also advised them to do so only if they were "convinced" their prior vote was "wrong." The instruction did not advise the jurors to acquiesce in the majority decision, but stressed that each juror should carefully weigh the evidence and "decide the case for yourself."
>
> The second relevant factor is the length of time the jurors in petitioner's case deliberated after receiving the trial court's supplemental instruction. . . . In any event, the timing of a verdict in relation to the giving of the instruction alone has proven to be an insufficient basis upon which to find that a verdict was coerced.
>
> [T]he third factor [is whether there is a] . . . circumstance present in this case indicating coercion of the jury stemming from the trial court's responsive instruction. The trial court's supplemental instruction was not directed toward a specific juror or set of jurors, but was addressed to the entire jury.

trial if the request is expressly and intelligently made.[110] The Supreme Court has found that the defendant can make an intelligent choice to waive, even if he made the request while representing himself.[111] But such a waiver will not be valid if the defendant is unaware of essential facts regarding the sentence sought by the prosecution.[112]

Under the Federal Rules of Criminal Procedure the waiver must be in writing, the government must consent to the waiver, and the court must approve the waiver before the defendant can successfully waive the right to a jury trial.[113] In *Singer v. United States*, the Court affirmed the rule requiring that the court and government assent to a defendant's jury waiver.[114] The justices emphasized that there is no constitutional right for a criminal defendant to have a case heard by the judge, without a jury.[115]

---

110. Fed. R. Crim. P. 23. Most courts scrutinize such decisions with care. *See, e.g.*, State v. Baker, 319 P.3d 1009, 1014 (Haw. 2014) (trial judge's responsibility is "serious and weighty"); Hinsley v. State, 280 P.3d 354, 355 (Okla. App. 2012) (must be "clear showing that the waiver was competent, knowing and intelligent."). Problems can be especially acute if the defendant has a "low I.Q. and . . . is learning disabled." United States v. Shorty, 741 F.3d 961, 967 (9th Cir. 2013).

111. Adams v. United States *ex rel.* McCann, 317 U.S. 269, 275 (1942).

112. As explained by Justice Marshall, the burden is on the prosecution to show such awareness:

> The court [in this case] did not determine whether petitioner had signed the waiver "with sufficient awareness of the relevant circumstances and likely consequences" of his act. Nor did the waiver itself cure this defect, since it did no more than inform petitioner of his "constitutional right to a trial by jury." When a defendant purports to waive a fundamental constitutional right, "it is the State that has the burden of establishing a valid waiver."

Jells v. Ohio, 498 U.S. 1111 (1991) (Marshall, J., dissenting from denial of writ of certiorari).

113. Fed. R. Crim. P. 23. The rule, though, is not absolute. Courts rarely overrule the objection of the government to a bench trial, but unusual circumstances may necessitate a trial without a jury. The most recent decision arose during the height of the COVID-19 pandemic. In United States v. Cohn, 19-CR-097 (GRB) (E.D.N.Y. Aug. 26, 2020), the defendant sought a nonjury trial over the government's objection. The bases of the request were the "extraordinary circumstances presented by the COVID-19 pandemic . . . [and the] desire to have a speedy trial . . . ." The court granted the motion, relying heavily on the special dangers presented during the pandemic: "the problem of conducting a trial with reasonable safeguards [at this time is] exquisitely difficult."

114. 380 U.S. 24 (1965).

115. "There is no federally recognized right to a criminal trial before a judge sitting alone, but a defendant can . . . in some instances waive his right to a jury trial." *Id.* at 34. The Court did, though, keep open the possibility that in some situations a requirement of government assent would not be constitutional: "We need not determine in this case whether there might be some circumstances where a defendant's reasons for wanting to be tried by a judge alone are so compelling that the Government's insistence on trial by jury would result in the denial to a defendant of an impartial trial." *Id.* at 39.

Several states follow the federal standard; they mandate that both the government and the court must consent to the jury waiver before a defendant's waiver request is granted.[116] Other states merely require that the defendant make the request to waive a jury trial in writing; no agreement by the government or the trial judge is needed.[117] Some states allow the defendant simply to make an oral or written request to waive the right to a jury trial. The request will be granted as long as the court finds that the waiver is made knowingly, voluntarily, and intelligently.[118] And in still other states a waiver shall be found if the defendant fails to request a jury trial.[119] A few states take the process a step further by requiring—as in the federal system—that the court approve the waiver. Unlike the federal model, however, in these states the prosecution does not have to agree to the waiver.[120]

Capital cases are treated differently in most states.[121] For instance, Texas, the leading state for death penalty prosecutions, will allow jury waiver "only if the attorney representing the State, in writing and in open court, consents to the waiver."[122]

---

116. *See, e.g.*, ARIZ. R. CRIM. P. 18.1; IND. CODE ANN. § 35-37-1-2; ALA. R. CRIM. P. 18.1; MASS. GEN. LAWS ch. 263, § 6.

117. *See* 725 ILL. COMP. STAT. ANN. 5/115-1 (1992).

118. COLO. REV. STAT. ANN. § 18-1-406(2); FLA. R. CRIM. P. 3.260.

119. CONN. GEN. STAT. § 54-82(b).

120. *See, e.g.*, MO. CONST. art. I, § 22(a).

121. But not in the federal system, where one process governs when waiver can be successful, even in death penalty prosecutions. FED. R. CRIM. P. 7.

122. TEX. CRIM. PROC. CODE ANN. art. 1.13 (2010). Some courts are unyielding in requiring the waiver to be made in open court, even in noncapital cases. See, for instance, this discussion in *State v. Haggard*, 465 P.3d 1097, 1102 (Idaho 2020):

> When a defendant waives the right to trial by jury and its associated protections, the trial court is required to abide by certain procedural guidelines. The Idaho Constitution explains how one may waive the right to a jury trial:
>
> The right of trial by jury shall remain inviolate; . . . . A trial by jury may be waived in all criminal cases, by the consent of all parties, expressed in open court, . . . signified in such manner as may be prescribed by law . . . .
>
> Here, there is some evidence that Haggard's waiver was knowing, intelligent, and voluntary. For example, Haggard's signature on the Pre-Trial Stipulation raises the presumption that it was voluntary. Likewise, there are multiple sources of evidence suggesting that his waiver was knowing and intelligent. For one, Haggard signed and initialed two separate forms that apprised him of his rights. In addition, the magistrate court's dialogue with Haggard at his arraignment revealed that Haggard had some experience and savvy with the criminal justice system. Haggard pleaded not guilty, asked for counsel, and stated that he had no questions concerning his rights.

VII. Jury Selection

A. Eligibility for Service

Under federal law, each district court must adopt a written plan for the random selection of jurors. The plan must include provisions for the creation of the master jury wheel from which prospective jurors are drawn.[123] The procedure must be designed to ensure (1) the random selection of a fair cross section of the community in the district where the court convenes; (2) that the names of persons from all counties or similar political subdivisions within the district are placed in the wheel; and (3) that each political subdivision is proportionately represented.[124]

Many states have similar systems for creating a master list of qualified persons, and the means by which unlawful distinctions and discriminations in the selection of a jury are to be avoided. Common sources for the names of prospective jurors for the master list include voter registrations, lists of actual voters, and driver license records.[125] Then, periodically, a clerk or judge will publicly draw at random the names of as many such persons as are needed for jury service.[126]

B. Qualifications

In routine cases, there are several requirements that limit some members of the community from serving as jurors. For example, a potential juror must be a U.S. citizen and at least eighteen years old.[127] Status as a registered voter or an elector is also a common means of selection for potential jurors. An individual is not qualified to serve on a jury if incapable by reason of mental or physical infirmity to

---

But while this evidence shows some general knowledge or familiarity with court procedures, it does not alter Idaho's constitutional requirement that the waiver and the parties' consent be "expressed in open court."

123. 28 U.S.C.A. § 1863.

124. *Id.*

125. The North Carolina process is typical: "At least every two years, a three-person Jury Commission for each county oversees the compiling of a master jury list of licensed drivers and/or registered voters. Names are drawn at random from this list. A jury summons is printed and issued to jurors by U.S. mail." N.C. Jud. Branch, *Jury Service*, https://www.nccourts.gov/help-topics/jury-service/jury-service (last visited Mar. 30, 2021).

126. As in the federal procedure, 28 U.S.C.A. § 1864(a): "From time to time as directed by the district court, the clerk or a district judge shall draw at random from the master jury wheel the names of as many persons as may be required for jury service."

127. *See, e.g.*, N.Y. State Unified Court Sys., *General Information Questions and Answers (FAQs)*, http://www.nyjuror.gov/juryQandA.shtml.

render satisfactory jury service. There is, however, no per se disqualification of a potential juror with a physical or mental impairment, so long as it will not interfere with court service.[128] Exclusion of jurors based on gender[129] or race[130] is prohibited. Many states also have broader criteria, confining the selection of jurors to those possessing sound judgment, fair character, or a general reputation for honesty,[131] as well as the ability to understand English.[132] Many jurisdictions also bar convicted felons from serving as jurors.[133]

---

128. 28 U.S.C.A. § 1865(b)(4): "The chief judge . . . shall deem any person qualified to serve . . . unless he is incapable, by reason of mental or physical infirmity, to render satisfactory jury service." The Utah explanation here is common:

> Judges can excuse people who show that they have a physical or mental disability that renders them incapable of jury service. Judges can also grant a postponement of jury service when they decide that such service would result in great hardship or inconvenience. But these postponements are rare. Everyone is inconvenienced to some degree by jury service, but for the system to work, people from all walks of life must be willing to serve. Those who refuse to complete the juror questionnaire or to appear when called to serve are subject to the imposition of fines and jail time.

UTAH STATE COURTS, *Selected to Serve—A Guide to Jury Service*, http://www.utcourt.gov/courts/dist/jury/selserve.htm.

129. Taylor v. Louisiana, 419 U.S. 522, 533 (1975) ("Women cannot be systematically excluded from jury panels from which petit juries are drawn. This conclusion is consistent with the current judgment of the country, now evidenced by legislative or constitutional provisions in every State and at the federal level qualifying women for jury service.").

130. Powers v. Ohio, 499 U.S. 400, 404 (1991) ("For over a century, this Court has been unyielding in its position that a defendant is denied equal protection of the laws when tried before a jury from which members of his or her race have been excluded by the State's purposeful conduct.").

131. Carter v. Jury Comm'r, 396 U.S. 320, 332 (1970) ("It has long been accepted that the Constitution does not forbid the States to prescribe relevant qualifications for their jurors. The States remain free to confine the selection to . . . those possessing good intelligence, sound judgment, and fair character."). Of course, individuals cannot, on this basis, be unconstitutionally discriminated against. *Id.*

132. 28 U.S.C.A. § 1865(b)(2), (3) ("The chief judge of the district . . . shall deem any person qualified to serve . . . unless he . . . is unable to read, write, and understands the English language with a degree of proficiency sufficient to fill out satisfactorily the juror qualification form [or] is unable to speak the English language."). For a good explanation, see CAL. COURTS, *Frequently Asked Questions*, http://www.courts.ca.gov/2954.htm. *See generally* United States v. Pineda, 743 F.3d 213, 217 (7th Cir. 2014).

133. 28 U.S.C.A. § 1865(b)(5) ("The chief judge of the district . . . shall deem any person qualified to serve . . . unless he . . . has been convicted in a State or Federal court of record of, a crime punishable by imprisonment for more than one year and his civil rights have not been restored."). Only two states, Kentucky and Virginia, absolutely prohibit such service by a convicted felon without successful petition to the governor. For an explanation of the Virginia process, *see* SEC. OF THE COMMONWEALTH OF VIRGINIA, *Restoration of Rights*, https://www.restore.virginia.gov/.

In addition to the numerous qualifications just listed, there are also excuses, exemptions, and exclusions from jury service. Although some jurisdictions restrict individuals in certain law-related professions from service,[134] most do not.[135]

C. Death Penalty Prosecutions

In a capital murder case, both the state and the defendant may question prospective jurors about their views on capital punishment. Individuals who claim that they would never be able to render a death penalty can be challenged for cause by the prosecutor; those who state that they would always render a death penalty if murder is proven can be challenged for cause by the defense. However, a potential juror may not be removed for cause simply because he or she expresses doubts about capital punishment.[136] When selecting a "death-qualified" jury, the proper standard for determining whether a prospective juror should be excluded for cause is whether that person's views on capital punishment would "prevent or substantially impair the performance of his duties as a juror."[137]

---

134. *But see* SEMINOLE CNTY. CLERK OF COURTS, *About Jury Duty Service*, https://www.seminoleclerk.org/departments/courts/jury-duty/jury-duty-information/ (last visited Mar. 30, 2021).

135. As is explained by one New Jersey law firm, these exclusions often consist of the following:

- The individual is 75 years of age or older;
- The individual previously served as a juror;
- Jury service would impose a severe hardship;
- The individual has personal obligations to care for others;
- The person is employed in firefighting or rescue, healthcare, or elementary education.

Wells, Jaworski & Liebman, *Have You Been Called for Jury Duty?: Exemption from Jury Service*, http://wellslaw.com/haveyoubeen.html.

136. Witherspoon v. Illinois, 391 U.S. 510, 522 (1968) ("[W]e hold that a sentence of death cannot be carried out if the jury that imposed or recommended it was chosen by excluding veniremen for cause simply because they voiced general objections to the death penalty or expressed conscientious or religious scruples against its infliction."). As the California Supreme Court further explained in *People v. Peterson*, 472 P.3d 382, 392 (Cal. 2020): "While a court may dismiss a prospective juror as unqualified to sit on a capital case if the juror's views on capital punishment would substantially impair his or her ability to follow the law, a juror may not be dismissed merely because he or she has expressed opposition to the death penalty as a general matter." *See also* Morgan v. Illinois, 504 U.S. 719 (1992).

137. Wainwright v. Witt, 469 U.S. 412, 424 (1985). For discussions of the process of "death qualifying" jurors, see Cohen & Smith, *The Death of Death-Qualification*, 59 CASE W. RES. L. REV. 87 (2008); Blume et al., *Probing "Life Qualification" Through Expanded Voir Dire*,

D. Jury Makeup

It is fair to say that for much of our history juries have not been representative of our citizenry, particularly with regard to race and gender.[138] It was only a full century after the adoption of the Constitution that the Supreme Court substantively addressed the matter, and then another several decades before it began to forcefully consider the exclusion of entire classes of individuals from jury service. The two key early cases are *Strauder v. West Virginia*[139] and *Ballard v. United States*.[140]

Well over a century ago, in *Strauder*, the Court considered the constitutionality of a state statute that limited those who could serve as jurors to "white male persons who are twenty-one years of age and who are citizens of this State." The *Strauder* Court had little difficulty striking down this law as unconstitutionally discriminatory.

> That the West Virginia statute respecting juries—the statute that controlled the selection of the grand and petit jury in the case of the plaintiff in error—is such discrimination ought not to be doubted. Nor would it be if the persons excluded by it were white men. . . . [It is] a stimulant to that race prejudice which is an impediment to securing to individuals of the race that equal justice which the law aims to secure to all others.[141]

While deciding the matter under federal statutory law, the justices made clear that prohibiting nonwhites and women from serving on juries would surely be found unconstitutional. As the Court would later state in *Ballard*, "The evil lies in the admitted exclusion of an eligible class or group in the community in disregard of the prescribed standards of jury selection. The systematic and intentional exclusion of women . . . deprives the jury system of the broad base it was designed by Congress to have in our democratic society."[142]

---

29 Hofstra L. Rev. 1209 (2001); Gross, *The Risks of Death: Why Erroneous Convictions Are Common in Capital Cases*, 44 Buff. L. Rev. 469, 494 (1996); Schnapper, *Taking* Witherspoon *Seriously—The Search for Death-Qualified Jurors*, 62 Tex. L. Rev. 977 (1984).

138. For good overviews of the issues raised in this section, see Chernoff, *Wrong About the Right: How Courts Undermine the Fair Cross-Section Guarantee by Confusing It with Equal Protection*, 64 Hast. L.J. 141 (2012); Stevenson, *Jury Selection and the Coase Theorem*, 97 Iowa L. Rev. 1645 (2012); Fowler, *Gender and Jury Deliberations: The Contributions of Social Science*, 12 Wm. & Mary J. Women & L. 1 (2005); Alschuler & Deiss, *A Brief History of the Criminal Jury in the United States*, 61 U. Chi. L. Rev. 867 (1994).

139. Strauder v. West Virginia, 100 U.S. 303 (1879).

140. Ballard v. United States, 329 U.S. 187 (1946).

141. *Strauder*, 100 U.S. at 308. *See also* discussion *supra* section VII.B.

142. *Ballard*, 329 U.S. at 195.

The clear and admitted exclusion of groups of individuals on the basis of race or gender was a relatively simple question for the Supreme Court. Much more difficult problems arise when the exclusion is not explicitly race or gender based. The justices have struggled to define and apply a standard of review of jury composition in those cases. Attempting to determine whether a fair representation of the citizenry is reflected in juries in particular cases is no easy task. This has been especially difficult because the Court has consistently noted that no particular system involving the random selection of jurors is required under the constitutional standards.[143] The thinking in the area is best reflected in three key cases.

In *Taylor v. Louisiana*,[144] the Supreme Court held that a "representative cross section of the community" is part of a fundamental right to a jury trial under the Sixth Amendment. Thus, a male defendant could demonstrate that the systematic exclusion of women from juries violated his constitutional right. The facts there were stark, as more than half of those eligible for jury service in the judicial district in which the defendant was being tried were women, but fewer than 10 percent of those in the jury pool were women. The parties agreed that this exclusion of women resulted from the application of state law in which women were not eligible for jury service unless they had filed a written declaration of desire to be subject to jury duty, something not required of men. The language of the opinion is quite strong:

> We accept the fair cross section requirement as fundamental to the jury trial guaranteed by the Sixth Amendment and are convinced that requirement has solid foundation. The purpose of a jury is to guard against the exercise of arbitrary power—to make available a common sense judgment of the community as a hedge against the overzealous or mistaken prosecutor and in preference to the professional, or perhaps over conditioned or bias response of a judge.
>
> This prophylactic vehicle is not provided if the jury pool is made up of only special segments of the populace or if large, distinctive groups are excluded from the pool. Community participation in the administration of the criminal law, moreover, is not only consistent with our democratic heritage but is also critical to public confidence in the fairness of the criminal justice system. Restricting jury service to only special groups or excluding identifiable segments playing

---

143. For discussions of this point, *see* Chernoff and Alschuler & Deiss, *supra* note 138.
144. Taylor v. Louisiana, 419 U.S. 522 (1975).

> major roles in the community cannot be squared with the constitutional concept of jury trial.[145]

The procedure in *Duren v. Missouri*[146] was a bit more subtle than found in *Taylor*, but equally unconstitutional. There the state jury system automatically excused from jury service any woman who requested exemption or failed to appear. No such automatic exclusion existed for men. In striking down the state system, the justices applied a three-prong test that required the moving party to show:

> (1) that the group alleged to be excluded is a "distinctive" group in the community; (2) that the representation of this group in venires from which juries are selected is not fair and reasonable in relation to the number of such persons in the community; and (3) that this underrepresentation is due to systematic exclusion of the group in the jury-selection process.[147]

With a showing that the defendant's all-male jury (taken from a larger pool in which women represented only 10 percent of the group) violated the standards, the defendant's conviction was reversed.[148]

---

145. *Id.* at 530.

146. Duren v. Missouri, 439 U.S. 357 (1975).

147. *Id.* at 364.

148. The opinion did make clear, however, that the states would have some room to argue that a disproportionate percentage was not necessarily unconstitutional:

> States remain free to prescribe relevant qualifications for their jurors and to provide reasonable exemptions so long as . . . the jury list or panels are representative of the community. . . . The right to a proper jury cannot be overcome on merely rational grounds. Rather, it requires that a significant state interest be manifestly and primarily advanced by those aspects of the jury-selection process, such as exemption criteria, that result in the disproportionate exclusion of a distinctive group.

Id. at 367–68. Numerous scholars have researched the question of why, even with appropriate selection criteria, there are fewer minority jurors in cases as a general matter.

> Although racially explicit barriers to minority participation in jury service have been pulled down, many factors continue to disproportionately exclude minorities from jury selection and service. Courts commonly generate lists of potential jurors from voter registration records—a database that tends to underrepresent the minority population residing in the jury district. Also, because racial minorities are statistically more mobile than whites, a greater number fail to receive jury summons mailed to outdated addresses. Even when they are contacted, minority residents are less likely to complete a jury questionnaire or to respond to a jury summons due to apathy or resentment of a criminal justice system from which many feel alienated.

The most recent Supreme Court decision on this matter did not bring much clarity to these complex matters. The criminal defendant in *Berghuis v. Smith*[149] established that in his county in Michigan, African Americans constituted over 7 percent of the jury-eligible population and 6 percent of the pool from which potential jurors were drawn. Yet, an all-white jury convicted him of various offenses. The Supreme Court once again emphasized that an individual challenging the composition of a jury must demonstrate that the imbalance arose from the deliberate and systematic exclusion of a particular class of individuals. The criminal defendant here could not make such a showing, and the Court was unwilling to find any particular method of jury selection as being constitutionally required. As a consequence, the justices did not accept the defendant's argument because they were unpersuaded that this case was analogous to *Duren.*

> [N]either *Duren* or any other decision of this court specifies the method or test courts must use to measure the representation of distinctive groups in jury pools. . . . Three methods [are] employed or identified in lower federal court decisions: absolute disparity, comparative disparity, and standard deviation. . . . Each test is imperfect. Absolute disparity and comparative disparity measurements, courts have recognized, can be misleading when, as here, "members of the distinctive group compose [only] a small percentage of those eligible for jury service." And to our knowledge, "[n]o court . . . has accepted [a standard deviation analysis] alone. . . . No "clearly established" precedent of this court supports Smith's claim that he can make out a prima facie case merely by pointing to a host of factors that, individually or in combination, *might* contribute to a group underrepresentation. . . . [We have previously] "recognized broad discretion in the States" to "prescribe relevant qualifications for their jurors and to provide reasonable exemptions."[150]

Forde-Mazrui, *Jural Districting: Selecting Impartial Juries Through Community Representation*, 52 Vand. L. Rev. 353, 356 (1999); *see generally* Chhablani, *Re-Framing the "Fair Cross-Section" Requirement*, 13 U. Pa. J. Const. L. 931 (2011).

149. Berghuis v. Smith, 559 U.S. 314 (2010).

150. *Id.* at 318. The courts continue to see extended litigation on claims alleging unconstitutional underrepresentation. *See, e.g.*, State v. Lilly, 930 N.W.2d 293 (Iowa 2019); Garcia-Dorantes v. Warren, 801 F.3d 584 (9th Cir. 2015); United States v. Hernandez-Estrada, 749 F.3d 1154 (9th Cir. en banc 2014); People v. Bryant, 822 N.W.2d 124 (Mich. 2012). For an excellent overview, see Hannaford-Agor, *Systematic Negligence in Jury Operations: Why the Definition of Systematic Exclusion in Fair Cross Section Claims Must Be Expanded*, 59 Drake L. Rev. 761 (2011).

VIII. Challenging Jurors

A. Information Given to the Lawyers, Understanding Voir Dire

Voir dire (which is derived from the French for "to speak the truth") is the process by which an impartial jury is selected from a larger group of prospective jurors. Attorneys can prepare questions to ask the prospective jurors during voir dire, based on information collected from juror questionnaires and made available earlier to the prosecution and the defense. The information contained in juror questionnaires generally includes a range of matters such as a person's name, age, occupation, education, employer, recent places of residence, homeowner status, marital status, age and educational background of spouse and children, union membership, military service, hobbies, previous service as a juror, literacy level, and medical conditions that would prevent the juror from sitting through a trial.[151]

B. Process of Voir Dire

Federal Criminal Procedural Rule 24 governs voir dire in the federal courts, and states have similar rules.[152] Prospective jurors may be questioned individually and/or as a group.[153] Voir dire can occur through oral and/or written questions,[154] although a local rule may more strictly define the question form that counsel must use. Most jurisdictions give the trial judge discretion as to whether the court will conduct voir dire, or allow counsel to do so.[155]

Although the process of voir dire varies considerably, the subject matters of voir dire questions are more consistent. Usually, the questions inquire into individuals' awareness of pretrial publicity, to determine whether a prospective juror has developed a preconceived notion about the guilt or innocence of the defendant.[156] If someone

---

151. *See, e.g.*, Pa. R. Crim. P. 632. Of course, questions can be directed to jurors apart from the standard questionnaire.

152. For a good overview, *see* Bamberger, *Jury Voir Dire in Criminal Cases*, N.Y. St. B.A. J., Oct. 2006, at 24.

153. Skilling v. United States, 561 U.S. 358, 359 (2010).

154. Gannett Co. v. DePasquale, 443 U.S. 368, 402 (1979).

155. Fed. R. Crim. P. 24. But not all jurisdictions give such broad discretion. *See, e.g.*, N.Y. Crim. Proc. Law § 270.15(1)(c) (lawyers ask questions, judge may then follow up). As a general matter, judges are more likely to conduct voir dire in federal cases, and lawyers more likely to do it in state cases.

156. United States v. Hall, 536 F.2d 313, 326 n.13 (10th Cir. 1976). The court is not required to inquire into the specific content of the publicity to which each juror was exposed. Mu'Min v. Virginia, 500 U.S. 415, 424–25 (1991).

has developed such a preconceived notion that would interfere with the ability to arrive at a verdict based solely on the evidence presented at the trial, then that person will be dismissed for cause.[157] Additionally, prospective jurors may be asked about whether they have a relationship with any participant or party,[158] and whether they have a bias relating to the type of defendant or the type of crime.[159] There may also be inquiry into each person's experience with—or opinion of—the relevant law, or with the criminal justice system.[160]

Very specific voir dire questions are required in death penalty cases because in such cases, the court cannot designate as a juror anyone who would never impose the death penalty or anyone who would always do so.[161] In noncapital cases, the trial judge has considerable authority to structure how potential jurors are to be questioned, and by whom. But the court is not necessarily required to ask every useful question. "To be constitutionally compelled . . . it is not enough that [voir dire] questions might be helpful. Rather, the trial court's failure to ask these questions must render the defendant's trial fundamentally unfair."[162] And, of course, potential jurors have a duty to honestly answer the questions asked of them. An individual who fails to truthfully answer voir dire questions may be charged with contempt or even perjury.[163]

C. Challenges for Cause

In all criminal trials the defendant has the right to a fair and impartial trier of fact.[164] If the defense or the prosecution can establish that an individual cannot serve as an unbiased and capable juror, that person must be dismissed for cause. In the federal and state courts, there is no limitation on the number of prospective jurors who may be challenged for cause. However, the moving party must specifically allege the ground for the concern that a potential juror is not qualified to

---

157. *Hall*, 536 F.2d at 326.

158. For questions that probe into possible relationships of prospective jurors to trial participants, see *Williams v. Taylor*, 529 U.S. 420, 440 (2000).

159. *Skilling*, 561 U.S. at 372.

160. United States v. Stewart, 317 F. Supp. 2d 432, 435 (S.D.N.Y. 2004).

161. *See* discussion *supra* section VII.C.

162. Mu'Min v. Virginia, 500 U.S. 415, 425–26 (1991).

163. Clark v. United States, 289 U.S. 1, 10 (1933).

164. *See* United States v. Gonzalez, 214 F.3d 1109, 1111 (9th Cir. 2000) (the bias or prejudice of even a single juror is enough to violate the constitutional guarantee). *See generally* United States v. Olsen, 704 F.3d 1172 (9th Cir. 2013); United States v. Sampson, 820 F. Supp. 2d 151 (D. Mass. 2012).

serve.[165] Challenges for cause may include the potential juror's appearance and expressions,[166] an inability to be unbiased due to prior experience in a similar matter,[167] any obvious prejudice, or any other inability to serve as stated by the potential juror or as a reasonable inference from information provided by the potential juror. As with peremptory challenges, the failure to challenge for cause before the trial begins will result in a waiver of the challenge, unless facts develop during the trial that reveal that the juror should be dismissed.[168]

D. Peremptory Challenge

In the federal and state courts, prosecutors and defense attorneys can use peremptory challenges to dismiss potential jurors without cause and without disclosure of their strategy or rationale.[169] There is no constitutional mandate for peremptory challenges; they "are permitted only when the government, by statute or decisional law, deems it appropriate to allow parties to exclude a given number of people who otherwise would satisfy the requirements for service on the petit jury."[170]

The number of peremptory challenges a party is authorized to use is generally determined by rule or statute. Under the Federal Rules of Criminal Procedure, for minor crimes, each side receives three peremptory challenges.[171] When a defendant is charged with a crime punishable by imprisonment of more than one year, the government is granted six peremptory challenges and the defendant is

---

165. *See generally* Gray v. Mississippi, 481 U.S. 648 (1987).

166. *See* People v. Johnson, 706 N.E.2d 742, 743 (N.Y. 1998). There the trial court made the determination, after having the advantage of observing a prospective juror's overall demeanor and body language, that the individual had a state of mind that was likely to preclude her from rendering an impartial verdict, and on that basis discharged the juror for cause. The trial court's ruling was affirmed on appeal. *See generally* Toomer v. State, 734 S.E.2d 333 (Ga. 2012); United States v. Allen, 644 F.3d 748 (8th Cir. 2011).

167. *See* Segura v. State, 921 So. 2d 765, 767 (Fla. Dist. Ct. App. 2006) (trial court erred in denying the cause challenges to a juror as he clearly expressed doubts as to his ability to be fair based on his experience with a family member victim of a similar crime). *See generally* Knox v. State, 29 A.3d 217 (Del. 2011); Underwood v. State, 252 P.3d 221 (Ok. Cr. App. 2011).

168. *See* United States v. Johnson, 688 F.3d 494, 502 (8th Cir. 2012); United States v. Diaz-Albertini, 772 F.2d 654, 657 (10th Cir. 1985).

169. J.E.B. v. Alabama, 511 U.S. 127, 148–49 (1994).

170. Edmonson v. Leesville Concrete Co., 500 U.S. 614, 620 (1991).

171. FED. R. CRIM. P. 24(b).

given ten peremptory challenges.[172] If the government is seeking the death penalty, each side has twenty peremptory challenges.[173] Most state rules are similar. For instance, Iowa allows each side four peremptory challenges for minor crimes, six for more serious crimes, and ten in a first-degree murder trial.[174] When there is more than one defendant at a joint trial, the court may grant additional peremptory challenges and these challenges may be exercised separately or jointly.[175] As a matter of procedure, in both the federal and state courts, a juror must be challenged before he or she is sworn in, otherwise the right is considered to have been waived.[176]

Historically, peremptory challenges were not subject to judicial review. That changed in 1986. In response to growing concerns that prosecutors were using peremptory challenges in a racially discriminatory manner, the Supreme Court acted in *Batson v. Kentucky*.[177] In *Batson*, the justices ruled that race could not be used overtly or covertly by prosecutors to support a peremptory challenge.

> Racial discrimination in the selection of jurors harms not only the accused whose life or liberty they are summoned to try. Competence to serve as a juror ultimately depends on an assessment of individual qualifications and ability impartially to consider evidence presented at a trial. A person's race simply "is unrelated to his fitness as a juror." . . . [B]y denying a person participation in jury service on account of his race, the State unconstitutionally discriminated against the excluded juror. . . .
>
> The harm from discriminatory jury selection extends beyond that inflicted on the defendant and the excluded juror to touch the entire community. Selection procedures that purposefully exclude black persons from juries undermine public confidence in the fairness of our system of justice.[178]

Specifically, *Batson* held that, if a defendant wished to challenge the prosecutor's use of a peremptory strike as race-based, a three-step inquiry was required. First, the trial court must determine whether the defendant had made a prima facie showing that the prosecutor's peremptory challenge had been based on the prospective juror's race.

---

172. *Id.*
173. Fed. R. Crim. P. 24(b)(1).
174. Iowa Court Ann. R. 2.18(9).
175. Fed. R. Crim. P. 24(b).
176. Snyder v. Louisiana, 552 U.S. 472, 475 (2008).
177. Batson v. Kentucky, 476 U.S. 79 (1986).
178. *Id.* at 87.

Second, if the showing was made, the burden shifted to the prosecutor to present a race-neutral explanation for striking the juror in question. Third, the court then determines whether the defendant had met her burden of proving purposeful discrimination.[179]

---

179. The justices' language here is instructive:

> [A] defendant may establish a *prima facie* case of purposeful discrimination in selection of the petit jury solely on evidence concerning the prosecutor's exercise of peremptory challenges at the defendant's trial. To establish such a case, the defendant first must show that he is a member of a cognizable racial group, and that the prosecutor has exercised peremptory challenges to remove from the venire members of the defendant's race. Second, the defendant is entitled to rely on the fact, as to which there can be no dispute, that peremptory challenges constitute a jury selection practice that permits "those to discriminate who are of a mind to discriminate." Finally, the defendant must show that these facts and any other relevant circumstances raise an inference that the prosecutor used that practice to exclude the veniremen from the petit jury on account of their race. This combination of factors in the empaneling of the petit jury, as in the selection of the venire, raises the necessary inference of purposeful discrimination. . . .
>
> Once the defendant makes a *prima facie* showing, the burden shifts to the State to come forward with a neutral explanation for challenging black jurors. Though this requirement imposes a limitation in some cases on the full peremptory character of the historic challenge, we emphasize that the prosecutor's explanation need not rise to the level justifying exercise of a challenge for cause. But the prosecutor may not rebut the defendant's *prima facie* case of discrimination by stating merely that he challenged jurors of the defendant's race on the assumption—or his intuitive judgment—that they would be partial to the defendant because of their shared race. Just as the Equal Protection Clause forbids the States to exclude black persons from the venire on the assumption that blacks as a group are unqualified to serve as jurors, so it forbids the States to strike black veniremen on the assumption that they will be biased in a particular case simply because the defendant is black. The core guarantee of equal protection, ensuring citizens that their State will not discriminate on account of race, would be meaningless were we to approve the exclusion of jurors on the basis of such assumptions, which arise solely from the jurors' race. Nor may the prosecutor rebut the defendant's case merely by denying that he had a discriminatory motive or "affirm[ing] [his] good faith in making individual selections." If these general assertions were accepted as rebutting a defendant's *prima facie* case, the Equal Protection Clause "would be but a vain and illusory requirement." The prosecutor therefore must articulate a neutral explanation related to the particular case to be tried. The trial court then will have the duty to determine if the defendant has established purposeful discrimination.

Id. at 96–98. *See generally Snyder*, 552 U.S. 472 (trial judge must make factual findings). For good discussions of the process, *see* Price, *Expanding Reach: The Importance of* Batson v. Kentucky *Thirty Years On*, 105 Ky. L.J. 609 (2017); Mazzone, Batson Remedies, 97 Iowa L. Rev. 1613 (2012); Bellin & Semitsu, *Widening* Batson's *Net to Ensnare More Than the Unapologetically Bigoted or Painfully Unimaginative Attorney*, 96 CORNELL L. REV. 101 (2011); Burgess & Smith, *The Proper Remedy for a Lack of* Batson *Findings: The Fall-out from* Snyder v. Louisiana, 101 J. CRIM. L. & CRIMINOLOGY 1 (2011).

In 2019, the Supreme Court followed up and refocused the *Batson* ruling in *Flowers v. Mississippi*.[180] In *Flowers*, remarkably, the defendant was tried and convicted of murder five times, and each time the conviction was reversed. He was convicted again at the sixth trial. He claimed on appeal that jurors had been improperly excused on the basis of race. In the six combined trials, the prosecuting attorney had used his challenges to strike 41 of 42 black prospective jurors. The trial judge in the sixth trial concluded that the peremptory strike of the black prospective juror there was not "motivated in substantial part by discriminatory intent."[181] A seven-justice majority of the Supreme Court sharply disagreed: "The state's relentless, determined effort to rid the jury of black individuals strongly suggests that the state wanted to try Flowers before a jury with as few black jurors as possible, and ideally before an all-white jury . . . . We cannot ignore that history." [182]

In 1992, the prohibition against using race-based peremptory challenges was extended to criminal defense attorneys.[183] Two years later, the Court further limited the exercise of peremptory challenges by holding it unconstitutional to use gender as a basis to challenge a juror.[184] As these cases illustrate, the peremptory challenge litigation

180. 139 S. Ct. 2228 (2019).

181. *Id.* at 2246.

182. *Id.*

183. Georgia v. McCollum, 505 U.S. 42, 59 (1992). While litigation involving such challenges is less common then cases looking at prosecution actions, they can present thorny issues. *See, e.g.*, State v. Bennett, 322 P.3d 815, 816–17 (Wash. App. 2014) (court will carefully review defense counsel's "race-neutral explanation for challenging jurors.").

184. J.E.B. v. Alabama, 511 U.S. 127, 146 (1994). Since *Batson* was decided, there has been considerable debate concerning the wisdom of the peremptory challenge, and also the way in which it is utilized in practice. For good discussions, *see* Offit, *Race-Conscious Jury Selection*, 82 Ohio St. L.J. 1 (2021); Hatoum, *Injustice in Black and White: Eliminating Prosecutors' Peremptory Strikes in Interracial Death Penalty Cases*, 84 Brooklyn L. Rev. 165 (2018); Johnson, *Arresting Batson: How Striking Jurors Based on Arrest Records Violates Batson*, 34 Yale L. & Pol'y Rev. 387 (2016); Tetlow, *Solving Batson*, 56 Wm. & Mary L. Rev. 1859 (2015); King, *Procedurally Criminal: How Peremptory Challenges Create Unfair and Unrepresentative Single-Gender Juries*, 21 Wm. & Mary J. Women & L. 187 (2014); Smith, *A Call to Abolish Peremptory Challenges by Prosecutors*, 27 Geo. J. Legal Ethics 1163 (2014); Caldwell & Hewitt, *Shades of Guilt: Combating the Continuing Influence Upon Jury Selection of Racial Stereotyping in Post-*Batson *Trials*, 38 Am. J. Trial Adv. 67 (2014); Weddell, *A Jury of Whose Peers? Eliminating Racial Discrimination in Jury Selection Procedures*, 33 B.C. J. L. & Soc. Just. 453 (2013); Grosso & O'Brien, *A Stubborn Legacy: The Overwhelming Importance of Race in Jury Selection in Post-*Batson *Northern Carolina Capital Trials*, 97 Iowa L. Rev. 1531 (2012). Efforts continue to extend the *Batson* doctrine beyond race and gender. *See*, for instance, the focus on sexual orientation, which has split the courts. *See* Smith v.

issues can be substantial.[185] Courts often must respond to defendants' assertion that "the government's proffered race-neutral justification for excluding [a juror] was simply a pretext for racial discrimination."[186] Whether an error in this area is automatically reversible has been open to much debate.[187] The moving party must raise the matter in a timely fashion or the issue will be deemed waived.[188] The Supreme Court has held that an error in denying a peremptory challenge does not require automatic reversal,[189] leading to challenges as to the

MacEachern, 2019 U.S. Dist. LEXIS 103431 (D. Mass. 2019); SmithKline Beecham v. Abbot Laboratories, 740 F.3d 471 (9th Cir. 2014); United States v. Blaylock, 421 F.3d 758 (8th Cir. 2005).

185. *See, e.g.*, Felkner v. Jackson, 562 U.S. 594, 596–97 (2011) (per curiam) (unanimous reversal of the court of appeals on the question of whether the prosecution's use of peremptory challenges to eliminate two of three black jurors violated *Batson*). *See also* People v. Jones, 247 P.3d 82 (Cal. 2011), where the majority of the California Supreme Court could find no constitutional problem with the government's eliminating three of five prospective black jurors. "The record here shows that the prosecutor exercised his peremptory challenges to obtain a jury as favorable to his side as possible . . . and not to eliminate African Americans for racial reasons." *Id.* at 369. *But see id.* at 382 (Werdegar, J., dissenting) ("[T]he prosecutor offered for each challenge important, even dramatic reasons—reasons the record does not support. That the record does not support the prosecutor's reasons suggests they were pretextual."). In some cases, the prosecutor may not remember, years later, the voir dire process. In *Lark v. Secretary of Pennsylvania Department of Corrections*, 645 F.3d 596 (3d Cir. 2011), the court held that even with such a memory problem, the criminal defendant still has the burden of showing intentional discrimination by the government lawyer. *See generally* United States v. Brasher, 962 F.3d 254 (7th Cir. 2020); Sells v. State, 109 A.3d 568 (Del. 2015); McCoy v. State, 112 A.3d 239 (Del. 2015); People v. Cisneros, 184 Cal. Rptr. 3d 1 (Cal. App. 2015); Murray v. Schriro, 745 F.3d 984 (9th Cir. 2014); State v. Giles, 745 S.E.2d 261 (S.C. 2014); United States v. Thompson, 735 F.3d 291 (5th Cir. 2013); State v. Wilkins, 94 So. 3d 983 (La. App. 2012).

186. United States v. Cecil, 615 F.3d 678, 685–88 (6th Cir. 2010). *See generally* Mendoza v. State, 2012 WL 1922666 (Nev. 2012); United States v. Gooch, 665 F.3d 1318 (D.C. Cir. 2012); Stevens v. Epps, 618 F.3d 489, 496–98 (5th Cir. 2010). To be sure, the Supreme Court did not accept the contention that "a demeanor-based explanation must be rejected if the judge did not observe or cannot recall the juror's demeanor." Thaler v. Haynes, 559 U.S. 43, 48 (2010).

187. *See* State v. Inman, 760 S.E.2d 105 (S.C. 2014); State v. Sutherland, 745 S.E.2d 448 (W. Va. 2013); Hardison v. State, 94 So. 3d 1092 (Miss. 2012); Winston v. Boatwright, 649 F.3d 618 (7th Cir. 2011); United States v. McFerron, 163 F.3d 952 (6th Cir. 1998).

188. United States v. Reid, 746 F.3d 528, 533, n.4 (6th Cir. 2014); United States v. Tomlinson, 764 F.3d 535, 538 (6th Cir. 2014); Denis v. State, 137 So. 3d 583, 585 (Fla. App. 2014). State v. Harris, 289 P.3d 591, 595 (Utah 2012); Commonwealth v. Daniels, 963 A.2d 409, 433 (Pa. 2009).

189. Rivera v. Illinois, 556 U.S. 148 (2009). *United States v. Lindsey*, 634 F.3d 541 (9th Cir. 2011) nicely explains the Supreme Court's reasoning. Some states, under their own constitutions, do not agree with *Rivera*. *See, e.g.*, State v. Mootz, 808 N.W.2d 207 (Iowa 2012); People v. Hecker, 942 N.E.2d 248 (N.Y. 2010).

impact of such an error.[190] Quite intense controversies and debates continue as to the reach and application of the *Batson* doctrine.[191]

---

190. One notable case is Robinson v. State, 255 P.3d 425 (Okla. Crim. App. 2011). *See* Note, *Due Process—Peremptory Challenges—Harmless Error Doctrine:* Rivera v. Illinois, 123 HARV. L. REV. 212, 216–18 (2009).

191. The latest Supreme Court decisions applying the *Batson* line of cases are Foster v. Chatman, 136 S. Ct. 1737 (2016), and Davis v. Ayala, 576 U.S. 257 (2015). In Foster v. Chatman, the defense argued that a review of the prosecutor's pretrial notes would show purposeful discrimination. The government contended that references in the files to minority jurors did not prove that it had exercised strikes in anything other than a "color-blind" manner. The Court disagreed. "[T]he focus on race in the prosecution's file plainly demonstrates a concerted effort to keep black prospective jurors off the jury." *Id.* at 1755. Davis v. Ayala was a habeas corpus case in which the justices reaffirmed the Fourteenth Amendment principle. "As we have held, the Fourteenth Amendment prohibits a prosecutor from striking potential jurors based on race. Discrimination in the jury selection process undermines our criminal justice system and poisons public confidence in the evenhanded administration of justice." *Id.* at 285. The trial judge had allowed the prosecutor to explain the basis for the use of peremptory challenges of prospective jurors without the participation of the defense lawyer so as not to share trial strategy. The Court assumed, without deciding, that an error had occurred but concluded that any such error was harmless under standards developed under earlier habeas cases and the Antiterrorism and Effective Death Penalty Act of 1996, 28 U.S.C. § 2254 (d). The Washington Supreme Court in Washington v. Saintcalle, 309 P.3d 326, *cert. denied*, 134 S. Ct. 831 (2013), expressed grave concerns about the inadequacies inherent in the U.S. Supreme Court's *Batson* decision:

> In short, *Batson*, like *Swain* before it, appears to have created a "crippling burden" making it very difficult for defendants to prove discrimination even where it almost certainly exists. . . .
>
> Unconscious stereotyping upends the *Batson* framework. *Batson* is only equipped to root out "purposeful" discrimination, which many trial courts probably understand to mean conscious discrimination. But discrimination in this day and age is frequently unconscious and less often consciously purposeful. That does not make it any less pernicious.
>
> Problematically, people are rarely aware of the actual reasons for their discrimination and will genuinely believe the race-neutral reason they create to mask it. Since *Batson*'s third step hinges on credibility, this makes it very difficult to sustain a *Batson* challenge even in situations where race has in fact affected decision-making.

309 P.3d at 335–36.

The state justices, however, took no action in the case before it, feeling a need for greater study and argument: "As urgent as the need for a new framework may be, we cannot create one in this case. Neither party has asked for a new standard or framework, nor have they briefed or argued what that framework might be or how it would apply in this case. The issue also was not raised or decided at the Court of Appeals or the trial court." *Id.* at 339. *See also* State v. Ornelas, 330 P.3d 1085 (Idaho App. 2014).

IX. Disclosing the Identity of Jurors

Historically, jurors' names were made publicly available as a routine matter. Over the past two decades, growing concerns over individual safety and privacy have made courts more willing to empanel anonymous jury members, though still on a very limited basis.[192]

A. Standards to Enforce Anonymity

In several prominent cases, judges have withheld jurors' home addresses and, in some instances, their names.[193] However, judges remain reluctant to withhold juror identities because of the Sixth Amendment implications. Juror anonymity "may hinder the defendant's ability to conduct an informed voir dire examination and to challenge effectively the seating of individual jurors."[194] "Unquestionably, the empanelment of an anonymous jury is a drastic measure, one which should be undertaken only in limited and carefully delineated circumstances."[195] It should occur "only in rare circumstances."[196]An anonymous jury "raises the specter that the defendant is a dangerous person from whom the jurors must be protected, thereby implicating the defendant's constitutional right to a presumption of innocence."[197]

While concerns are present, many courts have found that use of an anonymous jury is appropriate "only in rare circumstances when two conditions are met: (1) there is stong reason to conclude that the jury needs protection from interference or harm, or that the integrity of the jury's function will be compromised absent anonymity; and (2) reasonable safeguards have been adopted to minimize the risk

---

192. *See generally* United States v. Wecht, 537 F.3d 222 (3d Cir. 2008). For good overviews of the area, *see* Forster, *Between a Rock and a Hard Place: Maryland Criminal Defendants, Already Subject to Severely Limited Voir Dire, Now Also Face the Prospect of Anonymous Juries*, 40 U. Balt. L.F. 229 (2010); Wegner, *Juror Anonymity in Criminal Trials: The Media, The Defendant, and the Juror—Providing for the Rights of All Interested Parties*, 3 Alb. Gov't L. Rev. 429, 432 (2010).

193. *See, e.g.*, United States v. Pica, 692 F.3d 79 (2d Cir. 2012); United States v. Candelario-Santana, 909 F. Supp. 2d 68 (D.P.R. 2012); United States v. Edwards, 303 F.3d 606 (5th Cir. 2002).

194. United States v. Dinkins, 691 F.3d 358, 373 (4th Cir. 2012). *See also* United States v. Morales, 655 F.3d 608 (7th Cir. 2011); People v. Rizo, 302 P.3d 284 (Colo. App. 2011); State v. Sandoval, 788 N.W.2d 172 (Neb. 2010).

195. United States v. Ross, 33 F.3d 1507, 1519 (11th Cir. 1994). *See also* United States v. Hager, 721 F.3d 167 (4th Cir. 2013); Perez v. People, 302 P.3d 222 (Colo. 2013).

196. *Dinkins*, 691 F.3d at 373.

197. United States v. Morales, 655 F.3d 608, 620 (7th Cir. 2011). *See also* Lechunga v. United States, 15 F. Supp. 3d 788 (N.D. Ill. 2014); United States v. White, 698 F.3d 1005 (7th Cir. 2012).

that the rights of the accused will be infringed."[198] Numerous courts note that under the right circumstances, anonymity is necessary and should be allowed.[199] The question, of course, is what are the right circumstances?

The definitive answer is hard to state. Whether a jury should remain anonymous is determined on a case-by-case basis,[200] with courts weighing numerous factors such as:

> (1) The defendant's involvement in organized crime, (2) the defendant's participation in a group with the capacity to harm jurors, (3) the defendant's past attempts to interfere with the judicial process, (4) the potential that, if convicted, the defendant will suffer a lengthy incarceration and substantial monetary penalties, and (5) extensive publicity that could enhance the possibility that jurors' names would become public and expose them to intimidation or harassment. "[T]he presence of any one factor or set of factors [does not] automatically compel a court to empanel an anonymous jury" because the list of factors is only "instructive" and not "exhaustive."[201]

---

198. United States v. Mathis, 932 F.3d 242, 252-53 (4th Cir. 2019), *cert. denied*, 140 S. Ct. 639; United States v. McGill, 815 F.3d 846 (D.C. Cir. 2016); United States v. Prado, 634 F. App'x 323 (2d Cir. 2016); United States v. Ramírez-Rivera, 800 F.3d 1 (1st Cir. 2015); United States v. Darden, 70 F.3d 1507, 1532 (8th Cir. 1995). *See generally* State v. Nadeem, 809 N.W.2d 825 (Neb. App. 2012); State v. Sandoval, 788 N.W.2d 172 (Neb. 2010). The reference to "an anonymous jury" is a bit misleading. There are certainly "modified" versions as in *Perez v. People*, 302 P.3d 222 (Colo. 2013) (referring to jurors by numbers, yet parties had access to jurors' personal information), and *State v. Rogers*, 288 P.3d 544 (Or. 2012) (names of jurors withheld from defendant and public, but made available to defense counsel).

199. United States v. Mostafa, 7 F. Supp. 3d 334 (S.D.N.Y. 2014); United States v. Herron, 2 F. Supp. 3d 391 (E.D.N.Y. 2014); United States v. Vario, 943 F.2d 236, 242 (2d Cir. 1991); United States v. Scarf, 850 F.2d 1015, 1026 (3d Cir. 1988).

200. Green v. State, 994 N.E.2d 1276 (Ind. App. 2013); United States v. Candelario-Santana, 909 F. Supp. 2d 68 (D.P.R. 2012); United States v. Moore, 651 F.3d 30 (D.C. Cir. 2011); Major v. State, 873 N.E.2d 1120 (Ind. 2007). For a sharp critique of the practice, *see* Forster, *supra* note 192, at 231.

201. United States v. Gutierrez, 963 F.3d 320, 329 (4th Cir. 2000). See also *Ross*, 33 F.3d at 1520; United States v. Krout, 66 F.3d 1420, 1427 (5th Cir. 1995). The court in *State v. Sundberg*, 247 P.3d 1213, 1220 (Or. 2011), explained:

> [A]nonymous juries are permissible only if the trial court "concludes that there is a strong reason to believe that the jury needs protection" and the court takes "reasonable precautions to minimize any prejudicial effects on the defendant and to ensure that his fundamental rights are protected." . . . [T]he trial court must make a determination that the circumstances of the particular trial provide sufficient grounds to believe that jurors need the protection provided by anonymity. [Many] factors [must] be considered in deciding when it is appropriate to withhold juror names. . . .

The weighing process has resulted in some prominent prosecutions in which jurors' names have not been disclosed. In one case, the appeals court affirmed the district court's decision to empanel an anonymous jury, as the appellants were members of a dangerous gang linked to several murders in the state where they resided and were being tried. Furthermore, the case was the focus of much publicity, which the court thought would persist until the end of the trial.[202] In another federal prosecution, the court focused on the defendants' prior criminal behavior. There was strong evidence of defendants' past attempts to interfere with the judicial process, and defendants were alleged to be part of a group that possessed the means to harm jurors.[203]

Perhaps the most prominent example of the weighing process is *United States v. Blagojevich*,[204] the public corruption trial of the former governor of Illinois. Here the district court judge reached a compromise. He denied a pretrial motion by news outlets to reveal the names of the jurors in the incredibly high-profile case.[205] This decision was

---

> While we do not endorse any particular list of "factors," we believe that a trial court has the authority to protect jurors from the risk of physical harm, intimidation, or harassment—whether by parties, the press, or the public—by withholding juror names and other identifying information. But a determination that such a risk exists must be made on the facts of each case—and not on the basis of a generalized desire to protect the anonymity of all jurors in all cases in the interests of juror privacy.

See generally United States v. Jackson, 2014 WL 121976 (E.D. La. Cr. 2014); Green v. State, 994 N.E.2d 1276 (Ind. App. 2013); United States v. Pica, 692 F.3d 79 (Ind. Cir. 2012). In *United States v. Portillo*, 969 F.3d 144, 163 (5th Cir. 2020), the appeals court approved of the anonymous jury where

> the evidence at trial established the highly structured nature of the [defendant's] organization, which frequently resorted to violence to assure its power in Texas motorcycle society. . . . [I]t had the capacity to harm jurors and had previously attempted to interfere with the judicial process and intimidate witnesses . . . . [The group] instills a climate of fear of reprisal for witnesses who cooperate with law enforcement. The culture of the [group] underscored the potential danger to jurors. [A] history of witness threats provided a "reasonable basis to conclude that similar threats and attempts at intimidation were likely to be made to the jurors if their identities were known."

202. *Krout*, 66 F.3d 1420. *See also Dinkins*, 691 F.3d at 373. As the court wrote in *Morales*, while "the use of anonymous juries is discouraged . . . we have never held that it is presumptively inappropriate to rely on anonymity." 655 F.3d at 620.

203. United States v. Thomas, 757 F.2d 1359 (2d Cir. 1985). *See generally Gutierrez*, 963 F.3d 320; United States v. Persico, 2012 WL 1188243 (E.D.N.Y. 2012).

204. No. 08 CR 888-1 (N.D. Ill. 2010).

205. *See* Chase, *Blagojevich Jurors' Names Stay Under Wraps: Judge Says They Won't Be Identified Until After a Verdict*, Chi. Trib., July 26, 2010, http://articles.chicagotribune.com/2010-07-26/news/ct-met-blagojevich-juror-names-20100726_1_jurors-names-ver

based on his concern that people would contact the jurors, which could hinder and influence deliberations. However, the judge agreed to release the jurors' names after a verdict was reached.[206]

dict-rod-blagojevich. The judge relied upon the Jury Selection and Service Act of 1968, 28 U.S.C. §§ 1861–1869. The statute indicates that federal courts must adopt plans that would determine when trial judges have to allow prospective jurors' names be given to the parties and the public. The courts are not mandated to make the names of prospective jurors public at any particular time. The Act specifically gives the judges considerable discretion: "If the plan permits these names to be made public, it may nevertheless permit the chief judge of the district court, or such other district court judge as the plan may provide, to keep these names confidential in any case where the interests of justice so require." 28 U.S.C. § 1863(b)(7). The Massachusetts Supreme Judicial Court more recently decided that names of jurors must generally be made public once the trial is over.

> [T]he public's long-term interest in maintaining an open judicial process, as embodied in the United States Constitution and Massachusetts common law, requires that a list identifying the names of jurors who have been empanelled and rendered a verdict in a criminal case be retained in the court file of the case and be made available to the public in the same manner as other court records. Only on a judicial finding of good cause, which may include a risk of harm to the jurors or to the integrity of their service, may such a list be withheld. Insofar as the only basis for the order in this case was the judge's aversion to exposing jurors to press interviews and the personal preferences of the jurors, his order must be set aside in part, and a list identifying the names of jurors (without addresses) be disclosed.

Commonwealth v. Fujita, 23 N.E.3d 882, 885 (Mass. 2015).

206. Sweeney et al., *Many Blagojevich Jurors Disappointed*, Chi. Trib. (Aug. 18, 2010), http://articles.chicagotribune.com/2010-08-18/news/ct-met-blagojevich-verdict-jury-20100818_1_female-juror-deliberation-senate-seat. Even this decision in an extremely high-publicity prosecution, though, was not without substantial controversy. The judge's initial order was appealed, with the court of appeals directing the trial judge to consider carefully the presumption in favor of disclosure. United States v. Blagojevich, 612 F.3d 558, 561–65 (7th Cir. 2010). The court stated:

> But no one contends (or should contend) that jurors' names always must be released. Anonymous juries are permissible when the jurors' safety would be jeopardized by public knowledge, or the defendant has attempted to bribe or intimidate witnesses or jurors. . . . The right question is not whether names may be kept secret, or disclosure deferred, but what justifies such a decision. . . .
>
> [There is a] presumption in favor of disclosure. . . . [There must be] an overriding interest that is likely to be prejudiced. . . . That's also true of orders providing for the anonymity of jurors. Although deferred release of jurors' names requires less justification than does anonymity, an appropriate inquiry into the facts remains necessary. . . . [A] judge must find some unusual risk to justify keeping jurors' names confidential; it is not enough to point to possibilities that are present in every criminal prosecution. The great public interest in this prosecution may indeed create exceptional risks, and the trial's length may make sequestration exceptionally unattractive as an alternative, but these are questions that should be explored on the record.

The trial judge's decision in high-profile cases is quite complex, looking to both Sixth Amendment and First Amendment considerations. As one court wrote, "[If jurors were to feel] . . . that their personal safety was at risk, they might not only be reluctant to serve, but might tailor verdicts so as to forestall harm to themselves, thus depriving the parties of an impartial jury."[207]

B. First Amendment Analysis

The Supreme Court has not addressed the First Amendment implications of juror anonymity. Instead, the Court's main concern has been the related—but distinctly different—matter of closing trial proceedings to the public. This issue is discussed further in Chapter 2. The seminal case is *Press-Enterprise Co. v. Superior Court*,[208] where the Court reviewed a trial judge's decision to close several weeks of voir dire proceedings. This, the justices found, was unconstitutional under the public's First Amendment right to open proceedings, without careful consideration by the trial judge of less restrictive alternatives.[209] Thus, the Court interpreted the First Amendment to include a "presumptive openness of the jury selection process."[210]

This constitutional presumption enables the press to regularly argue that the rights of the public and the media are infringed if a court restricts access to juror identities. Recently, this argument has

---

The trial judge in the case of the prosecution of Baltimore police officers accused (but not convicted) of manslaughter in the death of Freddie Gray also ruled that jurors were to remain anonymous. Zapotosky, *Justice at the Hands of the Nameless in Baltimore Prosecution*, Wash. Post, Nov. 29, 2015, https://www.washingtonpost.com/local/public-safety/justice-at-the-hands-of-the-nameless/2015/11/28/d3ad3898-92d9-11e5-8aa0-5d0946560a97_story.html?hpid=hp_hp-cards_hp-card-local%3Ahomepage%2Fcard. *See* also Romo, *Judge Rules That 'El Chapo' Jury Will Remain Anonymous*, NPR (Feb. 6, 2018), https://www.npr.org/sections/thetwo-way/2018/02/06/583739445/judge-rules-that-el-chapo-jury-will-remain-anonymous.

207. *In re* Globe Newspaper Co., 920 F.2d 88, 91 (1st Cir. 1990). *See generally Morales*, 655 F.3d at 620–21; United States v. Loughner, 807 F. Supp. 2d 828 (D. Ariz. 2011).

208. Press-Enterprise Co. v. Superior Court, 464 U.S. 501 (1984).

209. *Id.* at 511.

210. *Id.* The guarantee was extended to criminal defendants, under the Sixth Amendment, in *Presley v. Georgia*, 558 U.S. 209, 213 (2010) ("the accused does have a right to insist that the voir dire of the jurors be public"). The anonymity issue also arises regularly with witness identifications. Here, of course, the chief concern is the claim under the Confrontation Clause, as explained in Chapter 7, *infra*. For recent cases looking to balance the various confrontation issues with witnesses, see *United States v. Gutierrez de Lopez*, 761 F.3d 1123, 1140 (10th Cir. 2014), and *United States v. Celis*, 608 F.3d 818, 832 (D.C. Cir. 2010).

been quite effective. In fact, one court has specifically found that there is a "presumptive First Amendment right of access to obtain the names of both trial jurors and prospective jurors prior to the empanelment of the jury."[211] To limit that right, the trial court must find a specific, strong reason for nondisclosure even if the jurors' own preference is to the contrary.[212]

The court rulings make clear that judges are to be sensitive to jurors' fears regarding safety and invasions of privacy. Still, empaneling an anonymous jury remains an unusual occurrence. Anonymous juries are "a last resort in a court's efforts to protect the jurors from intimidating or prejudicial influences."[213] "Empaneling an anonymous jury is an extreme measure that is warranted only where there is strong reason to believe the jury needs protection."[214] The Nevada Supreme Court emphasized the point:

> Yet we are mindful that juror anonymity may implicate a defendant's constitutional rights. By withholding certain biographical information, the district court denies a defendant information that may be helpful to strike biased jurors during voir dire, thereby threatening that defendant's Sixth Amendment right to an impartial jury. By referring to jurors by number instead of name, the district court may imply that a defendant's dangerousness required juror anonymity, "thereby implicating defendants' Fifth Amendment right to a presumption of innocence."

---

211. United States v. Wecht, 537 F.3d 222, 235 (3d Cir. 2008). For a different perspective, see Comment, United States v. Wecht*: When Anonymous Juries, the Right of Access, and Judicial Discretion Collide*, 40 Seton Hall L. Rev. 763 (2010).

212. *In re Globe Newspaper*, 920 F.2d at 91.

213. United States v. Edwards, 303 F.3d 606, 613 (5th Cir. 2002).

214. United States v. Mansoori, 304 F.3d 635, 650 (7th Cir. 2002). The issue continues to arise in connection with high-profile, intensely publicized prosecutions. *See, e.g.*, Alexander, *Defense Team for Man Held in Chandra Levy Killing Can't See Jury Pool*, Wash. Post, Aug. 21, 2010, http://www.washingtonpost.com/wp-dyn/content/article/2010/08/20/AR2010082005352.html. In *United States v. Solomon*, 387 F. App'x 258 (3d Cir. 2010), the trial judge decided to empanel a partially anonymous jury, that is, the names and personal residences of the jurors were withheld from the court and the parties. Jurors did, however, fill out an extensive eighty-five-question questionnaire developed by the government and by Solomon, and approved by the court. Included in this questionnaire was an inquiry into the general area of residence of each venireperson. Both parties were also permitted to question the venirepersons individually, and exercise peremptory challenges.

The court on appeal approved the action, as the crime charged there was a homicide in which the defendant paid someone "to kill the victim in order to intimidate and/or retaliate against the victim's son who was expected to testify against the Defendant. . . . Solomon stood accused of murdering a witness's father."

> We therefore emphasize that "empaneling an anonymous jury is an unusual measure," and caution that a district court should employ such a measure only after careful consideration of the competing individual and institutional interests at stake.[215]

X. Jury Nullification

Jury nullification is "the *de facto* ability of the jury to refuse to apply the law as instructed by the court, choosing instead 'to acquit out of compassion or compromise or because of the jury's assumption of a power which they had no right to exercise, but to which they were disposed through lenity.'"[216] The jury's inherent power to nullify has been acknowledged for hundreds of years, dating back—in the United States—to the prosecution of John Peter Zenger in 1735. Zenger wrote articles criticizing the royal governor and was charged by the government with seditious libel. Though the facts showed that Zenger was guilty as charged, the jurors opted to acquit him as a show of political protest.[217]

Jury nullification has always been widely accepted in the United States. In terms of practice, however, three issues have emerged regarding the application of this power: the need to instruct the jury on nullification, the right of defense counsel to argue the doctrine, and the ability of the lawyers to inform jurors of the potential sentence in order to persuade them to use nullification. On all three issues, the overwhelming judicial response has been more favorable to the prosecution than the defense.

The Supreme Court first addressed the jury instruction issue late in the nineteenth century in *Sparf v. United States*.[218] In *Sparf*, the Court rejected the suggestion that it is proper to instruct the jury regarding nullification: "Congress did not intend to invest juries in criminal cases with power arbitrarily to disregard the evidence and the

---

215. Menendez-Cordero v. State, 445 P.3d 1235, 1238–39 (Nev. 2019).

216. United States v. Scarmazzo, 554 F. Supp. 2d 1102, 1108 (E.D. Ca. 2008) (quoting Standefer v. United States, 447 U.S. 10, 22 (1980)). *See* United States v. Duval, 865 F. Supp. 2d 803, 808 (E.D. Mich. 2012). For a good discussion of the concept, see GERTNER & MIZNER, THE LAW OF JURIES 191 (2009).

217. *See* Linder, *The Trial of John Peter Zenger: An Account*, *in* FAMOUS AMERICAN TRIALS (2001), *available at* http://law2.umkc.edu/faculty/projects/ftrials/zenger/zenger.html.

218. Sparf v. United States, 156 U.S. 51 (1895).

principles of law applicable to the case on trial."[219] Over the years, this view has been consistently followed. One of the strongest statements on point comes from a California court:

> Jurors have a duty to follow the law as stated to them by the trial court. Nevertheless, although it is "a power which they ha[ve] no right to exercise" jurors have "the ability to disregard, or nullify, the law." "But the circumstance that the prosecution may be powerless to challenge a jury verdict or finding that is prompted by the jury's refusal to apply a particular law does not lessen the obligation of each juror to obey the court's instructions."
>
> Accordingly, "it is important not to encourage or glorify the jury's power to disregard the law. While that power has, on some occasions, achieved just results, it also has led to verdicts based upon bigotry and racism. A jury that disregards the law and, instead, reaches a verdict based upon the personal views and beliefs of the jurors violates one of our nation's most basic precepts: that we are 'a government of laws and not men.'"[220]

The problem of jury instructions regarding nullification is tricky, as seen in two recent decisions of the Ninth Circuit. In one 2017 case, the court on appeal found error in the trial judge's instruction to the jury regarding nullification.

> Although a court has "the duty to forestall or prevent [nullification]," including "by firm instruction or admonition," a court should not state or imply that (1) jurors could be punished for jury nullification, or that (2) an acquittal resulting from jury nullification is

---

219. *Id.* at 63.

220. People v. Estrada, 46 Cal. Rptr. 3d 111, 115–16 (Cal. Ct. App. 2006). *See also* United States v. Appolon, 695 F.3d 44, 64 (1st Cir. 2012); United States v. Fell, 571 F.3d 264 (2d Cir. 2009); State v. Paredes-Solano, 222 P.3d 900 (Ariz. Ct. App. 2009); United States v. Powell, 955 F.3d 1206, 1212–13 (9th Cir. 1992). For a sharply different view, *see* United States v. Courtney, 960 F. Supp. 2d 1152, 1198 (D.N.M. 2013), where the court, feeling bound by circuit precedent, would not instruct the jury. The judge added the following:

> At a minimum, it appears that the Court should not be lying to or misleading the jury—telling the jurors that they do not have the power to nullify or mitigate—when in fact the jury does have that power. Nevertheless, because of controlling precedent, the Court will deny Courtney's request to qualify its instruction to the jury about faithfully applying the law that the Court gives to it by inviting them not to do so if they "are left with a firm belief that application [of the law] in this case would be fundamentally unjust."

Id. at 1198–99.

> invalid. More specifically, the court's statement that the jury "would violate [its] oath and the law if [it] willfully brought a verdict contrary to the law given to [it] in this case," could be construed to imply that nullification could be punished, particularly since the instruction came in the midst of a criminal trial. Moreover, the statement that "[t]here is no such thing as valid jury nullification" could be understood as telling jurors that they do not have the power to nullify, and so it would be a useless exercise.[221]

In another case, however, decided just one year later, the Ninth Circuit found this instruction to potential jurors (during voir dire) permissible:

> Nullification is by definition a violation of the juror's oath which, if you are a juror in this case, you will take to apply the law as instructed by the court. As a . . . juror, you cannot substitute your sense of justice, whatever it may be, for your duty to follow the law, whether you agree with the law or not. It is not your determination whether the law is just or when a law is unjust. That cannot be and is not your task.[222]

Courts also generally prohibit counsel from discussing nullification in their closing arguments because it will not be an element of

---

221. United States v. Kleinman, 880 F.3d 1020, 1032–33 (9th Cir. 2017).

222. United States v. Lynch, 903 F.3d 1061, 1079 (9th Cir. 2018). The dissenting judge could not understand the majority view here when relying on the earlier decision.

> The court in this case crossed the line we drew in *Kleinman*. During voir dire, the court gave prospective jurors an instruction that largely tracked the one we approved [earlier] . . . . Critically, though, the court went further by stating: "Nullification is by definition a violation of the juror's oath which, if you are a juror in this case, you will take to apply the law as instructed by the court." In *Kleinman*, we held that a materially indistinguishable instruction—stating "[y]ou would violate your oath and the law" by engaging in nullification—was not only improper but an error of "constitutional dimension," for it carried with it the implicit threat of punishment. That implicit threat is no less present here, even though the court referred only to the jurors' oath without explicitly mentioning "the law." Telling jurors that nullification is a violation of their oath, standing alone, implies the potential for punishment because violating one's oath could be deemed either perjury or contempt, both of which are punishable by fine and imprisonment.

Id. at 1088–89. For a thoughtful discussion of the broad issue, along with consideration of these two cases, see Yorke, *Jury Nullification Instructions as Structural Error*, 95 WASH. L. REV. 1441 (2020).

the instructions to the jury from the court. This principle was stated in *United States v. Manzano*:[223]

> [W]e emphatically reject the rule . . . that district courts are free to permit jury nullification arguments whenever they feel justice so requires – in other words, in any case in which the court strongly disagrees with the government's charging decisions and the attendant sentencing consequences. As a practical matter, there is no meaningful difference between a court's knowing failure to remove a juror intent on nullification, a court's instruction to the jury that encourages nullification, and a court's ruling that affirmatively permits counsel to argue nullification. In each of these situations, the conduct in question subverts the jury's solemn duty to "take the law from the court, and apply that law to the facts of the case as they find them to be from the evidence." Sparf v. United States . . . . "We therefore join with those courts which hold that defense counsel may not argue jury nullification during closing argument." District courts have a duty to forestall or prevent such conduct, and the district court in this case abdicated its duty by ruling that defense counsel could argue jury nullification.[224]

Defense lawyers also have had little success in raising the nullification power through the process of informing the jury of an overly harsh sentence likely to be given in the particular case.[225] The courts overwhelmingly refuse to allow evidence or argument on point.

> Chesney claims that the district court violated his Fifth Amendment right to a fair trial by refusing to permit him to argue to the jury about the punishment he would receive if convicted. . . . The Supreme Court has stated that, unless juries have roles in sentencing, such as in capital sentencing proceedings, juries should be instructed not to consider defendants' possible sentences during deliberations. "It is well established that when a jury has no sentencing function, it should be admonished to 'reach its verdict without regard to what sentence might be imposed.'"

---

223. United States v. Manzano, 945 F.3d 616 (2d Cir. 2019).

224. *Id.* at 626–27. *See generally* United States v. Wilkerson, 966 F.3d 828, 834–35 (D.C. Cir. 2020); People v. Moore, 662 N.E.2d 1215 (Ill. 1996); United States v. Sepulveda, 15 F.3d 1161 (1st Cir. 1993); United States v. Trujillo, 714 F.2d 102, 105 (11th Cir. 1983).

225. Though at least a few judges have agreed with the defense position. *See, e.g.*, the dissent in *Manzano*, 945 F.3d at 632; United States v. Datcher, 830 F. Supp. 411, 415 (M.D. Tenn. 1993).

In Chesney's trial, the jury had no sentencing function, and no statute required that the jury be informed of the consequences of its verdict. Thus, argument about possible punishment in Chesney's case is foreclosed by well-settled precedent, and the district court did not err in refusing to permit Chesney to argue about his possible punishment.[226]

226. United States v. Chesney, 86 F.3d 564, 574 (6th Cir. 1996). *See also* United States v. Manning, 79 F.3d 212, 219 (1st Cir. 1996). One thoughtful commentator has opined that, "the constitutionality of prohibiting jury nullification is under attack." Bressler, *Reconstruction and the Transformation of Jury Nullification*, 78 U. Chi. L. Rev. 1133, 1135 (2011). *See generally* Carroll, *Nullifications as Law*, 102 Geo. L.J. 579 (2014). In an unusual move the New Hampshire legislature recently enacted this law: "In all criminal proceedings the court shall permit the defense to inform the jury of its right to judge the facts and the application of the law in relation to the facts in controversy." N.H. Rev. Stat. Ann. § 519:23-a. The defendant in *State v. Paul*, 104 A.3d 1058 (N.H. 2014), asserted that the intent of the legislators in this law was to allow the jury to learn of its ability to nullify. The state supreme court disagreed. "[The law] is decidedly not a direction that the jury is to have the right to sit in judgment of the law—the prerogative which, the defendant claims, lies at the heart of jury nullification. Instead the statute merely delineates the jury's traditional function of determining how the law applies to the facts as it has found them, which it must necessarily perform in every case in order to reach a verdict." *Id.* at 1061.

CHAPTER 4

Place of Prosecution

I. Historical Basis

The origins of our constitutional rules for place of prosecution reside in the *Magna Carta*, which states: "nor will We not pass upon him, nor condemn him, but by lawful judgment of his Peers, or by the Law of the land."[1] The English colonists carried this right with them to North America in the form of a trial by a local jury, and the colonists reacted with anger to King George III when he and Parliament eliminated this right for treason charges in 1769.[2] The English government decided to bring colonists charged with treason to England for trial after colonists in the Massachusetts Bay Colony rebelled against taxes imposed on them by Parliament.[3] The revolutionaries complained in the Declaration of Independence that the King "has combined with others to subject us to a jurisdiction foreign to our constitution, and unacknowledged by our laws; giving his Assent of pretended Legislation: . . . [f]or transporting us beyond Seas to be tried for pretended offenses."[4] The adoption of the Constitution in 1787 and the ratification of the Bill of Rights in 1791 formally established a "place of prosecution" right for U.S. citizens.

Article III of the U.S. Constitution states in part that "[t]he Trial of all Crimes, except in Cases of Impeachment, shall be by jury; and such Trial shall be held in the State where the said Crimes shall have been committed; but when not committed within any State, the Trial shall be at such Place or Places as the Congress may by Law have

1. MAGNA CARTA, cl. 29 (1297).

2. William Wirt Blume, *The Place of Trial of Criminal Cases: Constitutional Vicinage and Venue*, 43 MICH. L. REV. 59, 64 (1944).

3. *Id.* at 63.

4. THE DECLARATION OF INDEPENDENCE 15, 21 (U.S. 1776).

directed."[5] This venue provision provides a defendant with the right to be tried for a crime in the district where the crime allegedly occurred.[6]

The Sixth Amendment further established a vicinage[7] right for the citizens of the new United States: "In all criminal prosecutions, the accused shall enjoy the right to a speedy and public trial, by an impartial jury of the State and district wherein the crime shall have been committed, which district shall have been previously ascertained by law."[8] Because of limited travel in the early days of the United States, the vicinage requirement usually resulted in a jury selected from the district of the defendant's residence.[9] In modern times, the vicinage provision guarantees a jury selected from the district in which the crime allegedly occurred.[10]

The distinction between these two similar provisions is that the venue provision requires that an offender be *tried* in the district in which the crime was committed, while the vicinage provision requires that the *jury be selected* from the district in which the crime was committed.[11] These constitutional provisions also produce a variety of other issues. First, if the jury pool is restricted to the district of the crime, the defendant may be unable to attain a fair and impartial jury. Further, the crime may have allegedly occurred in multiple districts, all of which could claim proper venue to hear the case. Finally, these provisions provide no solution for venue selection for cases in which the crime was not committed within any district of the United States. As discussed below, modern statutes have attempted to solve these venue problems by allowing for cases to be transferred.

---

5. U.S. CONST. art. III, § 2.

6. "Venue (ven-yoo). [Law French 'coming'] (16c) *Procedure*. 1. The proper or a possible place for a lawsuit to proceed, usu. because the place has some connection either with the events that gave rise to the lawsuit or with the plaintiff or defendant. 2. The territory, such as a country or other political subdivision, over which a trial court has jurisdiction." BLACK'S LAW DICTIONARY 1790 (10th ed. 2014).

7. "Vicinage (vis- ə-nij). [Law French 'neighborhood'] (14c) 1. Vicinity; proximity. 2. The place where a crime is committed or a trial is held; the place from which jurors are to be drawn for trial; esp., the locale from which the accused is entitled to have jurors selected." BLACK'S LAW DICTIONARY 1797 (10th ed. 2014).

8. U.S. CONST. amend. VI.

9. Comment, *Multi-Venue and the Obscenity Statutes*, 115 U. PA. L. REV. 399, 413 (1967).

10. *See* Johnston v. United States, 351 U.S. 215, 220–21 (1956) (public policy fixes the situs of the trial in the vicinage of the crime rather than the residence of the accused).

11. *See* United States v. Means, 409 F. Supp. 115, 116–17 (D.N.D. 1976) (venue in criminal cases is governed by "a complicated interplay of constitutional provisions, statutes and rules, and important considerations of policy with deep historical roots").

The Supreme Court has not applied either the Sixth Amendment vicinage provision or the Article III venue provision to the states.[12] Even though the Sixth Amendment is mentioned in some cases discussing state law venue and vicinage issues, state cases are almost always decided on state law grounds without an analysis of the U.S. constitutional provisions.[13] Therefore, most of the state law examples in this chapter do not rely on the U.S. constitutional provisions.

II. Venue

A. Distinguished from Jurisdiction

A federal district court has jurisdiction over a criminal case when either (1) the crime occurred on federal land or (2) the Constitution grants federal jurisdiction over a criminal act, thereby making the crime a federal crime.[14] By contrast, venue dictates which specific federal court will hear the case, and the proper district, for venue purposes, is always determined by a district judge.

B. In General

Proper venue is determined by the nature of the crime and the location of the alleged act.[15] Unless Congress has provided a venue provision in the statute, the government generally must prosecute a crime in the district in which the alleged offense was committed,[16] the *locus*

---

12. Steven A. Engel, *The Public's Vicinage Right: A Constitutional Argument*, 75 N.Y.U. L. Rev. 1658, 1706 (2000). See *id.* at 1704–10 for a discussion of the application of the vicinage clause to the states; *see also* Wayne R. LaFave et al., Criminal Procedure § 2.6(b) (3d ed. 2014).

13. *See* Price v. Superior Court, 25 P.3d 618, 624–33 (Cal. 2001) (comprehensive review of the law leading to the court's conclusion that the federal vicinage clause does not apply to the states); *contra* Mareska v. State, 534 N.E.2d 246, 249–50 (Ind. Ct. App. 1989).

14. *See* 18 U.S.C. § 3231 ("The district courts of the United States shall have original jurisdiction, exclusive of the courts of the States, of all offenses against the laws of the United States."); *see also* United States v. Knott, 722 F. Supp. 1365, 1367 (E.D. Va. 1989) (federal magistrate judge did not have authority to revoke a defendant's state-issued driver's license and could instead forward defendant's DUI conviction to Virginia's Department of Motor Vehicles for consideration).

15. United States v. Anderson, 328 U.S. 699, 703 (1946) (the court had jurisdiction in the district where the defendant's crime of refusal occurred).

16. *Id.*

delicti,[17] as opposed to the location of the defendant.[18] In performing the inquiry into the *locus delicti*, "a court must initially identify the conduct constituting the offense (the nature of the crime) and then discern the location of the commission of the criminal acts."[19] The leading case is *United States v. Cabrales*, where the Supreme Court concluded that venue in Missouri was not proper for a money-laundering conspiracy charge.[20] Although the alleged drug sale took place there, the government could not prove that an agreement or any other part of the money-laundering crime with which the defendant was charged occurred in Missouri.[21] As in *Cabrales*, venue has traditionally been used to protect defendants from the burden of being forced to mount a defense in an inconvenient district unless the crimes were actually committed in that district.[22]

C. State Practice

The Sixth Amendment vicinage provision applies to all criminal prosecutions. Nearly five decades ago, the Supreme Court held that a state statute preventing a defendant from requesting a change of

---

17. "Locus Delicti (loh-kəs də-lik-ti). [Latin 'place of the wrong'] (18c) The place where an offense was committed; the place where the last event necessary to make the actor liable occurred." BLACK'S LAW DICTIONARY 1083 (10th ed. 2014).

18. *See* Travis v. United States, 364 U.S. 631, 631–32 (1961) (venue for continuing offenses is proper "wherever the wrongdoer roamed").

19. United States v. Rodriguez-Moreno, 526 U.S. 275, 279 (1999) (venue was proper in any district where defendant's crime of violence was committed, even if the firearm was only used or carried in a single district).

20. United States v. Cabrales, 524 U.S. 1 (1998).

21. *Id.* Justice Ginsburg explained:

> The counts before us portray her and the money she deposited and withdrew as moving inside Florida only. . . . But if Cabrales is in fact linked to the drug-trafficking activity [in Missouri], the Government is not disarmed from showing that is the case. She can be, and indeed has been, charged with conspiring with the drug dealers in Missouri. If the Government can prove the agreement it has alleged, Cabrales can be prosecuted in Missouri for that confederacy, and her money laundering in Florida could be shown as overt acts in furtherance of the conspiracy.

Id. at 9.

22. In response to *Cabrales*, Congress amended the venue provisions of the money-laundering statute to provide that venue is proper in "any district where a prosecution for the underlying specified unlawful activity could be brought, if the defendant participated in the transfer of the proceeds of the specified unlawful activity from that district to the district where the financial or monetary transaction is conducted." 18 U.S.C. § 1956(i)(B). This is an example of Congress changing the outcome of a Supreme Court opinion within the bounds of the Constitution.

venue, even for a misdemeanor trial, was unconstitutional under the Sixth and Fourteenth Amendments.[23]

States vary on the treatment of venue. In some states, venue is considered an element of the case and therefore must be proven by the prosecutor beyond a reasonable doubt;[24] in others, it need only be proven by a preponderance of the evidence.[25]

III. Transfer for Trial

Whether a motion to change venue should be granted is a case-specific and fact-intensive inquiry.[26] For example, although the current district may inconvenience the defendant, this fact may be outweighed by the likelihood of jury prejudice in other districts. If a court finds prejudice, though, it must transfer to a new venue.[27] When considering transfer for convenience, only an examination of the facts will determine whether the benefit to the defendant of a change in venue outweighs other considerations.[28] For this reason, trial courts are given great

---

23. Groppi v. Wisconsin, 400 U.S. 505, 507–08 (1971) (the Fourteenth Amendment's Due Process Clause requires that the defendant be given an opportunity to show why a change of venue is necessary).

24. *See, e.g.*, State v. Dixon, 691 S.E.2d 207, 209 (Ga. 2010) (under the Georgia state constitution, venue is an element of *every* crime); Hill v. State, 797 So. 2d 914 (Miss. 2001).

25. *See, e.g.*, Black v. State, 645 S.W.2d 789 (Tex. Crim. App. 1983).

26. *See* United States v. Parr, 17 F.R.D. 512, 517 (S.D. Tex. 1955) (a defendant in a criminal case has the burden of proving that the facts of his case authorize or require a change of venue to another district or division).

27. Examples of statutory and case law tests used by states for granting a transfer include CAL. PENAL CODE § 1033 ("[T]he court *shall* order a change of venue . . . [o]n motion of the defendant, to another county when it appears that there is a reasonable likelihood that a fair and impartial trial cannot be had in the immediate county.") (emphasis added); N.Y. CRIM. PROC. LAW § 230.20 (McKinney's 2011) (a court may remove an indictment and action to another county if the defendant or the state demonstrates "reasonable cause to believe that a fair and impartial trial cannot be had in" the originating county); Chandler v. State, 848 So. 2d 1031, 1036 (Fla. 2003) ("The test for determining a change of venue is whether the general state of mind of the inhabitants of a community is so infected by knowledge of the incident and accompanying prejudice, bias, and preconceived opinions that jurors could not possibly put these matters out of their minds and try the case solely on the evidence presented in the courtroom."); People v. Pelo, 942 N.E.2d 463, 491 (2010), *appeal denied*, 949 N.E.2d 663 (Ill. 2011) ("[R]easonable apprehension exists that [defendant] cannot receive a fair and impartial trial.").

28. *E.g.*, United States v. Valdes, 2006 WL 738403 (S.D.N.Y. 2006) (referencing ten nonexclusive factors that a court may consider in granting a venue transfer, originally promulgated in *Platt v. Minnesota Mining & Manufacturing Co.*, 376 U.S. 240 (1964)); *In re* Briscoe, 976 F.2d 1425, 1428 (D.C. Cir. 1992) (the slight benefit to the defendant did not warrant transfer because of the inconvenience it would cause other parties).

deference with respect to transfer decisions, and will only be overturned for an abuse of discretion.[29]

A. Waiver of Venue

Constitutional rights can only be *intentionally* and voluntarily waived by defendants.[30] However, under the relevant case law, choice of venue can be either expressly or impliedly waived.[31] Numerous courts have held that venue is a waivable privilege because it is "not a jurisdictional prerequisite and does not affect the power of a court to hear a case."[32] Inaction on the part of the defendant, by not objecting to venue prior to trial, is considered waiver of the right to object to the choice of venue.[33] By regarding venue as "a nonfundamental aspect of jurisdiction which may be waived either by defendant's consent or by failure to object," several courts have held that the defendant's failure to raise a timely objection to venue before trial waived any venue violation.[34] Objections to venue must be raised in a timely manner[35] in order to preserve the claim of error.[36] A defendant must make

29. *See, e.g.*, Skilling v. United States, 561 U.S. 358 (2010).

30. As the Supreme Court has repeatedly written, when constitutional rights are involved, the government must prove "an intentional relinquishment or abandonment." Johnson v. Zerbst, 304 U.S. 458, 464 (1938).

31. *See* United States v. Pomranz, 43 F.3d 156, 162 (5th Cir. 1995) ("[T]he standard for finding waiver of venue is much more relaxed than the rigorous standard for finding waivers of the right to trial by jury, the right to confront one's accusers or the privilege against compulsory self-incrimination. As opposed to waiver of these later rights, a defendant can waive venue rights by his silence."). *See generally* Note, *Change of Venue in Criminal Cases: The Defendant's Right to Specify the County of Transfer*, 26 STAN. L. REV. 131, 145–46 (1973).

32. *See, e.g.*, McClellion v. State, 858 So. 2d 379, 381 (Fla. Dist. Ct. App. 2003); *see also* People v. Greenberg, 678 N.E.2d 878, 879 (N.Y. 1997) ("To be sure, venue issues—which relate only to the proper place of trial, rather than to the power of the court to hear and determine the case—are waivable."); Brown v. Commonwealth, 207 S.E.2d 833, 836 (Va. 1974) (a venue statute does not limit the general criminal jurisdiction of the circuit courts).

33. People v. Gray, 783 N.E.2d 170, 179 (Ill. App. Ct. 2003) ("By pleading guilty or failing to object before trial, a defendant waives, *i.e.*, forfeits, any objection to the improper venue.").

34. *See, e.g.*, People v. Gbadebo-Soda, 45 Cal. Rptr. 2d 40, 45–46 (Cal. Ct. App. 1995) (distinguishing venue from fundamental aspects of jurisdiction, such as subject matter jurisdiction).

35. Comment, *Proper Venue as a Jury Issue in Federal Criminal Cases: The "In Issue" Approach to When Venue Presents a Fact Question for the Jury as Opposed to a Question of Law for the Court*, 76 TEMP. L. REV. 883, 886–87 (2003).

36. *See* FED. R. CRIM. P. 51(b); *see also* United States v. Carreon-Palacio, 267 F.3d 381, 391 (5th Cir. 2001).

objections to venue before the commencement of the trial in both federal and state courts,[37] keeping in mind that any significant change in the circumstances of the case, including dismissal of parties[38] or changes to the defendant's personal or health conditions,[39] might be sufficient to justify a later objection and transfer. Yet the court has the discretion to deny a transfer motion if a transfer of venue no longer promotes the interests of justice.[40]

If the defendant waives the right to prosecution in the local venue, the court can transfer the case to another district.[41] Defendants may request particular transferee districts, but the court is free to use its discretion in selecting the transferee district. By moving to change venue, the defendant communicates that she does not want the trial to take place in the district in which the alleged crime was committed even though that is her constitutional right.[42] Once she has waived that right, the defendant cannot later object to a new venue as improper, because she voluntarily left the proper venue. Once in the new venue, the defendant may object to the venue of the new district court only on the basis of substantial concerns regarding convenience or impartiality of the community.[43] The defendant must suggest a specific district in her transfer motion. If the case is transferred to that district, she automatically waives any right to object to venue in that district.[44] A case may be transferred back to the original district if the circumstances that caused the transfer no longer exist.[45] Once venue has been waived, the court's jurisdiction is valid even if a defect is eventually discovered.

---

37. *See, e.g.*, 720 Ill. Comp. Stat. 5/1–6 (a)(2013) ("All objections of improper place of trial are waived by a defendant unless made before trial."); People v. Simon, 25 P.3d 598, 615 (Cal. 2001) ("A specific objection to venue by a defendant should be considered timely if made *prior to the commencement of trial*."); People v. McClain, 376 N.E.2d 774, 776 (Ill. App. Ct. 1978) (venue must be waived explicitly or implicitly before trial).

38. United States v. Ashland Oil, Inc., 457 F. Supp. 661, 663 (W.D. Ky. 1978).

39. *See, e.g.*, United States v. Lopez, 2002 WL 31498984 (D. Kan. 2002); United States v. Liska, 1995 WL 704775 (N.D. Ill. 1995).

40. *See* United States v. Keuylian, 602 F.2d 1033, 1038–39 (2d Cir. 1979) (inconvenience to the parties and unnecessary delay of trial are factors that may be considered when deciding an untimely motion for transfer).

41. Darryl K. Brown, *The Role of Race in Jury Impartiality and Venue Transfers*, 53 Md. L. Rev. 107, 134–36 (1994).

42. United States v. Wilson, 26 F.3d 142, 151 (D.C. Cir. 1994).

43. *Id.* ("It seems to us beyond doubt that appellant Briscoe by initiating the move to transfer to D.C. waived any subsequent objections based on improper venue.").

44. *Id.*

45. United States v. Blackwell, 946 F.2d 1049, 1052 n.1 (4th Cir. 1991).

Pretrial publicity can significantly prejudice a jury pool.[46] It is for the defendant and her attorney to determine whether adverse pretrial publicity is so pervasive that the defendant should waive her right to be tried in the state and district in which the alleged crime was committed.[47]

B. Federal Rule of Criminal Procedure 21

Federal Rule of Criminal Procedure 21 provides two independent reasons for granting a motion to transfer. Subsection (a) states that "[u]pon the defendant's motion, the court must transfer the proceeding against that defendant to another district if the court is satisfied that so great a prejudice against the defendant exists in the transferring district that the defendant cannot obtain a fair and impartial trial here."[48] This type of prejudice can be personal prejudice by a juror against the defendant, known as "actual prejudice," or community prejudice spawned by pretrial publicity. However, the judge must find that community prejudice makes it impossible to empanel an impartial jury, keeping the defendant from a fair trial.[49] Based on this finding, the court may select the district to which the case is transferred.[50] Factors for selecting a transferee district may include a location outside of media coverage of the incident (although this concern is less prevalent in an age of global media), the size and schedule of

46. *See* Vineet R. Shahani, *Change the Motion, Not the Venue: A Critical Look at the Change of Venue Motion*, 42 Am. Crim. L. Rev. 93, 101–02 (2005).

47. United States v. Stratton, 649 F.2d 1066, 1077–78 (5th Cir. 1981). Recent examples of defendants seeking a change of venue based on prejudicial pretrial publicity include: Colin Campbell and Ian Duncan, *Officers in Freddie Gray Case File for Change of Venue*, Balt. Sun, May 27, 2015, http://www.baltimoresun.com/news/maryland/freddie-gray/bs-md-freddie-gray-venue-change-motion-20150527-story.html (six white and black police officers are charged with acts that are alleged to have caused the death of the victim while in police custody); Lauren Pack, *Fired University Officer to Seek Change of Venue*, Dayton Daily News, Aug. 18, 2015, http://www.daytondailynews.com/news//news/crime-law/lawyer-for-ex-cop-wants-trial-moved-out-of-hami/nnMH3/ (white police officer is indicted for murder after shooting a black victim during a traffic stop for no front license plate).

48. Fed. R. Crim. P. 21(a).

49. This burden is extremely high and almost impossible to meet, even in the case of highly publicized trials. For example, Boston Marathon bomber Dzhokhar Tsarnaev moved for and was denied change of venue three times before he was ultimately tried and convicted in Boston, Massachusetts. United States v. Tsarnaev, No. 14-10200-GA) (D. Mass. Feb. 6, 2015) (order denying defendant's third motion for change of venue).

50. Fed. R. Crim. P. 21(b).

the transferee court, ease of accessibility to the transferee district, and the presence of facilities to house witnesses who are in custody.[51]

Rule 21(b) continues: "Upon the defendant's motion, the court may transfer the proceeding, or one or more counts, against that defendant to another district for the convenience of the parties, any victim, and the witnesses, and in the interest of justice."[52] This subsection provides grounds for transfer independent of any finding of prejudice. Under Rule 21(b), transfer of venue can occur for any one of the stated reasons, although none is determinative. For example, even if a venue is inconvenient for the defendant, a motion for transfer may still be denied if other factors outweigh the benefits of transfer. Rule 21(b) instructs that actions may be wholly or partially transferred; thus, transfer may be granted to some or all of the defendants, or transfer may be granted for some or all of the counts charged to one defendant.[53] In cases of convenience there may be only parts of a criminal proceeding that require a more convenient venue for the defendant(s), witnesses, or evidentiary findings.[54]

As noted previously, the grant or denial of a motion for change of venue is within the trial court's discretion. Absent abuse of discretion by the trial court, the ruling will not be disturbed on appeal.[55] The

---

51. United States v. Moody, 762 F. Supp. 1485, 1490–91 (N.D. 1991) (discussing how the court selected the transferee district); *see also* State v. Walters, 426 N.W.2d 136, 138–39 (Iowa 1988) (offering a list of factors courts may use in deciding where to transfer a case).

52. Fed. R. Crim. P. 21(b).

53. *Id.; see also* United States v. Choate, 276 F.2d 724, 727–28 (5th Cir. 1960) ("[W]e conclude that Rule 21(b) is carefully drafted so as to permit the court to act upon the motion of any one defendant or any number of defendants and, in connection with Rule 14, to sever and transfer the proceeding under each count separately which charges the commission of the offense in the transferee district.").

54. Fed. R. Crim. P. 21(c) states, "When the court orders a transfer, the clerk must send to the transferee district the file, or a certified copy, and any bail taken. The prosecution will then continue in the transferee district." The transferee district also has the responsibility for the disposition of the case and any appeals. Fed. R. Crim. P. 21(d) states, "A motion to transfer may be made at or before arraignment or at any other time the court or these rules prescribe." This rule provides a change of venue only upon the defendant's motion. *See* Marcus, *Conflicts Among Circuits and Transfers Within the Federal System*, 93 Yale L.J. 677, 679–80 (1984).

55. United States v. Neal, 718 F.2d 1505, 1510 (10th Cir. 1983) (affirming trial court's denial of a venue change motion in a mail fraud case). The Supreme Court in *Skilling v. United States*, 561 U.S. 358, 378 n.11 (2010), made the point clearly: "As the language of the Rule suggests, district-court calls on the necessity of transfer are granted a healthy measure of appellate-court respect." In the trial against Boston Marathon bomber Dzhokhar Tsarnaev, the defendant sought review of the trial court's denial of change of venue by petitioning for a writ of mandamus from the First Circuit. The defendant's writ was

receiving court does not decide whether the transfer was in the interest of justice, because the decision to transfer is in the sole discretion of the transferring court. However, the question of whether the alleged offense was committed in the receiving district *is* reviewable by the transferee court.[56]

Furthermore, a defendant cannot be forced to accept a change in venue.[57] If the defendant chooses to exercise his constitutional right to have the case tried in the district where the crime was committed, the government may not object to this venue. Because the government initially brought the charges in the district, it has impliedly agreed to the venue.[58]

C. State Rules on Venue Transfer in Criminal Cases

Many states rules regarding transfer of venue in a criminal case mirror Rule 21, by separating prejudice and convenience as independent grounds for a motion to transfer.[59] For example, California allows for transfer when there is a "reasonable likelihood" that a fair and impartial trial cannot be had in the present county.[60] California also conducts a fact-specific evaluation of any motion to transfer.[61] Massachusetts has adopted the same time frame as the federal rule, such that motions to change venue must be made before trial.[62] Massachusetts, like other states, has further identified factors a court should consider in granting a motion to transfer for convenience of the parties.[63] Overall, state law governing venue transfers

---

denied because "[t]o compel the district court to change course, a petitioner must show not only that the district court was manifestly wrong, but also that the petitioner's right to relief is clear and indisputable, irreparable harm will result, and the equities favor such drastic relief." *In re* Tsarnaev, 780 F.3d 14, 16 (1st Cir. 2015).

56. *See* United States v. Bryson, 16 F.R.D. 431, 434 (N.D. Cal. 1954).

57. *See* United States v. DiJames, 731 F.2d 758, 761 (11th Cir. 1984); United States v. Abbott Labs., 505 F.2d 565, 572 (4th Cir. 1974).

58. *See generally* State v. Manning, 495 S.E.2d 191, 195 (S.C. 1997); State v. House, 978 P.2d 967, 977 (N.M. 1999). Research found no case where the government was successful in changing venue without the defendant's consent.

59. Fed. R. Crim. P. 21.

60. Cal. Penal Code § 1033 (West 2012).

61. In *People v. Davis*, 94 Cal. Rptr. 3d 322, 359–61 (Cal. 2009), defendant's motion to transfer was granted after extensive inquiry into the media coverage and bias of potential jurors.

62. Mass. R. Crim. P. 37.

63. Commonwealth v. Aldoupolis, 457 N.E.2d 268, 273 (Mass. 1983) (evaluating potential hardships to parties that a transfer might cause).

in criminal cases is very similar to federal law, except that states have all drafted their own codes and constitutions protecting a defendant's venue rights.[64]

D. Motion to Transfer

A motion to transfer must be made in the court in which the prosecution of the case is pending.[65] The motion will be dismissed if brought in the incorrect court. Absent a request, a court may not order a change of venue *sua sponte*.[66] A motion to transfer must also be made after indictment because prior to indictment offenders are not defendants within the meaning of the Rule, and the court has no authority to transfer grand jury proceedings from one district to another.[67] Furthermore, in a multidefendant case, a defendant who did not move to transfer may not be transferred against his will.[68]

A motion to transfer venue should be made as early as possible. If the motion is made later in the trial preparations, a greater showing of inconvenience may be required.[69] Courts may also deny motions to transfer when a defendant has previously announced that she is prepared to go to trial in that district.[70] Additionally, before granting a

64. FED. R. CRIM. P. 21 Advisory Committee Notes, n.2.

65. United States v. Winston, 267 F. Supp. 555, 562 (S.D.N.Y. 1967) (denying defendant's motion for transfer from a Nebraska court to a New York court because the motion was improperly filed in New York).

66. United States v. Abbott Labs., 505 F.2d 565, 572 (4th Cir. 1974) ("Because of a defendant's sixth amendment right to be tried in the district where the crime was allegedly committed, Rule 21 . . . conditions a change of venue, *inter alia*, upon the defendant's request therefor.").

67. *In re* Investigation of World Arrangements, Etc., of Petroleum, 107 F. Supp. 628, 630 (D.D.C. 1952) (denying movants' transfer request because no indictment yet existed, thus movants were not defendants entitled to transfer within the meaning of Rule 21); *see also* United States v. Crow Dog, 532 F.2d 1182, 1188 (8th Cir. 1976) (an indictment is a prerequisite for transferring venue).

68. *See, e.g.*, United States v. Aronoff, 463 F. Supp. 454, 458 (S.D.N.Y. 1978) (the court is powerless to transfer an entire case when one or more defendants did not motion for transfer); United States v. Clark, 360 F. Supp. 936, 945–46 (S.D.N.Y. 1973) (under Rule 21(b) transfer shall be granted only upon defendant's motion and the transfer shall apply only as to movant defendant).

69. United States v. Polizzi, 500 F.2d 856, 901 (9th Cir. 1974) (trial court's denial of change of venue was proper because trial was imminent and defendants could not show that transfer to another jurisdiction would be less of an inconvenience than the present jurisdiction); *see also* United States v. Taylor, 562 F.2d 1345, 1363 (2d Cir. 1977).

70. United States v. Tremont, 351 F.2d 144, 146 (6th Cir. 1965) (upholding trial court's denial of defendant's motion to transfer because "Rule 22 requires that [such a] motion be

change of venue on the ground that a jury would be prejudiced against the defendant, a judge must determine, at voir dire, that an impartial jury cannot be empaneled.[71] The court may delay a ruling on a transfer motion until it has adequate time to establish that an unprejudiced jury cannot be selected.[72] A judge may summon a large jury pool in order to achieve the selection of an impartial jury.[73]

In certain very limited situations, the prosecution can move to transfer the case out of the transferee district, but this requires a much stronger evidentiary showing than that proffered by the defendant.[74] In all cases, the court must make a fact-intensive inquiry when determining whether a case should be transferred.

1. Transfer for the Convenience of Parties

Most states do not recognize a transfer for convenience of the parties.[75] When determining if a motion for transfer should be granted on convenience grounds, the court may consider the physical location of parties, witnesses, and evidence. A transfer for convenience protects the defendant from an unfair prosecutorial advantage, thus protecting the defendant from districts where it may be more difficult to gather defense

---

made 'at or before arraignment' unless otherwise prescribed by the rules or the court"). Note: FED. R. CRIM. P. 22 was abrogated Dec. 1, 2002, but the substance of the Rule was transferred to FED. R. CRIM. P. 21(d).

71. *See* United States v. Dioguardi, 20 F.R.D. 33, 36 (S.D.N.Y. 1956) (denying motion to transfer until trial court has conducted voir dire and has determined whether the jury can issue a fair and impartial verdict despite national prejudicial publicity about defendant's actions); People v. Boudin, 87 A.D.2d 133, 135 (N.Y. App. Div. 1982) (stating that the determination of whether an emotional atmosphere exists should be made after voir dire). The Supreme Court in *Skilling v. United States*, 561 U.S. 358 (2010), upheld denial of defendant's motion to transfer, in favor of "effective voir dire . . . to ferret out any [juror] bias" (internal quotations omitted).

72. *See Dioguardi*, 20 F.R.D. 33 at 35–36.

73. *See* Matthew Mastromauro, *Pre-Trial Prejudice 2.0: How YouTube Generated News Coverage Is Set to Complicate the Concepts of Pre-Trial Prejudice Doctrine and Endanger Sixth Amendment Fair Trial Rights*, 10 J. HIGH TECH. L. 289, 315–16 (2010).

74. Note, *supra* note 31, at 152–53.

75. LAFAVE ET AL., CRIMINAL PROCEDURE: WEST'S CRIMINAL PRACTICE SERIES § 16.3(c) (3d ed. 2007) (discussing state variations for transfers for convenience).

evidence.[76] The primary reason for granting a transfer is to avoid hardships to the defendant, the defense attorney, and witnesses.[77]

a. Relative Locations

A defendant may request a change of venue for convenience of the defense, the parties, or witnesses. Motions to transfer can be based on the physical location of any of the following:

- the distance from the defendant's legal residence
- the location of defendant's witnesses and evidence,[78] such as records and documents
- the location of the alleged events
- the ability of the defendant's family and friends to attend trial[79]
- any disruption of the defendant's business if transfer is not affected
- expenses to the parties
- any other special elements that might affect the transfer[80]

When more than one venue would be proper, convenience to parties plays a role in determining the place of prosecution.

76. People v. Davis, 208 P.3d 78, 109 (Cal. 2009) ("[C]onsiderations of relative hardship, and the conservation of judicial resources and public funds, are important factors in deciding between various possible venue sites. This may include choosing a new venue site near the original venue site for the convenience of witnesses, attorneys, and interested residents of the original venue site." (internal quotations and citations omitted)).

77. *Cf.* United States v. Benjamin, 623 F. Supp. 1204, 1212 (D.D.C. 1985) (discussing Congress's stated preference that tax prosecutions be "brought as close to the defendant's residence as possible" (internal quotations omitted)). Although a court can consider convenience to the prosecution and its witnesses in deciding whether to grant a motion to transfer, the prosecution on its own may not motion for transfer as noted earlier.

78. *See* Fed. R. Crim. P. 21(b); *see also* United States v. Atwood, 538 F. Supp. 1206, 1207–08 (E.D. Pa. 1982) (granting defendant's motion for transfer in light of the residence of defendant, location of possible witnesses, cost of witness travel, and location of the illegal activity); United States v. Daewoo Indus. Co., 591 F. Supp. 157, 160 (D. Or. 1984) (transfer to California appropriate when the majority of material witnesses resided near the Los Angeles area).

79. *See* United States v. Garza, 593 F.3d 385, 390 (5th Cir. 2010) (vacating defendants' convictions after finding that judge abused her discretion by, *sua sponte*, ordering transfer at great inconvenience to the parties); *see also Davis*, 208 P.3d at 109 (transfer considerations should include "the convenience of witnesses, attorneys, and interested residents of the original venue site").

80. Platt v. Minn. Mining & Mfg. Co., 376 U.S. 240, 243–44 (1964) (involving the transfer of an antitrust prosecution against a corporation).

If the defendant and witnesses for the defendant reside in the transferee jurisdiction, and all books and papers relevant to the prosecution are also located in the transferee district, a court may grant a motion to transfer a criminal proceeding.[81] However, a defendant has no absolute right to be tried in the jurisdiction where she is domiciled.[82] The defendant's residence is a factor to be considered on a transfer motion, but it is not a determinative factor.[83] The court may deny the transfer of a criminal case if the transfer would greatly inconvenience, so long as the burden is greater than the defendant's inconvenience of remaining in the district.[84] For example, a court may refuse to transfer a case to the district in which the defendant resides if all other attorneys, witnesses, and evidence reside in the district where the crime was committed.[85]

b. Burden of Proof and Test for Transfer

If a defendant does not make a motion for a change of venue, she waives any future claims of inconvenience.[86] The defendant's motion, when premised on convenience, must prove that the interests of justice outweigh any inconvenience that would be suffered by the

---

81. *See* United States v. Erie Basin Metal Prods. Co., 79 F. Supp. 880, 881–82 (D. Md. 1948) (considering the location of evidence as well as the number of witnesses and defendants to be transferred as factors favoring a change of venue).

82. United States v. Bagnell, 679 F.2d 826, 832–33 (11th Cir. 1982).

83. *Id.*; United States v. Jones, 43 F.R.D. 511, 514 (D.D.C. 1967) (denying motion for transfer, especially because the other defendants in the case did not have the same state of residence as the movant).

84. *Cf.* United States v. Tellier, 19 F.R.D. 164, 167–68 (E.D.N.Y. 1956) (denying defendant's request for change of venue because the location of witnesses and physical evidence weighed against transfer).

85. Similarly, there must be a substantial difference between the current district and the transferee district. If the district courthouses are geographically close to each other, transfer will almost certainly be denied. *See* United States v. Smallwood, 293 F. Supp. 2d 631, 640 (E.D. Va. 2003). Geographic closeness not only eliminates any issues with convenience but also *lessens greatly* any difference in the prejudice of the jury. Other geographical factors may also play a role in determining the proper venue for trials that are scheduled for extended periods of time. For example, a court may decide to transfer a case to another district if there is a substantial chance that a volcanic eruption or earthquake could affect the continuation of the trial for a prolonged period of time. *See* United States v. McDonald, 740 F. Supp. 757, 763–64 (D. Alaska 1990).

86. *See* United States v. Vinieris, 606 F. Supp. 1390, 1395–96 (S.D.N.Y. 1985), *aff'd*, 779 F.2d 40 (2d Cir. 1985) ("The failure of defense counsel 'specifically [to] articulate[ ]' improper venue as a basis for a judgment of acquittal at the close of either the Government's or the entire case constituted a waiver of the issue.").

prosecution and its witnesses by changing districts.[87] However, "inconvenience to a defendant alone is not sufficient to require a transfer."[88] The district court may consider the inconvenience to the attorneys as a factor in considering a transfer motion.[89]

In determining whether the transfer of a criminal proceeding is "in the interest of justice,"[90] the court must take into account the rights of the accused, government, and public; the promotion of a speedy and fair trial; and the potential to curtail unnecessary expenditures or prolonged litigation should a transfer be granted.[91] The expense of a case transfer may not be justified if the benefits of the transfer are minimal. The court, preferring to avoid a trial delay, may be more apt to deny a weakly supported motion for transfer.

2. Transfer to Avoid Prejudice

Rule 21(a) and most state rules expressly *require* transfer if the defendant cannot obtain a fair and impartial trial, due to actual jury prejudice. A transfer *may* be granted when the risk of jury prejudice is so prevalent in the community that a change of venue is warranted.[92] The defendant has a right to be heard about her concerns of prejudice in the community. If the defendant can establish that the community is biased, a transfer of the case may be necessary in order to protect her constitutional rights.[93]

---

87. United States v. Dakota, 197 F.3d 821, 826–27 (6th Cir. 1999) (the district court did not abuse its discretion by transferring case where "the interests of justice outweighed the expense and inconvenience" of the transfer).

88. *See* United States v. Pozos, 697 F.2d 1238, 1244 (5th Cir. 1983).

89. *Cf.* United States v. Benjamin, 623 F. Supp. 1204, 1212 (D.D.C. 1985) ("The government is represented by two attorneys from the Department of Justice whose duty and practice is to try cases in any federal court in the United States," while attorneys in multiple-defendant cases have no such duty and would be at a severe disadvantage if each had to relocate and develop a base of resources and logistical support from scratch).

90. *See* United States v. McDonald, 740 F. Supp. 757, 761 (D. Alaska 1990) (it is in the interest of justice to transfer a case when the current district is inconvenient for the defendant).

91. United States v. Erie Basin Metal Prods. Co., 79 F. Supp. 880, 885 (D. Md. 1948).

92. McCleskey v. Kemp, 481 U.S. 279, 310 (1987) (denying change of venue in capital case where defendant failed to establish that any of the jurors acted with racial bias or discriminatory purpose in violation of his Fourteenth and Eighth Amendment rights); *see also* N.Y. C.P.L.R. § 510 (McKinney); Ohio R. Crim. P. 18.

93. *See* Paul G. Cassell, *Recognizing Victims in the Federal Rules of Criminal Procedure: Proposed Amendments in Light of the Crime Victims' Rights Act*, 2005 BYU L. Rev. 835, 879–880 (2005); *see also* Va. Code Ann. § 19.2-251 (West 2012) (protecting a defendant's right to an impartial jury through venue transfer).

a. Actual Prejudice

"A well-grounded fear of jury prejudice" may be sufficient to necessitate a change of venue.[94] Still, qualified jurors need not be totally ignorant of the facts and issues involved in the case.[95] The mere existence of a preconceived notion as to guilt or innocence of the accused is, without more, insufficient to rebut the presumption of impartiality, so long as the juror can lay aside impressions or opinions and render a verdict based solely on the evidence presented in court.[96] A reviewing court will look to the sufficiency of voir dire, inclusive of any questionnaires, to determine whether the jury has been infected by actual prejudice.[97] The defendant bears the burden of proving that the jury's prejudice provides a necessary ground for a transfer.

b. Presumption of Prejudice and Publicity

For half a century the Supreme Court has reviewed pretrial publicity issues. In the 1961 case of *Irvin v. Dowd*, the Court decided that the defendant's right to a fair trial was prejudiced by massive pretrial publicity, which included statements released by police and prosecutors describing the six murders.[98] During voir dire, eight of the twelve

---

94. *See* Singer v. United States, 380 U.S. 24, 35 (1965) (voir dire, challenges for cause, and peremptory challenges are all methods that may be used to ensure fairness and alleviate fears of jury prejudice); People v. Jenkins, 997 P.2d 1044, 1074–75 (Cal. 2000) (ordering transfer "if there is a reasonable likelihood that a fair and impartial trial cannot be had in the county" (internal quotations omitted)).

95. Irvin v. Dowd, 366 U.S. 717, 722 (1961) (discussing generally the test of impartiality of jurors in response to a habeas corpus petition); *In re* Tsarnaev, 780 F.3d 14, 15 (1st Cir. 2015) ("Thus, any high-profile case will receive significant media attention. It is no surprise that people, in general, and especially the well-informed, will be aware of it. Knowledge, however, does not equate to disqualifying prejudice."); People v. Pelo, 942 N.E.2d 463, 493 (Ill. 2010) (reviewing courts are hesitant to second-guess a trial judge's estimation of a juror's impartiality because the trial judge is in the best position to assess a prospective juror's "inflection, sincerity, demeanor, candor, body language, and apprehension of duty").

96. Murphy v. Florida, 363 F. Supp. 1224, 1227–28 (S.D. Fla. 1973), *aff'd*, 495 F.2d 553 (5th Cir. 1974), *aff'd.* 421 U.S. 794, 95 (1975) ("In these days of swift, widespread and diverse methods of communication, an important case can be expected to arouse the interest of the public in the vicinity. . . . To hold that the mere existence of any preconceived notion as to the guilt or innocence of an accused, without more, is sufficient . . . would be to establish an impossible standard."); *Jenkins*, 997 P.2d at 1075–76 (even if jurors had been exposed to media about the case, such exposure is harmless so long as the jurors are not themselves biased because of it).

97. *See Skilling*, 561 U.S. 358.

98. *Irvin*, 366 U.S. at 719–20.

jurors seated for the trial thought Irvin was guilty, yet stated that they could give the defendant a fair trial.[99] The justices found that the trial judge erred in accepting the potential jurors' statements that they could be impartial, due in large part to the substantial publicity surrounding the trial.[100] In other words, in cases where pretrial publicity is extremely pervasive and prejudicial to the defendant, a presumption of prejudice may be raised that will require a transfer regardless of venire members' assertions that they can be fair and impartial. The precedential impact of *Irvin* may be lessened, however, in cases involving national media attention.

The Court soon thereafter detailed the media circus both before and during the *Sheppard v. Maxwell* trial.[101] The Court ruled that the trial judge, who was interviewed by the media during the trial, lost control of the courtroom and courthouse before and during the trial, ultimately depriving the defendant of a fair trial.[102] The jurors were repeatedly exposed to, and involved in, the media coverage, including being asked to pose for a newspaper photograph during a lunch break from their deliberations.[103] The justices provided many suggestions for dealing with media interest, such as adopting strict rules for press access to the courtroom, insulating the witnesses and jurors from the press, and prohibiting extrajudicial statements by counsel, witnesses, the coroner, and the police.[104]

In some cases, a thorough voir dire may cure a presumption of prejudice. In 1991, the Supreme Court held that the trial judge is not required to ask jurors in voir dire specific information about the case that they have seen or heard in the media, even in a high-publicity, racially charged case. [105] If the jurors do not state that their views have been shaped by pretrial publicity, the impartial jury requirement will be satisfied.[106] More recently, the Court examined the pretrial publicity and voir dire process in the prosecution of two former Enron

---

99. *Id.* at 727.

100. *Id.*

101. 384 U.S. 333 (1966).

102. *Id.* at 355.

103. *Id.* at 345.

104. *Id.* at 357–62. The conviction was reversed and Sheppard was acquitted in the second trial.

105. Mu'Min v. Virginia, 500 U.S. 415 (1991) (the defendant requested voir dire questions testing the racial bias of the potential jurors in a capital murder case where a white police officer was the victim and the defendant was black).

106. *Id.* at 431–32.

Corporation chief executives in the home district of the corporation.[107] The justices observed that there were four years between the bankruptcy of the company and the trial.[108] There also was a jury selection process, including a detailed jury questionnaire, which screened out any prejudiced jurors.[109] These factors provided a fair trial for the defendant.[110]

The court may question the jurors on whether exposure to media coverage has caused them to form an opinion about the case.[111] In general, however, the judge will accept a juror's assertion that she has not formed an opinion about the case.[112]

The court does not have the option of waiving the defendant's right to be tried in the district of the crime, even if the trial judge sincerely believes that waiver would benefit the defendant.[113] Judicial convenience and multiple defendant trials are not sufficient reasons to overlook the constitutional right of a defendant to be tried in the district where the crime took place.

In most cases, a claim of prejudicial publicity is more appropriately tested by voir dire, as opposed to a motion to change venue.[114] A court will not grant a change of venue based on pretrial publicity where much of the publicity appears in nationally circulated publications,[115] as a change in venue under these circumstances would have no effect.[116] Further, pretrial publicity will likely not be considered prejudicial when it is largely based in fact.[117] For example, "[f]actual publicity consist[ing] of plain news reports detailing a defendant's previous conviction"[118] does not warrant a transfer.

Denying a motion for a change of venue is proper where a substantial amount of time has passed since the occurrence of the publicity, or when pretrial public statements were made by the defendant or

---

107. *Skilling*, 561 U.S. 358 (a massive fraud case that sent the Enron Corporation into bankruptcy and cost thousands of people their jobs and savings).

108. *Id.* at 361.

109. *Id.* at 391.

110. *Id.* at 392–83.

111. Mastromauro, *supra* note 73, at 347.

112. *Id.* at 347–48.

113. United States v. Stratton, 649 F.2d 1066, 1077 (5th Cir. 1981).

114. *See* United States v. Caesar, 368 F. Supp. 328, 335 (E.D. Wis. 1973).

115. United States v. Cohn, 230 F. Supp. 589, 590–91 (S.D.N.Y. 1964).

116. *Id.* at 591 (nationwide publicity can lead to a prejudicial jury in multiple districts).

117. United States v. Murphy, 495 F.2d 553, 555–56 (5th Cir. 1974).

118. Shahani, *supra* note 46, at 102.

her attorney.[119] The Supreme Court has stated that the standard for determining if the pretrial publicity warrants a change of venue is flexible and dependent upon both the intensity of coverage prior to trial and the amount of time since the peak of publicity.[120] The rationale for this standard is that time "soothes and erases" the memory of a case.[121] The prejudice of pretrial publicity must be proven through evidence,[122] and any members of the jury who maintain that they have formed a fixed opinion due to such publicity must be excused from the case for cause.[123] The role of the government in creating the prejudicial atmosphere for the jury is also relevant. If the prejudice was caused by government actions,[124] the court may find that a transfer of venue is necessary to protect the defendant from an unfair trial.

The court may decide against transfer if it is unlikely that a change in venue would enable the selection of an impartial jury.[125] It may be difficult to overcome the prejudicial effect of nationwide publicity, even after a transfer of venue.[126] The claim made in *United States v. Dioguardi* was that a transfer of venue would actually cause an even larger "avalanche" of publicity.[127] Because the story was distributed nationwide, prejudice could be found in any district and a transfer would only call more media attention to the case.[128] Therefore, even though an alternate venue may seem more appropriate,

---

119. United States v. McDaniel, 449 F.2d 832, 841–42 (8th Cir. 1971) (finding no error where record was not made as to the extent of pretrial publicity and where no members of the jury indicated that they had formed an opinion on the case due to newspaper publicity). The Supreme Court in *Skilling v. United States*, 561 U.S. 358, 383 (2010), distinguished the period of four years that transpired between the initial publicity and trial there from *Rideau v. Louisiana*, 373 U.S. 723 (1963), where coverage and trial were contemporaneous.

120. Patton v. Yount, 467 U.S. 1025, 1034 (1984).

121. Note, Michael Jacob Whellan, *What's Happened to Due Process Among the States? Pretrial Publicity and Motions for Change of Venue in Criminal Proceedings*, 17 Am. J. Crim. L. 175, 182–83 (1990).

122. Irvin v. Dowd, 366 U.S. 717, 722 (1961).

123. *Id.* at 723–24.

124. *Id.* at 725–26; Att'y Griev. Comm'r of Md. v. Gansler, 835 A.2d 548 (Md. 2003) (discipline of prosecutor for repeated prejudicial pretrial comments); *see* Dorothy J. Imrich, Charles Mullin & Daniel Linz, *Measuring the Extent of Prejudicial Pretrial Publicity in Major American Newspapers: A Content Analysis*, 45 J. Comm. 94 (1995).

125. United States v. Dioguardi, 20 F.R.D. 33, 35–36 (S.D.N.Y. 1956) ("Because there is no claim or indication of another district with a climate more conducive to a fair trial, there is no assurance, should a transfer be granted, that defendant would be content with the granting of his motion.").

126. *Id.* at 36.

127. *Id.* at 35.

128. *Id.*

publicity might become a greater problem after the transfer occurs. As noted previously, the 24-hour national and online news cycle makes it possible for potential jurors thousands of miles away to be exposed to news reports, images, unofficial blogs and commentary, and other media so that transferring venue may not help alleviate prejudice.[129]

The trial court, when selecting a new venue, may take into consideration "(a) the amount of change in racial demographics, (b) the distance to the new venue and the inconvenience or expense that would be imposed on the parties, and (c) the likelihood that the new venue would reduce the bias that infects the original locale."[130] These factors allow the judge to make an informed decision as to whether a change in venue is needed to protect the constitutional rights of the defendant.

E. The Judicial Test

The proper test to determine whether a fair trial can be administered in any district is whether prospective jurors can lay aside preexisting impressions or opinions and render a verdict based on the evidence presented in court.[131] The defendant ordinarily has the burden of showing any material unfairness in the adjudicatory process.[132] Both state and federal trial courts begin with the presumption that the jurors were not exposed to, or prejudiced by, pretrial publicity.[133] To

---

129. *See generally* Erika Patrick, *Protecting the Defendant's Right to a Fair Trial in the Information Age*, 15 Cap. Def. J. 71 (2002). Also note that the courts generally do not consider whether the government receives a fair trial.

130. Brown, *supra* note 41, at 153.

131. *See* United States v. McNally, 485 F.2d 398 (8th Cir. 1973) (the trial court did not abuse its discretion in denying a motion for change of venue where the empaneled jurors could remain impartial despite a community news article about the defendant's actions); People v. Davis, 208 P.3d 78 (Cal. 2009) (one factor to consider when deciding a motion to transfer venue is whether the jurors state that they can set aside their opinions and follow the applicable laws in reaching their verdict); Chandler v. State, 848 So. 2d 1031, 1036 (Fla. 2003) ("The test for determining a change of venue is whether the general state of mind of the inhabitants of a community is so infected by knowledge of the incident and accompanying prejudice, bias, and pre-conceived opinions that jurors could not possibly put these matters out of their minds and try the case solely on the evidence presented in the courtroom."). *See generally* United States v. Ringland, 497 F.2d 1250, 1252 (8th Cir. 1974).

132. *See* United States v. Delay, 500 F.2d 1360, 1365 (8th Cir. 1974) (denial of defendant's motion for change of venue was proper because defendant did not meet the burden of showing that pretrial publicity prejudiced the empaneled jury).

133. *See* Lilly v. Commonwealth, 499 S.E.2d 522, 570 (Va. 1998) *rev'd on other grounds sub nom.* Lilly v. Virginia, 527 U.S. 116, 119 (1999) ("A presumption exists that the

justify a change of venue, publicity must be (1) recent, (2) widespread, and (3) highly damaging.[134] The passage of time is crucial in determining the effects of pretrial publicity on a jury panel.[135] Further, a transfer of venue is not warranted where the publicity "at the time of trial was neither intensive nor extensive."[136]

The court generally does not consider whether the government is able to receive a fair trial. However, the court may take into consideration convenience factors relating to the prosecutors and their witnesses. Additionally, the judge may choose to deny a transfer if the inconvenience to the prosecutor outweighs the convenience for the defendant. The court will grant a transfer of venue only if the defendant's ability to have a fair and impartial trial at the current venue is substantially hindered or inconvenienced. In general, however, the "[v]enue statutes are to be liberally construed so as to minimize inconvenience to a defendant."[137]

F. Multiple Transfers

The defendant ordinarily will only receive one transfer, but there are certain exceptions for having the case transferred a second time. A subsequent transfer of the case is warranted when (1) pretrial publicity causes personal prejudice against the defendant in the second location, (2) cultural bias is present in the new district, and (3) geographical bias toward specific types of offenses is evident.[138] Other factors to be considered include inconvenience to the defendant's witnesses, counsel, and the fact-finding abilities of the parties in a particular district.[139]

---

defendant will receive a fair trial in the jurisdiction in which the offense occurred."); *see also* United States v. Tokoph, 514 F.2d 597, 607 (10th Cir. 1975) (trial court's questioning of potential jurors as to their prior knowledge of the case was important in concluding that the defendant received a fair and impartial trial that was not pervasively prejudiced by pretrial publicity).

134. *See, e.g.*, Wansley v. Slayton, 487 F.2d 90, 93 (4th Cir. 1973).

135. Murphy v. Florida, 363 F. Supp. 1224, 1229 (S.D. Fla. 1973) (denying habeas corpus petition after agreeing that change of venue was improper because jurors only had a vague recollection of their prior knowledge of the case).

136. *Id.* at 1228.

137. United States v. Casanas, 233 F. Supp. 1001, 1003 (D.D.C. 1964) (granting motion for transfer of venue from Washington, D.C., to Puerto Rico in mail and wire fraud case where all four defendants were residents of Puerto Rico, many of the government's and defendants' witnesses were from Puerto Rico, and the Puerto Rican courts had a less congested docket).

138. Note, *supra* note 31, at 142.

139. *See, e.g.*, People v. Cooper, 809 P.2d 865, 882–84 (Cal. 1991).

IV. Specific Venue Issues

A. Multiple Jurisdiction Crimes

Criminal conspiracies that allegedly occur over a broad range of counties, states, or districts can be prosecuted in any place in which an act in furtherance of the crime occurred.[140] "Congress has provided by statute for offenses 'begun in one district and completed in another;' such offenses may be 'prosecuted in any district in which [the] offense was begun, continued, or completed.'"[141] If a crime constitutes a single continuous act committed in a series of places, and the provision in the law making such an offense triable in any of those places confers jurisdiction on the court therein, then that law does not violate the Sixth Amendment.[142] An example of this situation is the crime of transporting an illegal substance across state and district lines. That case could be prosecuted in any one of several different places. The legal rationale behind having venue in multiple districts is that transportation is an essential part of the offense and occurs equally over any and all of the traveled routes.[143]

Venue is always proper in the district in which the scheme of the crime was devised.[144] An offender who travels through various districts may be tried in any of the districts in which it can be proved that actions in furtherance of the scheme occurred.[145] Similarly, in a conspiracy case, venue is proper in any district in which the agreement

---

140. United States v. Cabrales, 524 U.S. 1, 7 (1998). As explained in United States v. Heatherly, 982 F.3d 871, 881 (3d Cir. 2020), "For conspiracy, venue lies 'wherever a co-conspirator has committed an act in furtherance of the conspiracy.'"

141. *Cabrales*, 524 U.S. at 7 (quoting 18 U.S.C. § 3237(a)); *see, e.g.*, United States v. Barfield, 969 F.2d 1554 (4th Cir. 1994) (upholding venue in the district of the bank where the checks were drawn in transportation of forged securities case); Hedrick v. Warden of Sussex I State Prison, 570 S.E.2d 840 (Va. 2002) (holding that venue for robbery was proper in county where victim was murdered because the robbery was a continuing offense that was not completed until the victim was killed); *see also* United States v. Oceanpro Indus., 2012 WL 975710 (4th Cir. 2012) (defendant who made a false statement in D.C. may be prosecuted in Maryland because the false statement had a material effect in Maryland).

142. Armour Packing Co. v. United States, 209 U.S. 56, 76–77 (1908).

143. *Id.* at 76; *see also* Recent Case, 111 Harv. L. Rev. 1134, 1135–36 (1998) (venue can exist in multiple districts if the crime was partially committed in the district or the district was reasonably related to the crime).

144. *See* 18 U.S.C. § 3237(a).

145. United States v. Rodriguez-Moreno, 526 U.S. 275, 279–81 (1999) ("Where a crime consists of distinct parts which have different localities the whole may be tried where any part can be proved to have been done." (quoting United States v. Lombardo, 241 U.S. 73, 77 (1916))).

was made or any act occurred in furtherance of the conspiracy.[146] The act need not be substantial to support a finding of proper venue; any act will do.[147] In *United States v. Rommy*, the court stated that a phone call involving a member of the conspiracy made to or from the judicial district could be an act sufficient to support venue.[148] Thus, venue could be proper in one district even though most of the activity in furtherance of the conspiracy occurred in a different district.[149] Furthermore, the particular act giving rise to venue can be committed by the defendant or any member of the conspiracy.[150] Using the actions of coconspirators to find venue has led some courts to uphold venue in a district that the defendant has never even entered.[151] Even if the overt act was committed by or at the direction of a government agent, venue is proper if the act was part of the offense.[152] In many cases, these rules assume that a fair and impartial trial may be held in numerous districts, enabling the prosecution to find a district that is sufficiently convenient.

---

146. Whitfield v. United States, 543 U.S. 209, 218 (2005) (venue proper in a district where an overt act occurred even though the overt act was not an element of the offense); Hyde v. United States, 225 U.S. 347, 365 (1912) (comparing the common law and statutes' similar approach to finding venue in any county where an overt act was done in furtherance of conspiracy); *see also* United States v. Perez, 280 F.3d 318, 329 (3d Cir. 2002); United States v. Ochoa, 229 F.3d 631, 636 (7th Cir. 2000); United States v. Dabbs, 134 F.3d 1071, 1077–79 (11th Cir. 1998); United States v. Gaviria, 116 F.3d 1498, 1517 (D.C. Cir. 1997); United States v. Record, 873 F.2d 1363, 1366 (10th Cir. 1989); Bos. Med. Supply Co. v. Lea & Febiger, 195 F.2d 853, 855–56 (1st Cir. 1952).

147. United States v. Smallwood, 293 F. Supp. 2d 631, 637–38 (E.D. Va. 2003) (upholding venue in a district "barely brushe[d]" by the activities of the conspiracy); *see also* United States v. Levy Auto Parts, 787 F.2d 946, 951 (4th Cir. 1986).

148. United States v. Rommy, 506 F.3d 108, 116 (2d Cir. 2007).

149. *Levy Auto Parts*, 787 F.2d at 951; United States v. Abdallah, 840 F. Supp. 2d 584 (E.D.N.Y. 2012).

150. Dixon v. State, 486 So. 2d 67, 68–69 (Fla. Dist. Ct. App. 1986) ("[A] prosecution for a criminal conspiracy may be brought in the county where the unlawful combination is formed or in any county where the overt act is committed by any of the conspirators in furtherance of the unlawful confederacy." (internal quotations omitted)); *see also* United States v. Romero, 150 F.3d 821, 824 (8th Cir. 1998); *Smallwood*, 293 F. Supp. 2d at 637–38; Zuniga v. Commonwealth, 375 S.E.2d 381, 387 (Va. 1988) ("[V]enue in conspiracy cases is proper at places where agreement was made or where any act in furtherance of the conspiracy occurs.").

151. United States v. Caldwell, 16 F.3d 623, 624 (5th Cir. 1994) (it would ultimately be possible to find venue in a district where the defendant had "never even set foot"); *see also* United States v. Bucio-Sanchez, 2006 WL 3354649 (N.D. Iowa 2006); *Smallwood*, 293 F. Supp. 2d at 637–38.

152. United States v. Chi Tong Kuok, 671 F.3d 931, 938 (9th Cir. 2012); United States v. Kirk Tang Yuk, 885 F.3d 57, 71 (2018) (a telephone call made by a government agent can create proper venue so long as the call was made to further the conspiracy).

B. Crimes Not Committed in a District

Crimes allegedly committed outside the United States are not in any state or district's jurisdiction. Venue for such crimes is proper in the place in which the defendant is arrested or the district in which he is "first brought."[153] An offender who committed crimes outside of the jurisdiction of any district and was captured outside the United States may be tried in the district in which he enters the country.[154] Venue may also be proper in other districts in which parts of the crime were allegedly committed or in the district of the last known residence of the offender.[155] For example, proper venue for the trial of a conspirator who is apprehended outside of the United States may be in the district in which he enters the country, as well as any district in which any part of the crime was committed.[156]

C. Multiple Defendant Crimes

When a crime was allegedly committed by multiple defendants tried together, the case may be tried in any district in which any defendant committed any act in furtherance of the scheme.[157] In prosecutions of multiple defendants, the district judge is less likely to transfer the case to accommodate one of the defendants because of the probability that another defendant will allege that the chosen venue is inconvenient or that the particular cultural makeup of the district does not provide for a fair and impartial jury.[158]

---

153. *See* 18 U.S.C. § 3238. *See* United States v. Yousef, 327 F.3d 56, 114–15 (2d Cir. 2003) (discussing 18 U.S.C. § 3238, which sets forth venue rules for crimes committed outside the United States). Although the offense in *Yousef* was committed in the Philippines, the Southern District of New York was a proper venue because that is where the defendant was first arrested and brought before the court. *Id.*

154. United States v. Rendon, 354 F.3d 1320, 1326 (11th Cir. 2003) (holding that a federal district court has the jurisdiction to try a defendant brought before it on a federal indictment for violating a federal law, and conferring venue "at the point of entry where that person enters the United States.").

155. 18 U.S.C. § 3238.

156. *Id.*

157. Paul Marcus, *Re-evaluating Large Multiple-Defendant Criminal Prosecutions*, 11 Wm. & Mary Bill Rts. J. 67, 82–83 (2002) (discussing the issues with transferring venue in large multidefendant cases).

158. *Id.*

D. Failure to Act Crimes

Where the crime that is charged is the failure to do a required act—such as failure to register as a sex offender;[159] misprision of a felony;[160] and failure to report child abuse[161]—the place where the act was required to be performed is the proper venue for persecution.[162] Where various duties are imposed, some to be performed at a distant place and others at home, the government may prosecute in either location, as either would be proper venue for trial.[163]

E. Accessories

Defendants who aided and abetted an alleged crime can be tried in the places or districts in which the crime was aided, as well as the place or district in which the crime occurred.[164]

F. Crimes Furthered through Electronics

A novel issue created by the advent of the Internet is that it is increasingly difficult to ascertain the exact location where a crime was committed because of the wide range of venues to which illegal content can be easily transferred.[165] This ambiguity causes serious

---

159. 18 U.S.C. § 2250; United States v. Spivey, 956 F.3d 212, 217 (4th Cir. 2020) (prosecution of a convicted state sex offender for failing to register as required by the Sex Offender Registration and Notification Act may lie in the district where interstate travel began); contra United States v. Haslage, 853 F.3d 331, 335 (7th Cir. 2017).

160. 18 U.S.C. § 4.

161. Cal. Penal Code §§ 11166(c), 11166.01.

162. Johnston v. United States, 351 U.S. 215, 220–21 (1956).

163. Travis v. United States, 364 U.S. 631, 634–35 (1961); *see* United States v. Cores, 356 U.S. 405, 407 (1958) ("The provision for trial in the vicinity of the crime is a safeguard against the unfairness and hardship involved when an accused is prosecuted in a remote place."); United States v. Menendez, 291 F. Supp. 3d 606, 638 (D.N.J. 2018) (venue proper in the district where the defendant falsified a mandatory federal filing that was required to be filed in the District of Columbia).

164. *See, e.g.*, United States v. Valdez-Santos, 457 F.3d 1044, 1046 (9th Cir. 2006) ("[T]he crime of drug possession with intent to distribute, or aiding and abetting such possession, occurs where the principal commits it." (quoting United States v. Mendoza, 108 F.3d 1155, 1156 (9th Cir. 1997))).

165. *See* United States v. Rodriguez-Moreno, 526 U.S. 275, 281 (1999) (a crime may be tried in any district where any part of the crime occurred); *see also* United States v. Rodriguez, 581 F.3d 775, 784 (8th Cir. 2009); United States v. Kuehne, 547 F.3d 667, 677 (6th Cir. 2008); United States v. Smith, 452 F.3d 323, 335 (4th Cir. 2006); United States v. Ramirez, 420 F.3d 134, 139 (2d Cir. 2005); United States v. Rowe, 414 F.3d 271, 279 (2d Cir. 2005); United States v. Pace, 314 F.3d 344, 350 (9th Cir. 2002); United States v. Scott, 270 F.3d 30,

constitutional and practical problems.[166] Examples of such crimes include wire fraud;[167] advertisement of child pornography;[168] and electronic transmission of false statements to the Securities and Exchange Commission.[169]

Internet crimes, as with other offenses, can be tried in any district in which the crime was begun, continued, or completed.[170] This broad application means that in cases of conspiracy or the distribution of child pornography, any district that receives the illegal communication constitutes a proper venue to try the crime.[171] Consequently, defendants who use the Internet or other forms of electronic communication may be tried in districts they have never physically entered.

---

35 (1st Cir. 2001); United States v. Tingle, 183 F.3d 719, 726 (7th Cir. 1999); DeRosier v. United States, 218 F.2d 420, 423 (5th Cir. 1955); United States v. Aiken, 76 F. Supp. 2d 1346, 1350 (S.D. Fla. 1999).

166. Jacob Taka Wall, *Where to Prosecute Cybercrimes*, 17 Duke L. & Tech. Rev. 146 (2019).

167. United States v. Ebersol, 411 F.3d 517, 526 (4th Cir. 2005) (venue is proper if any payment-related wire communications were transferred to or from the district of prosecution); United States v. Shusterman, No. WQD-13-0460, 2014 WL 6835161 (D. Md. Dec. 2, 2014) (emails sent by a conspirator in the prosecuting district to a co-conspirator in another district establish venue for the co-conspirator in the prosecuting district).

168. *Rowe*, 414 F.3d at 275 (venue is proper in any district where the advertisement was accessible in a chat room and the chat room was actually accessed by anyone).

169. United States v. Johnson, 510 F. 3d 521, 525 (4th Cir. 2007) (venue is proper because the false statements were transmitted to the SEC's computer servers in the prosecuting district); United States v. Hassanshahi, 185 F. Supp. 3d 55, 58 (D.D.C. 2016) (The defendant failed to secure a license to export goods to trade-embargoed Iran. Venue is proper in the District of Columbia because an application for the license required to be sent to, received by, and approved by the Department of the Treasury. Venue was proper even though most of the acts occurred overseas.).

170. *Rowe*, 414 F.3d at 279 (quoting 18 U.S.C. § 3237(a): "Except as otherwise expressly provided by enactment of Congress, any offense against the United States begun in one district and completed in another, or committed in more than one district, may be inquired of and prosecuted in any district in which such offense was begun, continued, or completed."); *see also* United States v. Royer, 549 F.3d 886, 895 (2d Cir. 2008) ("Receipt of electronic transmissions in a district is sufficient to establish venue activity there.").

171. *Id.* The states, too, have been dealing with this problem. *See, e.g.*, Fla. Stat. Ann. § 910.15 ("A person charged with committing a crime facilitated by communication through use of the . . . Internet . . . may be tried in the county in which the dissemination originated, in which the dissemination was made, or in which any act necessary to consummate the offense occurred."); Va. Code Ann. § 19.2-249.2 (2015); People v. Federico, 120 Cal. Rptr. 3d 349, 355 (Cal. Ct. App. 2011) (venue is proper in the county where the offender used the Internet to commit the crime and in the jurisdiction where the victim was located when he or she received the harmful information).

G. Crimes Furthered through the United States Mail

Crimes furthered through the U.S. mail originate in the district where a package was mailed and culminate in the district in which the package was received.[172] Venue is proper in these two districts as well as any district through which the package traveled.[173] For example, a package of drugs mailed from Washington State to the District of Guam could be prosecuted in either district.[174]

H. Crimes Committed on Airplanes in Flight

Congress provides for the prosecution of certain federal crimes committed on airplanes in the special aircraft jurisdiction of the United States.[175] There is no specific provision in the statute to determine the venue for the trials of these cases.

The Ninth Circuit Court of Appeals, acting en banc, decided in a comprehensive opinion on venue for aircraft crimes that the offenses may be prosecuted in the district where the plane first lands after the offense.[176] The court relied on the second paragraph of a general venue statute, 18 U.S.C. § 3237(a), to support its decision.[177] Two other circuits previously arrived at the same conclusion.[178]

---

172. Any offense involving the use of the mails, transportation in interstate or foreign commerce, or the importation of an object or person into the United States is a continuing offense and, except as otherwise expressly provided by enactment of Congress, may be inquired of and prosecuted in any district from, through, or into which such commerce, mail matter, or imported object or person moves. 18 U.S.C. § 3237(a) (2015).

173. *Id.*

174. United States v. Obak, 884 F.3d 934, 937 (9th Cir. 2018).

175. 49 U.S.C. § 46501(2).

176. United States v. Lozoya, 982 F.3d 648, 657 (9th Cir. 2020).

177. Any offense involving . . . transportation in interstate or foreign commerce . . . is a continuing offense and, except as otherwise expressly provided by enactment of Congress, may be inquired of and prosecuted in any district from, through, or into which such commerce . . . moves.

178. United States v. Cope, 676 F.3d 1219, 1225 (10th Cir. 2012); United States v. Breitweiser, 357 F.3d 1249, 1253 (11th Cir. 2004).

CHAPTER 5

The Right to Be Informed of the Nature and Cause of the Accusations

I. When an Indictment or Information Is Required in Federal Prosecutions

A. Definitions

The Sixth Amendment to the U.S. Constitution states that an accused shall "be informed of the nature and cause of the accusation." The Fifth Amendment further elaborates on this principle by providing that for the most serious crimes, such notice of accusation be issued in the form of an indictment, a charge that is reviewed and approved by a grand jury.

There are several ways in which a criminal defendant is given notice of the accusation against him. The first is an indictment, which is a formal written statement made by a grand jury accusing a person of a crime. The Federal Rules of Criminal Procedure require that an indictment include a "plain, concise, and definite written statement of the essential facts" of the alleged crime, and that each count alleged be supported by the applicable statute, rule, or regulation.[1] An information, a criminal charge brought by the prosecutor without a grand jury indictment, is another form of accusation. A criminal complaint

1. Fed. R. Crim. P. 7(c)(1).

is also a formal charging document, often filed before an indictment or information can be prepared.[2]

B. The Indictment

An indictment is required for federal felony offenses, for under the Fifth Amendment "[n]o person shall be held to answer for a capital, or otherwise infamous crime, unless on a presentment or indictment of a Grand Jury except in cases arising in the land or naval forces, or in the Militia, when in actual service in time of War or public danger." "Infamous crimes" have been determined to be those crimes that result in imprisonment in a penitentiary.[3] The phrase "capital, or otherwise infamous crime" is thus interpreted in modern criminal procedure as meaning any offense punishable by death or by imprisonment in a penitentiary for more than one year—in other words, a felony.

When deciding whether an indictment is necessary, federal courts have interpreted the Fifth Amendment mandate to mean that an indictment must be returned by a grand jury whenever death or imprisonment of more than one year is possible.[4] This liberal requirement is based on both English common law principles and the intent of the Founders in the passage of the Bill of Rights. Thus, an actual order that the criminal defendant receive punishment of death or imprisonment for more than one year is not determinative. Where a defendant is in danger of being subjected to such a punishment, the Constitution mandates a grand jury indictment. The Fifth Amendment's requirement of an indictment for felony offenses has been laid out in Federal Rule of Criminal Procedure 7.[5]

---

2. Under Rule 3 of the Federal Rules of Criminal Procedure, the criminal complaint must be made under oath. The complaint is a written statement of the essential facts constituting the offense charged. It must be made under oath before a magistrate judge or, if none is reasonably available, before a state or local judicial officer. It is the only federal charging document that is required to be made under oath.

3. United States v. Moreland, 258 U.S. 433, 440 (1922).

4. Green v. United States, 356 U.S. 165, 183 (1958).

5. FED. R. CRIM. P. 7(a) ("An offense (other than criminal contempt) must be prosecuted by an indictment if it is punishable (A) by death; or (B) by imprisonment for more than one year."). Courts have carved out an exception to this with regard to criminal contempt, however. Although those found guilty of criminal contempt may in fact face punishments of greater than one year in prison, an indictment is not necessary. *Green,* 356 U.S. at 187. The Supreme Court has held that criminal contempts "possess a unique character under the U.S. Constitution," and are thus exempted from some of the normal rules of criminal procedure. *Id.* Contempt of Congress must be charged by an indictment. 2 U.S.C. §§ 192, 194; Russell v. United States, 369 U.S. 749 (1962).

A federal indictment must be issued prior to the defendant's arraignment before the district court. In fact, "[a]n arraignment must be conducted in open court and must . . . [ensure] that the defendant has a copy of the indictment or information."[6] The requirement that indictment precede arraignment enables a felony defendant to receive the notice of accusation early enough in the course of proceedings to prepare an adequate defense for trial.

C. Waiver

Felony defendants may waive the grand jury indictment requirement. Waiver is codified in the Federal Rules of Criminal Procedure.[7] If the defendant waives the indictment "in open court and after being advised of the nature of the charge and of [these] rights," she may be prosecuted by information.[8] Such a waiver must be made knowingly and voluntarily, to the satisfaction of the court.[9]

The Federal Rules allow waiver in the interest of the accused, as it gives a defendant the ability to expedite proceedings. It is especially helpful to those defendants "who, because of inability to give bail, are incarcerated pending action of the grand jury, but desire to plead guilty."[10] Given the gravity of punishment by death, however, a defendant may not waive an indictment for a capital offense:

> To construe the provisions of the Rule loosely to permit the use of informations, where, as here, the charge states a capital offense, would do violence to that Rule and would make vulnerable to summary treatment those accused of one of our most serious crimes. We cannot do this in view of the traditional canon of construction which calls for the strict interpretation of criminal statutes and rules in favor of defendants where substantial rights are involved.[11]

---

6. FED. R. CRIM. P. 10(a).
7. FED. R. CRIM. P. 7(b).
8. *Id.*
9. *Id.*
10. FED. R. CRIM. P. 7 Advisory Committee Note. This is a very common practice: initial appearance, waiver, arraignment, plea of guilty, and decision on bond all in one proceeding.
11. Smith v. United States, 360 U.S. 1, 9 (1959).

D. The Information

The Federal Rules of Criminal Procedure allow the prosecutor to proceed by information for misdemeanor offenses, which are those offenses punishable by imprisonment of one year or less.[12] Hence, the trial of a misdemeanor may proceed on an indictment, information, or complaint.[13] Given the low severity of a misdemeanor offense compared to a felony, the American criminal justice system deems the heightened protection of a grand jury return of an indictment to be unnecessary.[14]

II. When an Indictment Is Required in State Prosecutions

A. Generally

Whether an indictment is necessary in state prosecutions is solely within the discretion of the individual state, as no right to an indictment has been held to exist under the U.S. Constitution.[15] More than half of the states allow prosecution of felonies by either information or indictment.[16] The remaining jurisdictions require indictments in certain circumstances.[17]

---

12. Fed. R. Crim. P. 7(a)(2).

13. "The trial of a petty offense may also proceed on a citation or violation notice." Fed. R. Crim. P. 58(b)(1).

14. *See* Duke v. United States, 301 U.S. 492, 494–95 (1937) (permitting the prosecution of misdemeanors without an indictment).

15. *See* Hurtado v. California, 110 U.S. 516, 538 (1884) ("The substitution for a presentment or indictment by a grand jury of the proceeding by information . . . is not [prohibited by] due process of law.").

16. Arizona, Arkansas, California, Colorado, Connecticut, Hawaii, Idaho, Illinois, Indiana, Iowa, Kansas, Maryland, Michigan, Missouri, Montana, Nebraska, Nevada, New Mexico, North Dakota, Oklahoma, Oregon, South Dakota, Utah, Vermont, Washington, Wisconsin, and Wyoming.

17. Full indictment states are Alabama, Alaska, Delaware, Georgia, Kentucky, Maine, Massachusetts, Mississippi, New Hampshire, New Jersey, New York, North Carolina, Ohio, South Carolina, Tennessee, Texas, Virginia, and West Virginia. The District of Columbia is also full indictment. Four states are in the clear minority as partial indictment states: Florida, Louisiana, Minnesota, and Rhode Island.

B. Indictment

1. Indictment in All Cases

In some states, defendants have the right to an indictment issued by a grand jury for all, or virtually all, felonies.[18] Most of these jurisdictions have state constitutional provisions that include the right to an indictment;[19] in three states, indictments are mandated by statute or by common law.[20]

2. Indictment in a Limited Number of Cases

Some states recognize the right to an indictment, but only with a very few felonies. Usually, only murder charges require an indictment.[21] As a result, in these states, relatively few charges involve indictments.

C. Waiver of the Indictment

Most, but not all, states permit a defendant to waive the right to an indictment, even in the absence of constitutional or statutory language allowing waiver. States that permit waiver typically do not allow it if the crime charged is a capital offense or carries the penalty of life imprisonment.[22] As in the federal system, in order for the waiver to be valid, it must be made knowingly and voluntarily, and—in many states—the defendant must be in open court at the time of waiver.[23] Most states also mandate that the waiver be in writing.[24]

D. States That Use an Information

A majority of states allow for an information to substitute for the indictment. In fact, some states do not even have a grand jury or indictment system, thereby allowing prosecutors to use an

---

18. A felony is generally seen as a crime punishable by death, more than a year imprisonment, or imprisonment in a penitentiary.

19. *E.g.*, ALA. CONST. art. I, § 8; N.Y. CONST. art. I, § 6; TEX. CONST. art. I, § 10.

20. The three states are New Hampshire, Virginia, and Georgia. See N.H. Rev. Stat. Ann. § 601:1; Va. Code Ann. § 19.2-217; Webb v. Henlery, 74 S.E.2d 7, 8 (Ga. 1953).

21. *See* Fla. Const. art. I, § 15(a); LA. CONST. art. I, § 15; MINN. R. CRIM. P. 17.01; R.I. CONST. art. 1, § 7.

22. *See, e.g.*, OHIO. R. CRIM. P. 7(a).

23. *See, e.g.*, TEX. CODE CRIM. PROC. ANN. art. 1.141.

24. *See, e.g.*, ME. R. CRIM. P. 7(b).

information.[25] Prosecutions by information are established in state constitutional provisions, as well as in statutes and court rules.

III. Grand Juries

A. Historical Basis

The grand jury, "the voice of the community," has been an integral part of the English and American criminal justice systems for centuries.[26] Historically, only prominent landowners and other important individuals throughout the community served on this panel and were asked to share their opinions about the potential viability of cases brought before the jury.[27] Grand juries have traditionally been seen as a part of the governmental checks and balances system,[28] helping to prevent cases from going to trial solely on the word of government officials.[29] The Fifth Amendment of the U.S. Constitution includes a grand jury indictment clause: "No person shall be held to answer for a capital, or otherwise infamous crime, unless on a presentment or indictment of a grand jury." As noted previously, this provision is not included in the incorporation doctrine of the Fourteenth Amendment, and as result states are not required to utilize grand juries when attempting to bring criminal charges against an individual.[30]

---

25. *See, e.g.*, Conn. Super. Ct. R. § 36-11, *in* Conn. Practice Book 348, 350.

26. Brenner, *The Voice of the Community: A Case for Grand Jury Independence*, 3 Va. J. Soc. Pol'y & L. 67, 78 (1995).

27. *Id. See also* Kuckes, *The Useful, Dangerous Fiction of Grand Jury Independence*, 41 Am. Crim. L. Rev. 1, 43 (2004).

28. *See* United States v. Dionisio, 410 U.S. 1, 17 (1973) (the federal grand jury is a "protective bulwark," whose central mission is to protect civil liberties and shield citizens from unfounded or abusive criminal charges).

29. *See* United States v. Cotton, 535 U.S. 625, 634 (2002).

30. Hurtado v. California, 110 U.S. 516, 538 (1884). A clear expression of this point is found in Warren v. Craven, 271 P.3d 725, 728 (Idaho 2012):

> For over a century, the United States Supreme Court has held that while federal felony prosecutions must be brought before a grand jury, the same is not required in state prosecutions. A state felony prosecution proceeding by information, as a substitute for indictment, is not violative of the due process required in the Fifth and Fourteenth Amendments where there is an examination and commitment by a magistrate certifying a finding of probable cause, aid of counsel, and a right to cross-examine the prosecution's witnesses.

B. Composition and Selection

In both federal and state jurisdictions, the charging grand jury decides whether there is probable cause to believe that a crime has occurred and whether there is probable cause to believe that the persons identified by the prosecutor or by the investigation have committed that crime. Grand juries, unlike trial juries, do not usually convene on a daily basis. Regular grand juries typically sit for a set term; in the federal system the period is eighteen months, but a court can extend this time for an additional six months.[31] The Jury Selection and Service Act requires grand jurors in the federal system to be selected at random from a "fair cross-section" of the local community in which the court convenes.[32] Any list, such as those involving voter registration, motor vehicle licenses, or public utility users, can be utilized to select prospective grand jurors. State and federal grand jury systems automatically excuse certain individuals from serving, among them people over or under a certain age, people who have to care for ill or otherwise incapacitated dependents, and those who serve in public safety professions. Other individuals can be excused if they are able to convince the court that serving would be a hardship, either because of work commitments or family obligations.[33]

The Federal Rules of Criminal Procedure establish that a grand jury must comprise between sixteen and twenty-three members and most states have similar requirements.[34] The issuance of an indictment requires the approval of the majority of jurors.[35]

C. The Process

Once a grand jury has been charged and sworn in, it is the responsibility of the government to present relevant evidence upon which the grand jury can decide if a crime has been committed and a particular individual committed it. If so convinced, the jurors can then issue an

---

31. *See* Fed. R. Crim. P. 6(g). The federal code and many state laws also provide for a "special grand jury," which has more of an investigatory function than a charging function. *See, e.g.*, 18 U.S.C. §§ 3331–3333, Va. Code Ann. §§ 19.2-207 to 209.

32. 28 U.S.C. § 1861. *See* discussion in Chapter 3, section VII.D.

33. In *Taylor v. Louisiana*, 419 U.S. 522, 534 (1975), the Supreme Court emphasized that court officials may grant exemptions from jury service to individuals in case of special hardship or incapacity and to those engaged in particular occupations the uninterrupted performance of which is critical to the community's welfare. Still, some across-the-board restrictions—such as those based on gender—are unconstitutional.

34. Fed. R. Crim. P. 6(a), (b).

35. *See* Fed. R. Crim. P. 6(f) (twelve grand jurors must vote to approve an indictment).

indictment.[36] The Supreme Court has made clear that the grand jury must be allowed to come to conclusions about the existence of probable cause without outside influence.[37] After considering all of the evidence made available to them, both testimonial and tangible, jurors may vote to "return" an indictment if there is probable cause to believe a crime has been committed, thus beginning the criminal process against the accused.[38] The government attorneys—but no defense lawyers—are permitted to be present in the grand jury room at all times, except during the grand jury's deliberations.[39] Grand jury secrecy is the goal,[40] yet there have been strongly stated concerns as to the need for such secrecy and the effectiveness in keeping the proceedings secret.[41]

---

36. *See* discussion *supra* section I.B.

37. *See* United States v. Mechanik, 475 U.S. 66, 74 (1986). In Illinois v. Gates, 462 U.S. 213, 238 (1983), the Court set out the probable cause standard.

> [W]e reaffirm the totality-of-the-circumstances analysis that traditionally has informed probable cause determinations. The task of the issuing magistrate is simply to make a practical, common-sense decision whether, given all the circumstances set forth in the affidavit before him, including the "veracity" and "basis of knowledge" of persons supplying hearsay information, there is a fair probability that contraband or evidence of a crime will be found in a particular place.

38. As noted earlier, a defendant has the option of waiving the right to be indicted by a grand jury so that a government attorney can charge the individual by using an "information." *See* discussion *supra* section I.C.

39. *See* FED. R. CRIM. P. 6(d) (the Federal Rules limit who may be present in the grand jury room in order to ensure strict secrecy for grand jury proceedings and to provide for confidentiality of the grand jury's deliberations).

40. FED. R. CRIM. P. 6(e).

41. For a good overview of the concerns here, *see* Kadish, *Behind the Locked Door of an American Grand Jury: Its History, Its Secrecy, and Its Process*, 24 FLA. ST. U. L. REV. 1 (1996). A powerful judicial statement on secrecy is found in State v. Ross, 144 So. 3d 932, 937 (La. 2014):

> It is a long established policy that the secrecy of grand jury proceedings should be carefully maintained. Many reasons for this have been stated. Secrecy helps prevent the escape of prospective indictees by providing no forewarning to them of the investigation in progress; it insures that the grand jury investigation can proceed freely by protecting the grand jurors from outside influences and threats of reprisal; it serves to prevent the subordination of perjury and tampering of witnesses by targets of the investigation; it promotes free and open disclosure of information by witnesses without fear of retaliation; and it acts as a shield by protecting innocent people under investigation from the injury to their reputations that could be caused by the disclosure of baseless accusations. However, the secrecy of grand jury proceedings is not absolute. This court has stated that in some situations, justice may demand that discrete portions of transcripts be made available for use in subsequent proceedings.

D. The Critique

For many years, critics have harshly complained about the grand jury system in the United States. The most common critique is that grand juries no longer are actually independent decision-making bodies; they are seen as existing only to fulfill the needs of law enforcement and prosecutors.[42] Today—often reflecting such criticism and a desire to cut costs—just half of the states in the United States still utilize the grand jury system.[43] Jurisdictions that no longer require the use of grand juries hold preliminary hearings during which a judge hears evidence concerning an alleged offense and then makes the decision whether the prosecution can proceed with the charges against an individual.[44]

IV. The Preliminary Hearing

The preliminary hearing is conducted by a trial judge or magistrate judge. In federal jurisdictions, the preliminary hearing must be within fourteen days of a prisoner's first appearance if that person is held in custody, or within twenty days of the first appearance before the magistrate judge if the defendant has made bail.[45] Most states have similar sorts of timing rules.[46]

The preliminary hearing is designed to decide whether enough evidence can be offered to justify holding a defendant for trial. As one state court described it, the hearing acts as a

---

42. *See* Roots, *Grand Juries Gone Wrong*, 14 RICH. J.L. & PUB. INT. 331, 331–32 (2010) ("Today's federal grand juries fail to provide even a modicum of resistance to the government, and serve as a machine of government expansion and caprice."); Dession, *From Indictment to Information—Implications of the Shift*, 42 YALE L.J. 163, 163 (1932) ("[U]nder modern conditions, the grand jury is seldom better than a rubber stamp of the prosecuting attorney. . . ."); Boudin, *The Federal Grand Jury*, 61 GEO. L.J. 1, 35 (1972) ("[The grand jury] is no longer a group of peers sitting to protect citizens; instead, it is an arm of the state, more powerful than ever before, serving the ends of the prosecution[.]"). *See generally* Brenner, *supra* note 26.

43. Alabama, Alaska, Delaware, Georgia, Kentucky, Maine, Massachusetts, Mississippi, New Hampshire, New Jersey, New York, North Carolina, Ohio, Pennsylvania, South Carolina, Tennessee, Texas, Virginia, and West Virginia maintain grand jury indictment requirements. Florida, Louisiana, Minnesota, and Rhode Island require use of the grand jury only for crimes that could result in capital punishment or life imprisonment. *See* Simmons, *Re-examining the Grand Jury: Is There Room for Democracy in the Criminal Justice System?*, 82 B.U. L. REV. 1, 19 n.85 (2002).

44. *See* discussion *infra* section IV.

45. 18 U.S.C.A. § 3060(b). Note, though, that there is a conflict between this section and FED. R. CRIM. P. 5.1(c), which provides for 21 days.

46. *See, e.g.*, COLO. R. CRIM. P. 5(a)(4)(I); OR. REV. STAT. § 135.070(2).

> screening device to ferret out groundless and improvident prosecutions [, thereby] reliev[ing] the accused of the substantial degradation and expense attendant to a criminal trial, but also conserv[ing] judicial resources and promot[ing] confidence in the judicial system. It is at this hearing that the State must establish a factual and legal basis to bind over a charge for trial by introducing sufficient evidence to persuade the magistrate that there is probable cause to believe that the crime charged has been committed and that the defendant committed it. To meet its burden, the State must produce believable evidence of all the elements of the crime charged. If the State fails to produce evidence of all the elements, then a magistrate must dismiss the charge and discharge the defendant.[47]

Another wrote:

> Although a preliminary hearing may serve other purposes, i.e., (1) expose weaknesses in the prosecution's case; (2) lay the groundwork for impeachment of prosecution's witnesses at trial; (3) result in a plea; (4) demonstrate the futility of a motion to suppress; (5) provide discovery of the prosecution's case; or (6) result in dismissal of the charges, its stated purpose is to determine whether there is probable cause to hold the defendant for the grand Jury.[48]

Federal prosecutors may seek and obtain an indictment before the preliminary hearing. If that effort is successful, no preliminary hearing is necessary.[49] Rules regarding preliminary hearings vary from state to state. One fundamental difference pertains to the charging document. Most states that use the grand jury indictment system for felonies permit prosecutors to bypass the preliminary hearing by obtaining an indictment before the scheduled preliminary hearing.[50] However, in other states a preliminary hearing is not required in order to seek an indictment before a grand jury.[51] In states that allow

---

47. State v. Dykes, 283 P.3d 1048, 1052 (Utah Ct. App. 2012).

48. Friess v. Morgenthau, 383 N.Y.S.2d 784, 787, 856 (Sup. Ct. 1975). *See also* Thies v. State, 189 N.W. 539, 541 (Wis. 1922).

49.
> If a defendant is charged with an offense other than a petty offense, a magistrate judge must conduct a preliminary hearing unless (1) the defendant waives the hearing; (2) the defendant is indicted; (3) the government files an information . . . charging . . . a felony (4) the government files an information charging . . . a misdemeanor (5) the defendant is charged with a misdemeanor and consents to a trial before a magistrate judge.

FED. R. CRIM. P. 5.1(a).

50. *See, e.g.*, LA. CODE CRIM. PROC. ANN. art. 292 (2009).

51. *See, e.g.*, KAN. STAT. ANN. § 22-2902 (2010).

an information (previously discussed), a prosecutor does not need to seek an indictment from a grand jury in order to take a defendant to trial.[52] Generally, though, in these states the prosecutor must make her case at a preliminary hearing or she will not be allowed to seek an information charging the defendant.

States also differ as to the waiving of preliminary hearings. Some states waive preliminary hearings only upon timely requests by the defense or the government.[53] Other states require a defendant seeking to avoid a preliminary hearing to file a waiver request,[54] though the prosecutor may have to agree with the request.[55] Generally, the right to a preliminary hearing is lost if the issue is not raised before a plea is entered.[56]

At the preliminary hearing the defendant has the right to counsel.[57] The role of the lawyer, here, is seen as important:

> Plainly the guiding hand of counsel at the preliminary hearing is essential to protect the indigent accused against an erroneous or improper prosecution. First, the lawyer's skilled examination and cross-examination of witnesses may expose fatal weaknesses in the State's case that may lead the magistrate to refuse to bind the accused over. Second, in any event, the skilled interrogation of witnesses by an experienced lawyer can fashion a vital impeachment tool for use in cross-examination of the State's witnesses at the trial, or preserve testimony favorable to the accused of a witness who does not appear at the trial. Third, trained counsel can more effectively discover the case the State has against his client and make possible the preparation of a proper defense to meet that case at the trial. Fourth, counsel can also be influential at the preliminary hearing in making effective arguments for the accused on such matters as the necessity for an early psychiatric examination or bail.[58]

---

52. *See, e.g.*, 725 ILL. COMP. STAT. ANN. 5/111-2(a) (2010). A few states allow the prosecutor to file an information without a preliminary hearing, but there are other safeguards present, so that a judge may have to approve the information.

53. *See, e.g.*, MD. CODE ANN., CRIM. PROC. § 4-103 (2010).

54. *See, e.g.*, IDAHO CODE ANN. § 19-1308 (2010). The federal rules require a preliminary hearing unless the defendant actively waives the hearing. FED. R. CRIM. P. 5.1(a)(1).

55. *See, e.g.*, KY. R. CRIM. P. 3.10(3).

56. *See, e.g.*, Ashworth v. Addison, 132 Fed. App'x. 752, 753 (10th Cir. 2005); Norton v. State, 43 P.3d 404, 408 (OK. Crim. App. 2002); Lingo v. Hann, 71 N.W.2d 716, 722 (Neb. 1955).

57. Coleman v. Alabama, 399 U.S. 1, 9 (1970).

58. *Id.* at 9. For further explanation, *see* Baatz v. State, 849 N.W.2d 225, 229 (N.D. 2014).

At the end of the preliminary hearing, the judge decides whether there is enough evidence against the defendant to hold him until a trial, to be "bound over." In the event of a bindover, the defendant remains in custody.[59] If the judge determines that there is too little evidence, the judge issues a dismissal. With a dismissal, the defendant is discharged, though in many states a prosecutor can still seek an indictment from a grand jury.[60] A prosecutor may, in some states, appeal the outcome of the preliminary hearing.[61] Some states also allow for a prosecutor to refile the complaint and obtain a second preliminary hearing.[62]

V. Waiver of the Indictment Requirement

A. Federal

Federal Rule of Criminal Procedure 7(b) allows for defendants to waive the indictment requirement. Although the Fifth Amendment mandates grand jury indictments in federal prosecutions, the Supreme Court has held that a defendant can constitutionally waive that requirement in noncapital cases.[63] Waiver in this context, like many others, requires the defendant do so "knowingly, intelligently and voluntarily."[64] However, courts often demand more, as an indictment is designed to protect the potentially innocent defendant.[65] As such, Rule 7(b) explicitly requires that a waiver be made in open court,

---

59. If the defendant is out on conditions of release, the defendant ordinarily stays on release and is not in custody. If the judge decides to release the defendant after the preliminary hearing, she may so order.

60. *See, e.g.,* Burke v. Commonwealth, 365 N.E.2d 811, 814 (Mass. 1977).

61. *See, e.g.,* COLO. R. CRIM. P. 5(a)(4)(v).

62. *See, e.g.,* State v. Rubek, 371 N.W.2d 115, 118 (Neb. 1985).

63. Smith v. United States, 360 U.S. 1, 9 (1959). An exception is carved out for capital offenses, as to hold otherwise "would make vulnerable to summary treatment those accused of one of our most serious crimes." *Id.* It can at times be difficult to ascertain what is a capital offense, as in situations where a homicide offense can be elevated due to the presence of certain statutory aggravating factors. *See* Matthews v. United States, 622 F.3d 99, 101–03 (2d Cir. 2010).

64. United States v. Ferguson, 758 F.2d 843, 851 (2d Cir. 1985). *See* United States v. Daughenbaugh, 549 F.3d 1010 (5th Cir. 2008); United States v. Gaudet, 81 F.3d 585 (5th Cir. 2006).

65. Swail v. Hunt, 742 F. Supp. 2d 352, 363 (W.D.N.Y. 2010); United States v. Macklin, 523 F.2d 193, 196 (2d Cir. 1975). Of course, it may well be to the advantage of the defendant to waive. The defendant then may be allowed "to obtain a speedier disposition of the charges against him and the State is spared the time and expense of Grand Jury proceedings." People v. Milton, 989 N.E.2d 962, 964 (N.Y. 2013).

after the defendant has been advised of the nature of the charge and of her rights.[66]

Rule 7(b) envisions the ability to waive to be most helpful to those defendants who are held awaiting a grand jury decision, but who wish to plead guilty nonetheless.[67] Due to the formality requirements designed to protect defendants, a guilty plea is insufficient to act as a waiver to indictment.[68] The explicit authorization to waive, therefore, allows admittedly guilty defendants to expedite the judicial process, especially in jurisdictions where grand juries meet sporadically.[69]

B. States

The law on indictment waivers varies considerably among the states, as the Fifth Amendment's indictment requirement, as previously noted, does not apply to the states.[70] Each state, therefore, can promulgate its own version of the requirement and, consequently, its own version of waiver. All states that require prosecution by indictment have explicit legislative authority to recognize waivers of indictments, in the form of a state constitutional provision,[71] a statute,[72] or a court rule.[73]

States have enacted a number of requirements in order to protect a defendant from involuntarily, unknowingly, or unintelligently waiving the indictment requirement. Many states follow the federal rule that the waiver must be made in open court, after the defendant has been advised of the nature of the charge and his rights.[74] Another

---

66. United States v. Bastian, 770 F.3d 212, 217–18 (2d Cir. 2014); *Matthews*, 622 F.3d at 101. *See* Ramirez v. Lempke, 2014 WL 3106218 (N.D.N.Y. July 7, 2014): "At Ramirez's plea hearing, defense counsel represented that Ramirez had signed a 10-page waiver of indictment . . . The court required Ramirez to re-execute the form in open court after swearing him in."

67. Fed. R. Crim. P. 7(b) Advisory Committee Note to Subdivision (b)(1).

68. *See, e.g., Macklin*, 523 F.2d at 196 ("[T]he waiver of indictment has been deliberately clothed in formal procedure. It must be made in open court and the defendant must be told the nature of the charge and informed of his rights before he is allowed to consent to the waiver.").

69. Fed. R. Crim. P. 7(b) Advisory Committee Note to Subdivision (b)(1) (some defendants must spend "many weeks, and even months, in jail before [they] can begin the service of [the] sentence").

70. Hurtado v. California, 110 U.S. 516, 535 (1884).

71. *E.g.*, N.C. Const. art. I, § 22.

72. *E.g.*, Ga. Code Ann. § 17-7-70 (2010); Mass. Gen. Laws Ann. ch. 263, § 4 (2010).

73. *E.g.*, N.H. R. Crim. P. 9.

74. *See* Alaska R. Crim. P. 7(b); Tenn. Code Ann. *§ (1c)103-3-40. See* People v. Catnott, 937 N.Y.S.2d 470 (N.Y. App. Div. 2013).

common requirement is that the waiver be in writing, which precludes the possibility of an implied waiver because the defendant must explicitly state the request.[75] Some states mandate that a defendant cannot waive without counsel.[76]

VI. Challenging the Sufficiency of the Indictment

The indictment, as we have seen, is designed to put the defendant and counsel on notice as to the crimes that are being charged and all the necessary elements of those crimes that must be proved beyond a reasonable doubt.[77] "An indictment is sufficient if it '(1) contains the elements of the offense intended to be charged, (2) sufficiently apprises the defendant of what he must be prepared to meet, and (3) allows the defendant to show with accuracy to what extent he may plead a former acquittal or conviction in the event of a subsequent prosecution.'"[78]

Challenges to the sufficiency of the indictment are not often successful unless serious substantive drafting errors are present.[79] "The

---

75. *See* VA. CODE ANN. § 19.2-217.

76. *See* N.Y. CONST. art. I, § 6, as explained in People v. Simmons, 973 N.Y.S.2d 865 (N.Y. Sup. Ct. App. 2013).

77. *See generally* United States v. O'Brien, 560 U.S. 218 (2010). As stated in United States v. Chrurchill, 2021 WL 862306 *2 (ED. Tx. 2021), "the fundamental purpose of an indictment is to inform a defendant of the charges against him."

78. United States v. Islam, 2021 WL 963580 *5 (ED. Pa. 2021). *See also* United States v. Schaffer, 586 F.3d 414, 422 (6th Cir. 2009):

> An indictment is generally sufficient if it fully, directly, and expressly . . . set[s] forth all the elements necessary to constitute the offense intended to be punished. In particular, the indictment must (1) set out all of the elements of the charged offense and must give notice to the defendant of the charges he faces and (2) be sufficiently specific to enable the defendant to plead double jeopardy a subsequent proceeding, if charged with the same crime based on the same facts.

79. As in *United States v. Steffen*, 687 F.3d 1104, 1113 (8th Cir. 2012), where the defendant was indicted on several counts of fraud. The indictment was struck down with the court writing,

> "An indictment is normally sufficient if its language tracks the statutory language." However, where an indictment alleges a scheme to defraud under the bank, mail, or wire fraud statutes, it must specify facts "not merely in the general words of the statute, but with such reasonable particularity as will apprise [the defendant], with reasonable certainty, of the nature of the accusation and as will enable the court to say that the facts stated are sufficient in law to support a conviction."

Numerous other sorts of challenges can be made to a prosecution going forward, of course, such as those dealing with right to a speedy trial, selective prosecution, and statutes of limitations. With sufficiency challenges, the moving party has a difficult burden. It is not enough, for instance, to show that the prosecutor did not sign the document.

sufficiency of an indictment [should] be determined on the basis of practical rather than technical consideration. . . . Hair splitting is to be eschewed."[80] As the Supreme Court has consistently held, "An indictment is sufficient if it, first, contains the elements of the offense charged and fairly informs a defendant of the charge[s] against which he must defend, and second, enables him to plead an acquittal or conviction in bar of future prosecutions for the same offense."[81] Sufficiency is frequently achieved by prosecutors tracking the elements of the appropriate statute in the indictment.[82] And if the result is somewhat conclusory and not helpful to the defense lawyer in preparing for trial, counsel may request a bill of particulars spelling out the allegations in some more detail.[83] The requirement is that the motion challenging an indictment be filed in a timely manner, normally well before the trial commences. If the motion is not made then, the challenge will be deemed waived.[84]

VII. Claims of Duplicity and Multiplicity

A. Duplicity

A duplicitous indictment "sets out separate and distinct crimes in a single count."[85] Courts can determine whether more than one offense is charged in a single count by assessing whether multiple

---

See, e.g., United States v. Bergrin, 650 F.3d 257 (3rd Cir 2011); United States v. Chess, 610 F.3d 965, 968 (7th Cir. 2010). For the extreme case where the indictment was clearly inadequate, see *United States v. Gonsalves*, 691 F.2d 1310, 1320 (9th Cir. 1982) (indictment "was 'such a complex monstrosity' as to be unmanageable").

80. United States v. Medina–Garcia, 918 F.2d 4, 8 (1st Cir. 1990). As stated in United States v. Yihao Pu, 15 F. Supp. 3d 846, 849 (N.D. Ill. 2014): "The test for validity is not whether the indictment could have been framed in a more satisfactory manner, but whether it conforms to minimal constitutional standards."

81. Hamling v. United States, 418 U.S. 87, 117 (1974).

82. Nix v. State, 401 S.W.3d 656, 662 (Tex. App. 2013) ("[A]n indictment is legally sufficient if it tracks the language of the statute in question."). *See also* United States v. McNair, 605 F.3d 1152, 1186 (11th Cir. 2010); State v. Noel, 690 S.E.2d 10, 16 (N.C. Ct. App. 2010).

83. *See infra* section VIII.

84. Fed. R. Crim. P. 12(b)(3)(B), (C). *See* United States v. Whitfield, 590 F.3d 325, 359 (5th Cir. 2009); United States v. Keller, 916 F.2d 628, 636 (11th Cir. 1990). *But see* United States v. Anderson, 605 F.3d 404, 411 (6th Cir. 2010) ("A party may raise an allegation that the indictment does not state an offense at any time, including post-trial or on appeal.").

85. United States v. Lombardo, 582 F. App'x 601 (6th Cir. 2014). *See* Fed. R. Crim. P. 8(a) (requiring that there be a separate count for each offense). *See generally* State v. Samuels, 743 S.E.2d 773, 776 (S.C. 2013); State v. Butler, 286 P.3d 1074, 1079 (Az. App. 2012); United States v. Anderson, 605 F.3d 404 (6th Cir. 2010).

punishments can be imposed for the single offense.[86] An indictment is not duplicitous if the charged crime may be committed by one of many alternative acts, and the indictment charges the crime by several or all of those acts.[87] The issue arises often in conspiracy prosecutions; the law is clear that a single count of a single conspiracy that alleges that the defendant agreed to commit one crime—or even several crimes—is not duplicitous.[88]

A duplicitous indictment undermines several rights of a criminal defendant. It may not provide a defendant with sufficient notice of the charge against her,[89] or it may disguise a guilty verdict as a unanimous verdict, when jurors have not, in fact, found the defendant guilty of the same offense.[90] Also, if jurors have not found the defendant guilty of the same offense, the court cannot levy an appropriate sentence,[91] and the guilty verdict may infringe upon the defendant's Fifth Amendment protection against double jeopardy.[92]

A defendant who wishes to challenge the indictment as duplicitous typically must do so before trial.[93] By failing to object before trial,

---

86. Bell v. United States, 349 U.S. 81, 83–84 (1955).

87. *See* United States v. Caldwell, 302 F.3d 399, 408 (5th Cir. 2002). *See also* United States v. Martin, 516 F. App'x 433, 446 (6th Cir. 2013) *cert. denied*, 571 U.S. 919 (2013) and 571 U.S. 936 (2013). As explained in *United States v. Mancuso*, 718 F.3d 780, 792 (9th Cir. 2013), the court is "not to review the evidence presented at trial to determine whether it would support charging several crimes rather than one, but rather solely to assess whether the indictment itself can be read to charge only one violation in each court."

88. This is because conspiracy, rather than the individual offenses, is the crime charged. United States v. Ohle, 678 F. Supp. 2d 215 (S.D. NY 2010); United States v. Lewis, 408 F. App'x 423, 426 (2d Cir. 2010); United States v. Lawson, 618 F. Supp. 2d 1251, 1258 (E.D. Wash. 2009).

89. United States v. Steiner, 847 F.3d 103, 114 (3d Cir. 2017); United States v. Tairod Nathan Webster Pugh, 2015 WL 9450598, at *16 (E.D.N.Y. Dec. 21, 2015); United States v. Sanford, Ltd., 859 F. Supp. 2d 102, 116 (D.D.C. 2012); United States v. Place, 757 F. Supp. 2d 60, 62 (D. Mass. 2010); United States v. Root, 585 F.3d 145, 154 (3d Cir. 2009).

90. United States v. Robinson, 855 F.3d 265, 269 (4th Cir. 2017); United States v. Lombardo, 582 F. App'x 601 (6th Cir. 2104); United States v. Pietrantonio, 637 F.3d 865 (8th Cir. 2011); *Crisci*, 273 F.3d at 238; United States v. Haddock, 956 F.2d 1534, 1546 (10th Cir. 1992).

91. *See generally* Guerraro-Clavjo v. United States, 242 F. Supp. 3d 57, 61 (D. Mass. 2017); United States v. McCafferty, 2011 WL 933771 (N.D. Ohio Mar. 16, 2011); *Crisci*, 273 F.3d at 238.

92. *Id.* If it is unclear from the indictment what crime is charged, then, in turn, it will be unclear for which crime the defendant was found guilty and punished; as a result, she could be charged with the same crime again. *Caldwell*, 302 F.3d at 412. *See also* United States v. Brown, 2016 WL 6093308, at *2 (N.D. Tex. 2016); United States v. Washington, 653 F.3d 1251, 1262 (10th Cir. 2011).

93. United States v. Lombardo, 582 F. App'x 601 (6th Cir. 2014); State v. Butler, 286 P.3d 974, 1079 (Ariz. App. 2012); United States v. Barrington, 648 F.3d 1178, 1189–90 (11th Cir.

the defendant generally waives the claim[94] and "the case proceeds under the presumption that the court's instructions to the jury will clear up any ambiguity created by the . . . indictment."[95] Thus, a jury instruction would be the defendant's only remedy in the trial court. When the requested jury instruction fails to clear up the ambiguity and the court on appeal examines an indictment, the standard of review depends on whether at trial the defendant objected to the insufficient jury instruction.[96] If she failed to object to the jury instruction, the appellate court will overturn a conviction on the ambiguous indictment only if there was "plain error" in the trial court.[97]

B. Multiplicity

A multiplicitous indictment charges a single offense in multiple counts.[98] Like duplicity, multiplicity violates a criminal defendant's Fifth Amendment protection against double jeopardy because a multiplicitous indictment could result in multiple punishments for a single offense.[99] Consequently, an indictment that is multiplicitous "may

---

2011); United States v. Kakos, 483 F.3d 441, 444 (6th Cir. 2007). An exception is allowed for the claim that the duplicitous nature of the indictment was not apparent on its face and thus could not be discovered until trial, when facts previously unknown to the parties and the court arose. *See* United States v. Sturdivant, 244 F.3d 71, 75–77 (2d Cir. 2001). If the defendant objects to the indictment before the trial, he may move the court to dismiss the indictment, to require the prosecution to select one charge in the duplicitous count, or to "particularize the distinct offenses contained within a count." *Kakos,* 483 F.3d at 444.

94. *Kakos,* 483 F.3d at 444 ("[A] defendant's objections to the indictment made after trial has begun are properly addressed not to the indictment itself but to the harm stemming from the . . . indictment."). *See* Fed. R. Crim. P. 12(b)(3)(B), (C). *But see* United States v. Robinson, 627 F.3d 941, 957 (4th Cir. 2010) (even if the defendant did not object prior to the trial, "[some courts hold] that newly raised duplicity claims that go beyond technicalities to allege that the conviction could have rested on an impermissibly divided jury deserve plain error review"). *Id.*

95. *Kakos,* 483 F.3d at 444.

96. *Id.* at 445.

97. United States v. Barrington, 648 F.3d 1178, 1190 (11th Cir. 2011): "[Defendant's] failure to object to the [jury] instruction or submit an alternative instruction results in a waiver unless the instructions which were given constitute plain error"; *see also* United States v. Davis, 471 F.3d 783 (7th Cir. 2006).

98. *See* United States v. Cooper, 886 F.3d 146, 152 (D.C. Cir. 2018); United States v. Abdi, 2014 WL 3828165 (N.D. Ga. Aug. 4, 2014); State v. Thums, 837 N.W.2d 177 (Wis. App. 2013); Elnicki v. State, 2012 WL 718966 (Kan. App. 2012); United States v. Wachumwah, 710 F.3d 862, 868 (9th Cir. 2012).

99. United States v. Leal, 330 F. Supp. 3d 1257, 1269 (D.N.M. 2018); State v. Sprung, 277 P.3d 1100, 1105 (Kan. 2012); United States v. Richards, 659 F.3d 527, 547 (6th Cir. 2011);

lead to multiple sentences for the same conduct and may suggest to the jury that the defendant committed more than one crime."[100]

Multiplicity is not "fatal to the indictment."[101] However, the defendant must generally object to an indictment as multiplicitous before trial, or she will have waived the objection.[102] If the defendant waives the objection to the indictment, she nonetheless may later object to multiplicity of sentencing, if the sentences are not to be served concurrently.[103] When she objects to the indictment, the defendant has the burden of proving that the indictment is multiplicitous.[104] To repair the multiplicitous indictment, the court may dismiss some counts of the indictment,[105] or the prosecutor can either elect to dismiss a charge[106] or request a jury instruction to clarify the multiplicitous charge.[107] If the defendant is convicted, and the indictment is subsequently found to be multiplicitous, then the court on appeal will vacate those convictions that are multiplicitous.[108]

United States v. Shrader, 737 F. Supp. 2d 589, 594 (S.D. W. Va. 2010); *Johnson*, 130 F.3d at 1424.

100. United States v. Haddock, 956 F.2d 1534, 1546 (10th Cir. 1992). *See* United States v. Maynard, 2019 WL 1505875, at *2 (D. Colo. Apr. 5, 2019); United States v. Frierson, 698 F.3d 1267, 1269 (10th Cir. 2012).

101. United States v. Ganadonegro, 854 F. Supp. 2d 1068, 1079 (D. N.M. 2012); *Johnson*, 130 F.3d at 1424.

102. Fed. R. Crim. P. 12(b)(3)(B), (C). *See* United States v. Kokayi, 2019 WL 2997384, at *2 (E.D. Va. 2019); United States v. Davis, 306 F.3d 398, 417–18 (6th Cir. 2002).

103. United States v. Reedy, 304 F.3d 358, 364 (5th Cir. 2002).

104. United States v. Askarkhodjaev, 2010 WL 3940450 (W.D. Mo. 2009).

105. United States v. Mann, 701 F.3d 274, 286 (8th Cir. 2012); United States v. Ganadonegro, 854 F. Supp. 2d 1068, 1079 (D. NM 2012); United States v. King, 713 F. Supp. 2d 1207, 1218 (D. Haw. 2010); United States v. Barner, 441 F.3d 1310, 1313 (11th Cir. 2006).

106. *King*, 713 F. Supp. 2d at 1218.

107. *See* United States v. Roy, 408 F.3d 484, 491 (8th Cir. 2005) ("[M]ultiplicitous indictments may be saved at the trial stage if the district court submits an appropriate instruction to the jury."); *Ganadonegro*, 854 F. Supp. 2d at 1079.

108. *See, e.g.*, United States v. Chilaca, 909 F.3d 289, 297 (9th Cir. 2018).

VIII. Bill of Particulars

A bill of particulars is a document used to specify the nature and character of the charges against a defendant.[109] It does not function as an indictment, nor can it save a faulty indictment.[110] The bill serves several purposes, such as helping a defendant better prepare for trial, making certain a defendant is not surprised at trial as to charges, and preventing a defendant from being tried twice for the same offense due to a vague or indefinite indictment.[111]

There is no right to a bill of particulars.[112] The decision to grant or deny a defendant's motion for a bill of particulars is within the discretion of the trial court,[113] and the court's decision to deny the request will be affirmed unless the defendant demonstrates that actual surprise or prejudice resulted from the denial and thus the court's action

---

109. Dzikowski v. State, 82 A.3d 851, 857 (Md. 2013); United States v. Brown, 2014 WL 3909116, at *2 (W.D. La. Aug. 11, 2014) ("The purpose of a bill of particulars 'is to apprise a defendant of the charges against him with enough detail to allow him to prepare his defense.'"); United States v. Page, 575 F. App'x 641, 643 (6th Cir. 2014) ("The purpose of a bill of particulars is to give a defendant key factual information not contained in the indictment, so as to enable him or her to prepare a defense and avoid surprise at trial."); United States v. Bowie, 618 F.3d 802, 817 (8th Cir. 2010); United States v. Hernandez, 299 F.3d 984, 989 (8th Cir. 2002).

110. *See* United States v. Ortiz, 2016 WL 4239370, at *3 (N.D. Cal. 2016); United States v. Huggans, 650 F.3d 1210 (8th Cir. 2011); Russell v. United States, 369 U.S. 749, 770 (1962).

111. United States v. Vaid, 2017 WL 3891695, at *10 (S.D.N.Y. 2017); United States v. Ramirez, 609 F.3d 495, 503 (2d Cir. 2010).

112. United States v. Rosso, 2019 WL 4397333, at *1 (N.D. Okla. 2019); United States v. Perryman, 881 F. Supp. 2d 427, 430 (E.D.N.Y. 2012); United States v. Shabazz, 2012 WL 5334480 (M.D. Pa. 2012); United States v. Dulin, 410 F.2d 363, 364 (4th Cir. 1969).

113. As noted by the Supreme Court in *Will v. United States*, 389 U.S. 90, 98–99 (1967), "[F]ederal trial courts have always had very broad discretion in ruling upon requests for such bills." Most codes of criminal procedure have specific provisions regarding bills of particulars, as in Federal Rule 7(f). One court laid out the rule regarding the bill:

> The decision to grant a bill of particulars is left to the discretion of the [trial] court. The standard for determining whether a bill of particulars is appropriate is based on necessity: "In deciding a motion for a bill of particulars '[t]he important question is whether the information sought is necessary, not whether it is helpful.'" The purpose of a bill of particulars is to "supplement the allegations in the indictment when necessary to (1) enable the defendant to prepare his defense, (2) avoid unfair surprise to the defendant at trial, and (3) preclude a second prosecution of the same offense." A bill of particulars is appropriate "only where the charges of the indictment are so general that they do not advise the defendant of the specific acts of which he is accused."

United States v. Mandell, 710 F. Supp. 2d 368, 384 (S.D.N.Y. 2010). *See generally Bowie*, 618 F.3d at 817.

was an abuse of discretion.[114] However, if an indictment sufficiently details the charges against a defendant or the government agrees to provide full discovery to the defense, there is no need for a bill of particulars to be issued and the request will be routinely denied.[115] A court will deny a motion for a bill of particulars where the facts sought by a defendant are either already known, or the means of ascertaining those facts are otherwise available to the defense.[116]

Under the Federal Rules of Criminal Procedure, a motion for a bill of particulars must be made before or within fourteen days after arraignment.[117] The motion must also specify which portion of the indictment needs better explanation; the request cannot simply allege that the entire indictment is insufficient.[118]

When deciding whether to issue an order requiring a bill of particulars, the court must strike a balance between use of the government's available evidence and the defendant's protection against surprise at trial.[119] Fear that a defendant will attempt to use a bill of particulars as a way to create broad discovery or "freeze" the government's evidence in advance of trial is often stated as a reason for the hesitancy to grant motions for bill of particulars.[120]

---

114. *See generally Bowie*, 618 F.3d at 817; *Hernandez*, 299 F.3d at 990.

115. *See* United States v. Mitchell, 744 F.2d 701, 705 (9th Cir. 1984) (not an abuse of discretion to deny the defendant's motion for a bill of particulars because the government satisfied its obligation to inform him of the charges against him by disclosing the contents of its files to defense counsel). *See also* United States v. Perryman, 881 F. Supp. 2d 427, 439 (E.D.N.Y. 2012); United States v. Schembari, 484 F.2d 931, 934–35 (4th Cir. 1973).

116. United States v. Pirk, 282 F. Supp. 3d 603, 608 (W.D.N.Y. 2017) ("A district court judge . . . has the discretion to deny a bill of particulars if the information sought by the defendant is provided in the indictment or in some acceptable alternate form."); United States v. Abakporo, 959 F. Supp. 2d 382, 389 (S.D.N.Y. 2013) ("In deciding whether a bill of particulars is needed, the court must determine whether the information sought has been provided elsewhere").

117. Fed. R. Crim. P. 7(f). State standards are similar, as in the Colorado rule that the motion must be filed within ten days after arraignment. Colo. R. Crim. P. 7(g). Some states, though, are less specific. *See, e.g.*, 725 Ill. Comp. Stat. Ann. 5/114-2(a) ("motion . . . shall be filed before or within a reasonable time after arraignment").

118. *See, e.g.*, United States v. Ellison, 442 F.Supp. 3d 491, 498 (D.P.R. 2020).

119. *See* United States v. Livingstone, 576 F.3d 881, 883 (8th Cir. 2009); United States v. Martin, 822 F.2d 1089 (6th Cir. 1987).

120. *See* United States v. Abakporo, 959 F. Supp. 2d 382, 389 (S.D.N.Y. 2013) ("The court must be cognizant of the fact that a bill of particulars confines the government's evidence at trial to the particulars furnished. The bill of particulars may not be used for the purpose of discovering the government's evidence."); United States v. Gibson, 175 F. Supp. 2d 532, 537 (S.D.N.Y. 2001) ("A bill of particulars is not a general investigative tool, a discovery device or a means to compel the government to disclose evidence or witnesses to be offered prior to trial."). *See also* United States v. Rigas, 258 F. Supp. 2d 299,

IX. Secret Indictments

Secret indictments—which are sealed upon issuance—are unusual, but not rare.[121] There are few reported state cases because most of the law in the area comes from the federal courts.[122] Under federal law, specific procedures have not been published to direct courts regarding the sealing of an indictment.[123] The magistrate judge to whom an indictment is returned may direct that the indictment be kept secret until the defendant is in custody or has been released pending trial; this decision is wholly within the judge's discretion.[124] Some—but not all—judges additionally require that the government give a detailed factual basis containing the essential facts forming the basis for the request for secrecy.[125]

Generally, courts construing the federal rule[126] are deferential to requests to seal an indictment. Indeed, judges have held that the reasons for sealing an indictment are not limited to facilitating arrest and found that sealing is not a substantive judicial determination but merely a ministerial act.[127] As a result, courts have provided that a magistrate judge "may grant the government's motion to seal an indictment for any legitimate prosecutorial need" so long as the government provides a factual basis for the request.[128] The rationale here is that the defendant's right to challenge the propriety of sealing is fully protected by affording her the right to a hearing after the indictment is unsealed.[129] At that time, the government, upon defendant's

305 (S.D.N.Y. 2003) ("The combination of the lengthy [i]ndictment, the early discovery, and the further particularization to be provided by the government goes well beyond the minimum level of detail necessary to prepare a defense and to avoid surprise.").

121. *See* Stinson, *Secret Indictments: How to Discourage Them, How to Make Them Fair,* 2 Drexel L. Rev. 104 (2009).

122. People v. Leavitt, 22 N.E.3d 430, 446 (Ill. App. 2014), is a detailed discussion of secret indictments in state court.

123. United States v. Srulowitz, 819 F.2d 37, 41 (2d Cir. 1987).

124. United States v. Ellis, 622 F.3d 784, 792 (7th Cir. 2010); *Srulowitz,* 819 F.2d at 41.

125. United States v. Laliberte, 131 F.R.D. 20, 21 (D. Mass. 1990) (These courts may also direct the government to give "some reasonable estimate as to when [it] will be able to request that the indictment be unsealed.").

126. Fed. R. Crim. P. 6(e)(4).

127. *Srulowitz,* 819 F.2d at 41. Secret indictments must be returned in open court before they can be sealed. Fed. R. Crim. P. 6(f).

128. United States v. Lakin, 875 F.2d 168, 170 (8th Cir. 1989). Some courts have upheld the sealing of indictments where the only reason was to toll the running of the statute of limitations. United States v. Edwards, 777 F.2d 644, 648 (11th Cir. 1985). *See generally In re* Midland Nat. Life Ins. Co. Annuity Sales Practices Lit., 686 F.3d 1115, 1119 (9th Cir. 2012).

129. *See generally* United States v. Southland Corp., 760 F.2d 1366, 1378 (2d Cir. 1985).

showing of prejudice occurring during the period when the indictment was sealed, must demonstrate legitimate prosecutorial purposes for the secrecy of the indictment.[130]

Federal courts use a "prejudice only" standard of review. They require the defendant to demonstrate substantial actual prejudice occurring between the date of sealing and the date of unsealing. This is true even when an indictment remains secret beyond the original statute of limitations period.[131]

The use of secret indictments is controversial, as it raises concerns about due process and speedy trial protections.[132] Still, defendants challenging the sealing process have a heavy burden. They will prevail "only upon a showing of substantial, irreparable prejudice."[133]

---

130. United States v. Cherico, 769 F. Supp. 2d 560, 569 (S.D.N.Y. 2011); *Edwards,* 777 F.2d at 649; United States v. Cosolito, 488 F. Supp. 531, 537 (D. Mass. 1980).

131. *See* United States v. Maling, 737 F. Supp. 684, 695 (D. Mass. 1990) ("A properly sealed indictment extending beyond the limitations period should not be dismissed unless the defendant can show substantial, irreparable, actual prejudice."); *Srulowitz,* 819 F.2d at 41.

132. For a sharp critique of current practice, *see* Stinson, *supra* note 121.

133. United States v. Goff, 400 F. App'x 507, 511 (11th Cir. 2010); *Edwards,* 777 F.2d at 649. For discussions of such showings, see *United States v. Delgomini,* 111 F. Supp. 2d 198, 199 (E.D.N.Y. 2000); *United States v. Rogers,* 781 F. Supp. 1181 (S.D. Miss. 1991); and *United States v. Heckler,* 428 F. Supp. 269, 272 (S.D.N.Y. 1976).

CHAPTER 6

The Confrontation Clause[1]

I. The History of Confrontation

Confrontation has been a component of criminal trials throughout legal history,[2] but until the 1990s, the Supreme Court paid little attention to the Confrontation Clause or its history.[3] Starting less than three decades ago, Justice Scalia and Justice Thomas began to advance the view that the Confrontation Clause, with its roots in seventeenth-century English law, must be understood as they believed it was

1. This chapter is separately dedicated to the memory of Associate Justice Antonin Scalia (1936–2016)—a vital, eloquent, and fearsome proponent of a robust Confrontation Clause.

2. Roman law required confrontation, although scholars disagree about the nature and scope of the ancient right. Some legal historians believe that confrontation under Roman law was "a production requirement unconnected to cross-examination . . . designed to ensure fair criminal procedure by requiring witnesses to testify live before both the accused and the trier of fact." *See* Raymond LaMagna, *(Re)constitutionalizing Confrontation: Reexamining Unavailability and the Value of Live Testimony*, 79 S. Cal. L. Rev. 1499, 1500 (2006) (citing Herrmann & Speer, *Facing the Accuser: Ancient and Modern Precursors of the Confrontation Clause*, 34 Va. J. Int'l L. 481, 539 n.290 and accompanying text (1994)). Others argue that confrontation under Roman law was "not a trial device but an investigative tool akin to a line-up." Kenneth Graham, *Confrontation Stories: Raleigh on the Mayflower*, 3 Ohio St. J. Crim. L. 209, 211 (2005). Although the legal history of the right to confront one's accusers is uncertain, it appears that confrontation (in some form) continued to exist under Roman law until the "late twelfth century, [when] both Church and secular courts abandoned a defendant's right to be present during testimony in favor of secret inquisitorial proceedings." LaMagna, *supra* at 1513. English courts would eventually follow a similar inquisitorial model that relied on secret interrogations, exemplified by the notorious 15th-century Court of the Star Chamber. *See* Randolph N. Jonakait, *The Origins of the Confrontation Clause: An Alternate History*, 27 Rutgers L.J. 77, 79–84 (1995).

3. Crawford v. Washington, 541 U.S. 36 (2004).

intended, to prevent abuses common to the English criminal trials of that era.[4]

Over the past few decades, there has been heated academic debate challenging the historical accuracy of the Court's legal history in a range of contexts including confrontation. For example, one commentator has called the modern Court's "conventional history of the right to confrontation[,] . . . [that] the right of confrontation was created by common law judges seeking to preserve the English tradition of liberty,"[5] a "romantic myth"[6] wholly at odds with the fact that "the English common law has never recognized a right to confrontation."[7] Another has argued that the Court purports to adhere to historical assertions plainly "inconsistent with the basic premises that shaped the framer's understanding of the [confrontation] right."[8] Although some experts agree in principle with the Court that "seventeenth century English history, and other English actions, may have affected the development of American constitutional rights,"[9] they argue that "English abuses focused on by the standard histories were not the prime or immediate cause of the Confrontation Clause."[10]

A competing historical view posits that "the Confrontation Clause, and related Sixth Amendment provisions, sought to constitutionalize criminal procedure as it then existed in the states."[11] This approach differs from the historical view of the Court, because it is not focused on the time of the framing but instead on the 1791 ratification date.[12] But law professors cannot resist an irresolvable debate. So a third historical approach focuses on intentionality circa 1868, the year the

---

4. *See, e.g.*, White v. Illinois, 502 U.S. 346, 361–62 (1992) ("The Court consistently has indicated that the primary purpose of the [Confrontation] Clause was to prevent abuses which had occurred in England.").

5. Graham, *supra* note 2, at 209.

6. *Id.*

7. *Id.* (emphasis added).

8. Thomas Y. Davies, *Not "The Framers' Design": How the Framing-Era Ban Against Hearsay Evidence Refutes the Crawford-Davis Testimonial Formulation of the Scope of the Original Confrontation Clause,* 15 J.L. & POL'Y 349, 352 (2007); *see also* Fisher, *The Crawford Debacle,* 113 MICH. L. REV. FIRST IMPRESSIONS 17, 20 (2014) (neither the Confrontation Clause's history nor its text can "sustain Justice Scalia's distinction between *testimonial* hearsay, generally excluded unless the defendant can cross-examine the declarant, and *nontestimonial* hearsay, regulated only by evidence rules") (emphasis in original).

9. Jonakait, *supra* note 2, at 80–81 (emphasis added).

10. *Id. at 81.*

11. *Id.*

12. *Id.*

Fourteenth Amendment was adopted.[13] In the midst of this academic fracas, one refreshingly skeptical constitutional scholar has argued that "originalist claims that have appeared in recent criminal procedure decisions have usually reflected the ideological proclivities of the justices who made them, but have rarely resembled the historical legal doctrines that actually shaped the Framers' understanding."[14]

Whatever your view of the accuracy of the Supreme Court's legal history or the manifold alternatives promoted by its critics, even a cursory glance at the modern confrontation cases demonstrates that the Court is likely to continue to interpret the scope and nature of confrontation through a historical lens. In 2006, in the watershed case *Crawford v. Washington*, the Supreme Court, led by Justice Scalia, relied on its understanding of the historical record to revive confrontation and, more specifically, to disentangle the right from the rules of evidence.[15] Today, academics and practitioners seeking to understand and predict how federal and state criminal courts will treat confrontation-based arguments need not agree on its legal history, but even as we struggle to accommodate new and future concerns raised by the COVID-19 pandemic,[16] we should expect our jurisprudence to remain intertwined with the Sixth Amendment's evolution.

---

13. *See Peter* Nicolas, *I'm Dying to Tell You What Happened: The Admissibility of Testimonial Dying Declarations Post-*Crawford, 37 Hastings Const. L.Q. 487, 504 (010) (objecting to the *Crawford* Court's microfocus on 1791 when the clause was adopted).

14. Davies, *supra* note 8, at 350. *See also* Stephanos Bibas, *The Limits of Textualism in Interpreting the Confrontation Clause*, 37 Harv. J.L. & Pub. Pol'y 737 (2014).

15. Crawford v. Washington, 541 U.S. 36 (2004). This game-changing decision is discussed *infra* section V.

16. *See* United States v. Crittenden, No. 4:20-CR-7 (CDL), 2020 U.S. Dist. LEXIS 151950 (M.D. Ga. Aug. 21, 2020) ("Under the specific circumstances presented by the global COVID-19 pandemic, the Court is satisfied that the current mask requirement does not violate the Confrontation Clause." . . . "Here, the mask requirement is necessary to further an important public policy: ensuring the safety of everyone in the courtroom in the midst of a unique global pandemic."); United States v. Casher, No. CR 19-65-BLG-SPW, 2020 U.S. Dist. LEXIS 106293 (D. Mont. June 17, 2020) (the court is sympathetic to witnesses who must travel during these times but finds that the potential risks COVID-19 poses do not present the requisite necessity under *Maryland v. Craig* to forgo the defendant's confrontation rights or allow the witnesses to testify via video); United States v. Donziger, No. 19-CR-561 (LAP), 2020 U.S. Dist. LEXIS 157797 (S.D.N.Y. Aug. 31, 2020) (finding that limiting the spread of COVID-19 and protecting at-risk individuals from exposure to the virus are critically important public policies that justified an exception to the ordinary "face-to-face confrontation" requirement and allowed a witness to testify via a two-way videoconference system). *See also* Michael Shammas & Michael Pressman, *Advocacy Through the Computer Screen: The Permissibility & Constitutionality of Jury Trial by Video Conference* (July 30, 2020), https://ssrn.com/abstract=3664014, http://dx.doi.org/10.2139/ssrn.3664014; Matthew T. Mangino, The Confrontation Clause and the

II. The Supreme Court's Early Confrontation Jurisprudence

The text of the Confrontation Clause of the Sixth Amendment guarantees every criminal defendant the right "to be confronted with the witnesses against him."[17] The Supreme Court first addressed the meaning and operation of this language over a century ago in *Mattox v. United States*.[18]

A. Confrontation Defined

The *Mattox* Court was the first to define the "primary object" of the Confrontation Clause.[19] The right to confrontation was intended to "prevent depositions or *ex parte* affidavits, such as were sometimes admitted in civil cases, being used against the prisoner in lieu of a personal examination and cross-examination of the witness."[20] According to the Court, the Sixth Amendment guarantees the defendant an "opportunity . . . [(1) to] test the recollection and sift the conscience of the witness, [and (2) to] . . . compel him to stand face to face with the jury in order that they may look at him, and judge by his demeanor upon the stand and the manner in which he gives his testimony whether he is worthy of belief."[21] After *Mattox*, confrontation would become fully synonymous with cross-examination.

Mattox is frequently invoked as both a seminal and an expansive interpretation of the defendant's right to confrontation. However, closer examination reveals that at the time, three Justices envisioned an even broader guarantee of rights. The precise question before the *Mattox* Court was whether the Sixth Amendment barred admission of a transcribed copy of a newspaper reporter's stenographic notes taken during the defendant's first murder trial.[22] The reporter's notes described the trial testimony of two crucial prosecution witnesses. After the first trial, one of the witnesses (Whitman) fully recanted his

---

Return of Jury Trials, The Times (July 31, 2020), https://www.timesonline.com/story/opinion/columns/2020/08/05/matthew-t-mangino-confrontation-clause-and-return-of-jury-trials/112822240 (discussing the potential problems face masks will present in relation to the Confrontation Clause once post-COVID jury trials resume); Julia Ann Simon-Kerr, Unmasking Demeanor, 88 Geo. Wash. L. Rev. Arguendo 158 (2020).

17. U.S. Const. amend. VI.
18. 156 U.S. 237 (1895).
19. *Id.* at 257.
20. *Id.* at 242.
21. *Id.* at 242–43.
22. *Id.* at 241.

testimony but died before the second trial.[23] Defense counsel argued that because cross-examination was now impossible, the right to confrontation should be interpreted to encompass the opportunity to impeach Whitman's written statement using testimony from two new witnesses who would describe his recantation.[24]

Three members of the *Mattox* Court agreed. In their view, if

> the right of the accused to confront the witnesses against him, although formally secured to him by the express terms of the Constitution, and being of importance and value to him, as are recognized by the courts, may be dispensed with because of the death of a witness, it would seem justly to follow that neither should that death deprive the accused of his right to put in evidence, valid and competent in nature, to show that the witness was unworthy of belief.[25]

These justices viewed confrontation as including both cross-examination of Whitman and the right to alternatives to cross-examination that could achieve the same impeachment objectives. They also believed that the prosecutor's inability to repair Whitman's credibility should not prevent the defendant from exercising his right to confront.

The *Mattox* majority did not adopt this expansive view of confrontation. Instead, the Court articulated the more limited approach that confrontation guarantees *only* cross-examination. The broader interpretation was rejected, according to the majority, because "say[ing] that a criminal, after having once been convicted by the testimony of a certain witness should go scot free simply because death has closed the mouth of that witness, would be carrying his constitutional protection to an unwarrantable extent."[26] This led the Court to conclude that "the rights of the public shall not be wholly sacrificed in order that an *incidental benefit* [of confrontation] may be preserved to the accused."[27] The Court's instrumental diminution of the value of confrontation served the majority's short-term purpose (denying the defendant the ability to present potentially exonerating evidence), but in the long term the Court would eventually disavow its blatant mischaracterization of confrontation as a mere "incidental benefit."

---

23. *Id.* at 244.
24. *Id.*
25. *Id.* at 260 (Shiras, J., dissenting) (joined by Justices Gray and White).
26. *Id.* at 243.
27. *Id.* (emphasis added).

B. Incorporation to the States

Mattox had little impact on criminal prosecutions for the next seventy years because the right to confrontation was not incorporated to the states until 1965. That year, the Supreme Court held in *Pointer v. Texas*[28] that confrontation is a "fundamental right essential to a fair trial in a criminal prosecution."[29] According to the *Pointer* Court, "the right of an accused to be confronted with the witnesses against him must be determined by the same standards whether the right is denied in a federal or state proceeding."[30]

Unlike *Mattox, Pointer* was an unequivocal expansion of the scope of the confrontation guarantee. Specifically, the *Pointer* Court held that not all prior opportunities to confront prosecution witnesses satisfy the Sixth Amendment. In *Pointer*, the defendant's confrontation rights were violated when the state trial court admitted the transcript of a prosecution witness's preliminary hearing testimony.[31] The defendant had been present at the preliminary hearing but was not yet represented by counsel. The *Pointer* Court reasoned that if confrontation guarantees cross-examination, the witness's preliminary hearing statement could not be admitted because the statement had not been "taken at a time and under circumstances affording petitioner *through counsel* an adequate opportunity to cross-examine."[32] As discussed in the following sections, post-*Pointer* courts uniformly presume that cross-examination through defense counsel is constitutionally required.[33]

III. The Right to Confrontation, 1968 to 2004

A. Defining the Scope of Confrontation

1. Confrontation as a Trial Right

In 1968, in *Barber v. Page*, the Supreme Court briefly interpreted the Confrontation Clause to also require that cross-examination occur *at trial*.[34] In dictum addressing the scope of the Confrontation Clause, the *Barber* Court explicitly agreed with the *Mattox* view that the Sixth

28. Pointer v. Texas, 380 U.S. 400 (1965).
29. *Id.* at 404.
30. *Id.* at 407–08.
31. *Id.* at 400.
32. *Id.* at 407 (emphasis added).
33. *See infra* section III(B).
34. Barber v. Page, 390 U.S. 719 (1968).

Amendment required prosecution witnesses "to stand face to face with the jury."[35]

In *Barber*, defense counsel had been present at defendant's preliminary hearing representing both the defendant (Barber) and his codefendant (Woods). Obviously, when Woods testified at the hearing, defense counsel could not cross-examine his own client.[36] As discussed later, the Supreme Court held that the admission of Woods's preliminary hearing testimony violated Barber's confrontation rights because the prosecutor had not established that Woods was unavailable to testify at trial (noting that, at the time of trial, Woods was incarcerated in a nearby federal prison).[37] However, in dictum discussing whether confrontation must occur *at trial in front of the jury*, the *Barber* Court commented as follows:

> We would reach the same result on the facts of this case had petitioner's counsel actually cross-examined Woods at the preliminary hearing. The right to confrontation is basically a trial right. It includes both the opportunity to cross-examine and the occasion for the jury to weigh the demeanor of the witness.[38]

Barber represents the short-lived apotheosis of confrontation. According to the *Barber* Court, a defendant's right to confront is so robust that cross-examination during a preliminary hearing, outside the presence of the trial jury, did not satisfy the Sixth Amendment.[39]

Just two years later in *California v. Green*,[40] the Court would retreat from *Barber* in a case involving the admission of a witness's prior inconsistent statement during a preliminary hearing. In direct contrast to *Barber*, the *Green* Court held that a defendant's Confrontation Clause rights were satisfied by the opportunity to cross-examine a prosecution witness during a pretrial hearing.[41] By 1970, the Court had apparently abandoned the idea that confrontation is a trial right

---

35. *Id.* at 721.

36. *Id.* at 720.

37. *Id.* at 724–25.

38. *Id.* at 725.

39. For an excellent discussion of the independent constitutional significance of live in-court testimony under the Sixth Amendment, *see* LaMagna, *supra* note 2. Professor Josephine Ross has also commented on the long-standing assumption that "it was thought that a man would more easily state a false accusation if he did not have to do so publicly and in front of the person he unfairly accused." Josephine Ross, *What's Reliability Got to Do with the Confrontation Clause After* Crawford, 14 WIDENER L. REV. 383, 405 (2009).

40. California v. Green, 399 U.S. 149 (1970).

41. *Id.* at 166.

because a defendant is entitled to have a jury observe the cross-examination of prosecution witnesses, to assess their demeanor and credibility.

2. Witness Unavailability

Barber v. Page was also the Supreme Court's first exploration of witness unavailability for confrontation purposes.[42] According to the Court, the Sixth Amendment burden on the prosecutor to establish that her witness is unavailable is greater than the burden of proof required under the handful of hearsay exceptions requiring unavailability.[43] After *Barber*, "a witness is not 'unavailable' for purposes of the . . . confrontation requirement unless the prosecutorial authorities have made a good-faith effort to obtain his presence at trial."[44]

Over the next three decades, the Supreme Court would repeatedly revisit the scope of the witness unavailability requirement, occasionally developing special rules for child alleged victims in sex crimes cases[45] and for statements that fit certain well-rooted hearsay exceptions.[46] In 2004, in *Crawford v. Washington*, the Court clarified its adherence to *Barber* by holding that "[t]estimonial statements of witnesses absent from trial have been admitted *only* where the declarant is unavailable, and *only* where the defendant has had a prior opportunity to cross-examine."[47] Post-*Crawford*, the Court has entertained the possibility of admitting testimony from unavailable witnesses only in the context of child sexual assault cases, which are discussed in more detail later, where prosecutors seek to avoid face-to-face encounters between alleged child victims and the defendant.[48]

3. Confrontation and Evidentiary Reliability

By 1980, in *Ohio v. Roberts*, the Confrontation Clause had become handmaiden to the rules of evidence.[49] Fifteen years post-incorporation, Roberts involved the admissibility of preliminary hearing testimony

---

42. *See supra* section III.A.1.

43. *See, e.g.*, Fed. R. Evid. 804.

44. Barber v. Page, 390 U.S. 719, 724–25 (1968).

45. *See infra* section IV.

46. *See, e.g.*, United States v. Inadi, 475 U.S. 387, 396–400 (1986) (prosecutors seeking admission of out-of-court statements from coconspirators need not establish witness unavailability).

47. Crawford v. Washington, 541 U.S. 36, 59 (2004) (emphasis added).

48. Ohio v. Clark, 576 U.S. 237 (2015).

49. Ohio v. Roberts, 448 U.S. 56 (1980).

from a defense witness. The *Roberts* Court held that confrontation and hearsay could be understood as overlapping and even duplicative protections because they share the same goal of "augment[ing] accuracy in the factfinding process by ensuring the defendant an effective means to test adverse evidence."[50] The *Roberts* Court, which represents the nadir of confrontation power, found that the right was functionally superfluous for most or all criminal defendants because hearsay protections "stem from the same roots"[51] and "are generally designed to protect similar values."[52]

For the next 15 years, *Roberts* would guide confrontation analysis in the federal and state criminal courts. If, under the operating rules of evidence, the prosecution proffered presumptively reliable out-of-court statements by an unavailable witness, confrontation was unnecessary because it could not make the statement more reliable.[53] Post-*Roberts* defendants had no constitutional grounds to oppose the admission of statements by out-of-court witnesses insulated from defense cross-examination, assuming the prosecutor successfully argued that the statement (1) fit a "firmly rooted hearsay exception"[54] or (2) had "particularized guarantees of trustworthiness."[55]

4. The Formality of the Out-of-Court Statement

The Supreme Court's modern confrontation jurisprudence has also repeatedly focused on the "formality" of the prosecution proffered out-of-court statement, as a means of determining whether the speaker acted as a "witness against the accused." The first substantive discussion of formality and confrontation actually appeared four years before *Crawford*, in Justice Thomas's 1992 concurring opinion in *White v. Illinois*.[56]

In *White*, the Court held that the Confrontation Clause was not violated by the admission of out-of-court statements from a four-year-old alleged sexual assault victim who was available but did not testify at trial.[57] Justice Thomas (joined by Justice Scalia) initially and quite candidly acknowledged, "[t]here is virtually no evidence of

50. *Id.* at 65.
51. *Id.*
52. *Id.* at 66.
53. *Id.*
54. *Id.*
55. *Id.*
56. White v. Illinois, 502 U.S. 346, 348–66 (1992) (Thomas, J., concurring).
57. *Id.* at 359.

what the drafters of the Confrontation Clause intended it to mean."[58] According to Justice Thomas, although the "strictest reading" would limit confrontation to witnesses who testify at trial, this interpretation would conflict with the history of confrontation at common law, during which courts had long considered a defendant's right to confront a wide range of out-of-court statements.[59] The United States, as *amicus curiae*, argued, "the Confrontation Clause should apply *only* to those persons who provide in-court testimony or the functional equivalent, such as affidavits, depositions, or confessions that are made in contemplation of legal proceedings."[60] Justice Thomas, who had joined the Court that same year, articulated (for the first time) a view that he continues to hold, that "the Confrontation Clause is implicated by extrajudicial statements *only* insofar as they are contained in formalized testimonial materials, such as affidavits, depositions, prior testimony, or confessions."[61] Justice Thomas also presciently anticipated the coming legal morass when he predicted that the creation of a confrontation standard that "[a]ttempt[s] to draw a line between statements made in contemplation of legal proceedings and those not so made would entangle the courts in a multitude of difficulties."[62]

B. Limiting the Scope of Confrontation

In the century since *Mattox*, the Supreme Court has consistently held that confrontation guarantees the defendant the right to cross-examination by counsel, but not the right to fruitful or effective cross-examination. For example, in 1984 in *Delaware v. Fensterer*,[63] a case involving a state-sponsored expert witness who testified that he could not recall his own methodology, the Court clarified that confrontation "includes no guarantee that every witness called by the prosecution will refrain from giving testimony that is marred by forgetfulness, confusion, or evasion."[64] Thus, a defendant's confrontation right is satisfied by cross-examination of a prosecution expert witness who cannot recall the bases for his opinion because the defendant has been provided an "opportunity to probe and expose . . . [these] infirmities through crossexamination, . . . [by] calling to

58. *Id.*
59. *Id.* at 361–63.
60. *Id.* at 364 (emphasis added).
61. *Id.* at 365 (emphasis added).
62. *Id.* at 364.
63. Delaware v. Fensterer, 474 U.S. 15, 21–22 (1985).
64. *Id.*

the attention of the factfinder the reasons for giving scant weight to the witness' testimony."[65]

Fensterer was reaffirmed and expanded three years later in *United States v. Owens*.[66] The *Owens* Court found the Confrontation Clause satisfied by cross-examination of a prosecution witness who remembered speaking to the Federal Bureau of Investigation but claimed to have forgotten all of the relevant facts that formed the subject matter of his previous testimony.[67] The vast majority of federal and state courts continue to follow *Fensterer/Owens*,[68] but post-*Crawford*, a handful of courts have explored whether confrontation might require more than mere physical presence on the witness stand.[69]

---

65. *Id.* at 22. *But see* United States v. Rosalez, 711 F.3d 1194, 1217 (10th Cir. 2013) (the denial of confrontation was harmless error, but explaining that "a violation of this constitutional right occurs when the defendant is prohibited from engaging in otherwise appropriate cross-examination that, as a result, precludes him from eliciting information from which jurors could draw vital inferences in his favor") (citation omitted).

66. United States v. Owens, 484 U.S. 554 (1988).

67. *Id.* at 560.

68. *See, e.g.*, State v. Baker, 200 P.3d 696, 698 (Mont. 2013) (the "right to confront includes only the opportunity for cross-examination, but not any guarantee that it will elicit helpful evidence" thereby precluding the defendant's argument that his right to confrontation was violated by the introduction of the alleged child victim's out-of-court statement after she testified at trial); State v. Davis, 128 So. 3d 1161 (La. 2013) ("a declarant's appearance and subjection to cross-examination at trial are all that is necessary to satisfy the Confrontation Clause, even if the declarant suffers from memory loss"); United States v. Mohamud, 941 F. Supp. 2d 1303, 1317–18 (D. Or. 2013) (the defendant's right to confrontation is not violated by incomplete or ineffective cross-examination when the defendant had extensive information about the witnesses' background, training, and the bias inherent in the testimony of a government agent, from which to fashion cross-examination questions); United States v. Alaniz, 726 F.3d 586, 610–11 (5th Cir. 2013) (the defendant's right to confrontation is not violated when confidential informants testify at trial and are subject to cross-examination, but are not required to disclose their dates of birth and social security numbers).

69. Some post-*Owens* cases have suggested that the physical presence of the witness on the witness stand may not always be constitutionally adequate. In *Goforth v. State*, 70 So. 3d 174, 186 (2011), the state supreme court (relying in part on the Mississippi Constitution) found the Confrontation Clause unsatisfied by defendant's opportunity to cross-examine a prosecution witness who, "though physically present at trial, did not have the requisite minimal ability or capacity to act" because he suffered from physical disabilities and mental impairments resulting in complete memory loss regarding *both* the underlying events and his statement to the police. On narrower grounds, in *People v. Learn*, 919 N.E.2d 1042, 1049 (2009), the court found that "[a] child witness is considered unavailable if the child is unwilling or unable to testify because of fear, unable to communicate in the courtroom setting, or declared incompetent because she is incapable of expressing herself so as to be understood concerning the matter. . . . [and that] [i]t makes no difference whether the witness becomes "unavailable" before or after she takes the witness stand."

C. Special Confrontation Cases: Statements from Child Witnesses

Starting in the late 1980s, the Supreme Court decided a series of confrontation cases involving a defendant's right to confront child alleged victims in sexual assault cases. In 1988, in *Coy v. Iowa*,[70] the Court found that despite prosecutors' concerns about potential psychological harm to this class of alleged victim, "the Confrontation Clause guarantees the defendant a face-to-face meeting with witnesses appearing before the trier of fact."[71] In *Coy*, the prosecutor had been permitted to place a screen between the two teenage alleged rape victims and the defendant (which blocked the defendant from their view, but allowed him to see and hear their testimony). According to Justice Scalia, who wrote for the *Coy* majority, this testimony violated the Confrontation Clause.[72] More specifically, the Court upheld "the right to face-to-face confrontation[, which] serves much the same purpose as a less explicit component of the Confrontation Clause that we have had more frequent occasion to discuss, the right to cross-examine the accuser; both ensure the integrity of the fact-finding process."[73]

The *Coy* Court's "face-to-face" analysis appears, at first glance, to echo the century-old "face-to-face" understanding of *Mattox*,[74] but it is not the same. The *Mattox* Court interpreted the Confrontation Clause to require that prosecution witnesses "stand face to face with the jury in order that they may look at him, and judge by his demeanor upon the stand and the manner in which he gives his testimony whether he is worthy of belief."[75] In contrast, the *Coy* Court understood the

---

70. Coy v. Iowa, 487 U.S. 1012 (1988).

71. *Id.* at 1016.

72. *Id.* at 1020.

73. *Id.* at 1019–20 (quotations omitted).

74. Mattox v. United States, 156 U.S. 237 (1895).

75. *Id.* at 242–43 (emphasis added). For an interesting recent discussion of confrontation as a face-to-face requirement, see *People v. Ketchens*, No. B282486, 2019 WL 2404393 (Cal. Ct. App. June 7, 2019). In this case, the defendant alleged that a witness wearing a partially face-covering scarf violated the Confrontation Clause. The California appellate court deferred to the trial court's determination that it did not violate the Confrontation Clause because it was worn for religious reasons and after objection, the witness had uncovered her eyes and nose (therefore allowing the defendant to see her facial expressions). One commentator has also argued that the face-to-face requirement of confrontation should not be required in cases alleging elder abuse because these cases are highly "witness-centric" and more likely to involve witnesses who are unavailable to testify. *See* Anna Corcoran, *The Primary Purpose for Admitting Hearsay over Confrontation Challenges in Elder Abuse Cases: A Framework for Bringing Unavailability Concerns into the Light in a Post-*Crawford *World*, 25 ELDER L.J. 161 (2017) (describing a range of approaches for dealing with unavailable elderly witnesses). *See also* People v. Wrotten, 923 N.E.2d 1099 (N.Y. 2009) (the trial court had the authority to allow a prosecution witness, found to be elderly,

Confrontation Clause to guarantee not the jury, but the defendant, "a face-to-face meeting with witnesses appearing before the trier of fact."[76] There are obvious and manifold theoretical, conceptual, and practical differences between a confrontation right understood to require a witness/accuser to face the jury and one understood to require her to face the accused.

Just two years later, the Supreme Court found a technological workaround to the problem of confrontation in cases involving child alleged sexual assault victims. In *Maryland v. Craig*, the prosecutor introduced expert testimony explaining that the alleged victim would suffer serious emotional harm if forced to testify in the courtroom and forced to see the defendant.[77] The judge agreed to allow the alleged victim to testify using one-way closed circuit television, which enabled the jury to view the victim but blocked the defendant from the alleged victim's view.[78] In a decision echoing *Roberts*, Justice O'Connor, writing for the *Craig* majority, concluded that "[t]he central concern of the Confrontation Clause is to ensure the reliability of the evidence against a criminal defendant by subjecting it to rigorous testing."[79] However, confrontation objectives must be interpreted "in a manner sensitive to its purposes and sensitive to the necessities of trial and the adversary process."[80] After balancing these competing interests, the *Craig* Court held that face-to-face courtroom confrontation could be denied without violating the Confrontation Clause if a court determined that a less traumatic procedure could further the important public policy interest in protecting child witnesses.[81]

---

infirm, and physically incapable of traveling interstate, to testify via live, two-way television, subject to cross-examination).

76. *Coy*, 487 U.S. at 1016.

77. *Craig*, 497 U.S. at 842.

78. *Id.* at 850. *See also* Harris v. State, 964 N.E.2d 920, 925 (Ind. Ct. App. 2012) (the admission of testimony by a child witness not present in the courtroom is not an inherent violation of the defendant's right to confront witnesses against him); People v. Lujan, 150 Cal. Rptr. 3d 727, 732 (Cal. Ct. App. 2012) (same). For an interesting discussion of the future of virtual testimony and confrontation, see James W. Kraus & Pietragallo G. Alfano, *Virtual Testimony and Its Impact on the Confrontation Clause*, 34 CHAMPION 26 (2010).

79. *Craig*, 497 U.S. at *845*.

80. *Id.* at 849. *See also* Lipsitz v. Nevada, 442 P.3d 138 (Nev. 2019) (upholding use of two-way video under Craig because the alleged victim was in treatment program and would not be available for months, waiting for her availability would violate speedy trial concerns, and "the audiovisual transmission procedure . . . adequately ensure[d] the reliability of the testimony, as it allowed [the defendant] to cross-examine the victim and the jury could hear and observe the victim").

81. *Craig*, 497 U.S. at 856–57. *See also* Will Resnik, *Get with the Times: Why the Use of Live Two-Way Video Testimony Does Not Violate the Confrontation Clause*, 45 AM. J. CRIM. L.

In two subsequent cases, the Supreme Court addressed the related confrontation problem of the admissibility of out-of-court statements by available child alleged sex crimes victims who did *not* testify at trial. In *Idaho v. Wright*, decided the same year as *Craig*, the Court addressed the admissibility of a child's out-of-court statement to her doctor under a residual hearsay exception.[82] According to the *Wright* Court, admission of the out-of-court statement violated the Confrontation Clause because the evidence did not fit any of the firmly rooted hearsay exceptions.[83] This presumptive lack of reliability could not be ameliorated with corroborating evidence.[84] Two years later, in *White v. Illinois*,[85] the Court held, under rather different circumstances, that the admission of out-of-court statements by a four-year-old alleged sexual assault victim through third-party witnesses did not violate the Confrontation Clause.[86] Despite the fact that the prosecutor had failed to establish that the alleged victim was unavailable to testify, the *White* Court held that the Confrontation Clause was not violated because her statements fit the firmly rooted "excited utterance" and "statements for the purpose of medical treatment" exceptions to the hearsay rule.[87] The *White* decision significantly elevated the presumptive reliability of certain hearsay exceptions over the defendant's constitutional concerns. *White* is also notable because the decision echoes and expands *Roberts* by finding that the defendant's right to confront can simply be ignored by any court that believes it would serve no credibility-determining function.[88] According to the *White* Court, cross-examination of a statement that fits a firmly rooted hearsay exception serves no fact-finding purpose, because the out-of-court statement is presumed to be "so trustworthy that *adversarial testing can be expected to add little to its reliability*."[89] *White* seems an obvious

---

461 (2019); *Sixth Amendment—Confrontation Clause—New Mexico Supreme Court Holds Two-Way Video Testimony Violates Confrontation Clause*, 130 HARV. L. REV. 801 (2016).

82. Idaho v. Wright, 497 U.S. 805 (1990).

83. *Id.* at 816–17.

84. *Id.* at 822–23.

85. White v. Illinois, 502 U.S. 346 (1992).

86. *Id.* at 357–58.

87. *Id.* at 357.

88. Ohio v. Roberts, 448 U.S. 56, 66 (1980).

89. *White*, 502 U.S. at 357 (emphasis added).

antecedent to *Crawford v. Washington*, decided just four years later, although the *Crawford* Court notably declined to overrule *White*.[90]

Much more recently, in 2019, the Ninth Circuit addressed the (slightly different) question of whether two-way video of the testimony of a child alleged victim violated the Confrontation Clause.[91] In *United States v. Carter*, the court agreed, in principle, that the *Craig* Court's requirement of face-to-face confrontation should not "easily be dispensed with" because the "defendant's right to physically confront an adverse witness (whether child or adult) cannot be compromised by permitting the witness to testify by video (whether one-way or two-way) unless *Craig*'s standard is satisfied."[92] But these concerns must be balanced against considerations of whether "denial of such confrontation is necessary to further an important public policy" and "the reliability of the testimony is otherwise assured."[93] Finally, the *Carter* Court considered, in some detail, the constitutional import of various pragmatic courtroom issues including the size and quality of the monitor and the viewing angles.[94]

IV. The Revitalized Confrontation Clause: *Crawford v. Washington*

A. The Facts

In 2004, *Crawford v. Washington* resurrected the Confrontation Clause by severing the constitutional command from notions of presumptively reliable statements based on "firmly rooted" hearsay exceptions and baseless judicial assumptions of evidentiary reliability.[95] Initially, *Crawford* appeared to signal a more robust understanding of defendants' Confrontation Clause protections, but more recent cases suggest that this expansive view may be ephemeral.

---

90. Crawford v. Washington, 541 U.S. 36, 58 n.8 (2004) ("[T]he only question presented in *White* was whether the Confrontation Clause imposed an unavailability requirement on the types of hearsay at issue. The holding did not address the question whether certain of the statements, because they were testimonial, had to be excluded *even if* the witness was unavailable.") (citations omitted).

91. United States v. Carter, 907 F.3d 1199, 1202 (9th Cir. 2018).

92. *Id.* at 1206.

93. *Id.*

94. *Id.*

95. *Crawford*, 541 U.S. at 40. For a more expansive (but related) discussion of *Crawford* and the implications of the post-*Crawford* cases through *Bryant* written by one of the authors, see Moreno, *Finding Nino: Justice Scalia's Confrontation Clause Legacy from Its (Glorious) Beginning to (Bitter) End*, 44 U. Akron L. Rev. 1212 (2011).

Crawford involved the admission of a tape-recorded out-of-court statement obtained from the defendant's wife, Sylvia Crawford, who was a witness to the charged crime.[96] Mrs. Crawford made a statement to the police during a stationhouse custodial interrogation after receiving Miranda warnings and waiving her rights.[97] At trial, she invoked the state marital privilege and did not testify. The prosecutor introduced her out-of-court statement (which undermined her husband's self-defense claim by suggesting that the victim had been unarmed) under the firmly rooted state hearsay exception for statements against interest.[98]

B. *Ohio v. Roberts* (Partially) Overruled

By the time *Crawford* reached the Supreme Court, the justices—especially Justice Scalia—were loaded for bear.

The Court emphatically rejected the *Roberts* rule permitting judges to substitute their own ad hoc determinations of reliability for the "crucible of cross-examination."[99] The long-standing practice of supplanting the Confrontation Clause with the rules of evidence bore the full brunt of Justice Scalia's estimable ire. Writing for a unanimous Court, Justice Scalia declared that "[d]ispensing with confrontation because testimony is obviously reliable is akin to dispensing with jury trial because a defendant is obviously guilty."[100] In the *Crawford* Court's view, "the Clause's ultimate goal is to ensure reliability of evidence, . . . [which] is a procedural rather than a substantive guarantee."[101] The Sixth Amendment "commands, not that evidence be reliable, but that reliability be assessed in a particular manner: by testing in the crucible of cross-examination."[102] Disavowing *Roberts*

---

96. *Crawford,* 541 U.S. at 40.

97. *Id.* at 38–39.

98. *Id.* at 40.

99. *Id.* at 61. *See also* Eileen A. Scallen, *Coping with* Crawford*: Confrontation of Children and Other Challenging Witnesses,* 35 WM. MITCHELL L. REV. 1558, 1560–63 (2009) (describing the post-*Roberts,* pre-*Crawford* expansion of the category of "firmly rooted hearsay exceptins" along with the steady erosion of the witness unavailability requirement).

100. *Crawford,* 541 U.S. at 37 ("The unpardonable vice of the *Roberts* test, however, is not its unpredictability, but its demonstrated capacity to admit core testimonial statements that the Confrontation Clause plainly meant to exclude.").

101. *Id.* at 61.

102. *Id.* (emphasis added). "The clause thus reflects a judgment not only about the desirability of reliable evidence (a point on which there could be little dissent), but about how reliability can best be determined." *Id.*

and its modern progeny, the Court held that the Confrontation Clause cannot be circumvented by reliance on hearsay exceptions because statements from "witnesses against the accused" are only admissible if the defendant has an opportunity to confront.

C. A New Focus on the Text and History of the Confrontation Clause

The *Crawford* Court supported its decision with an analysis of both the text and history of the Confrontation Clause.

The Court began its textual analysis with a dictionary definition of "witnesses against the accused" borrowed from an 1828 edition of *Webster's American Dictionary of the English Language.*[103] *Webster's* defined a witness as one who "bears testimony" and defined "testimony" as "a solemn declaration or affirmation made for the purpose of establishing or proving some fact."[104] Justice Scalia, as lexicologist, reasoned that the Framers could not have intended to refer *only* to those who actually testify in court, nor could they have intended to include *all* out-of-court declarants.[105] "Witnesses" must, therefore, include those who testify in courtrooms but also those who testify outside courtrooms by making "testimonial statements." Unsurprisingly, this second group of out-of-court (yet testifying) witnesses has proved very difficult for subsequent courts to define and identify.[106]

---

103. *Id.* at 51. This approach seems borrowed from Justice Thomas's concurring opinion in *White v. Illinois,* in which he noted that "the critical phrase within the [Confrontation] Clause. . . . is 'witnesses against him. . . . ;' [thus] [a]ny attempt at unraveling and understanding the relationship between the Clause and the hearsay rules must begin with an analysis of the meaning of that phrase." White v. Illinois, 502 U.S. 346, 359 (1992).

104. *Crawford,* 541 U.S. at 51. *But see* Randolph N. Jonakait, *"Witness" in the Confrontation Clause:* Crawford v. Washington, *Noah Webster, and Compulsory Process,* 79 TEMP. L. REV. 155 (2006) (stating that the dictionary cited by the *Crawford* Court actually gives five definitions for the noun "witness" and that Justice Scalia selected the last of the five and ignored the first four). *See also* Adam Liptak, *Justices Turning More Frequently to Dictionary, and Not Just for Big Words,* N.Y. TIMES (June 13, 2011) (noting that the use of dictionaries by Supreme Court Justices to decide legal questions has been booming over the past 20 years, despite the fact that lexicographers rely on select source material and that it is easy to find a dictionary that highlights a predetermined interpretation).

105. *Crawford,* 541 U.S. at 51.

106. *Id.* By 2009, four members of the Court would criticize *Crawford* for its "fundamental mistake . . . [of] read[ing] the Confrontation Clause as referring to a kind of out-of-court statement—namely a testimonial statement—that must be excluded from evidence." Melendez-Diaz v. Massachusetts, 557 U.S. 305, 343 (2009) (Kennedy, J., dissenting). More recently, Justice Kennedy (writing for Chief Justice Roberts and Justices Breyer and Alito) commented that "[s]even years after its initiation, it bears remembering that the *Crawford* approach was not preordained. This Court's missteps have produced an

The *Crawford* Court's decision was also rooted in its own historical analysis, which included a lengthy disquisition of the treason trial of Sir Walter Raleigh, along with other materials.[107] According to Justice Scalia, the history of confrontation demonstrated that "the principal evil at which the confrontation clause was directed was the civil-law mode of criminal procedure, and particularly its use of *ex parte* communications as evidence against the accused."[108] The Court reasoned, "the Framers would not have allowed the admission of *testimonial statements* made by a witness who did not appear at trial unless he was unavailable to testify, and the defendant had had a prior opportunity for cross-examination."[109] Thus, *Crawford* shifted the focus of the confrontation inquiry to the question of whether the prosecution-sponsored statement was "testimonial," because this would determine whether the Sixth Amendment guaranteed the defendant an opportunity to confront.

D. The Advent of the "Testimonial Statement"

After *Crawford,* the act of identifying a "testimonial statement" would be of critical constitutional and practical import.[110] Although the Court

---

interpretation of the word 'witness' at odds with its meaning elsewhere in the Constitution, including elsewhere in the Sixth Amendment and at odds with the sound administration of justice." Bullcoming v. New Mexico, 564 U.S. 647, 684 (2011) (Kennedy, J., dissenting) (internal citations omitted).

107. As discussed above, the accuracy of the *Crawford* Court's legal history has been the subject of lively academic debate. However, as Professor Robert P. Mosteller astutely observed, "[t]he opinion in *Crawford* provides the Court's (Justice Scalia's) view of the historical purpose of the Confrontation Clause [and] [t]hese historical materials and the perspective adopted are obviously selective, but they are now the essential materials and the privileged perspective." Mosteller, Crawford v. Washington*: Encouraging and Ensuring the Confrontation of Witnesses,* 39 U. Rich. L. Rev. 511, 514 (2005).

108. *Crawford,* 541 U.S. at 50. *But see* Thomas Y. Davies, *Selective Originalism: Sorting out Which Aspects of* Giles's *Forfeiture Exception to Confrontation Were or Were Not "Established at the Time of the Founding,"* 13 Lewis & Clark L. Rev. 605, 628 (2009) (noting that "it does not appear that [Sir Walter] Raleigh explicitly framed his objection in terms of the lost opportunity for cross-examination").

109. *Crawford,* 541 U.S. at 53–54 (emphasis added).

110. *See* Hensley v. Roden, 755 F.3d 724, 732 (1st Cir. 2014) (noting that the "threshold question" in Confrontation Clause claims is "whether the challenged statement is testimonial") (internal citations omitted); United States v. Lyons, 740 F.3d 702, 719–20 (1st Cir. 2014) (noting that the Confrontation Clause does not confer a "general right to cross-examine the source of all evidence introduced at trial" because it only applies to testimonial evidence such that introducing a nontestimonial directory of customers and agents of a gambling business at trial did not violate the Confrontation Clause).

failed to define testimonial statements,[111] it clarified that "[w]hatever else the term covers, it applies at a minimum to prior testimony at a preliminary hearing, before a grand jury, or at a former trial; and to police interrogations."[112] *Crawford* also contained dicta identifying, but not adopting, three possible definitions. The narrowest would be limited to statements "contained in formalized testimonial materials, such as affidavits, custodial examinations, prior testimony, or confessions."[113] A second definition (suggested by the *Crawford* petitioner) would expand "testimonial statements" to include all out-of-court statements that are the functional equivalent of ex parte in-court testimony such as "affidavits, custodial examinations, prior testimony that the defendant was unable to cross-examine, or similar pretrial statements that declarants would reasonably expect to be used prosecutorially."[114] Finally, the third and broadest definition (suggested in an amicus brief filed by the National Association of Criminal Defense Lawyers) would include all statements "made under circumstances that would lead an objective witness reasonably to believe that the statement would be available for use at a later trial."[115] As discussed herein, the Court subsequently relies on this third definition, although the two alternatives have never been explicitly rejected.

---

111. *Crawford*, 541 U.S. at 68 ("We leave for another day any effort to spell out a comprehensive definition of 'testimonial'").

112. *Id.* As Professor Eileen Scallen observed, "[t]he clear losers in the *Crawford* upheaval are the courts, especially the state trial court judges who are responsible for the lion's share of criminal trials in this country. State trial court judges struggle to apply the almost perversely cryptic formulations of 'testimonial hearsay' emanating from the Supreme Court to the messy real-life factual contexts that trial courts face every day." Scallen, *supra* note 99, at 1572–73. *But see* United States v. Tull-Abreu, 921 F.3d 294, 306 (1st Cir. 2019) (citations omitted) ("It is axiomatic that the confrontation clause does not come into play where a potential witness neither testifies nor provides evidence at trial. None of the five former patients that Tull-Abreu points to were called as witnesses by the prosecution or provided evidence at trial. Tull-Abreu was free to call them but chose not to do so. His Sixth Amendment rights were not violated.").

113. *Crawford*, 541 U.S. at 51–52.

114. *Id.*

115. *Id.*

V. The Right to Confrontation from 2004 to the Present: The *Crawford* Doctrine in the Federal and State Courts

A. A New Focus on the Primary Purpose of the Interrogation and the Ongoing Emergency Exception

Just two years after *Crawford*, the Court decided *Davis v. Washington* and its consolidated companion case *Hammon v. Indiana*.[116] Both cases were factually distinct from *Crawford* because the alleged victims made their out-of-court statements, not in the relative calm of the police station interrogation room, but (as many witness statements are made) during or immediately following violent crimes.

According to the *Davis* Court, statements are nontestimonial (i.e., do not raise confrontation concerns) under *Crawford* when they were made "under circumstances objectively indicating that the primary purpose of interrogation is to enable police assistance to meet an ongoing emergency."[117] In contrast, statements are testimonial (i.e., require confrontation) "when the circumstances objectively indicate that there is no such ongoing emergency, and that the primary purpose of the interrogation is to establish or prove past events potentially relevant to later criminal prosecutions."[118] By applying this refinement to the *Crawford* standard, the Court concluded in *Davis* that a frantic mid-assault 911 call by the victim is nontestimonial,[119] but in *Hammon* that a "battery affidavit" (prepared by the victim

---

116. Davis v. Washington, 547 U.S. 813 (2006).

117. *Id.* at 813–14.

118. *Id.* at 814. For an interesting discussion about how *Davis* creates the risk that police will mask their crime scene interrogations to focus on emergency matters while seeking accusatorial statements, see Scott G. Stewar, *The Right of Confrontation, Ongoing Emergencies, and the Violent-Perpetuator-at-Large Problem*, 61 STAN. L. REV. 751, 765–66 (2008). *See also* State v. Williams, 52 A.3d 911, 918 (Me. 2012) (statements made in "private, intimate conversations" were nontestimonial because they were not intended "to establish facts that could reasonably be anticipated to be used at a later trial").

119. *Davis*, 547 U.S. at 817. *See also* People v. Kenyon, 970 N.Y.S.2d 638, 640–43 (N.Y. App. Div. 2013) (victim's statement to 911 operator explaining that defendant, her boyfriend, had kicked down the door of her apartment and refused to leave was nontestimonial because its purpose was "to enable the police to meet an ongoing emergency and apprehend the perpetrator, not to provide evidence for later prosecution") (internal citation omitted); Hunt v. State, 218 P.3d 516 (Okla. Crim. App. 2009) (statements to 911 operator made weeks before the victim's death were testimonial); Commonwealth v. Nesbitt, 892 N.E.2d 299 (Mass. 2008) (victim's statements to 911 operator seeking medical help and identifying her attacker were nontestimonial because they were immediately post-assault and the police needed to know the location of the suspect).

post-assault during a secured-scene kitchen table police interview while the suspect was detained nearby) was testimonial.[120]

B. Defining the Primary Purpose of the Interrogation or Statement and the Ongoing Emergency Exception

To date, the Court has never answered the question of how judges should determine the objective primary purpose of a statement or interrogation. Five years after *Davis*, in *Michigan v. Bryant*,[121] the Court revisited the issue in a case involving police interrogation of a critically injured crime victim as he lay on the street bleeding from gunshot wounds, just hours before he died.[122] Justice Sotomayor wrote for a *Bryant* majority that included Chief Justice Roberts and Justices Kennedy, Breyer, and Alito.[123] The bottom line is that the *Bryant* Court held that the victim's statements identifying the defendant as the shooter were nontestimonial, so their admission at trial did not violate the Confrontation Clause. But the analytic path to the Court's conclusion was abstruse.

1. The Dual/Combined Objective Primary Purpose of the Interrogation

According to the *Bryant* majority, their decision rested on a finding that the objective primary purpose of the police interrogation of the victim was *not* to establish past events potentially relevant to a criminal prosecution. This conclusion was the result of a two-part inquiry. On the threshold question of *whose* purpose should govern, Justice Sotomayor explained that courts should use "a combined inquiry that accounts for both the declarant and the interrogator,"[124] because this dual focus "ameliorates problems that could arise from looking solely to one participant."[125] However, the Court undermined the clarity of its own guidance by simultaneously stating that the "relevant inquiry is not the subjective or actual purpose of the individuals in a

---

120. *Davis*, 547 U.S. at 829–30. However, because the Supreme Court found that the facts of *Davis* clearly indicated a nontestimonial purpose and the facts of *Hammon* clearly indicated a testimonial purpose, the justices did not address the problem of facts that reveal ambiguous, multiple, or conflicting nontestimonial and testimonial purposes. This problem would arise five years later in *Michigan v. Bryant*, 562 U.S. 344 (2011).

121. *Bryant*, 562 U.S. 344.

122. *Id.* at 348.

123. Justice Thomas concurred in the result, Justices Scalia and Ginsburg dissented separately, and Justice Kagan recused herself.

124. *Id.* at 367.

125. *Id.* at 368.

particular encounter, but rather the purpose that reasonable participants would have had, as ascertained from the individuals' statements and actions and the circumstances in which the encounter occurred."[126] Hence, post-*Bryant* courts are left with the unenviable task of gleaning an objective primary combined purpose from "the statements and actions of both the declarant and interrogators,"[127] including (1) "the contents of both the questions and answers,"[128] (2) whether the statement was made during an "ongoing emergency," and (3) the "informality of an encounter between a victim and police."[129]

In 2017, the Seventh Circuit engaged in an enlightening and rather entertaining *Bryant* analysis of a police informant's statement: "That was a big ass pistol."[130] Applying *Bryant*, the court considered and then rejected the possibilities that the informant's out-of-court statement was intended to prompt the suspect to say something admissible or to warn a police officer that the suspect had a gun.[131] Ultimately the appellate court simply gave up, concluding that for some nontestimonial statements, the court "need not say with certainty what the purpose was; indeed, there may have been 'no discernible purpose at all.'"[132]

Given the importance of *Bryant* to the developing confrontation analysis, the Court's objective primary combined inquiry is flabbergasting in its opacity.[133] Courts routinely balk when asked to divine past intent; but after *Bryant*, courts face the Herculean task of both

---

126. *Id.* at 360.

127. *Id.* at 367.

128. *Id.* at 368.

129. *Id.* at 366.

130. United States v. Amaya, 828 F.3d 518, 529 (7th Cir. 2019).

131. *Id.*

132. *Id.*

133. *See* Jeffery Bellin, *The Incredible Shrinking Confrontation Clause*, 92 B.U. L. Rev. 1865, 1868 (2012) (noting that "the *Bryant* Court erected a framework for analyzing 'primary purpose' that appears just as malleable as the *Roberts* test—a flexibility that, if *Roberts* is any guide, is more likely to favor the prosecution (by admitting hearsay) than the defense (by excluding it)" and that "[t]ogether, *Bryant* and *Davis* work a dramatic curtailment of the post-*Crawford* confrontation right"); Craig M. Bradley, *Further Confusion Over Confrontation*, 47 Trial 52, 53 (2011) (arguing that in *Bryant*, the Court "dug itself deeper into the hole of confusion created by its earlier decisions concerning the Confrontation Clause in *Crawford v. Washington* and *Davis v. Washington*"); Steven C. Berlowitz, *Hijacking Justice: Assessing the Emergency Driven Analysis of Confrontation Jurisprudence*, 36 Cardozo L. Rev. 1191, 1193. (2015) (arguing that "[t]he tendency of the emergency assessment to drive the [confrontation] analysis, in the context of 911 calls and crime scene interviews, is precisely what makes the assessment so difficult").

inferring and reconciling the objective primary combined purposes of two or more people who often have very different motives and perspectives. As Justice Scalia persuasively argued in his dissent, which addressed only the police interrogation circumstances at issue, "[s]orting out the primary purpose of a declarant with mixed motives is sometimes difficult[;] . . . [b]ut adding in the mixed motives of the police only compounds the problem."[134]

2. *Myriad Possible Ongoing Emergency Determinants*

In the wake of *Bryant*, the nature and circumstances of any alleged ongoing emergency have enhanced constitutional significance.[135] As the Sixth Circuit noted in 2017, after *Bryant*, "statements made during police interrogation are testimonial when the circumstances objectively indicate that the primary purpose of the interrogation is to prove past events potentially relevant to later criminal prosecution and non-testimonial when the circumstances objectively indicate that the primary purpose of the interrogation is to enable police to meet an ongoing emergency."[136] Although this standard can be made to sound simple, even in *Bryant*, the Court acknowledged its complexities, because the existence of an ongoing emergency is not determinative[137] but merely "an important factor—that informs the ultimate inquiry regarding the 'primary purpose' of the investigation."[138]

---

134. Justice Scalia elaborated on this argument:

> The Court claims one affirmative virtue for its focus on the purposes of both the declarant and the police: It "ameliorates problems that . . . arise" when declarants have "mixed motives." I am at a loss to know how. . . . Now courts will have to sort through two sets of mixed motives to determine the primary purpose of an interrogation. And the Court's solution creates a mixed-motive problem where (under the proper theory) it does not exist—viz., where the police and the declarant each have one motive, but those motives conflict. The Court does not provide an answer to this glaringly obvious problem, probably because it does not have one.

Bryant, 562 U.S. at 383 (Scalia, J., dissenting).

135. *See, e.g.*, United States v. McKinney, 713 F. App'x 910, 915 n.4 (relying on Bryant as support for the conclusion that "[g]enerally, where the purpose of a police interrogation is not to meet an ongoing emergency, statements made during a police interrogation are testimonial").

136. Dorsey v. Cook, 677 F. App'x 265, 267 (6th Cir. 2017).

137. *Bryant*, 562 U.S. at 366 (majority opinion) ("[O]ur discussion of the Michigan Supreme Court's misunderstanding of what *Davis* meant by 'ongoing emergency' should not be taken to imply that the existence *vel non* of an ongoing emergency is dispositive of the testimonial inquiry.").

138. *Id. But see* State v. Bruffey, 745 S.E.2d 540, 550–51 (W. Va. 2013) (although there was no ongoing emergency, out-of-court statements by unavailable witness to police that

Bryant has also been understood to limit testimonial statements to those for which, "in light of all the circumstances, viewed objectively, the primary purpose of the conversation was to create an out-of-court substitute for trial testimony."[139]

As the lower courts have been discovering for nearly a decade, *Bryant* has increased confrontation confusion.[140] As a threshold matter, *Bryant* does not even specify whether nontestimonial statements must be made during an *actual* ongoing emergency, or if a declarant's and/or the police officer's reasonable (but mistaken) belief that an emergency is ongoing governs.[141] If judges must decide whether an *actual*

---

he saw the defendant's car near the scene of the crime a few days before the crime took place were nontestimonial statements because they were "not introduced to inculpate Mr. Bruffey," but were "simply part of the *res gestae*" of the police officer's investigation "address[ing] an ancillary and uncontested fact," rather than "directed at establishing the facts of a past crime").

139. United States v. Hanro, 922 F.3d 1272, 1287 (2019) (citations omitted) (out-of-court statement was nontestimonial because, at the time it was made, "no future prosecution was on the horizon" so the declarant "had no reason to believe that his statements . . . would ever be used in court").

140. *See, e.g.*, United States v. Stimler, 864 F.3d 253, 272 (3d Cir. 2017) (citing *Bryant* as support for finding that a "statement is testimonial only if it meets two requirements: (1) it is a solemn declaration or affirmation made for the purpose of establishing or proving some fact; and (2) it was made primarily for the purpose of proving past events potentially relevant to later criminal prosecution" (citations omitted)); Commonwealth v. Smith, 951 N.E.2d 674, 682 (Mass. 2011) (attempting to understand and apply the *Bryant* Court's "nonexhaustive list of circumstances to consider when determining whether an emergency exists: (1) whether an armed assailant poses a substantial threat to the public at large; (2) the type of weapon that has been employed; (3) the severity of the victim's injuries; (4) the formality of the interrogation; and (5) the involved parties' statements and actions" along with "additional considerations includ[ing] whether the victim's safety is at substantial imminent risk"); Commonwealth v. Middlemiss, 989 N.E.2d 871, 878 (Mass. 2013) (factors that bear on whether there is an ongoing emergency include (1) whether the assailant is armed and is a threat to the victim or the public, (2) the type of weapon that was used, and (3) the severity of the victim's injuries or medical condition). *See generally* Moreno, *Finding Nino: Justice Scalia's Confrontation Clause Legacy from Its (Glorious) Beginning to (Bitter) End,* 44 U. Akron L. Rev. 1212, 124548 (2011) (explaining that the *Bryant* Court's "primary purpose" test is virtually inoperable and poorly supported by precedent).

141. *Bryant,* 562 U.S. at 370 ("[t]he existence of an emergency or the parties' perception that an emergency is ongoing is among the most important circumstances that courts must take into account in determining whether an interrogation is testimonial"). *See* Wright v. State, 434 S.W.3d 401, 408–09 (Ark. Ct. App. 2014) (statements to officer following a domestic violence incident were testimonial because an objectively reasonable person could not conclude there was an ongoing emergency because the crime was not committed by a stranger, defendant had already fled, and there was no indication that defendant posed a danger to the public or the "victim" (despite all other indicia); State v. Lewis, 125 So. 3d 1252, 1261 (La. Ct. App. 2013) ("Statements are testimonial when the

emergency was ongoing when the statement was made (as the *Davis* Court clearly assumed),[142] how will they decide? Instead of guidance, the *Bryant* Court simply alighted on myriad factors that might be used to determine whether there was an emergency and whether it was ongoing, including:

- the nature of the dispute;[143]
- the scope of the potential harm to the victim;[144]
- the threat to additional identifiable victims;[145]
- the existence of a more generalized threat to the public;[146]
- the suspect's choice of weapon;[147] and
- whether the suspect remained "at large" or had been located (but not yet apprehended) by the police and/or any other "first responders."[148]

In addition to juggling those six criteria, the *Bryant* Court further tasked judges with the job of assessing the "medical condition of the victim . . . to the extent that it sheds light on the ability of the victim to have any purpose at all in responding to police questions and on the likelihood that any purpose formed would be a testimonial

---

circumstances objectively indicate that there is no such ongoing emergency, and the primary purpose of the interrogation is to establish or prove past events potentially relevant to later criminal prosecution"). *But see* Ohio v. Clark, 576 U.S. 237, 245 (2015) ("the existence *vel non* of an ongoing emergency is not the touchstone of the testimonial inquiry" but instead, "whether an ongoing emergency exists is simply one factor . . . that informs the ultimate inquiry regarding the 'primary purpose' of an interrogation.") (citations omitted).

142. The Court's analysis of the "ongoing emergency" in both cases focused solely on what was actually happening at the time. *See* Davis v. Washington, 547 U.S. 813, 813–14 (2006). In contrast, more recently in *Ohio v. Clark,* 576 U.S. 237 (2015), the Court found that a child's statements made to his preschool teachers at school constituted an "ongoing emergency" based on the fact that the teachers were attempting to ascertain the source of his injuries and how best to secure his safety.

143. *Bryant,* 562 U.S. at 377 (noting that the emergency was likely to be ongoing because the victim "did not indicate any possible motive for the shooting, and thereby gave no reason to think that the shooter would not shoot again if he arrived on the scene").

144. *Id.* at 372 ("[T]he scope of an emergency in terms of its threat to individuals other than the initial assailant and victim will often depend on the type of dispute involved").

145. *Id.* at 373.

146. *Id.* at 363 ("An assessment of whether an emergency that threatens the police and public is ongoing cannot narrowly focus on whether the threat solely to the first victim has been neutralized because the threat to first responders and to public may continue.").

147. *Id.* at 364 ("[T]he duration and scope of an emergency may depend in part on the type of weapon employed.").

148. *Id.*

one."[149] As the beloved Bubby of one coauthor would have said, "Oh vey iz mir" (Yiddish for "woe is me").

In 2011, the Court decided *Bullcoming v. New Mexico*,[150] which is discussed in more detail in the following sections on expert testimony.[151] In *Bullcoming*, decided just months after *Bryant*, the four dissenting justices reflect the prevailing view—that seven years after *Crawford*, the Court was doing little to resolve "the elusive distinction between utterances aimed at proving past events, and those calculated to help police keep the peace."[152]

C. The Importance of the Formality of the Statement and Interrogation

In *Crawford* and the post-*Crawford* cases, the Court has repeatedly considered the constitutional significance of the formality of the statement and, where applicable, the interrogation. As discussed previously, as a conceptual matter, a formal statement makes an out-of-court declarant more like an in-court witness. At the practice level, unlike "ongoing emergencies" or a speaker's "objective intent," formality is an attractive confrontation criterion because it is typically relatively easy for judges to ascertain.

The *Crawford* Court held that "[a]n accuser who makes a formal statement to government officers bears testimony in a sense that a person who makes a casual remark to an acquaintance does not."[153] Building on this distinction, the *Davis* Court noted that "formality is

149. *Id.* at 364–65. This final factor might negate consideration of the preceding seven factors, if a court determines that (despite all other indicia that an emergency was not ongoing) the victim's medical condition rendered her incapable of formulating a testimonial purpose.

150. Bullcoming v. New Mexico, 564 U.S. 647 (2011).

151. *See infra* section VII.

152. *Bullcoming*, 564 U.S. at 678.

153. *Bryant*, 562 U.S. at 354 (quoting Crawford v. Washington, 541 U.S. 36, 51 (2004)). This conclusion is not undermined by the *Bryant* majority's confusing assertion that if the interrogation was "solely directed at establishing the facts of a past crime, in order to identify (or provide evidence to convict) the perpetrator," the resulting victim/witness statement will be akin to a "solemn declaration or affirmation." *Id.* at 353. The notion that all statements to the police regarding past crimes are, by definition, "formalized" is effectively refuted by Justice Thomas. He argued that "[t]he possibility that an oral declaration of past fact to a police officer, if false, could result in legal consequences to the speaker may render honesty in casual conversations with police officers important. It does not, however, render those conversations solemn or formal in the ordinary meanings of those terms." Davis v. Washington, 547 U.S. 813, 838 n.3 (2006) (Thomas, J., concurring in part and dissenting in part).

indeed central to testimonial utterance"[154] and specifically contrasted Sylvia Crawford's post-*Miranda* stationhouse custodial interrogation with Michelle McCottry's frantic mid-assault 911 call.[155] According to the Court, "the difference in the level of formality [between the two interrogations] is striking."[156] In *Crawford*, the declarant "was responding calmly, at the station house, to a series of questions, with the officer interrogator taping and making notes of her answers."[157] In contrast, in *Davis*, the declarant provided "frantic answers . . . over the phone, in an environment that was not tranquil, or even (as far as any reasonable 911 operator could make out) safe."[158] Thus, during informal interrogation, McCottry "was not acting as a *witness;* she was not testifying . . . [and] [w]hat she said was not 'a weaker substitute for live testimony' at trial."[159]

More recently, a majority of the Court agreed that the formality of statement and the interrogation (if one occurred) is always relevant to the confrontation inquiry.[160] The *Bryant* Court addressed formality in two ways. As a general matter, the Court found that "the most important instances in which the Clause restricts the introduction of out-of-court statements are those in which state actors are involved in a *formal,* out-of-court interrogation of a witness to obtain evidence for trial."[161] According to the *Bryant* majority, *formal* out-of-court interrogations are the most egregious confrontation violations because "the basic purpose of the Confrontation Clause was to 'target' the sort of 'abuses' exemplified at the notorious treason trial of Sir Walter

---

154. *Davis*, 547 U.S. at 830 n.5 (majority opinion)

155. *Id.* at 828.

156. *Id.* at 827.

157. *Id.*

158. *Id.*

159. *Id.* at 828. Most recently, in Ohio v. Clark, Justice Alito specifically explained that "a formal station-house interrogation, like the questioning in *Crawford*, is more likely to provoke testimonial statements, while less formal questioning is less likely to reflect a primary purpose aimed at obtaining testimonial evidence against the accused. (citations omitted). 576 U.S. 237, 245 (2015). Justice Alito's recent concerns echo a near-identical discussion of formality by Justices Thomas and Alito (each concurring separately) in *Giles v. California*, 554 U.S. 353, 377–81 (2008).

160. Michigan v. Bryant, 562 U.S. 344, 366 (2011). Formality concerns are also increasingly evident among the lower courts. *See, e.g.*, Helms v. State, 38 So. 3d 182 (Fla. Dist. Ct. App. 2010) (statement to undercover police officer deemed nontestimonial because it lacked formality and because the declarant did not know that her statement might be used in criminal prosecution); People v. Holmes, 150 Cal. Rptr. 3d 914, 915 (Cal. Ct. App. 2012) (forensic data and reports relied on by DNA experts were nontestimonial because they were unsworn and uncertified records of objective fact and thus lacked "formality").

161. *Bryant*, 562 U.S. at 358 (emphasis added).

Raleigh."[162] More specifically, the Court found that the Michigan Supreme Court had "too readily dismissed the informality of the circumstances in this case,"[163] despite the fact that "the questioning . . . [had] occurred in an exposed, public area, prior to the arrival of emergency medical services, and in a disorganized fashion."[164] According to Justice Sotomayor, who wrote for the majority, this "informality suggests that the interrogators' primary purpose was simply to address what they perceived to be an ongoing emergency"[165] and that "the circumstances lacked any formality that would have alerted . . . [the victim] to or focused him on the possible future prosecutorial use of his statements."[166]

Finally, although both *Melendez-Diaz v. Massachusetts*[167] and *Bullcoming v. New Mexico*[168] addressed the general question of a defendant's right to confront prosecution-sponsored experts,[169] the perceived formality of the proffered out-of-court statement was determinative in the first case and significant in the second. In *Melendez-Diaz,* Justice Thomas's fifth-vote concurrence was based solely on his conclusion that the affidavits at issue were formalized testimonial statements. Similarly, the Court in *Bullcoming* specifically found that even though the laboratory report was not in the form of an affidavit, it was adequately "formalized in a signed document."[170] Of course, if the Court increases its reliance on formality to determine whether a statement is testimonial, this approach (because it encompasses a smaller group of statements and because government agencies can avoid cross-examination of their employees by switching to less formal types of reporting) would effectively narrow the scope of defendants' constitutional protections.

---

162. *Id.* at 357–58.

163. *Id.* at 366.

164. *Id.*

165. *Id.* at 377.

166. *Id.* at 379 (Thomas, J., concurring) (internal quotations marks omitted). Justice Thomas, in his concurring opinion, commended the *Bryant* majority for highlighting the fact that the victim "interacted with the police under highly informal circumstances as he bled from a fatal gunshot wound," which "did not result in formalized testimonial materials such as a deposition or affidavit, and bore no indication of solemnity." *Id.* at 1167 (Thomas, J., concurring).

167. Melendez-Diaz v. Massachusetts, 557 U.S. 305 (2009).

168. Bullcoming v. New Mexico, 564 U.S. 647 (2011).

169. *See infra* section VII.

170. *Bullcoming*, 564 U.S. at 678 (Kennedy, J., dissenting).

D. Reliability Redux

Finally, in a rather strange bit of dictum, the *Bryant* Court appeared to revive some of the reliability concerns that *Crawford* resoundingly rejected. The Court, in two different contexts, raised concerns of evidentiary reliability.

First, the *Bryant* Court construed the *Davis* ongoing emergency exception as principally motivated by the "implicit" idea that people tend to speak truthfully during emergencies: "[B]ecause the prospect of fabrication in statements given for the primary purpose of resolving an ongoing emergency is presumably significantly diminished, the Confrontation Clause does not require such statements to be subject to the crucible of cross-examination."[171] This assumption (borrowed from the rationale for the "excited utterance" hearsay exception) is properly referred to as "implicit," because the *Davis* Court did not actually address the evidentiary reliability of either statement.

Second, the *Bryant* Court assumes that some out-of-court statements—where the objective primary purpose of the investigation was *not* to resolve an ongoing emergency—do not raise confrontation concerns.[172] According to the Court, if these statements are proffered by the prosecutor, "in making the primary purpose determination, standard rules of hearsay, designed to identify some statements as reliable, will be relevant."[173] The Court did not further define which specific out-of-court statements, or which type of out-of-court statements (not made to resolve an ongoing emergency), do not raise confrontation concerns. These opaque references to evidentiary reliability could threaten the *Crawford* doctrine if a future court finds that, in some as yet undefined set of circumstances, the admissibility of some testimonial statements may be determined using a pre-*Crawford* reliability/hearsay analysis.[174]

171. *Bryant*, 562 U.S. at 361.

172. "But there may be other circumstances, aside from ongoing emergencies, when a statement is not procured with a primary purpose of creating an out-of-court substitute for trial testimony." *Id.* at 358.

173. *Id.* at 358–59.

174. This language is quoted in Ohio v. Clark, 576 U.S. 237, 245–46 (2015) ("[U]nder our precedents, a statement cannot fall within the Confrontation Clause unless its primary purpose was testimonial. 'Where no such primary purpose exists, the admissibility of a statement is the concern of state and federal rules of evidence, not the Confrontation Clause.'") (quoting Michigan v. Bryant, 562 U.S. 344, 359 (2011), which suggests that a majority of the current Court would deem some nonemergency statements nontestimonial). *See also* State v. Gleason, 329 P.3d 1102 (Kan. 2014) (witness's post-arrest statements made to police officer when entering into plea agreement were testimonial hearsay governed by the Confrontation Clause rather than statutory hearsay exceptions); United

E. The U.S. Supreme Court Revisits the Primary Purpose Test and the Ongoing Emergency Requirement

In 2015, in *Ohio v. Clark*,[175] the Supreme Court addressed whether admission of out-of-court statements made by a three-year-old boy ("L.P.") to his teacher describing physical abuse at the hands of his mother's boyfriend violated the Confrontation Clause. L.P. did not testify at trial or during any pretrial hearing because, under Ohio State law, children under ten are presumed to be too young to provide competent trial testimony.[176]

1. Statements Made to People Other Than Police Officers

The *Clark* Court confronted a variety of questions relevant to future confrontation cases. On the threshold question of whether statements made to anyone other than a police officer might be testimonial, Justice Alito, writing for the majority, offered the following guidance:

> In this case, we consider statements made to preschool teachers, not the police. We are therefore presented with the question we have repeatedly reserved: whether statements to persons other than law enforcement officers are subject to the Confrontation Clause. Because at least some statements to individuals who are not law enforcement officers could conceivably raise confrontation concerns, we decline to adopt a categorical rule excluding them from the Sixth Amendment's reach. Nevertheless, such statements are much less likely to be testimonial than statements to law enforcement officers.[177]

States v. Smalls, 752 F.3d 1227, 1242 (10th Cir. 2014) (the Confrontation Clause does not apply to nontestimonial statements and allows "their admission even if they lack indicia of reliability") (citations omitted); United States v. Charles, 722 F.3d 1319, 1327–28 (11th Cir. 2013) (rejecting the argument that more reliable out-of-court statements are more likely to be admissible, because *Crawford* "rejected reliability as too narrow a test for protecting against Confrontation Clause violations. . . . [because] the Confrontation Clause commands, not that evidence be reliable, but that reliability be assessed in a particular manner: by testing in the crucible of cross examination") (internal citations omitted).

175. Ohio v. Clark, 576 U.S. 237 (2015).

176. *Id.* at 241–42 ("Under Ohio law, children younger than ten years old are incompetent to testify if they 'appear incapable of receiving just impressions of the facts and transactions respecting which they are examined, or of relating them truly.'").

177. *Id.* at 238. The *Clark* Court elaborated on the special nature of a student-teacher relationship as follows:

> [A]lthough we decline to adopt a rule that statements to individuals who are not law enforcement officers are categorically outside the Sixth Amendment, the fact that L.P. was speaking to his teachers remains highly relevant. Courts must evalu-

So statements made to people other than the police can raise confrontation concerns.

The Supreme Court also addressed the related question of the "formality" of the out-of-court statements; applying the general rule that informal questioning is less likely to raise confrontation concerns because it is "less likely to reflect a primary purpose aimed at obtaining testimonial evidence against the accused."[178] Thus, the *Clark* Court concluded that the out-of-court statements at issue were "informal and spontaneous," because the teachers had inquired about apparent injuries "immediately upon discovering them, in the informal setting of a preschool lunchroom and classroom, and they did so precisely as any concerned citizen would talk to a child who might be the victim of abuse."[179] As in other recent cases discussed herein, *Clark* suggests that formality will play an ongoing role in future confrontation determinations.

2. The "Primary Purpose" Test

The *Clark* Court relied on *Crawford*, along with the more recent "combined primary purpose" test articulated in *Michigan v. Bryant*,[180] to determine whether the out-of-court statements were testimonial. According to Justice Alito, if "the primary purpose of an interrogation is to respond to an 'ongoing emergency,' its purpose is not to create a record for trial and thus is not within the scope of the [Confrontation] Clause."[181] However, the Court clarified that the existence of an ongoing emergency "is not the touchstone of the testimonial inquiry."[182] Instead, "whether an ongoing emergency exists is simply one factor . . . that informs the ultimate inquiry regarding the 'primary purpose' of an interrogation."[183] Using this test, the Court held that the

---

> ate challenged statements in context, and part of that context is the questioner's identity. Statements made to someone who is not principally charged with uncovering and prosecuting criminal behavior are significantly less likely to be testimonial than statements given to law enforcement officers. It is common sense that the relationship between a student and his teacher is very different from that between a citizen and the police.

Id. at 249 (citations omitted).

178. *Id.* at 245–247 (citing Michigan v. Bryant, 562 U.S. 344, 366, 377 (2011)).

179. *Id.*

180. Michigan v. Bryant, 562 U.S. 344 (2011).

181. *Clark*, 576 U.S. at 254 (quoting *Bryant*, 562 U.S. at 358).

182. *Id.* (quoting *Bryant*, 562 U.S. at 374).

183. *Id.* (quoting *Bryant*, 562 U.S. at 366).

"statements occurred in the context of an ongoing emergency involving suspected child abuse."[184] The teachers' "immediate concern was to protect a vulnerable child who needed help"[185] and "their questions and L.P.'s [the child, alleged victim's] answers were primarily aimed at identifying and ending the threat."[186] This conclusion is bolstered by the finding that "[t]here is no indication that the primary purpose of the conversation was to gather evidence for Clark's prosecution."[187] It is significant that the *Clark* Court effectively expanded the definition of an "ongoing emergency" beyond the scope initially drawn in *Davis*. Previously, the Court had emphasized the urgency of the emergency (i.e., the fact that a 911 call was made while the domestic assault was ongoing[188] or that a gunshot victim lay bleeding on the sidewalk).[189] In *Clark*, L.P. was in no immediate danger at the time the teachers questioned him in an effort to identify his abuser, although their clear objective was to protect the child victim from future harm.

3. Testimonial Statements by Young Children

The *Clark* Court also addressed the specific question of testimonial statements by young children. According to Justice Alito,

> Statements by very young children will rarely, if ever, implicate the Confrontation Clause. Few preschool students understand the details of our criminal justice system. Rather, "[r]esearch on children's understanding of the legal system finds that" young children "have little understanding of prosecution." . . . Thus, it is extremely unlikely that a 3-year-old child in L.P.'s position would intend his

---

184. *Id.* at 246.

185. *Id.*

186. *Id.*

187. *Id.*

188. Davis v. Washington, 547 U.S. 813, 827 (2006) ("Moreover, any reasonable listener would recognize that McCottry (unlike Sylvia Crawford) was facing an ongoing emergency. Although one might call 911 to provide a narrative report of a crime absent any imminent danger, McCottry's call was plainly a call for help against bona fide physical threat.").

189. Michigan v. Bryant, 562 U.S. 344, 363 (2011) ("Domestic violence cases like Davis and Hammon often have a narrower zone of potential victims than cases involving threats to public safety. An assessment of whether an emergency that threatens the police and public is ongoing cannot narrowly focus on whether the threat solely to the first victim has been neutralized because the threat to the first responders and public may continue.").

> statements to be a substitute for trial testimony. On the contrary, a young child in these circumstances would simply want the abuse to end, would want to protect other victims, or would have no discernible purpose at all.[190]

These common-sense findings regarding the capacity of very young declarants to make testimonial statements should guide future courts.

Finally, the *Clark* majority noted that, as a historical matter "there is strong evidence that statements made in circumstances similar to those facing L.P. and his teachers were admissible at common law."[191] In Justice Alito's view, it is

> highly doubtful that statements like L.P.'s ever would have been understood to raise Confrontation Clause concerns. Neither Crawford nor any of the cases that it has produced has mounted evidence that the adoption of the Confrontation Clause was understood to require the exclusion of evidence that was regularly admitted in criminal cases at the time of the founding.[192]

While these conclusions add little to the decision, the Court seems intent on reiterating that *Crawford* did not supplant historical rules admitting certain types of hearsay evidence.

4. The Concurring Opinions

Justice Scalia, joined by Justice Ginsburg, concurred in the *Clark* decision. In their view, the case should have been simple. L.P.'s "primary purpose here was certainly not to invoke the coercive machinery of the State against Clark."[193] Moreover, the teachers did not "have the primary purpose of establishing facts for later prosecution," but instead "sought to ensure that they did not deliver an abused child back into imminent harm."[194] Additionally, the teachers' conversation with L.P. lacked "the requisite solemnity necessary for testimonial statements."[195] Taken together, these facts clearly establish that the statements at issue were nontestimonial.

The concurring justices wrote separately to object to "the Court's shoveling of fresh dirt upon the Sixth Amendment right of

190. *Clark*, 576 U.S. at 248 (internal citations omitted).
191. *Id.*
192. *Id.*
193. *Id.* at 251 (Scalia, J., concurring).
194. *Id.*
195. *Id.* at 252.

confrontation so recently rescued from the grave in *Crawford v. Washington*."[196] They specifically objected to the majority's characterization of *Crawford* as "nothing more than 'adopt[ing] a different approach,'—as though Crawford is only a matter of twiddle-dum twiddle-dee preference, and the old, pre-*Crawford* 'approach' remains available?"[197] In their view, the majority's mischaracterization of the Court's 2004 landmark decision overruling *Ohio v. Roberts* demonstrated Justice Alito's "hostility to *Crawford* and its progeny, perhaps aggravated by [his] inability to muster the votes to overrule them."[198]

Justices Scalia and Ginsburg also objected to "the opinion's statement that the primary-purpose test is merely *one* of several heretofore unmentioned conditions ('necessary, but not always sufficient') that must be satisfied before the Clause's protections apply."[199] In their view, the majority's finding "is absolutely false, and has no support in our opinions" because:

> [t]he Confrontation Clause categorically entitles a defendant *to be confronted with the witnesses against him*; and the primary-purpose test sorts out, among the many people who interact with the police informally, *who is acting as a witness and who is not*. Those who fall into the former category bear testimony, and are therefore acting as "witnesses," subject to the right of confrontation. There are no other mysterious requirements that the Court declines to name.[200]

Finally, Justices Scalia and Ginsburg complained that the majority incorrectly asserted that "future defendants, and future Confrontation Clause majorities, must provide 'evidence that the adoption of the Confrontation Clause was understood to require the exclusion of evidence that was regularly admitted in criminal cases at the time of the founding.'"[201] On this important point, the justices argued, the majority "gets the burden precisely backwards—which is of course precisely the idea" because "[t]he burden is upon the prosecutor who seeks to introduce evidence over this bar to prove a long-established practice of introducing *specific* kinds of evidence, such as dying declarations."[202]

---

196. *Id.* at 252.
197. *Id.*
198. *Id.*
199. *Id.*
200. *Id.* at 253 (emphasis in original).
201. *Id.*
202. *Id.* (emphasis in original).

Justice Thomas wrote his own *Clark* concurrence to reiterate his long-held view that only "extrajudicial statements that bear sufficient indicia of solemnity . . . fall within the original meaning of testimony."[203] Justice Thomas also noted that, for statements that are not made to police officers, he "would use the same test for statements to private persons that I have employed for statements to agents of law enforcement, assessing whether those statements bear sufficient indicia of solemnity to qualify as testimonial."[204] Although the *Clark* majority agreed in part, by finding that formality should play some role in the confrontation determination, to date a majority of the Court has never signed on to Justice Thomas's view that formality should be the single determinative criterion.

*5. Post-*Clark *Decisions in Child Witness Cases*

In the wake of *Clark*, courts continue to explore alternative means of satisfying the Confrontation Clause in child witness/alleged victim cases, with varying results. For example, in 2018 in *United States v. Carter*, the Ninth Circuit held that the Confrontation Clause was violated when the alleged child sex trafficking victim (now an adult unable to travel for medical reasons) was allowed to testify via video.[205] According to the court, "compelling adverse witnesses at trial to testify in the accused's presence thus enhances the accuracy of fact-finding at trial. . . . [as] does compelling witnesses to stand face to face with the jury as they tell their side of the story."[206] Under this broad understanding of confrontation, "any procedure that allows an adverse witness to testify remotely necessarily diminishes the profound truth-inducing effect upon a witness of standing in the presence of the person the witness accuses."[207] In contrast, in 2019 in *Lipsitz v. Nevada*,[208] the Nevada Supreme Court upheld the use of video testimony when the alleged victim was in a treatment program and would not be available for months and waiting for her would violate speedy trial concerns.[209] Under this narrower construction of confrontation protections, "the audiovisual transmission procedure

203. *Id.* at 255 (Thomas, J., concurring).

204. *Id.*

205. United States v. Carter, 907 F.3d 1199, 1202 (9th Cir. 2018) (testimony via two-way video of alleged child victim violated Confrontation Clause).

206. *Id.* at 1207 (citations omitted).

207. *Id.*

208. Lipsitz v. Nevada, 442 P.3d 138 (Nev. 2019).

209. *Id.*

. . . adequately ensure[s] the reliability of the testimony, as it allowed [the defendant] to cross-examine the victim and the jury could hear and observe the victim."[210] As these cases demonstrate, even post-*Crawford*, the scope of special exceptions to confrontation or special means of satisfying confrontation in cases involving alleged child victims remains in flux.[211]

VI. Forfeiture of the Right to Confrontation

In 2008, the Supreme Court in *Giles v. California*[212] squarely addressed the question of forfeiture of confrontation, although the Court had first applied the forfeiture doctrine more than a century earlier[213] and forfeiture was mentioned in both *Crawford* and *Davis*.[214] The prosecutor in *Giles* had introduced statements during the defendant's murder trial that had been made by the victim (defendant's former girlfriend) to the police. The victim's statements included defendant's threat to kill her if she cheated on him, made three weeks before her alleged murder.[215] On appeal, the defendant argued that admission of these statements violated his right to confrontation under *Crawford*.[216] The California Court of Appeals and the California Supreme Court disagreed, holding that the defendant had forfeited his right to confrontation under the state evidence rules by procuring the victim's unavailability at trial.[217]

---

210. *Id.*

211. *See infra* section V; *see also* People v. Brandon P., 10 N.E.3d 910, 919–20 (Ill. 2014) (the statements of an unavailable child witness made to a detective were testimonial because the purpose of the interview was to "establish or prove past events potentially relevant to later criminal prosecution").

212. Giles v. California, 554 U.S. 353 (2008).

213. *See* Reynolds v. United States, 98 U.S. 145, 158 (1897) ("The Constitution gives the accused the right to a trial at which he should be confronted with the witnesses against him; but if a witness is absent by [the accused's] wrongful procurement, he cannot complain if competent evidence is admitted to supply the place of that which he has kept away.").

214. *See* Davis v. Washington, 547 U.S. 813, 883 (2006) ("But when defendants seek to undermine the judicial process by procuring or coercing silence from witnesses and victims, the Sixth Amendment does not require courts to acquiesce. While defendants have no duty to assist the State in proving their guilt, they *do* have the duty to refrain from acting in ways that destroy the integrity of the criminal-trial system. We reiterate what we said in *Crawford:* that 'the rule of forfeiture by wrongdoing . . . extinguishes confrontation claims on essentially equitable grounds.' That is, one who obtains the absence of a witness by wrongdoing forfeits the constitutional right to confrontation.").

215. *Giles*, 554 U.S. at 356–57.

216. *Id.* at 357.

217. *See* People v. Giles, 19 Cal. Rptr. 3d 843, 850 (Cal. Ct. App. 2004), *aff'd*, 152 P.3d 433, 435 (Cal. 2007).

When *Giles* reached the Supreme Court, Justice Scalia, once again writing for the majority, found that a defendant does *not* forfeit his right to confrontation by his own wrongdoing, unless the prosecution can establish that the defendant intended through his actions to prevent the witness from testifying.[218] After *Giles*, it is not enough for the declarant to anticipate that his wrongdoing will procure the witness's absence from trial—that must be his intent. *Giles* has no impact, however, on the admissibility of nontestimonial statements.

Giles intended to limit forfeiture of confrontation to cases where courts have made a specific finding of prosecution proof (by a preponderance) of the defendant's purpose/intent.[219] Subsequent cases have clarified that the prosecutor need not prove that preventing the witness from testifying was the defendant's sole objective.[220] Post-*Giles*, lower courts have elaborated on this evidentiary requirement. For example, in *Commonwealth v. Szerlong*,[221] the Supreme Judicial Court of Massachusetts held that forfeiture need not be based on a criminal act if three criteria are satisfied: "(1) the witness is unavailable; (2) the defendant was involved in, or responsible for, procuring the unavailability of the witness; and (3) the defendant acted with the intent to procure the witness's unavailability."[222] Thus, the court in *Szerlong* found that a defendant who married the alleged victim of his domestic assault (with the purpose of enabling her to claim her spousal privilege and avoid testifying at trial) forfeited his right to

218. *Giles*, 554 U.S. at 365–67 (under the common law, "the 'wrong' and 'evil Practices' to which . . . statements [defining forfeiture] referred was conduct *designed* to prevent a witness from testifying"). *See also* United States v. Henderson, 626 F.3d 326, 333 (6th Cir. 2010) (the doctrine of forfeiture at common law was "not intended to permit introduction of unconfronted hearsay statements unless there was clear proof that the defendant engaged in conduct *designed* to prevent the declarant's testimony by procuring his or her unavailability"); United States v. Jackson, 706 F.3d 264, 265 (4th Cir. 2013). For an interesting discussion of the implications of *Giles* in cases involving coconspirator misconduct, see Adrienne Rose, *Forfeiture of Confrontation Rights Post-*Giles*: Whether a Co-Conspirator's Misconduct Can Forfeit a Defendant's Right to Confront Witnesses,* 14 N.Y.U. J. Legis. & Pub. Pol'y 281 (2011).

219. *See generally* Tim Donaldson, *A Reliable and Clear-Cut Determination: Is a Separate Hearing Required to Decide When Confrontation Forfeiture by Wrongdoing Applies?*, 49 New Eng. L. Rev. 167 (2015).

220. United States v. Cazares, 788 F.3d 956, 975 (9th Cir. 2015) (noting that the district court properly applied the proof by a preponderance-of-the-evidence standard and that "[t]he government is not required to show that a defendant's sole purpose was to silence the declarant").

221. Commonwealth v. Szerlong, 933 N.E.2d 633 (Mass. 2010).

222. *Id.* at 638. *See* Commonwealth v. Scionti, 962 N.E.2d 190, 201 (Mass. App. Ct. 2012) (the misconduct "sufficient to trigger the doctrine of forfeiture" does not have to be criminal).

confrontation.[223] More recently, the Supreme Court of New Mexico held that a defendant's affirmative action, necessary for forfeiture of the right to confront, need not take the form of an overt threat of violence.[224]

In sum, most courts agree that forfeiture can follow a defendant's noncriminal act and need not include a threat of violence, assuming proof by a preponderance of a defendant's affirmative act intended to cause the witness's unavailability.[225] In 2015, the Ninth Circuit articulated the evidentiary standard with precision:

> where there has been affirmative action on the part of the defendant that produces the desired result, non-appearance by a prospective witness against him in a criminal case[;] [s]imple tolerance of, or failure to foil, a third party's previously expressed decision either to skip town himself rather than testifying or to prevent another witness from appearing does not "cause" or "effect" or "bring about" or "procure" a witness's absence.[226]

In a case involving somewhat unusual facts, the First Circuit recently held that a defendant forfeited his right to confrontation by fleeing the jurisdiction, thereby depriving himself of the opportunity to confront a witness who testified at his coconspirators' trial five years earlier but died before defendant's trial.[227] The Second Circuit has held that forfeiture applies not just to the proceeding from which the defendant intended to procure the witness's absence but to all subsequent proceedings.[228]

Federal and state courts have also struggled, post-*Giles*, with adjacent forfeiture questions. Currently, courts are divided on the question of whether defense cross-examination that opens the door to a

223. *Szerlong*, 933 N.E.2d at 641.

224. State v. Maestas, 412 P.3d 79, 88–89 (N.M. 2018) ("[A]pplication of the forfeiture-by-wrongdoing exception requires no showing of overt threat of harm; it applies to any conduct intended to interfere with or undermine the judicial process. A threat of physical harm may suffice, as may persuasion, intimidation, murder, or other violent conduct. . . . Application of the exception, however, requires not just wrongdoing but both intent to cause, and causation of, unavailability by that wrongdoing.").

225. Anderson v. State, 2019 WL 6352774 (Nev. 2019) ("To apply the forfeiture-by-wrongdoing exception to the Confrontation Clause, the trial court must find by a preponderance of the evidence that the defendant intentionally procured the witness's absence.").

226. Carlson v. Attorney General of California, 791 F.3d 1003, 1010 (9th Cir. 2015).

227. United States v. Ponzo, 853 F.3d 558, 579 (1st Cir. 2017).

228. United States v. Stewart, 485 F.3d 666, 672 (2d Cir. 2007); *see also* Grayton v. Ercole, 691 F.3d 165, 171 (2d Cir. 2012) (determination of whether defendant has forfeited his right to confrontation should be made with "fundamental fairness in mind").

testimonial statement by a witness who cannot be cross-examined waives Confrontation Clause rights. The New York Court of Appeals has held that a defendant, who elicited an out-of-court statement made by a nontestifying eyewitness during cross-examination, by opening the door to admission of that statement, also waived his right to confront.[229] The specific concern, from that state's highest court, was

> [i]f evidence barred under the Confrontation Clause were inadmissible irrespective of a defendant's actions at trial, then a defendant could attempt to delude a jury by selectively revealing only those details of a testimonial statement that are potentially helpful to the defense, while concealing from the jury other details that would tend to explain the portions introduced and place them in context . . . with the secure knowledge that the concealed parts would not be admissible under the Confrontation Clause.[230]

In contrast, the Supreme Court of Minnesota refused to find that a defendant's Confrontation Clause right had been waived under similar circumstances.[231] Addressing ancillary challenges to evidence after confrontation has been forfeited, the Supreme Court of Illinois explained that such evidence must also be deemed reliable, because the defendant who waives the right to confront has also lost the right to challenge admission under the governing rules of evidence.[232]

VII. The Right to Confront Expert Witnesses

A. Recognizing the Right to Confront Experts

The Supreme Court in 2009 first addressed the question of whether prosecution-sponsored experts can be "witnesses against the accused" for confrontation purposes.[233] In *Melendez-Diaz v. Massachusetts*, the prosecutor had introduced three sworn and notarized "certificates of analysis"[234] that identified the white powder seized from the defendant as cocaine.[235] Under state law, the certificates provided prima

---

229. People v. Reid, 971 N.E.3d 382, 388 (N.Y. 2012).

230. *Id.*

231. State v. Hull, 788 N.W.2d 91, 101 (Minn. 2010).

232. *See* People v. Hanson, 939 N.E.2d 238, 254 (Ill. 2010); People v. Coleman, 24 N.E.3d 373 (Ill. App. Ct. 2014) (noting that the reliability of the statement must be considered in accordance with People v. Hanson).

233. Melendez-Diaz v. Massachusetts, 557 U.S. 305 (2009).

234. *Id.* at 308.

235. *Id.*

facie evidence of the composition, quality, and weight of a tested substance.[236]

In *Melendez-Diaz*, Justice Scalia wrote for Justices Stevens, Souter, and Ginsburg.[237] The plurality concluded that the laboratory certificates were testimonial statements requiring confrontation because (1) they were affidavits; (2) they were "made under circumstances which would lead an objective witness reasonably to believe that the statement would be available for use at a later trial";[238] and (3) "we can safely assume that the analysts were aware of the affidavits' evidentiary purpose."[239] The plurality's first rationale defined the limits of the Court's holding because it was the only point of agreement with Justice Thomas, who provided the fifth vote.[240]

Justice Kennedy, joined by Chief Justice Roberts and Justices Alito and Breyer, wrote for the four *Melendez-Diaz* dissenters. Their disagreement with the plurality was profound. In the dissenters' view, "witnesses against the accused" must be read as limited to typical conventional/adversarial prosecution witnesses and cannot be extended to experts who have "witnessed nothing to give them personal knowledge of the defendant's guilt."[241] These justices complained that the Court was now "dictat[ing] to the States, as a matter of constitutional law, an as-yet undefined set of rules governing what kinds of evidence may be admitted without in-court testimony. . . . [and] without guidance from any established body of law."[242] They also anticipated that future courts would struggle to identify the "analyst" among the "many people [who] play a role in a routine test for the presence of illegal drugs."[243] Finally, the four dissenters predicted that *Melendez-Diaz* would "disrupt forensic investigations across the country and put prosecutions nationwide at risk of

---

236. *Id.* at 311 (the "purpose of the affidavits was to provide 'prima facie evidence of the composition, quality, and the net weight' of the analyzed substance").

237. *Id.* at 306.

238. *Id.* at 310 (quoting Crawford v. Washington, 541 U.S. 36, 51 (2004)).

239. *Id.* at 311.

240. *Id.* at 329 (Thomas, J., concurring).

241. *Id.* at 330–31 (Kennedy, J., dissenting) (the plurality "makes no attempt to acknowledge the real differences between laboratory analysts who perform scientific tests and other, more conventional witnesses—'witnesses' being the word the Framers used in the Confrontation Clause").

242. *Id.* at 331.

243. *Id.* at 332. *See also* Michael H. Graham, *Justice Scalia's Fundamentally Flawed Confrontation Clause Analysis Continues in* Melendez-Diaz: *It's Time to Begin All Over Again*, 45 CRIM. L. BULL. 6 (2009) (positing that "the current state of the Confrontation Clause . . . is theoretically unsound, inconsistent, confused, and illogical").

dismissal based on erratic, all-too-frequent instances when a particular laboratory technician, now invested by the Court's new constitutional designation as the analyst, simply does not or cannot appear."[244]

B. Defining the Right to Confront Experts

Although *Melendez-Diaz* seemed to settle the question of whether out-of-court statements by prosecution experts raised confrontation concerns,[245] over the next three years the Supreme Court would grant certiorari in three more expert witness cases. The first was *Briscoe v. Virginia*,[246] which involved the question of whether providing a criminal defendant with the opportunity to subpoena prosecution experts adequately protects the right to confrontation. The case, which came to the Court in the wake of Justice Souter's departure and Justice Sotomayor's arrival, was argued but then remanded to the Supreme Court of Virginia based on a single-paragraph decision.[247] One year later, in *Bullcoming v. New Mexico*,[248] the Court held that the Confrontation Clause was violated when the prosecutor introduced a laboratory report through the in-court "surrogate testimony" of an expert witness (Razatos) who was familiar with the lab procedures, but "did not sign the certification or perform or observe the test reported in

---

244. *Melendez-Diaz*, 557 U.S. at 340–41 (Kennedy, J., dissenting). In 2011, in Justice Kennedy's dissenting opinion in *Bullcoming v. New Mexico*, he follows up on this concern by citing new supporting empirical evidence. This included a brief filed by the State of California describing how the ten toxicologists employed by the Los Angeles Police Department spent 782 hours at 261 court appearances during a one-year period, and a brief filed by the National District Attorneys Association indicating that each blood-alcohol analyst in California processes an average of 3,220 cases per year. Bullcoming v. New Mexico, 564 U.S. 647, 684 (2011).

245. *See, e.g.*, United States v. Roberts, 419 F. App'x 155, 160 (3d Cir. 2009) (a ballistics expert's trace summary report that identified the make, model, and serial number of a gun is testimonial because it "was made for the purpose of establishing some fact with the intent to be introduced at trial"). *But see* People v. Holmes, 150 Cal. Rptr. 3d 914, 915–19 (Cal. Ct. App. 2012) (forensic analysis relied on by DNA experts merely recorded objective facts, were unsworn and uncertified, and thus, lacked the requisite formality to be considered testimonial).

246. Briscoe v. Virginia, 559 U.S. 32 (2010). The specific question at issue in *Briscoe* was the constitutionality of a state law that shifted to the defense the burden of demanding the appearance at trial of any expert witness who had prepared a report that the prosecution had proffered for use at trial. On remand, the Virginia Supreme Court held that the statute violated the Confrontation Clause. Cypress v. Virginia, 699 S.E.2d 305 (Va. 2010).

247. *Briscoe*, 599 U.S. at 33.

248. *Bullcoming*, 564 U.S. 647.

the certification."[249] The justices rejected the argument that the prosecution expert (Caylor) who had performed the blood alcohol test (but did not testify) did not make a testimonial statement but was a mere scrivener who transcribed results generated by machines.[250] According to the *Bullcoming* majority, "the operation of the machines requires specialized knowledge . . . [s]everal steps are involved in the gas chromatograph process, and human error can occur at each step."[251] Thus, the admission of Caylor's testimonial statement via trial testimony from Razatos deprived the defendant of the opportunity to "raise before a jury questions concerning Caylor's proficiency, the care he took performing his work, and his veracity."[252] Although the laboratory report at issue in *Bullcoming* was unsworn, the Court found that it contained adequate formalities to qualify as a testimonial statement.[253]

In *Bullcoming*, Justice Sotomayor wrote a separate concurring opinion to emphasize that her conclusion was based on the fact that the laboratory report "has a primary purpose of creating an out-of-court substitute for trial testimony,"[254] and to map the limits of her concordance with the majority. According to Justice Sotomayor, "this is [a] *not* a case in which an expert was asked for his independent opinion about underlying testimonial reports that were not themselves admitted into evidence,"[255] which apparently would have led her to a different conclusion. As discussed in the following sections, the precise question anticipated by Justice Sotomayor subsequently came before the Court the following term in *Williams v. Illinois*.[256]

Unsurprisingly, the four *Melendez-Diaz* dissenters (Chief Justice Roberts and Justices Alito, Breyer, and Kennedy) also dissented in

---

249. *Id.* at 652. It is also notable that the prosecutor never argued that the expert who performed the blood alcohol test at issue was unavailable to testify at trial. *Id.* at 659. In fact, at the time of trial, he was on unpaid leave for undisclosed reasons. *Id.*

250. *Id.* at 657. *But see* Scott v. Mule Creek State Prison, 504 F. App'x 658 (9th Cir. 2013), *aff'g* 2010 WL 5563805, at *3–5 (C.D. Cal. 2010) (a laboratory report that only involved checking boxes and writing down the tests that were performed was not a testimonial statement under *Melendez-Diaz*).

251. *Bullcoming*, 564 U.S. at 654. *But see* United States v. Lamons, 532 F.3d 1251 (11th Cir. 2008) (call data from airline records relating to a false bomb threat was nontestimonial based on automated recording system); State v. Ziegler, 855 N.W.2d 551, 552 (Minn. Ct. App. 2014) ("data collected from a sensing and diagnostic module" in defendant's vehicle "are not testimonial statements within the meaning of the Confrontation Clause").

252. *Bullcoming*, 564 U.S. at 661 n.7.

253. *Id.* at 665.

254. *Id.* at 668–69 (Sotomayor, J., concurring).

255. *Id.* at 673.

256. People v. Williams, 939 N.E.2d 268 (Ill. 2010).

Bullcoming. In their view, *Bullcoming* was another unnecessary and unwarranted extension of *Crawford* that only "forbid[s] sworn, *ex parte*, out-of-court statements by unconfronted and available witnesses who *observed the crime* and do not appear at trial,"[257] a definition that does not include experts. Once again, the dissenters faulted the majority for displacing states' authority to impose their own fair trial procedures[258] and "extending and confirming *Melendez-Diaz*'s vast potential to disrupt criminal procedures"[259] as supported by new empirical evidence cited by various amici.[260]

Over the last decade, the Supreme Court has continued to revisit the confrontation of prosecution-sponsored experts.[261] In *People v. Williams*, the Illinois Supreme Court had permitted the prosecutor to introduce the in-court testimony of a prosecution expert (Lambatos) who did not perform or observe the DNA testing described in the laboratory report.[262] Instead, she testified that she had evaluated and analyzed the underlying data and the DNA report.[263] The state court found that Lambatos' testimony regarding the DNA report (which had not been proffered or admitted in evidence) did not violate the Confrontation Clause. The evidence had been admitted, not "for the truth of the matter asserted," but for the limited purpose of enabling the jury to assess the basis of the testifying expert's opinion under Rule 703 of the Federal Rules of Evidence.[264] This court's reasoning is analogous to the well-accepted view that a testimonial statement offered solely to impeach need not be confronted, because the

257. *Bullcoming*, 564 U.S. at 682 (Kennedy, J., dissenting) (emphasis added).

258. *Id.*

259. *Id.* at 677.

260. *Id.*

261. People v. Williams, 939 N.E.2d 268 (Ill. 2010).

262. *Id.*

263. *Id.*

264. *Id.* at 271–72. Federal Rule of Evidence 703 and its state court equivalents contemplate the admission of "otherwise inadmissible" facts or data, not for their truth but to enable the jury to assess the expert's opinion. This nonhearsay use is limited under Rule 703 as follows: (1) the expert must have been aware of or personally observed the inadmissible evidence, (2) "experts in the particular field would reasonably rely on those kinds of facts or data in forming an opinion," and (3) the court must determine that "their probative value in helping the jury evaluate the opinion substantially outweighs their prejudicial effect." Fed. R. Evid. 703. *See also* United States v. Roberts, 419 F. App'x 155, 160 (3d Cir. 2009) (a "trace summary" confirming the make, model, and serial number of a firearm was a testimonial statement because it was intended to be introduced at trial); Commonwealth v. Greineder, 984 N.E.2d 804, 807–08 (Mass. 2013) (applying state rule that only an expert's opinion and not the testimonial hearsay basis of the expert's opinion is admissible on direct examination).

statement was not offered for the truth of the matter asserted, but for the limited nontruth purpose of impeachment (i.e., jurors need not believe the impeaching statement to doubt the witness's credibility).

C. Narrowing the Right to Confront Experts

In June 2012, the case came before the Supreme Court as Williams v. Illinois. Justice Alito, writing for a plurality that included the other *Bullcoming* and *Melendez-Diaz* dissenters (Chief Justice Roberts, Justice Kennedy, and Justice Breyer), agreed that Lambatos' testimony did not violate the Confrontation Clause.[265] The plurality reasoned that the DNA report was not testimonial because it did not have "the primary purpose of accusing a targeted individual."[266] As Justice Alito explained, the primary purpose of the DNA testing and report was not "to accuse petitioner or to create evidence for use at trial" but "to catch a dangerous rapist who was still at large."[267] The plurality also concluded that Lambatos' testimony was not offered to prove the truth of the matter asserted.[268] Given the facts, it is notable that the plurality also reached beyond the facts to state that, even if the Cellmark report *had* been admitted into evidence at trial, there would have been no constitutional violation.[269] In their view, the report was nontestimonial for the independent reason that it was not "sought for the purpose of obtaining evidence to be used against petitioner, who was not even under suspicion at the time."[270] On this secondary issue, the plurality emphasized the factual distinction between *Williams* and both *Melendez-Diaz* and *Bullcoming*. In the two earlier cases, the lab reports at issue had been formally certified to ensure their

265. *Williams v. Illinois*, 567 U.S. 50, 57–58 (2012).

266. *Id.* at 58.

267. *Id.*

268. *Id.* at 79. As the plurality explained, the "expert witness referred to the report not to prove the truth of the matter asserted in the [Cellmark] report, *i.e.*, that the report contained an accurate profile of the perpetrator's DNA, but only to establish that the report contained a DNA profile that matched the DNA profile deduced from petitioner's blood." *Id.* It is worth noting that the force of this conclusion is significantly undermined by the plurality's subsequent admission that the dissent's argument (that Lambatos' testimony regarding the DNA match *was* admitted for the truth of the matter asserted) "would have force if petitioner had elected to have a jury trial . . . [because] there would have been a danger of the jury's taking Lambatos' testimony as proof that the Cellmark profile was derived from the sample obtained from the victim's vaginal swabs." *Id.* at 72.

269. *Id.*

270. *Id.* at 58.

admission at trial.[271] In *Melendez-Diaz*, the formalization of the report was the *sine qua non* for Justice Thomas's concurring decision and his only point of agreement with the plurality. In that case, Justice Thomas had focused on the statement's "lack[] [of] the requisite formality and solemnity to be considered testimonial for purposes of the Confrontation Clause."[272] Finally, in a rather odd bit of dictum, Justice Alito dismissed the risk that *Williams* could be construed by future courts to both permit an expert to express an opinion based on testimonial hearsay and to disclose that same testimonial hearsay to the trier of fact. According to Justice Alito, "this argument plainly has no application in a case like this one, in which a judge sits as the trier of fact." Despite Justice Alito's assurances, the mere lack of a jury in the underlying case does nothing to limit the ambit of future interpretations of *Williams*' scope.[273]

In his concurring decision, Justice Breyer objected to the Court's failure to resolve critical questions involving the application and scope of Confrontation Clause protections in the context of crime lab reports. In his view, doctrinal ambiguity posed practical problems because "laboratory reports frequently constitute a portion of the evidence in ordinary criminal trials. . . . [and] [o]bviously, judges, prosecutors, and defense lawyers have to know, in a definitive a form as possible, what the Constitution requires so they can try their cases accordingly."[274] As noted previously, Justice Thomas "agree[d] with the plurality that the disclosure of Cellmark's out-of-court statements through the expert testimony of Sandra Lambatos did not violate the Confrontation Clause."[275] But Justice Thomas criticized the plurality on two important points. First, he saw the plurality's new "primary purpose" test, which asked "whether an out-of-court statement has

---

271. *Id.* at 65 (noting that the forensic reports at issue in both *Melendez-Diaz* and *Bullcoming* "contain[ed] a testimonial certification, made in order to prove a fact at a criminal trial.").

272. *Id.* at 103–04 (Thomas, J., concurring). In earlier work predating *Bryant*, one of the authors predicted that Justice Scalia's leadership would wane and that a new confrontation jurisprudence would align more closely with Justice Thomas's focus on formality because this is a critical distinction between "witnessing" and speaking. *See supra* note 95.

273. *Id.* at 80 n.11 (majority opinion).

274. *Id.* at 92 (Breyer, J., concurring). Justice Breyer's principal concern is that "[o]nce one abandons the traditional rule [that the Cellmark statements are admissible under Federal Rule of Evidence 703 and not for their truth], there would seem often to be no logical stopping place between requiring the prosecution to call as a witness one of the laboratory experts who worked on the matter and requiring the prosecution to call all of the laboratory experts who did so." *Id.* at 89.

275. *Id.* at 103 (Thomas J., concurring).

'the primary purpose of accusing a targeted individual of engaging in criminal conduct,' . . . [as] lack[ing] any grounding in constitutional text, in history, or in logic."[276] Second, like the four dissenters, Justice Thomas rejected the plurality's conclusion that Cellmark's statements had not been offered for their truth.[277]

Justice Kagan, in her dissent on behalf of Justices Scalia, Ginsburg, and Sotomayor, argued that *Williams* is an "open-and-shut case"[278] that cannot properly be distinguished from *Bullcoming*. In their view, the Cellmark analyst who prepared the report referenced by Lambatos was a witness against the accused for confrontation purposes who could not be cross-examined by the defendant.[279] The dissenters complained that the plurality has somehow garnered "five votes to approve the admission of the Cellmark report, but not a single good explanation."[280] Like Justice Thomas, they also specifically rejected the plurality's argument that the report had not been offered for the truth of the matter asserted.[281] On this important final point, the dissenters persuasively argued that "when witness, expert or otherwise, repeats an out-of-court statement as the basis for a conclusion . . . the statement's utility is then dependent on its truth. . . . [because] [i]f the statement is true, then the conclusion based on it is probably true; if not, not."[282]

Because *Williams* raised—but did not resolve—the question of the interrelationship between Federal Rule of Evidence 703 (or its state equivalents) and the post-*Crawford* Confrontation Clause,[283] its lack of clarity has had a deleterious effect on the lower courts. Some post-*Williams* courts have concluded that the admission of evidence under Rule 703 does *not* violate the Confrontation Clause because a testifying expert can be cross-examined about the formulation of her

---

276. *Id.* at 114 (internal citations omitted).

277. *Id.* at 109 ("It remains the case that the prosecution is attempting to introduce a testimonial statement that has no relevance to the proceedings apart from its truth—and that the defendant cannot cross-examine the person who made it. Allowing the admission of this evidence would end-run the Confrontation Clause, and make a parody of its strictures."). Justice Thomas also expressed concern that this "holding . . . will reach beyond scientific evidence to ordinary out-of-court statements" including statements of uncertain reliability, such as those made by third parties interviewed by experts. *Id.*

278. *Id.* at 119 (Kagan, J., dissenting).

279. *Id.* at 119–20.

280. *Id.* at 120

281. *Id.*

282. *Id.* at 126.

283. Brief of Petitioner-Appellant at 20–24, Williams v. Illinois, No. 10-8505 (U.S. June 18, 2012).

opinion.[284] Other courts have found that the Confrontation Clause is not violated when prosecution experts rely on a laboratory test that (like the DNA report at issue in *Williams*) would have raised constitutional concerns but was not admitted in evidence or presented to the jury in the form of a sworn affidavit.[285] In recent cases, experts have been permitted to testify to opinions shaped by constitutionally inadmissible evidence based on an understanding that "[t]he holding in *Williams* indicates that the admission of an expert opinion based on a scientific DNA report prepared by another does not violate the right to confrontation."[286] For example, the Confrontation Clause is apparently not violated by testimony from a police chemist who based her opinions on DNA tests conducted by a nontestifying expert, although this finding was contingent on the fact that such tests were neither admitted nor described by the witness.[287] Construed most broadly, *Williams* has been understood to support the view that confrontation is required *only* based on a finding that the prosecution expert "is used as little more than a conduit or transmitter for testimonial hearsay."[288] Finally, as a practical matter, it appears clear that, under current doctrine, defendants cannot slow or obstruct the judicial process by demanding that "anyone whose testimony may be relevant in establishing the chain of custody, authenticity of the sample, or accuracy of the testing device must appear as part of the prosecution's case."[289]

284. Commonwealth v. Greineder, 984 N.E.2d 804 (Mass. 2013); State v. McLeod, 66 A.3d 1221, 1230 (N.H. 2013) ("We agree with the proposition that the Confrontation Clause is not violated when an expert testifies regarding his or her independent judgment, even if that judgment is based upon inadmissible testimonial hearsay.").

285. Littleton v. State, 372 S.W.3d 926, 931 (Mo. Ct. App. 2012) (no Confrontation Clause violation when a lab report prepared by an unavailable technician was not admitted into evidence and the expert testified as to her own findings relating to the DNA identification evidence based on her personal knowledge of the tests and results); Morris v. United States, 2010 WL 1752030, at *3 (D.S.D. 2010) (no Confrontation Clause violation when a DEA lab report was not admitted into evidence or presented to the jury in the form of a sworn affidavit and the two expert witnesses presented their independent judgments and expertise regarding the substances in question to the jury and were subject to cross-examination by the defendant).

286. Mattei v. Medeiros, 320 F. Supp. 3d 231 (D. Mass. 2018).

287. Commonwealth v. Banville, 931 N.E.2d 457, 540–41 (Mass. 2010); *see also* Speers v. State, 999 N.E.2d 850, 853–55 (Ind. 2013) (the right to confrontation is not violated where both DNA profiles at issue were analyzed by a single analyst who testified at trial even though one technician who prepared the glass swabs that the analyst eventually tested did not testify at trial because the state does not need to "establish a perfect chain of custody") (citations omitted).

288. Morris v. United States, 2010 WL 1752030 (D.S.D. 2010).

289. *Id.* (quoting Melendez-Diaz v. Massachusetts, 557 U.S. 305, 312 n.1 (2009)).

D. Changes to the Court and the Right to Confront Experts

Given the addition of three new Supreme Court justices from 2017 to 2020, any insight into their confrontation jurisprudence could be useful. Although the recent docket has not included confrontation cases, Justice Gorsuch (joined by Justice Sotomayor) wrote a very interesting and revealing dissent to the 2018 writ of certiorari denial in *Stuart v. Alabama*.[290]

In *Stuart*, to prove that the defendant was driving under the influence, the state introduced the results of a blood-alcohol test conducted hours after her arrest. At trial, the prosecutor failed to call the analyst who had performed the test but called a substitute analyst who extrapolated and estimated the defendant's blood-alcohol level at the time she was driving. The dissenting justices argued that the defendant had been deprived of her right to confrontation. Noting at the outset that "[m]ore and more, forensic evidence plays a decisive role in criminal trials today" and that such evidence is "hardly immune from the risk of manipulation," Justice Gorsuch bemoaned the fact that the fundamental promise of the Confrontation Clause had been violated.[291]

> That promise was broken here. To prove Vanessa Stuart was driving under the influence, the State of Alabama introduced in evidence the results of a blood-alcohol test conducted hours after her arrest. But the State refused to bring to the stand the analyst who performed the test. Instead, the State called a different analyst. Using the results of the test after her arrest and the rate at which alcohol is metabolized, this analyst sought to estimate for the jury Ms. Stuart's blood-alcohol level hours earlier when she was driving. Through these steps, the State effectively denied Ms. Stuart the chance to confront the witness who supplied a foundational piece of evidence in her conviction. The engine of cross-examination was left unengaged, and the Sixth Amendment was violated.[292]

This suggests that, had Justice Gorsuch been on the Court when *Williams* was decided, he would have shared the dissenters' view that the Confrontation Clause was violated because the Cellmark analyst

---

290. Stuart v. Alabama, 139 S. Ct. 36 (2018). *See also* Michael S. Pardo, *Confrontation After Scalia and Kennedy*, 70 Ala. L. Rev. 757 (2019) (discussing the future of the Confrontation Clause with Justices Gorsuch and Kavanaugh on the bench and predicting that Justice Gorsuch will be a defender of the clause).

291. *Stuart*, 139 S. Ct. 36 (Gorsuch, J., dissenting).

292. *Id.*

who prepared the report could not be cross-examined[293] and perhaps even their opinion that the plurality had "five votes to approve the admission of the Cellmark report, but not a single good explanation."[294] Summing up his thoughts on *Williams*, Justice Gorsuch remarked: "Respectfully, I believe we owe lower courts struggling to abide our holdings more clarity than we have afforded them in this area."

Justice Gorsuch held the current Court responsible for creating confrontation confusion: "To be fair, the problem appears to be largely of our creation. This Court's most recent foray in this field, *Williams v. Illinois*, 567 U.S. 50 (2012), yielded no majority and its various opinions have sown confusion in courts across the country."[295] He also complained that the Alabama court had misread *Williams* on the threshold question of whether a lab report can be admitted, without calling the preparing analyst, based on the prosecutor's claim that the report did not raise hearsay concerns because it was not being offered for the truth of its assertions.

> [W]hile *Williams* yielded no majority opinion, at least five Justices rejected this logic—and for good reason. After all, why would any prosecutor bother to offer in evidence the nontestifying analyst's report in this case except to prove the truth of its assertions about the level of alcohol in Ms. Stuart's blood at the time of the test? The whole point of the exercise was to establish—because of the report's truth—a basis for the jury to credit the testifying expert's estimation of Ms. Stuart's blood-alcohol level hours earlier.[296]

As Justice Gorsuch correctly observed, this was the view of the four dissenting justices and Justice Thomas, who, in his concurring decision, stated that "[t]here is no meaningful distinction between disclosing an out-of-court statement so that the factfinder may evaluate the [testifying] expert's opinion and disclosing that statement for its truth."[297]

E. New Cases and Statutes That May Limit the Right to Confront Experts

In recent cases, lower courts routinely complain that the current standard for confrontation of prosecution experts is ambiguous and

293. *Williams*, 567 U.S. at 119–20 (Kagan, J., dissenting).
294. *Id.* at 120.
295. *Stuart*, 139 S. Ct. at 36 (Gorsuch, J., dissenting).
296. *Id.*
297. *Williams*, 567 U.S at 106 (Thomas, J., concurring).

uncertain. The Supreme Court of Tennessee has bemoaned the "fractured decision in *Williams*[, which] provides little guidance and is of uncertain precedential value because no rationale for the decision—not one of the three proffered tests for determining whether an extrajudicial statement is testimonial—garnered the support of a majority of the Court."[298] Other courts have similarly objected to the fact that "each of those three opinions in *Williams* embraces a different approach to determining whether the use of forensic evidence violates the Confrontation Clause, and there is no narrow rule that would have the support of a majority of the Supreme Court that we can discern from the opinions in *Williams*,"[299] making "*Williams*'s force, as precedent, at best unclear."[300] A very recent Arkansas decision held that the Confrontation Clause was violated by both (1) trial testimony from a substitute analyst regarding the results of a DNA test and (2) admission of the DNA report because "[a]lthough in *Williams*, there were five votes to approve the admission of the report in question, the Court could not settle on a specific or particular reason why."[301] This led the court to the astute conclusion that "[t]he lack of common ground between the plurality opinion and Justice Thomas's opinion concurring in the judgment renders *Williams* of questionable utility."[302]

VIII. The Right to Confront Witness under Specific Circumstances

A. Official Records

Federal and state courts regularly address the confrontation implications of a wide range of official records.[303]

1. Laboratory Reports

Certificates of the chemical analysis of drugs, like those at issue in *Melendez-Diaz*, are generally considered testimonial because they are akin to the testimony a forensic analyst would be expected to give on

---

298. State v. Dotson, 450 S.W.3d 1, 68 (Tenn. 2014).
299. State v. Michaels, 95 A.3d 648, 666 (N.J. 2014).
300. *Id.*
301. Alejandro-Alvarez v. State, 587 S.W.3d 269, 273 n.2 (Ark. 2019).
302. *Id.*
303. *See also* 18 A.L.R. 7th Art. 6 (2017).

direct examination.[304] For example, courts have held that certificates describing the results of breath-alcohol tests are testimonial because their sole purpose is to assist the government in prosecuting DWI cases.[305] This same rationale has been applied to certificates of analysis containing results of DNA testing introduced by the prosecution in rape cases.[306]

2. Medical Examiner Reports

Autopsy reports and death certificates can serve both testimonial and nontestimonial purposes.[307] A recent federal district court deemed

---

304. *See, e.g.*, Cypress v. Commonwealth, 699 S.E.2d 206 (Va. 2010); State v. Brewington, 693 S.E.2d 182 (N.C. Ct. App. 2010); United States v. Maxwell, 724 F.3d 724, 726 (7th Cir. 2013) ("the government may not introduce forensic laboratory reports or affidavits reporting the results of forensic tests and use them as substantive evidence against a defendant unless the analyst who prepared or certified the report is offered as a live witness subject to cross-examination").

305. *See, e.g.*, Roseborough v. Commonwealth, 704 S.E.2d 414 (Va. 2011). *But see* State v. Benson, 287 P.3d 927, 931 (Kan. 2012) (noting that "most jurisdictions uniformly agree that documents certifying maintenance records of breath-test machines are not testimonial in nature").

306. *See, e.g.*, Aguilar v. Commonwealth, 699 S.E.2d 215 (Va. 2010); State v. Krodinger, 128 So. 3d 270, 277 (La. Ct. App. 2013) (DNA certificate of analysis admitted at trial was testimonial).

307. *See* United States v. James, 712 F.3d 79, 88 (2d Cir. 2013) (the autopsy reports were nontestimonial because they were not created "for the purpose of establishing or proving some fact at trial") (citation omitted); People v. Dungo, 286 P.3d 442, 449 (Cal. 2012) ("An autopsy report typically contains two types of statements: (1) statements describing the pathologist's anatomical and physiological observations about the condition of the body, and (2) statements setting forth the pathologist's conclusions as to the cause of the victim's death. The out-of-court statements at issue here—[a pathologist's] observations about the condition of [victim's] body—all fall into the first of the two categories. These statements, which merely record objective facts, are less formal than statements setting forth a pathologist's expert conclusions. They are comparable to observations of objective fact in a report by a physician who, after examining a patient, diagnoses a particular injury or ailment and determines the appropriate treatment. Such observations are not testimonial in nature."). *See also* Hensley v. Roden, 755 F.3d 724, 732–33 (1st Cir. 2014) (describing how the *Melendez-Diaz* Court "in no way . . . indicated that autopsy reports are testimonial in nature. It simply used autopsies as an example of a forensic test where do-overs are not possible."). *See generally* Dana Amato, *What Happens If Autopsy Reports Are Found Testimonial?: The Next Steps to Ensure the Admissibility of These Critical Documents in Criminal Trials*, 107 J. Crim. L. & Criminology 293 (2017); Daniel J. Capra & Joseph Tartakovsky, *Autopsy Reports and the Confrontation Clause: A Presumption of Admissibility*, 2 Va. J. Crim. L. 62 (2014); Andrew Higley, *Tales of the Dead: Why Autopsy Reports Should be Classified as Testimonial Statements Under the Confrontation Clause*, 48 New Eng. L. Rev. 171 (2013).

both types of statements testimonial, despite the fact that the medical examiner "did not perform an autopsy on Sgt. Johnson's body *solely* to gather evidence for use in a future prosecution."[308] According to that court, it was sufficient that she was "aware" that the autopsy report would be available for use at trial and that the statements at issue were "marked by a formality characteristic of documents to be introduced in court."[309] After deeming these statements testimonial, the court clarified that a prosecutor could not make an "end run around *Crawford*" by simply calling another medical examiner to testify to statements made in either document.[310]

3. Criminal Records

The Eighth Circuit has held that judgments of conviction are testimonial statements when offered to prove facts underlying the charged crime.[311] The D.C. Circuit Court of Appeal reached the same conclusion for a letter from the court clerk stating that the defendant had previously been convicted of a felony.[312] State courts have similarly found that a federal plea agreement was a testimonial statement.[313]

---

308. United States v. Williams, 740 F. Supp. 2d 4, 7 (D.D.C. 2010). *See* United States v. Ignasiak, 667 F.3d 1217, 1230–31 (11th Cir. 2012) (the admission of autopsy reports that were not authored by the testifying expert when the testifying expert did not personally observe or participate in the autopsies violated the Confrontation Clause).

309. *Williams*, 740 F. Supp. 2d at 7 (quoting Justice Thomas's concurring opinion in *Melendez-Diaz v. Massachusetts*, 557 U.S. 305, 329 (2009)). "The Confrontation Clause is implicated by extrajudicial statements only insofar as they are contained in formalized testimonial materials, such as affidavits, depositions, prior testimony, or confessions." *Id.*

310. *Id.* at 9.

311. *See* United States v. Head, 707 F.3d 1026, 1031 (8th Cir. 2013) (where defendant was charged with being an accessory after the fact, admission of principal's guilty plea as conclusive proof that he committed the offense violated defendant's Confrontation Clause rights); United States v. Causevic, 636 F.3d 998 (8th Cir. 2011).

312. *See* United States v. Smith, 640 F.3d 358, 363 (D.C. Cir. 2011) (the clerk's letter was made for the purpose of establishing a fact at trial). *But see* United States v. Dale, 494 F. App'x 317, 318 (4th Cir. 2012) (admission of fingerprint cards from prior convictions in absence of trial testimony from official who took the fingerprints did not violate Confrontation Clause because the "official did no analysis and came to no conclusions[,] . . . [t]he cards serve no prosecutorial function on their own" and "contain only ministerial, objective observations" such that they are nontestimonial in nature).

313. *See* State v. Tollardo, 275 P.3d 110, 117 (N.M. 2012) (admission of testimonial plea agreements violated the defendant's right to confront witnesses against him); People v. Hill, 120 Cal. Rptr. 3d 251 (Cal. Ct. App. 2011).

4. Certificates of Nonrecord

Certificates of nonexistence of official records have also been held to be testimonial statements. In *United States v. Martinez-Rios*,[314] the Fifth Circuit specified that certificates of nonexistence of records are testimonial and require confrontation because these statements are created *specifically* for use at trial and not produced in the ordinary course of regular government business.[315]

5. Nontestimonial Official Records

Various other types of official records have typically been deemed nontestimonial. For example, the Seventh Circuit has found that both a certification and affidavit authenticating cell phone records were nontestimonial business records.[316] According to a California federal district court, a fill-in-the-blank style laboratory report (where the statement was made by checking boxes and copying test results) does not raise confrontation concerns under *Melendez-Diaz*.[317] Courts have

---

314. United States v. Martinez-Rios, 595 F.3d 581 (5th Cir. 2010); State v. Jasper, 271 P.3d 876, 886 (Wash. 2012) (noting that "[a] substantial majority of courts have held since *Melendez-Diaz* that clerk certifications attesting to the nonexistence of a public record are testimonial statements subject to confrontation"). *But see* United States v. Montalvo-Rangel, 2010 WL 1484708 (W.D. Tex. 2010) (defendant's Confrontation Clause rights were satisfied despite unavailability of the INS agent who signed the CNR, by the opportunity to cross-examine another INS agent who testified that he reviewed the various databases "to assure himself that a diligent search was performed and there was no record found to indicate that Defendant obtained consent for re-admission").

315. *Martinez-Rios*, 595 F.3d at 586. *See also* United States v. Martinez-Sanchez, 522 F. App'x 355, 357 (7th Cir. 2013) (noting that after *Melendez-Diaz*, two courts of appeals overturned their circuit precedents and concluded that certificates of nonexistence of records "are testimonial because they are created for trial and used to prove a fact necessary for conviction"); United States v. Valdovinos-Mendez, 641 F.3d 1031, 1034 (9th Cir. 2011); United States v. Orozco-Acosta, 607 F.3d 1156, 1161 (9th Cir. 2010).

316. United States v. Yeley-Davis, 632 F.3d 673, 679 (10th Cir. 2011); United States v. Brinson, 772 F.3d 1314, 1323 (10th Cir. 2014) (finding *Yeley-Davis* dispositive, even when the records at issue were "debit cards rather than a cellphone," because "what matters is the nature of the certificate rather than the records" and that *Melendez-Diaz* does not apply because the certificate at issue did not contain any analysis such that the "certificate is simply a non-testimonial statement of authenticity").

317. Scott v. Mule Creek State Prison, 2010 WL 5563805, at *5 n.6 (C.D. Cal. 2010) aff'd, 504 F. App'x 658 (9th Cir. 2013) ("The lab report in this case states a mechanical result—that the substance found was determined to be cocaine. As noted in the trial transcript, filling out the lab report was merely a 'matter of checking boxes or writing down the type of tests that were performed' along with the results of the tests. The mechanically filled out lab report in this case does not appear to fall in the category of 'affidavits, depositions,

also determined that completed applications for Federal Emergency Management Agency assistance,[318] criminal records,[319] customer directories,[320] immigration records,[321] and motor vehicle records[322] are nontestimonial because these records were not created to provide evidence at a trial.[323]

---

prior testimony, or confessions.'") (quoting Melendez-Diaz v. Massachusetts, 129 S. Ct. 2527, 2542 (2009) (Thomas, J., concurring).

318. *See* United States v. Breland, 366 F. App'x 548, 554 (5th Cir. 2010) (warning on FEMA application that statements could be used at trial did not transform business records into testimonial statements).

319. *See* People v. Richie, 2014 WL 1631485, at *16 (Cal. Ct. App. 2014) ("records of prior convictions are business records, and, therefore, nontestimonial statements" because "[s]uch documents are not prepared for the purpose of use in a future court proceeding; rather, they are created primarily for the administrative purposes of the Department of Corrections and Rehabilitation") (citation omitted); People v. Moreno, 121 Cal. Rptr. 3d 669, 682 (Cal. Ct. App. 2011) (record of defendant's prior criminal history was not a testimonial statement).

320. *See* United States v. Santos, 947 F.3d 711, No. 18-14529, 2020 WL 102253 (11th Cir. Jan. 9, 2020) (naturalization form annotated by an adjudications officer was nontestimonial because it was "produced as a matter of administrative routine, for the primary purpose of determining [the applicant's] eligibility for naturalization") (citations omitted); United States v. Noria, 945 F.3d 837 (5th Cir. 2019) (the I-213 immigration "Record of Deportable/Inadmissible Alien" forms containing biographical data are nontestimonial); United States v. Lyons, 740 F.3d 702, 719–20 (1st Cir. 2014) (directory of the customers and agents of an illegal gambling business was nontestimonial because it was not produced with "a primary purpose of creating an out-of-court substitute for trial testimony") (citation omitted).

321. *See* United States v. Rojas-Pedroza, 716 F.3d 1253, 1268–69 (9th Cir. 2013) ("Like a warrant of removal, a Notice of Intent/Decision to Reinstate Prior Order is nontestimonial. Immigration officers complete these notices to comply with an agency regulation that requires the government to apprise the alien of its determination that the alien is removable and to give the alien an opportunity to contest the government's determination [and] . . . although there is a possibility, that the contents of these notices could be used in a criminal prosecution, the objective circumstances indicate that, like warrants of removal, their primary purpose is to effect removals, not to prove facts at a criminal trial.") (citation omitted).

322. *See* State v. Murphy, 991 A.2d 35 (Me. 2010) (state record indicating that defendant had been given notice that his driver's license had been suspended was not a testimonial statement); *see also* People v. Nunley, 821 N.W.2d 642, 652–53 (Mich. 2012) (certificate of mailing and circumstances under which certificate was created show "that it is a nontestimonial business record created primarily for an administrative reason and kept in the regular course of operations of a governmental agency rather than a testimonial affidavit or other record created for a prosecutorial or investigative reason" and is nontestimonial for confrontation purposes).

323. *See* United States v. Anekwu, 695 F.3d 967, 971 (9th Cir. 2012) (as an issue of first impression for the Ninth Circuit, the admission of certificates of authentication of foreign public records does not violate the Confrontation Clause).

6. Defense Stipulations and Waiver

It is not clear whether a defense stipulation constitutes a confrontation waiver. Most post-*Melendez-Diaz* courts have held that by stipulating to the admission of a prosecution-sponsored laboratory report, the defendant waives the right to argue a Confrontation Clause violation.[324] However, other courts have found that a similar stipulation does not constitute a waiver under circumstances where defense counsel entered into the stipulation over the defendant's objection.[325]

7. Testimonial Purpose

In a range of recent cases, the federal courts have explored the importance of a declarant's testimonial purpose as a factor relevant to a determination of the scope of a defendant's Confrontation Clause rights.[326]

B. Special Circumstances

1. Suppression Hearings

The Wisconsin Supreme Court recently held that the Confrontation Clause does not apply at suppression hearings.[327] It is quite likely that other courts would take a similar approach and find that the

324. *See* United States v. Smith, 632 F.3d 1043, 1047 (8th Cir. 2011); United States v. Robinson, 617 F.3d 984, 989 (8th Cir. 2010); *see also* People v. Witherspoon, 2013 WL 1352435, at *1 (Mich. Ct. App. 2013) (defendant (through defense counsel) waived his right of confrontation regarding a laboratory report because confrontation may be waived by counsel "as long as counsel's actions constitute reasonable trial strategy, which is presumed, and the defendant does not object on the record").

325. *See* United States v. Williams, 632 F.3d 129, 133 (4th Cir. 2011); State v. Humphries, 336 P.3d 1121, 1124 (Wash. 2014) (stipulation does not constitute waiver when made "over the defendant's known and express objection").

326. *See* Lucero v. Holland, 902 F.3d 979, 989 (9th Cir. 2018) (handwritten note meant only to be shared between gang members was not testimonial); United States v. Taylor, 688 F. App'x 638, 642 (11th Cir. 2017) (muted videotape not testimonial); United States v. Fryberg, 854 F.3d 1126, 1135–36 (9th Cir. 2017) (a return of service from a tribal court informing the defendant that he had been serviced with notice of hearing was not testimonial because its primary purpose was not for evidence at trial). *But see* United States v. London, 746 F. App'x 317 (5th Cir. 2018) (the introduction into evidence of notarized first-person statements that robbed bank was FDIC insured violated the Confrontation Clause because the statements had been created for the purpose of use at trial).

327. State v. Zamzow, 892 N.W.2d 637, 646–47 (Wis. 2017), *cert. denied*, Zamzow v. Wisconsin, 138 S. Ct. 501 (2017).

Confrontation Clause "protects defendants [only] at trial—when guilt or innocence is at stake."[328]

2. Notice-and-Demand Statutes

Some states have enacted notice-and-demand statutes to expedite and simplify prosecutions by limiting the circumstances under which prosecution experts are called to testify at trial regarding the contents of official records.[329] These statutes generally require the prosecutor to give "notice" to the defense that the state will seek to introduce an official record (such as a laboratory report) and then the burden shifts to the defense to "demand" that the expert witness testify at trial. One commentator has identified four different burden-shifting statues of this type: (1) notice-and-demand statutes; (2) notice-and-demand statutes that impose additional requirements on the defense; (3) statutes that require little if any notice, but require a defense demand; and (4) statutes that require the defense to subpoena prosecution experts.[330] It is reasonable to assume that the Supreme Court will eventually address the constitutionality of a notice-and-demand statute in this context.

3. Translated Statements

The lower courts are divided on the question of whether statements by a foreign language interpreter translating statements of a non-English-speaking defendant qualify as testimonial statements.[331] Most courts have held that the final statements of the interpreter should be treated like the original statements of the non-English-speaking defendant, because the interpreter functions as a "language conduit" for a defendant who does not have the right to "confront himself."[332]

---

328. *Id.*

329. *See, e.g.*, MD. CODE ANN., CTS. & JUD. PROC. § 10-306(b) (West 2008).

330. Paul C. Giannelli, *Right of Confrontation: Lab Reports*, 24 CRIM. JUST. 4 (2009); Metzger, *Cheating the Constitution*, 59 VAND. L. REV. 475, 481–91 (2006).

331. *See generally* Casen B. Ross, *Clogged Conduits: A Defendant's Right to Confront His Translated Statements*, 8 U. CHI. L. REV. 1931, 1932–33 (2014).

332. *See, e.g.*, United States v. Orm Hieng, 679 F.3d 1131, 1140 (9th Cir 2012) ("whether the interpreter must be considered a declarant, rather than a language conduit, is a threshold inquiry, and that confrontation concerns do not even arise if the statement may be fairly attributed directly to the speaker [and that only] [i]f a court were to hold that the statement must be attributed to the interpreter, it would, under Crawford, ask whether the statement, as applied to the interpreter, was testimonial") (citation omitted); United States v. Budha, 495 F. App'x 452, 454 (5th Cir. 2012) ("except in unusual circumstances,

Recently the Eleventh Circuit, in *United States v. Charles*, rejected this rationale finding that because language interpretation "does not provide for a one-to-one correspondence between words or concepts in different languages," a language interpreter is not a "language conduit."[333] The interpreter is instead a separate declarant from the non-English-speaking defendant, which entitles the defendant to confront the language interpreter about testimonial statements made by the interpreter.[334]

4. The Role of Federal Rule of Evidence 403

In 2018, the Seventh Circuit addressed the question of whether the Sixth Amendment bars a court from applying Rule 403 of the Federal Rules of Evidence to limit defense cross-examination of a prosecution witness.[335] Consistent with the general principle that the rules of evidence must cede to constitutional concerns, the court found that a trial court violates the Confrontation Clause when it "routinely applies Rule 403 to limit cross-examination by the accused on issues central to the defense."[336]

C. Nonhearsay Statements

Obviously, the Confrontation Clause does not eliminate all possible prosecution uses of testimonial statements. As the *Crawford* Court

---

interpreters may be considered language conduits, whose translations of the defendant's own statements are not hearsay and do not implicate defendant's confrontation rights"). *See also* Taylor v. State, 130 A.3d 509, 539 (Md. Ct. Spec. App. 2016) ("In sum, the Ninth Circuit's language-conduit doctrine does exactly what Crawford forbids: it leaves 'the Sixth Amendment's protection to the vagaries of the rules of evidence' and to 'amorphous notions of "reliability."'"); Lopez-Ramos v. Minnesota, No. 19-5936, 2020 WL 129679 (U.S. Jan. 13, 2020) (denial of certiorari by U.S. Supreme Court in a case where a defendant challenged the admission of an interpreter's translation of his statements to police).

333. United States v. Charles, 722 F.3d 1319, 1324–25 (11th Cir. 2013) (because the defendant "has the right, under the Confrontation Clause, to confront the 'declarant,' that is the person who made the out-of-court statement, she has the right to confront the Creole language interpreter about the statements to which the . . . officer testified to [sic] in court").

334. *Id.* at 1324–25 (11th Cir. 2013). *See also* Taylor v. State, 130 A.3d 509 (Md. Ct. Spec. App. 2016) (finding a confrontation violation because a language interpreter is a witness and not merely the defendant's conduit). *See generally* Zachary C. Bolitho, *The Hearsay and Confrontation Clause Problems Caused by Admitting What a Non-Testifying Interpreter Said the Criminal Defendant Said*, 49 N.M. L. Rev. 193 (2019).

335. Rhodes v. Dittmann, 903 F.3d 646, 657 (7th Cir. 2018).

336. *Id.* at 657.

explained, and most courts have agreed, defendants do not have the right to confront nonhearsay statements because the Confrontation Clause "does not bar the use of testimonial statements for purposes other than establishing the truth of the matter asserted."[337] For example, in 2018, the Eleventh Circuit admitted statements from the defendant's wife that implicated him in the crime, because they were not admitted for the truth of the matter asserted but "for the limited purpose of explaining subsequent events."[338] In contrast, in 2019, the Second Circuit held that the introduction of a codefendant's statement through police officer testimony violated the defendant's confrontation rights, despite a jury instruction not to consider the statement for the truth of the matter asserted.[339] According to the Second Circuit, the risk that the jury "will not, or cannot" follow the instructions was too great.[340]

I. Dying Declarations

In *Ohio v. Roberts*, the Court identified dying declarations as precisely the sort of out-of-court statements that fall within a firmly rooted hearsay exception.[341] The *Crawford* Court specifically suggested that testimonial dying declarations do not require confrontation.[342] More recently, some members of the current Court have expressed the view that testimonial dying declarations do not even implicate the Confrontation Clause. In *Giles*, Justice Breyer noted that a dying declaration is one made "when every motive to falsehood is silenced, and the mind is induced by the most powerful considerations to speak the truth."[343] Justice Ginsburg reached the same conclusion in her dissenting decision in *Bryant*.[344] Although the Supreme Court has yet to

---

337. Crawford v. Washington, 541 U.S. 36, 60 n.9 (2004). *See* State v. Williams, 52 A.3d 911, 918 (Me. 2012) (the admission of statements made "during the course and in furtherance of the conspiracy" in private, intimate conversations where the declarant "did not intend to establish facts that could reasonably be anticipated to be used at a later trial" did not violate the Confrontation Clause).

338. United States v. Davis, 742 F. App'x 435, 438 (11th Cir. 2018).

339. Orlando v. Nassau Cnty. Dist. Attorney's Off., 915 F.3d 113, 122 (2d Cir. 2019).

340. *Id.*

341. Ohio v. Roberts, 448 U.S. 56, 66 n.8 (1980).

342. The Confrontation Clause "is most naturally read as a reference to the right of confrontation at common law, admitting only those exceptions established at the time of the founding, [so] it follows that the common law pedigree of the exception for dying declarations poses no conflict with the Sixth Amendment." *Crawford*, 541 U.S. at 44.

343. Giles v. California, 554 U.S. 353, 397 (2008) (Breyer, J., dissenting).

344. According to Justice Ginsburg, the *Crawford* Court had acknowledged that "in the law we inherited from England, there was a well-established exception to the

decide a post-*Crawford* case involving the admissibility of a testimonial dying declaration, the federal and state courts regularly assume that dying declarations do not raise confrontation concerns.[345]

2. Statements Seeking Medical Treatment

The *Melendez-Diaz* Court noted in a footnote that "medical reports created for treatment purposes . . . would not be testimonial under our decision today."[346] In 2009, in *United States v. Santos*, the Fifth Circuit reached a similar conclusion, holding that admission of an stabbing victim's statement to a prison nurse describing his pain was not testimonial because (1) it was made during and to resolve an ongoing emergency and (2) the nurse was not gathering evidence but ascertaining the victim's level of pain.[347] Statements that relate to the

---

confrontation requirement: The cloak protecting the accused against admission of out-of-court testimonial statements was removed for dying declarations." Michigan v. Bryant, 562 U.S. 344, 395 (2011) (Ginsburg, J., dissenting). In her view, this would have been determinative if the prosecutor had not abandoned this argument. *Id.* at 396.

345. *See* State v. Hailes, 92 A.3d 544, 551–52 (Md. Ct. Spec. App. 2014) (regardless of whether the declaration was testimonial, the admission of a dying declaration that identified defendant as the shooter from a photographic array did not violate the Confrontation Clause); Commonwealth v. Middlemiss, 989 N.E.2d 871, 874 (Mass. 2013) (statements to a police officer at the scene were admissible as dying declarations and thus, were not subject to the Confrontation Clause). *But see* People v. Burns, 832 N.W.2d 738, 744 n.33 (Mass. 2013) (noting that the "United States Supreme Court has not expressly recognized that dying declarations are an exception to the Sixth Amendment's confrontation right"); Nesbitt v. St. Amand, 2011 WL 1232376, at *12 (D. Mass. Mar. 30, 2011) (reviewing recent cases from a range of federal courts and concluding that the post-*Crawford*/*Davis* admissibility of dying declarations has not been established); People v. Clay, 926 N.Y.S.2d 598, 608 (N.Y. App. Div. 2011) (stating "[a]lthough many dying declarations may not be testimonial, there is authority for admitting even those that clearly are" and joining "all of the other state courts that have decided this question . . . 'the Sixth Amendment incorporates an exception for testimonial dying declarations'"). *See generally* Nicolas, *supra* note 10, at 492, 545 (citing post-*Crawford* federal and state cases finding a confrontation exception for dying declarations, but also noting that the Supreme Court must still resolve three constitutional questions: (1) Can the dying declarations exception be invoked only in homicide cases?; (2) Is the exception limited to statements concerning the cause and circumstances of the declarant's impending death?; and (3) Must the declarant die?); Aviva Orenstein, *Her Last Words: Dying Declarations and Modern Confrontation Jurisprudence*, 2010 U. ILL. L. REV. 1411 (2010) (addressing the dying declarations exception in post-*Crawford* cases of femicide).

346. Melendez-Diaz v. Massachusetts, 557 U.S. 305, 312 n.2 (2009).

347. United States v. Santos, 589 F.3d 759, 763 (5th Cir. 2009). *See also* State v. Boggs, 185 P.3d 111, 123–24 (Ariz. 2008) (the admission of the victim's statements made as she lay dying on the ground describing the robbery and asking for help did not violate the Confrontation Clause because she was attempting to meet an ongoing emergency). *But see*

collection or preservation of medical evidence are especially likely to be deemed testimonial.[348] Statements are also more likely to be deemed testimonial if the declarant is responding to structured questions from medical professionals who have forensic training, such as sexual assault nurses[349] or members of a child protection team.[350]

3. *Statements Offered to Impeach*

Courts have consistently assumed that defendants do not have a right to confront testimonial statements admitted solely for impeachment purposes, because these statements are not offered for the truth of the matter asserted. For example, the Sixth Circuit has held that admission of a nontestifying codefendant's out-of-court statement (identifying the defendant as the shooter) did not violate the Confrontation Clause because the statement has been proffered solely for the nonhearsay purpose of impeaching the defendant's self-exculpatory trial

---

McCarley v. Kelly, 759 F.3d 535, 546 (6th Cir. 2014) (letters written by child psychologist to police officer detailing her therapy sessions with a child witness were "testimonial evidence where they were deliberately elicited in an interrogation-like atmosphere absent an ongoing emergency and used to prove past events in a later criminal prosecution") (internal citations omitted).

348. *See* McCarley v. Kelley, 801 F.3d 62 (6th Cir. 2015) (statements nontestimonial because primary purpose of a medical examination was to collect and preserve evidence).

349. *See* Hartsfield v. Commonwealth, 277 S.W.3d 239 (Ky. 2009) (interview conducted by the sexual assault nurse examiner was akin to a police interview). *But see* Miller v. Mitchell, 2014 WL 6472875, at *8 (D. Kan. 2014) (admission of testimony of sexual assault nurse examiner was not a violation of the defendant's right to confrontation because, although there was no emergency when the child made the statements to the nurse examiner, "there was an injury or a concern of injury which provided a medical purpose to the interview"). *See also* State v. Jones, 288 P.3d 140 (Kan. 2012) (determining whether a victim's statements to a sexual assault nurse examiner were testimonial is a highly context-dependent inquiry requiring an objective analysis of whether the nurse examiner is a state actor or agent, whether there was an ongoing emergency, whether the encounter was formal, and whether the primary purpose of the questioning is for a use other than the later prosecution of a crime).

350. *See* State v. Contreras, 979 So. 2d 896, 905 (Fla. 2008) (child protection team coordinator who took a statement from the alleged victim while in remote communication with the county sheriff was "serving as a police proxy"); McDonald v. Crews, 2014 WL 1328969, at *41 (N.D. Fla. 2014) (victim's statements to child protection team on video did not violate the right to confrontation because they fit the child hearsay exception in the Florida Statutes). *But see* People v. Jurewicz, 942 N.W.2d 116, 2019 WL 3642973 (Mich. Ct. App. 2019) (statements made by toddlers were not testimonial, despite the formality of the interviews because the purpose was to "ensure their safety and to aid a police investigation, and where the children were to young to understand the legal implications of their statements").

testimony.[351] Courts have specifically rejected defense arguments that *Crawford* bars the admission of testimonial statements offered for impeachment because "[t]he impeaching value of a prior inconsistent statement comes not from the fact that the prior statement is true and the later statement is false, but from the very fact of inconsistency."[352] Although this question appears generally well settled, one court has found—in an unusual situation—that a judgment of conviction used for impeachment was a testimonial statement.[353]

4. Statements Offered to Prove Notice

When out-of-court statements are offered not for the truth of the matter asserted, but instead to prove notice, they generally do not raise confrontation concerns. For example, the admission of Internal Revenue Service documents stating that certain payments to the defendant constituted "wages" was found not to violate the Confrontation Clause.[354] These records were offered by the prosecutor not to establish that the defendant had in fact received wages but solely for the limited purpose of showing that the IRS had placed the defendant on notice by communicating its opinion regarding such payments. Thus, even if the IRS statement was testimonial because it was prepared in anticipation of prosecution, the admission of the statements did not violate the Confrontation Clause.[355] The Eleventh Circuit reached a similar conclusion in a case involving out-of-court statements made

---

351. *See also* United States v. Davis, 577 F.3d 660 (6th Cir. 2009) (Confrontation Clause does not bar the nonhearsay use of testimonial statements). *But see* Mack v. State, 23 N.E.3d 742, 754–55 (Ind. Ct. App. 2014) (recorded statements made by confidential informant during a controlled drug buy, although not offered by the state to prove the truth of the matter asserted, were testimonial statements because "an objective witness would reasonably have believed that the purpose of the statements was to gather evidence of past events potentially relevant to a later criminal prosecution").

352. Jackson v. Stovall, No. 208-CV-10094, 2010 WL 1754446, at *13 (E.D. Mich. Apr. 12, 2010); Horton v. Martin, 509 F. App'x 762, 765 (10th Cir. 2013) (prosecutor's cross-examination of defendant's character witness using police reports and affidavits did not violate the Confrontation Clause because the testimonial statements were used for a purpose other than establishing the truth of the matter asserted).

353. United States v. Causevic, 636 F.3d 998, 1002 (8th Cir. 2011) ("At first blush, it seems that the Bosnian judgment, as a public record, differs significantly from Crawford's examples of testimonial statements, as well as the analysts' reports at issue in *Melendez–Diaz*, . . . [but finding a Confrontation Clause violation because] the defendant here challenges the government's use of a conviction for a significantly different purpose, namely, to show that he in fact committed the crime of which he was convicted.").

354. United States v. Henrickson, No. 08-20585, 2010 WL 1686799, at *5 (E.D. Mich. Apr. 26, 2010)

355. *Id.*

by unidentified witnesses because the statements had been admitted not for their substantive truth but solely to explain the police response.[356]

D. Statements to Nonofficials

In cases involving statements to people who are not government actors, courts have regularly found that testimonial statements do not raise confrontation concerns. In *Ohio v. Clark*, discussed earlier, the Court addressed the general question of "whether statements to persons other than law enforcement officers are subject to the Confrontation Clause."[357] According to *Clark*, "[b]ecause at least some statements to individuals who are not law enforcement officers could conceivably raise confrontation concerns, we decline to adopt a categorical rule excluding them from the Sixth Amendment's reach,"[358] but such statements "are much less likely to be testimonial than statements to law enforcement officers."[359]

For example, courts have admitted statements implicating the defendant made by an alleged child sexual assault victim ["J.B."] to a social worker and to her mother.[360] The fact that the social worker "had a duty to report child abuse to the Child Abuse Hotline[,]. . . . by itself, did not render all statements made by J.B. to her testimonial."[361] In this case, the court held that an "appropriate [confrontation] test should recognize the distinction between statements

356. United States v. Glover, 335 F. App'x 35 (11th Cir. 2009); United States v. Becknell, 601 F. App'x 709, 712 (10th Cir. 2015) ("conclusion that testimony is not hearsay because it was not offered for the truth of the matter asserted informs its Confrontation Clause status").

357. Ohio v. Clark, 576 U.S. 237, 244 (2015).

358. *Id.*

359. *Id.* The *Clark* Court elaborated on the special nature of a student-teacher relationship as follows:

> [A]lthough we decline to adopt a rule that statements to individuals who are not law enforcement officers are categorically outside the Sixth Amendment, the fact that L.P. was speaking to his teachers remains highly relevant. Courts must evaluate challenged statements in context, and part of that context is the questioner's identity. Statements made to someone who is not principally charged with uncovering and prosecuting criminal behavior are significantly less likely to be testimonial than statements given to law enforcement officers. It is common sense that the relationship between a student and his teacher is very different from that between a citizen and the police.

Id. at 249.

360. Seely v. State, 282 S.W.3d 778 (Ark. 2008).

361. *Id.* at 778.

to government officials and statements to nonofficials."[362] Here, the primary purpose of the communication was "ascertaining the nature of her injuries, providing comfort, and determining whether medical intervention was necessary"[363] and the statement was made in an informal setting.[364] Other courts have reached similar conclusions.[365] However, statements by children to police officers have been found to be testimonial when they were not spontaneous or made in the context of an ongoing emergency.[366] In a recent case involving allegations of sexual assault made by an eight-year-old child to a police officer, the court focused on the fact that the interrogations were more formal than those in *Clark* and "were memorialized in police reports and later introduce[d] into evidence at trial."[367] Additionally, the child was older than the three-year-old in *Clark*, making it more likely that the alleged victim understood that their statements could be used against the defendant in court.[368]

IX. The Right to Confrontation in Nontrial Proceedings

Federal and state cases have consistently rejected arguments that the right to confrontation should be recognized in a range of nontrial criminal proceedings.[369] A criminal defendant has no right to confrontation during a preliminary hearing.[370] A defendant also has no right

---

362. *Id.* at 787.

363. *Id.* at 788.

364. *See id.*

365. *See, e.g.*, Brown v. State, 703 S.E.2d 609 (Ga. 2010) (alleged victim's statements to family and friends nontestimonial because declarant had no reasonable expectation that they would be used at trial); State v. Code, 968 A.2d 1175 (N.J. 2009) (admission of an alleged victim's statements to her mother did not violate Confrontation Clause because the statements were not given in response to police evidence-gathering effort). *But see* N.W. v. State, 454 S.W.3d 271, 277–78 (Ark. App. Ct. 2015) (distinguishing the facts of this case from Seely and finding that the statements at issue were testimonial because "there was no evidence that the interview was to determine if any medical treatment was necessary . . . was watched by the police detective, the interviewer consulted with the detective to make sure all questions he wanted asked were asked, and the detective took a copy of the interview with him when he left").

366. Ramirez v. Tegels, No. 14-CV-802-JDP, 2019 WL 4721033 (W.D. Wis. Sept. 26, 2019).

367. *Id.*

368. *Id.*

369. In addition to the proceedings discussed herein, for an interesting analysis of the confrontation clause issues likely to arise in future terrorism prosecutions, see Norman Abrams, *Confrontation and Hearsay Issues on Federal Court Terrorism Prosecutions of Gitmo Detainees*, 75 Brook. L. Rev. 1067 (2010).

370. *See* Sheriff v. Witzenburg, 145 P.3d 1002 (Nev. 2006); State v. Rhinehart, 153 P.3d 830 (Utah App. 2006); State v. Woinarowicz, 720 N.W.2d 635 (N.D. 2006); People v. Brink,

to confrontation during a probation revocation proceeding,[371] transfer of custody hearing,[372] or a sentencing hearing.[373]

Courts have similarly refused to recognize a right to confrontation in quasi-judicial and administrative proceedings, even proceedings that may result in punitive consequences. For example, there is no right to confront government witnesses during a Transportation Security Administration hearing.[374] Detainees also may not confront government witnesses during immigration proceedings, regardless of the potential deportation or custodial consequences.[375] Courts have also refused to recognize a right to confrontation of witnesses for the state right during involuntary commitment proceedings.[376]

Although the clear trend is for courts to refuse to recognize confrontation outside the trial courtroom, one federal trial court has held that a defendant has a right to confrontation during both phases of federal capital sentencing.[377] In this case, the judge concluded that recent Supreme Court death penalty doctrine "strongly suggest[s] that a defendant's Sixth Amendment expansive trial rights extend

---

31 A.D.3d 1139, 818 N.Y.S.2d 374 (N.Y.A.D. 2006); People v. Felder, 129 P.3d 1072 (Colo. App. 2005); Vanmeter v. State, 165 S.W.3d 68 (Tex. App. 2005) (all of which held that *Crawford* is not applicable to pretrial suppression hearing because right of confrontation is a trial right). *See also* Commonwealth v. Tyler, 587 A.2d 326 (Penn. 1991); State v. Sherry, 667 P.2d 367 (Kan. 1983); Rex v. Sullivan, 575 P.2d 408 (Colo. 1978); Mitchell v. State, 267 N.W.2d 349 (Wis. 1978) (pre-*Crawford* decisions which held that the Sixth Amendment right to confrontation is not applicable to preliminary hearings).

371. Harris v. Fulwood, 989 F. Supp. 2d 64, 73 (D.C. Cir. 2015) (noting that the right to confront and cross-examine witnesses against the accused has been held inapplicable to parole revocation proceedings); Petty v. Wainwright, 917 F. Supp. 2d 4, 6 (D.D.C. 2012) (supervision revocation hearing is administrative in nature and is not a criminal proceeding to which "the full panoply of rights due a [criminal] defendant" attach) (citations omitted); Hawthorne v. State, 953 So. 2d 751 (Fla. 2007).

372. *In re* S.M., 207 S.W.3d 421 (Tex. 2006).

373. *See* United States v. Coonce, 932 F.3d 623, 640–41 (9th Cir. 2019) (citing Williams v. New York, 337 U.S. 241 (1949) (there is no right to confrontation during sentencing for capital murder); United States v. Smith, 751 F.3d 107, 116 (3d Cir. 2014) (the Confrontation Clause does not prevent the admissibility of testimonial statement at a sentencing hearing); United States v. Goodon, 742 F.3d 373, 375–76 (8th Cir. 2014) (admission at a sentencing hearing of a certified copy of a conviction does not violate the Confrontation Clause).

374. Sutera v. Transp. Sec. Admin, 708 F. Supp. 2d 304 (E.D.N.Y. 2010).

375. Stolaj v. Holder, 577 F.3d 651 (6th Cir. 2009); Sova v. Holder, 451 F. App'x 543, 547 (6th Cir. 2011) (immigration proceeding seeking discretionary relief "was not a criminal proceeding, so the Confrontation Clause does not apply").

376. People v. Sweeney, 95 Cal. Rptr. 3d 557 (Cal. Ct. App. 2009); People v. Sarpas, 172 Cal. Rptr. 3d 25, 52 (Cal. Ct. App. 2014) (Confrontation Clause does not apply to civil actions).

377. *See* United States v. Mills, 446 F. Supp. 2d 1115 (C.D. Cal. 2006); United States v. Umana, 762 F.3d 413, 414–15 (4th Cir. 2014) (the Confrontation Clause does not apply to capital sentencing).

into the eligibility and selection phases" of the capital sentencing process.[378] In light of these recent cases and because "all of the alleged aggravating factors—statutory or nonstatutory—are of constitutional significance[,]. . . . the jury's factfinding [in all phases of capital sentencing] . . . should be accompanied by the same constitutional protections as those which accompany the trial of elements."[379] The Arkansas Supreme Court has extended this reasoning to noncapital sentencing hearings if they are held before a jury.[380] According to this court, the same protections should inure in noncapital cases whenever defendants are sentenced by a jury because constitutional protections should not be limited by the available punishment and a sentencing body's need for evidence "does not sanction the admission of unconstitutional evidence against the defendant."[381]

X. Confrontation and Codefendant Confessions

A. The *Bruton* Rule

In 1968, in *Bruton v. United States*, the Supreme Court interpreted the Confrontation Clause to bar admission of a codefendant's confession implicating a nonconfessing defendant at a joint trial.[382] Prior to *Bruton*, federal and state criminal courts had generally assumed that when defendants were tried together, confessions by one defendant that implicated another defendant could be admitted without violating the Confrontation Clause *if* the judge instructed the jury that the confession was admissible only against the confessing codefendant.[383] The *Bruton* Court found that the admission of a confession under these circumstances "violated petitioner's right of cross-examination secured by the Confrontation Clause of the Sixth Amendment" based on "the substantial risk that the jury, despite instructions to the contrary, looked to the incriminating extrajudicial statements in determining petitioner's guilt."[384] According to the Court, "[t]he fact of the

378. *Mills*, 446 F. Supp. 2d at 1122.

379. *Id.* at 1135.

380. *See* Vankirk v. State, 385 S.W.3d 144, 147–48 (Ark. 2011). *But see* State v. Martinez, 303 P.3d 627, 632 n.8 (Idaho Ct. App. 2013) ("The only cases we have located where state courts have held *Crawford*'s protections extend to sentencing proceedings are those where the evidence in question, unlike in this case, was presented to a *jury* during the punishment phase of the trial").

381. *Vankirk*, 385 S.W.3d at 150.

382. Bruton v. United States, 391 U.S. 123 (1968).

383. *See* Delli Paoli v. United States, 352 U.S. 232 (1957) (it is possible for jurors to follow jury instructions to disregard inculpatory references to a nonconfessing codefendant).

384. *Bruton*, 391 U.S. at 126.

matter is that too often such admonition against misuse is intrinsically ineffective in that the effect of such a nonadmissible declaration cannot be wiped from the brains of the jurors."[385]

The *Bruton* Court understood the Confrontation Clause to protect defendants from this specific harm because "[a] basic premise of the Confrontation Clause . . . is that certain kinds of hearsay are at once so damaging, so suspect, and yet so difficult to discount, that jurors cannot be trusted to give such evidence the minimal weight that it deserves."[386] Thus, the Court held that prosecutors can admit a nontestifying codefendant's interlocking confession only if it has been effectively redacted or if the defendants' trials are severed and the confession is introduced only against the confessing defendant.

After *Bruton*, the Court clarified that the Confrontation Clause is violated by the admission of a nontestifying codefendant's confession, even when the defendant's own confession (reciting essentially the same information) has been admitted.[387] The justices also distinguished confessions that explicitly and directly incriminate codefendants from those that incriminate codefendants *only* inferentially when combined with other evidence.[388] In cases where a nontestifying codefendant's confession incriminates the defendant only when combined with other incriminating evidence, the Confrontation Clause is not violated if "the confession is redacted to eliminate not only the

385. *Id.* at 129. The *Bruton* justices clarified the scope of their decision writing that "in many such cases the jury can and will follow the trial judge's instructions to disregard such information. . . . [however,] there are some contexts in which the risk that the jury will not, or cannot, follow instructions is so great, and the consequences of failure so vital to the defendant, that the practical and human limitations of the jury system cannot be ignored." *Id.* at 135.

386. *Id.* at 138 (Stewart, J., concurring).

387. Cruz v. New York, 481 U.S. 186, 193 (1987) ("We hold that, where a nontestifying codefendant's confession incriminating the defendant is not directly admissible against the defendant, the Confrontation Clause bars its admission at their joint trial, even if the jury is instructed not to consider it against the defendant, and even if the defendant's own confession is admitted against him.").

388. In *Richardson v. Marsh*, 481 U.S. 200, 208 (1987), the Court found that when a confession "was not incriminating on its face, and became so only when linked with evidence introduced later at trial (the defendant's own testimony)[,] . . . it is a less valid generalization that the jury will not likely obey the instruction to disregard the evidence." *See also* United States v. Boyd, 78 F. Supp. 3d 1207, 1213 (N.D. Cal. 2015) (coded statement by declarant in which defendant is not mentioned and the pronouns used to refer to the male defendant were feminine is not so "powerfully incriminating" as to fall within the scope of *Bruton* because it is "not a confession directly referring to" the defendant and "several inferential leaps must be made in order for the statement to be incriminating at all"); United States v. Stevens, 778 F. Supp. 2d 683 (W.D. La. 2011) ("Confessions that are only 'incriminating by connection' to other evidence are not excluded under *Bruton*.").

defendant's name, but any reference to his or her existence."[389] However, the redaction must be full and effective. Thus, the Confrontation Clause is violated if the defendant's name is simply removed and the nontestifying codefendant's confession retains direct and obvious references to "someone" whose name has obviously been deleted.[390]

B. Applying *Crawford* to Limit *Bruton*

Prior to *Crawford*, courts applied *Bruton* to confessions and other incriminating statements made to nonstate actors, such as jailhouse informants, because the same prejudice inured to the nonconfessing codefendant.[391] Federal and state courts have now begun to read *Crawford* to limit the scope of *Bruton*. This has resulted in a series of recent cases approving the admission of a nontestifying codefendant's unredacted interlocking confessions based on the finding that the confession was not a testimonial statement under *Crawford*. The Seventh Circuit has held that "[a] *Bruton* violation occurs only if the confession of a non-testifying co-defendant facially incriminates the

389. *Richardson*, 481 U.S. at 211.

390. Gray v. Maryland, 523 U.S. 185, 192 (1998) ("Redactions that simply replace a name with an obvious blank space or a word such as "deleted" or a symbol or other similarly obvious indications of alteration, however, leave statements that, considered as a class, so closely resemble *Bruton*'s unredacted statements that, in our view, the law must require the same result."). *See also* United States v. Ashburn, 2015 WL 588704, at *28 (E.D.N.Y. 2015) ("where complete redaction would distort the confession . . . by excluding substantially exculpatory information, or changing the tenor of the utterance as a whole, district courts are permitted to replace the declarant's reference to a co-defendant with neutral pronouns, such as another person, my neighbor, this guy, friend, and similar language" and such redactions "are consistent with *Bruton* if the altered statement uses words that might actually have been said by a person admitting his own culpability in the charged conspiracy while shielding the specific identify of his confederate") (citations omitted); United States v. West, 790 F. Supp. 2d 687, 691 (N.D. Ill. 2011) ("a court does not consider a redacted statement in isolation, [r]ather, it can and should consider the surrounding circumstances in determining whether the redacted statement impermissibly identifies a non-testifying co-defendant"). *See generally* Kevin Wynosky, *Avoiding the Prisoner's Dilemma: Refining the Bruton Rule to Resolve the Split over Neutral Term Substitution*, 166 U. Pa. L. Rev. Online 205 (2018) (student-written comment discussing the divisions among the federal circuits—including internal circuit splits—regarding the use of neutral term substitution in codefendant confessions).

391. *See* United States v. Veltmann, 6 F.3d 1483 (11th Cir. 1993) (under *Bruton*, the Confrontation Clause was violated by the admission of a nontestifying codefendant's statements to a cellmate, incriminating defendant); United States v. Samson, 540 F. App'x 927, 932 (11th Cir. 2013) (although codefendant's "references to three other robbers might have helped incriminate Samson when linked with the other evidence presented at trial, this is insufficient to sustain a *Bruton* violation, as the statements were not incriminating on their faces").

non-confessing co-defendant."[392] This ruling is consistent with decisions from other courts,[393] and the Seventh Circuit's more sweeping conclusion that "it is now clear that the Confrontation Clause does not apply to non-testimonial statements by an out-of-court declarant."[394]

The case law reveals a trend in favor of viewing *Bruton* objections through a "*Crawford* lens," despite the fact that the harm that *Bruton* sought to prevent is not ameliorated by deeming the subject confession "nontestimonial."[395] In a conflicting decision rejecting the argument that *Crawford* limits *Bruton*, a California federal district court wrote that "[t]he *Bruton* Court did not draw a distinction between extra-judicial statements that are testimonial in nature (e.g., statements given to the police during interrogation) and statements that are not (e.g., casual remarks to acquaintances)."[396] This led that court to conclude that although *Crawford* identified testimonial statements as the "primary object" of the Confrontation Clause, the Supreme Court has not decided that the right to confrontation is limited to this "primary object."

---

392. United States v. Spagnola, 632 F.3d 981, 988 (7th Cir. 2011); United States v. Boyd, 78 F. Supp. 3d 1207, 1213 (N.D. Cal. 2015) ("the *Bruton* rule is limited to confessions of a non-testifying codefendant that are facially incriminating of another defendant").

393. *See* United States v. Johnson, 581 F.3d 320, 326 (6th Cir. 2009) (*Bruton* does not apply to nontestimonial statements); United States v. Avila Vargas, 570 F.3d 1004, 1009 (8th Cir. 2009) (same); United States v. Dargan, 738 F.3d 643, 651 (4th Cir. 2013) (same).

394. United States v. Dale, 614 F.3d 942, 955 (7th Cir. 2010). *See also* United States v. Smalls, 605 F.3d 765, 768 n.2 (10th Cir. 2010); United States v. Diaz, 2014 WL 1308601, at *8 (D. Nev. 2014) (applying the general rule "that statements made unwittingly by a non-testifying codefendant to an undercover officer or informant are nontestimonial" and finding that *Bruton* does not apply because the prosecutor will not elicit statements by codefendant to confidential informant incriminating defendant).

395. *See, e.g.*, United States v. Reyes-Garcia, 798 F. App'x 346 (11th Cir. 2019) (the admission of a nontestifying codefendant's statement does not violate the Confrontation Clause or *Bruton*, because they were statements to an acquaintance and are nontestimonial in nature); Wisconsin v. Nieves, 897 N.W.2d 363 (Wis. 2017) (Crawford limits *Bruton* to statements from codefendants that are testimonial in nature, in a case involving jailhouse statements by a codefendant to an informant implicating defendant in homicide offenses, because the setting was not formal and no facts suggested that these statements had been made for the primary purpose of creating evidence for defendant's prosecution).

396. Montiel v. Evans, 2011 WL 1135336, at *8 n.7 (C.D. Cal. 2011); Colin Miller, *Avoiding a Confrontation? How Courts Have Erred in Finding That Nontestimonial Hearsay Is Beyond the Scope of the* Bruton *Doctrine*, 77 Brook. L. Rev. 625 (2012). *But see* United States v. DeLeon, 341 P.3d 315, 334 (Wash. Ct. App. 2014) ("it is necessary to view *Bruton* through the lens of *Crawford* with the result that *Bruton*'s restriction on the admission of the inculpatory statements by a jointly tried codefendant is limited to testimonial hearsay") (internal quotes omitted).

CHAPTER 7

The Compulsory Process Clause

"In all criminal prosecutions, the accused shall enjoy the right to a speedy and public trial, by an impartial jury of the State and district wherein the crime shall have been committed, which district shall have been previously ascertained by law, and to be informed of the nature and cause of the accusation; to be confronted with the witnesses against him; *to have compulsory process for obtaining witnesses in his favor*, and to have the Assistance of Counsel for his defense."[1]

I. Historical Foundations of the Compulsory Process Clause

A. Development of Compulsory Process in England

Nestled near the end of the Sixth Amendment—but not to be forgotten—the Compulsory Process Clause enshrines the defendant's right to compel, through the power of a court's subpoena, a witness to give sworn testimony in order to present an adequate defense.[2]

When the Founders crafted the Sixth Amendment, they did not carry forward ages-old English common law. Under ancient civil law, the accused had no opportunity to rebut witnesses or to present his own.[3] As the modern trial started to develop during the fifteenth

1. U.S. CONST. amend. VI (emphasis added).

2. HELLER, THE SIXTH AMENDMENT TO THE CONSTITUTION OF THE UNITED STATES 108 (Univ. of Kan. Press 1951). *But see* Hoeffel, *The Sixth Amendment's Lost Cause: Unearthing Compulsory Process*, 2002 WIS. L. REV. 1275 (2002) ("The Compulsory Process Clause of the Sixth Amendment is overlooked, underutilized, and rarely discussed.").

3. *See* HELLER, *supra* note 2, at 107. *See also* Huff, *Witness for the Defense: The Compulsory Process Clause as a Limit on Extraterritorial Criminal Jurisdiction*, 15 TEX. REV. L. & POL. 130, 132 (2010) ("As late as the sixteenth century, English defendants were not permitted to call witnesses, even if they were present in the courtroom and prepared to testify.") (citing Westen, *The Compulsory Process Clause*, 73 MICH. L. REV. 71, 83 (1974)).

century, courts "began to separate the duty of a witness from the duty of a juror, allowing for independent witnesses and jurors without knowledge of the case."[4] At this time, defendants had the right to address the jury and provide their own unsworn testimony, but they had no other trial rights.[5] In fact, English defendants could not call witnesses, even if the witnesses were present in the courtroom and willing to testify.[6] As England entered the seventeenth century, courts began to allow defendants to call witnesses who could provide *unsworn* testimony on their behalf, which slightly blunted the power imbalance skewed to favor the Crown.[7]

It was not until the seventeenth century, after a series of high-profile treason trials and the Puritan rebellion, that criminal procedure reforms began to make their way through the British Parliament.[8] Although the Restoration briefly interrupted these developments, the widely known abuses of this period may have strengthened the protections contained in the Bill of Rights of 1689.[9] In 1695, the British Parliament enacted a statute granting a range of rights to those accused of treason, including the right to compel sworn testimony from reluctant witnesses. Six years later, Parliament extended these rights to all felony defendants.[10] Thus, by the time of the American Revolution, the two principal prongs of compulsory process—the defendant's right to compel witnesses and to obtain their sworn testimony—were firmly entrenched in English law.[11]

---

4. *See* Hoeffel, *supra* note 2, at 1279.

5. *See id.* at 1279–81 (citing HOLDSWORTH, A HISTORY OF ENGLISH LAW 224, 229, 232–33 (3d ed. 1944)).

6. *See* Huff, *supra* note 3, at 132.

7. *See* Westen, *supra* note 3, at 84. Westen, in the first of his three comprehensive law review articles about the clause, wrote that at the time, "[t]he accused, however, still lacked two advantages possessed by the Crown: the right to compel witnesses to appear and testify and the right to have his testimony sworn." *Id. See also* Hoeffel, *supra* note 2 (noting that a defendant's witnesses "somehow had to avoid directly contradicting the Crown's witnesses").

8. *See* Huff, *supra* note 3, at 134.

9. *See* Westen, *supra* note 3, at 89 (citations omitted) (noting that by the end of the seventeenth century, criminal defendants had the right to be free from excessive bail, to have pretrial detention reviewed by habeas corpus, to be informed of the charges against them, to have assistance of counsel, to refuse to answer incriminating questions, to be confronted with witnesses against them, and to be free from cruel and unusual punishment).

10. *See* Hoeffel, *supra* note 2, at 1281 (citing Clinton, *The Right to Present a Defense: An Emergent Constitutional Guarantee in Criminal Trials*, 9 IND. L. REV. 711, 720 (1976)).

11. *See* Westen, *supra* note 3, at 90. *See also* Huff, *supra* note 3, at 134.

B. Development of Compulsory Process during the American Colonial and Revolutionary Periods

American colonists, who were still British subjects, kept abreast of criminal procedure developments in England.[12] During the tumultuous Stuart period of the seventeenth and early eighteenth centuries, which was "experienced on both sides of the Atlantic,"[13] the colonists followed and supported a range of legal reforms.[14] The most progressive colony was Pennsylvania, which may be attributable to the fact that its founder William Penn "had been a criminal defendant in England subject to the panoply of limitations on his right to present a defense."[15] By 1750, Pennsylvania, along with Maryland, Massachusetts, and Virginia, allowed defendants to subpoena witnesses, order them to the stand, and elicit their sworn testimony for the defense.[16] In 1769, when Parliament debated a proposal "authorizing Americans charged with treason to be transferred to England for trial[,]. . . . [t]he Virginia House of Burgesses howled in protest. . . . immediately pass[ing] a series of resolutions condemning it as highly derogatory of the rights of British subjects."[17] By granting greater rights to the criminal defendant than were available in England, the colonies were expressing their specific disapproval of the possibility that they might be tried in England and their general and increasing alienation from England and English law.[18]

C. Compulsory Process as a Constitutional Right

As the emerging American states began to draft their respective constitutions and bills of rights, they included a range of criminal procedure principles, such as the subpoena power, the right to present evidence and sworn testimony, and the right to confront witnesses.[19] Although the precise definition of these rights varied among the states, these documents "reflected the principle that the defendant must have a meaningful opportunity . . . to establish the essential elements of his case."[20] Of the thirteen original colonies, nine included

12. *See* Huff, *supra* note 3, at 135.
13. *Id.* at 91.
14. *See* Clinton, *supra* note 10, at 728–29.
15. *See* Hoeffel, *supra* note 2, at 1281.
16. *See* Westen, *supra* note 3, at 93.
17. *See* Huff, *supra* note 3, at 135.
18. *Id.*
19. *See* Westen, *supra* note 3, at 95.
20. *See* Clinton, *supra* note 10, at 726.

specific provisions establishing compulsory process in their founding documents.[21]

The Articles of Confederation, which were ratified in 1781, and the Constitution of the United States, ratified in 1788, did not include similar criminal procedure protections and some Anti-Federalists explained their opposition to the Constitution on this ground.[22] Almost half of the states took a similar view and conditioned their ratification of the Constitution on the addition of various "bill of rights"-type amendments, including the right of the accused to present witnesses in his defense.[23] For example, representatives from Virginia, Pennsylvania, North Carolina, and New York specifically advocated for more aggressive language to protect a defendant's right to call for evidence in his favor.[24]

James Madison authored most of the Bill of Rights, including the Sixth Amendment.[25] His draft version of the Sixth Amendment contained language almost identical to the Virginia rule, except for the compulsory process provision, which suggests that he did not want to replicate the precise language of any state statute.[26] Instead of guaranteeing the defendant the right "to call for evidence in his favor," Madison's draft secured the defendant's right "to have compulsory process for obtaining witnesses in his favor."[27] Madison may also have altered the language to "make it perfectly clear that part of calling witnesses in one's favor includes, by necessity, the right to have them compelled."[28]

The draft Bill of Rights was introduced in the House in June 1789 and ratified and added to the Constitution in 1791. During two and a half years of debate, the Compulsory Process Clause was discussed just once and the only alteration to the initial draft was to change "*a* compulsory process" to "compulsory process."[29]

21. *See* Huff, *supra* note 3, at 136.
22. Clinton, *supra* note 10, at 731 n.96.
23. *See* Westen, *supra* note 3, at 95.
24. *See* Huff, *supra* note 3, at 136.
25. *Id.* at 136–37.
26. *See* Westen, *supra* note 3, at 97–98.
27. *Id.* at 97.
28. *See* Hoeffel, *supra* note 2, at 1287.
29. *See* Huff, *supra* note 3, at 137.

II. Compulsory Process and the Supreme Court

A. The Treason Trial of Aaron Burr

The first test of the scope of the Sixth Amendment Compulsory Process Clause occurred during the treason trial of former Vice President Aaron Burr in 1807. Burr was accused of plotting to go to war with Spain in the hope of establishing a separate government in the western states.[30] At issue were letters Burr sought to present in his defense, some of which were written by his archenemy, the president of the United States, Thomas Jefferson.[31] The Jefferson administration complied with the defendant's subpoena and produced the letters, including a heavily redacted letter at the center of the controversy. Still, the defendants sought additional evidence and filed a second motion requesting the unedited letters and demanding an indefinite postponement of the trial until the evidence was produced.[32]

Chief Justice John Marshall's opinion gave a defendant's right to compulsory process a broad and forceful interpretation.[33] The Chief Justice, who had been a member of the Virginia convention that advocated inclusion of the compulsory process right in the Constitution of the United States, explicitly recognized the centrality of the defendant's right "to present evidence on [his] own behalf."[34] Chief Justice Marshall described the *core purpose* of compulsory process as enabling a defendant to present evidence in support of his defense and to obtain subpoenas before and after indictment so that he can prepare his defense.[35] According to the *Burr* Court, the defendant's right to obtain information "essential to the defense" outweighed the president's interest in secrecy.[36] The Court's conclusion that the right secured by the Compulsory Process Clause "must be deemed sacred by the courts" gave force and meaning to the new right of compulsory process.[37]

30. *Id.*
31. *See* Westen, *supra* note 3, at 103.
32. *Id.*
33. *See* Clinton, *supra* note 10, at 770–71.
34. *Id.* at 771.
35. United States v. Burr, 25 F. Cas. 30, 33 (C.C.D. Va. 1807).
36. *Id.* at 37.
37. *Id.* at 33.

B. Incorporation of the Right to Compulsory Process to the States

After the Burr trial, the Supreme Court rarely considered the Compulsory Process Clause for over 150 years until the seminal case of *Washington v. Texas*,[38] which incorporated the right as a fundamental element of due process and made it applicable to the states via the Fourteenth Amendment.[39] There, the Court rejected a Texas rule that prevented a defendant from obtaining testimony from any alleged accomplice.[40]

Chief Justice Warren, who wrote for the Court, found that state efforts to avoid unreliable testimony cannot violate "[t]he right of an accused to have compulsory process for obtaining witnesses in his favor[, which] stands on no lesser footing than the other Sixth Amendment rights that we have previously held applicable to the States."[41] The Court also specifically noted that the Clause affords defendants the right to offer the testimony of witnesses *and* the right to compel reluctant witnesses to testify via the subpoena power of the courts.[42] The purpose of the Compulsory Process Clause, according to the Court, is "in plain terms" the protection of "the right to present a defense, the right to present the defendant's version of the facts as well as the prosecution's to the jury so it may decide where the truth lies."[43]

C. Defining the Scope of the Right to Compulsory Process

1. The Right to Compel Testimony from a Former Accomplice

In *Washington*, Texas law prevented persons charged as principals, accomplices, or accessories in the same crime from testifying as witnesses for each other, although they could testify for the state.[44] The defendant (Washington) had sought to call an alleged accomplice (Fuller) to testify that Fuller fired the shotgun that fatally wounded the deceased and that Washington tried to dissuade him and ran

38. Washington v. Texas, 388 U.S. 14, 23 (1967).

39. *Id.* at 23. *See also* Melendez-Diaz v. Massachusetts, 557 U.S. 305, 325 (2009) (discussing the functional difference from the defendant's perspective between compulsory process and confrontation rights).

40. *Washington*, 388 U.S. at 23. The rule at issue was based on the assumption that accomplice testimony is not reliable evidence. *Id.*

41. *Id.* at 18.

42. *Id.* at 19.

43. *Id.*

44. *Id.* at 16.

away before Fuller fired.[45] The trial judge applied the state law and did not allow Fuller to testify. Washington was convicted and his appeal was upheld by Texas Court of Criminal Appeals.[46] According to the U.S. Supreme Court, the Texas law precluding accomplice testimony was unconstitutional because the "Framers of the Constitution did not intend to commit the futile act of giving to a defendant the right to secure the attendance of witnesses whose testimony he had no right to use."[47]

Five years later, the Court confronted a related question in *Cool v. United States*[48] and applied a similar rationale. There, the jurors had been instructed that they should reject exculpatory testimony for the defense provided by an alleged accomplice unless they found the testimony true beyond a reasonable doubt.[49] The *Cool* Court held that this jury instruction violated the Compulsory Process Clause as construed in *Washington v. Texas* by preventing the defense from obtaining relevant exculpatory evidence because it *might* be unreliable.[50] One commentator has suggested that it is "natural to draw the inference from the *Cool* decision that the Court viewed the impermissible jury instruction as conflicting with *Washington*'s prohibition against assuming that some [defense] witnesses' testimonies are not worthy of belief."[51]

2. The Right to Compel Privileged or Confidential Information

In *Pennsylvania v. Ritchie*,[52] the defendant was charged with the rape of his teenage daughter. The defendant sought to compel the production of records maintained by the state department of children and youth services.[53] The prosecutor responded by arguing that the records were privileged.[54]

When the case reached the Supreme Court, Justice Powell began by noting that after *United States v. Burr* was decided in 1807, "the Compulsory Process Clause was rarely a factor in this Court's

45. *Id.*
46. *Id.* at 17.
47. *Id.* at 23.
48. Cool v. United States, 409 U.S. 100 (1972).
49. *Id.* at 104.
50. *Id.* at 101–02.
51. Garcia, *The Compulsory Process Clause and the "Sporting Theory of Justice": The Supreme Court Evens the Score*, 28 Duq. L. Rev. 619, 630 (1990).
52. 480 U.S. 39 (1987).
53. *Id.* at 43.
54. *Id.*

decisions during the next 160 years."[55] The *Ritchie* Court found that the Compulsory Process Clause guarantees, "at a minimum[,] . . . [that] criminal defendants have the right to the government's assistance in compelling the attendance of favorable witnesses at trial and the right to put before a jury evidence that might influence the determination of guilt."[56] However, the Court opted to analyze the defendant's claim under the Due Process Clause of the Fourteenth Amendment because "compulsory process provides no *greater* protections in this area than those afforded by due process."[57] Thus, the justices "need not decide today whether and how the guarantees of the Compulsory Process Clause differ from those of the Fourteenth Amendment."[58]

In a decision that explicitly balanced the defendant's rights against the state privilege, the *Ritchie* Court concluded that allowing full disclosure of the Department of Children and Youth Services files would "sacrifice unnecessarily the State's compelling interest in protecting its child abuse information."[59] Under these circumstances, in camera review by the trial court would serve to protect both the defendant's right to discovery of exculpatory evidence that "probably would have changed the outcome of the trial"[60] and the state's interest in protecting the sensitive information.[61]

An increasingly important limitation for compelling confidential information is the Classified Information Procedures Act, enacted in 1980. It provides for special procedural mechanisms in cases where information deemed by the government as sensitive to national security might otherwise be admitted into evidence in a criminal trial.[62] Of particular importance, section 6 allows the government to challenge the "use, relevance, or admissibility of classified information" to be offered at trial in a special hearing that the court is required to conduct.[63] The hearing may be conducted in camera.[64] Even if the court finds that the evidence would normally be admissible, the government

55. *Id.* at 55.
56. *Id*
57. *Id.*
58. *Id.*
59. *Id.* at 60.
60. *Id.* at 58.
61. *Id.* at 61.
62. 18 U.S.C. app. 3 §§ 1–16 (2006).
63. *Id.* § 6(a).
64. In order for the hearing to be conducted in camera, the attorney general must certify that such a hearing in public "may result in the disclosure of classified information." *Id.*

may move ex parte to have the classified information substituted by a government admission or a summary of the information, which the court must grant if it finds that disclosure "would cause identifiable damage to the national security of the United States."[65]

3. The Right to Compel Exculpatory Evidence

Although compulsory process guarantees defendants the right to call witnesses into court, it does not necessarily include, in all cases, the right to compel the prosecution to turn over exculpatory evidence.[66] In *United States v. Nixon*, the Supreme Court balanced concerns of executive privilege against the defendant's right to compulsory process:

> The allowance of the privilege to withhold evidence that is demonstrably relevant in a criminal trial would cut deeply into the guarantee of due process of law and gravely impair the basic function of the courts. A President's acknowledged need for confidentiality in the communications of his office is general in nature, whereas the constitutional need for production of relevant evidence in a criminal proceeding is specific and central to the fair adjudication of a particular criminal case in the administration of justice. Without access to specific facts a criminal prosecution may be totally frustrated.[67]

The *Nixon* Court decided that "[t]he President's broad interest in confidentiality of communications will not be vitiated by disclosure of a limited number of conversations preliminarily shown to have some bearing on the pending criminal cases."[68] The justices there clearly suggested that compulsory process could require the production of evidence relevant to the defense. Subsequently, some state courts decided that defendants have the right to access "present exculpatory evidence, including impeachment evidence, in the possession of a third party."[69] Nevertheless, the vast majority of production of evidence issues have been evaluated under the Due Process Clause.[70]

---

65. 18 U.S.C. app. 3 § 6(c) (2006).
66. *Ritchie*, 480 U.S. at 56.
67. United States v. Nixon, 418 U.S. 683, 712–13 (1974).
68. *Id.* at 713.
69. Commonwealth v. Barroso, 122 S.W.3d 554, 561 (Ky. 2003); *see also In re* Farber, 78 N.J. 259, 274 (1978).
70. *Ritchie*, 480 U.S. at 56 (citing United States v. Bagley, 473 U.S. 667 (1985)); Brady v. Maryland, 373 U.S. 83, 83 (1963). *See also* Wardius v. Oregon, 412 U.S. 470 (1973).

D. Limiting the Right to Compulsory Process

1. Discovery Sanctions

The Supreme Court did not address the question of limits to a defendant's right to compulsory process until the late 1980s. In *Taylor v. Illinois*,[71] defense counsel had violated a state reciprocal discovery rule that required the defendant and prosecutor to reveal the names and addresses of their witnesses before trial. On the second day of trial, defense counsel sought to amend his pretrial witness list.[72] He explained to the trial court that the two last-minute additions were necessary because "he had just been informed about them and that they had probably seen the entire incident."[73] Only one of the two witnesses arrived in court the following day.[74] During defense counsel's offer of proof, the witness indicated that he could provide relevant and exculpatory testimony, but also revealed that he had not observed the alleged crime and that defense counsel had visited him at his home a week before the trial began.[75] Because the witness directly contradicted defense counsel's explanation for the delay, the trial judge sanctioned the defense for a "willful and blatant" discovery violation by barring the witness's trial testimony.[76]

The Supreme Court affirmed. Justice Stevens, writing for the majority explained that the constitutional promise of compulsory process is limited by the nature of the right:

> There is a significant difference between the Compulsory Process Clause weapon and other rights that are protected by the Sixth Amendment—its availability is dependent entirely on the defendant's initiative. Most other Sixth Amendment rights arise automatically on the initiation of the adversary process and no action by the defendant is necessary to make them active in his or her case. While those rights shield the defendant from potential prosecutorial abuses, the right to compel the presence and present the testimony of witnesses provides the defendant with a sword that may be employed to rebut the prosecution's case. The decision whether to employ it in a particular case rests solely with the defendant. The very nature of

71. Taylor v. Illinois, 484 U.S. 400 (1988).
72. *Id.* at 403.
73. *Id.* at 417. *See also* Garcia, *supra* note 51, at 648.
74. *Taylor*, 484 U.S. at 417.
75. *Id.*
76. *Id.* at 416.

> the right requires that its effective use be preceded by deliberate planning and affirmative conduct.[77]

Accordingly, "[t]he accused does not have an unfettered right to offer testimony that is incompetent, privileged, or otherwise inadmissible under standard rules of evidence. The Compulsory Process Clause provides him with an effective weapon, but it is a weapon that cannot be used irresponsibly."[78] The Court further reasoned that the integrity of the adversarial process depends on the presentation of reliable evidence and the fair and efficient administration of trial procedure.[79] According to the justices, the sanction was necessary and proper because "[d]iscovery, like cross-examination, minimizes the risk that a judgment will be predicated on incomplete, misleading, or even deliberately fabricated testimony."[80]

The *Taylor* Court approved the trial judge's selection of the most onerous sanction available under the relevant state rules because a less severe penalty "would perpetuate rather than limit the prejudice to the State and the harm to the adversary process."[81] Finally, Justice Stevens cautioned that "[w]henever a lawyer makes use of the sword provided by the Compulsory Process Clause, there is some risk that he may wound his own client."[82] It is worth noting that the *Taylor* majority simply ignored both that there was no evidence that the witness's testimony was unreliable and that there was minimal prejudice to the prosecutor, who could have simply sought a brief delay to prepare for cross-examination.

In his dissent, Justice Brennan complained that the majority had failed to acknowledge the centrality of the excluded witness's testimony to Taylor's defense.[83] One commentator agreed that the *Taylor* Court "conveniently missed the primary lesson of *Washington*: that the defendant's right to present exculpatory evidence outweighs the court's interest in preventing perjured or otherwise potentially unreliable testimony."[84] Justice Brennan also viewed the extreme

---

77. *Id.* at 410 (citation omitted).

78. *Id.* at 410.

79. *Id.* at 412.

80. *Id.*

81. *Id.* at 413. *But see id.* at 419 for Justice Brennan's spirited dissent that the trial court's sanction was disproportionate in this case.

82. *Id.* at 418.

83. *Id.* at 419.

84. *See* Garcia, *supra* note 51, at 651.

sanction as especially inappropriate given that there was no evidence that the defendant himself engaged in any wrongful behavior.[85]

Three years after *Taylor*, the Supreme Court revisited the question of limiting the defendant's right to compulsory process, this time as a sanction for defense violation of a state notice-and-hearing requirement. In *Michigan v. Lucas*,[86] a defendant charged with a sex crime that sought to introduce evidence of a prior sexual history between the defendant and the alleged victim was required to comply with a notice-and-hearing rule.[87] According to the state rape shield law, a defendant had ten days after arraignment to file a written motion and offer of proof.[88] The court could then order an in camera hearing to determine the admissibility of the proposed evidence.[89] However, the statute mentioned no sanction for failing to meet the deadline.[90] The defendant did not file his motion in time and instead asked the court at the start of the trial to admit the evidence.[91] The trial judge refused and Lucas was convicted on two counts of sexual assault.[92] The Michigan Court of Appeals reversed, ruling that the state's notice-and-comment requirement was an unconstitutional violation of the Compulsory Process Clause in *all* sex crimes prosecutions whenever the rule was used to preclude evidence of past sexual behavior between the defendant and alleged victim.[93]

A majority of the U.S. Supreme Court disagreed, with Justice O'Connor writing that "[t]he Sixth Amendment is not so rigid. The notice-and-hearing requirement serves legitimate state interests in protecting against surprise, harassment, and undue delay. Failure to comply with this requirement may in some cases justify even the severe sanction of preclusion."[94] In a decision reminiscent of the analysis from *Taylor*, the *Lucas* Court found that the sanction under the state notice-and-hearing rule did not constitute a per se violation of the defendant's Sixth Amendment right to compulsory process because probative evidence may be excluded when the criminal

---

85. *Taylor*, 484 U.S. at 419.
86. Michigan v. Lucas, 500 U.S. 145 (1991).
87. *Id.* at 149.
88. *Id.* at 151.
89. MICH. COMP. LAWS ANN. § 750.520j.
90. *Id.*
91. *Lucas*, 500 U.S. at 151.
92. *Id.* at 147–48.
93. *Id.* at 159.
94. *Id.* at 152–53.

defendant fails to comply with a valid discovery rule.[95] However, Justice O'Connor left open the possibility that the Court's decision might not apply to *all* discovery sanctions, because "restrictions on a criminal defendant's rights to confront adverse witnesses and to present evidence 'may not be arbitrary or disproportionate to the purposes they are designed to serve.'"[96]

2. Deportation of Defendant's Witnesses

An emerging issue of note, in light of the post-9/11 political landscape and the demand for increased immigration enforcement, is how government deportation of witnesses whose testimony might assist the defendant implicates the right to compulsory process.[97] In *United States v. Valenzuela-Bernal*,[98] the defendant, who was charged with transporting illegal aliens, protested the deportation of two witnesses who had been passengers in his car when he was arrested by border patrol officers.[99] The defendant argued that the deportation of the witnesses violated his right to compulsory process and his due process right under the Fourteenth Amendment. He did not, however, show the likely significance of their testimony.

The Supreme Court rejected the defendant's argument, reasoning that the burden falls to the defendant to make "some plausible explanation of the assistance that he would have received" from the witnesses.[100] The justices also recognized that the defendant's interest must be weighed against the government's responsibility to promptly deport illegal aliens.[101] Prosecutors can readily determine, prior to deportation, which alien witnesses "possess no evidence favorable to the defendant in a criminal prosecution."[102] Thus, the Court decided that the defense position could not prevail unless "there is a reasonable likelihood that the testimony could have affected the judgment of the trier of fact."[103]

95. *Id.* at 151 (quoting United States v. Nobles, 422 U.S. 225 (1975)).
96. *Id.* (quoting Rock v. Arkansas, 483 U.S. 44, 56 (1987)).
97. *See, e.g.*, United States v. Damra, 621 F.3d 474, 489–90 (6th Cir. 2010), *cert. denied*, 131 S. Ct. 2930 (2011) (defendant failed to prove that the deportation of his brother, a potential witness, violated his right to compulsory process).
98. United States v. Valenzuela-Bernal, 458 U.S. 858 (1982).
99. *Id.* at 861.
100. *Id.* at 884 (citing Roviaro v. United States, 353 U.S. 53, 63–64 (1957)).
101. *Id.* at 865.
102. *Id.*
103. *Id.*

One commentator has noted that "the primary rationale of *United States v. Valenzuela-Bernal* rests on the dubious proposition that the defendant can depend on the prosecution to determine the materiality of the evidence; and that the defendant bears the burden of proving, without any means of interviewing the witness, that the witness' testimony would have been material and favorable to the defense."[104]

3. Trial Court Discretion and Subpoena Powers

The trial court is within its discretionary powers to abide by its jurisdictional limits and to establish financial limits on its subpoena powers. For example, well before *Washington v. Texas*, the Supreme Court found no Fourteenth Amendment due process violation when a trial court did not compel an out-of-state, material witness to testify on behalf of the defendant.

> Nor can we see how a person is deprived of life or liberty without due process of law, on account of not having the benefit of the testimony of witnesses who are beyond the jurisdiction of the court, when the lawmaking power of the state is powerless to make any provision which would result in the compulsory attendance of the witnesses, and the use of depositions in such cases is directly contrary to the usages, customs, and principles of the common law.[105]

Along these lines, courts have held that the Sixth Amendment does not require that the government compel a foreign citizen to appear in court from abroad, even if the witness's testimony would be otherwise material and favorable to the defense.[106] However, when a subpoena is issued, federal courts require the government's good-faith effort in serving subpoenas on behalf of defendants, including conducting "intensive searches" to demonstrate a reasonable effort.[107] The trial court has the discretion to determine how many

---

104. *See* Garcia, *supra* note 51, at 635. In the wake of *Valenzuela-Bernal*, the Second, Sixth, Seventh, Ninth, and Tenth Circuits have construed the decision to require that defendants prove that the government acted in bad faith and deported the witnesses with the intent to suppress defense evidence. Buie v. Sullivan, 923 F.2d 10, 11–12 (2nd Cir. 1990); United States v. Damra, 621 F.3d 474, 489–90 (6th Cir. 2010); United States v. Chaparro-Alcantara, 226 F.3d 616, 624 (7th Cir. 2000); United States v. Dring, 930 F.3d 687, 693–94 (9th Cir. 1991); United States v. Iribe-Perez, 129 F.3d 1167, 1173 (10th Cir. 1997).

105. Minder v. Georgia, 183 U.S. 559, 562 (1902).

106. *See* United States v. Sensi, 879 F.2d 888, 898 (D.C. Cir. 1989); United States v. Zabeneh, 837 F.2d 1249, 1259–60 (5th Cir. 1988).

107. United States v. Salzmann, 417 F. Supp. 1139, 1167 (E.D.N.Y. 1976), *aff'd*, 548 F.2d 395 (2d Cir. 1976). *See also* People v. Beyea, 38 Cal. App. 3d 176, 191 (Cal. Ct. App. 1974)

witnesses will be called before the court at the government's expense. For example, in *Goldsby v. United States*, the Supreme Court found no error in a trial court allowing fifteen witnesses for the defendant to be summoned at government expense, while denying ten others.[108]

4. Federal Rule of Criminal Procedure 17

Federal Rule of Criminal Procedure 17 provides for court-issued subpoenas for witnesses for the defense and for the payment of witness fees for indigent defendants consistent with the defendant's right to compulsory process.[109] Judges, however, maintain "wide discretion" over whether to issue Rule 17 subpoenas.[110] Trial courts are tasked with screening out subpoenas that represent the type of "abuses often attempted by defendants," while upholding defendants' rights to compulsory process under the Sixth Amendment, their rights not to be disabled by indigence under the Fifth Amendment, and the additional rights set forth in Rule 17.[111] To secure a subpoena, defendants must make a showing that a proposed witness is "necessary" to the defense, that is, that the testimony would be "relevant, material, and useful to an adequate defense."[112]

5. Uniform Act to Secure Attendance of Witnesses from without the State in Criminal Proceedings

Given the near universal adoption among the states of the Uniform Act to Secure Attendance of Witnesses from without the State in Criminal Proceedings,[113] state courts will usually produce witnesses

---

(the government demonstrated a sufficient effort to locate a witness by visiting friends, relatives' residences, and work sites, and checking with public utilities, county welfare, law enforcement agencies, and labor union offices). *But see* State v. Pereda, 529 P.2d 695, 697 (Ariz. 1974) (the government's effort was insufficient when it relied on telephone calls only, without checking a known place of residence and a place of business, or public utility and telephone services).

108. Goldsby v. United States, 160 U.S. 70, 73 (1895). *See also* United States v. Chapman, 954 F.2d 1352, 1362 (7th Cir. 1992); Poole v. Lambert, 819 F.2d 1025, 1029 (11th Cir. 1987).

109. Fed. R. Crim. P. 17(b).

110. United States v. Butler, 988 F.2d 537, 540 (5th Cir. 1993); United States v. Moore, 917 F.2d 215, 230 (6th Cir. 1990).

111. *Moore*, 917 F.2d at 230.

112. *Id.*

113. Unif. Act to Secure Attendance of Witnesses, 11 U.L.A. 6 (2003) (the District of Columbia and all states except North Dakota have adopted this act).

for criminal trials in another state.[114] While a defendant's right to compulsory process is not necessarily violated when a state court is unable to produce witnesses from outside its jurisdiction,[115] the Supreme Court has held in the confrontation clause context that the prosecutorial authority must, when able, attempt to secure such witnesses.[116] However, if the jurisdiction in which a witness is located refuses the state's request for a subpoena, no Sixth Amendment violation has occurred.[117]

6. Application of Conflicting Privileges and Evidentiary Rules

A defendant's power to compel witness testimony is not absolute and most notably yields to the Fifth Amendment privilege against compulsory self-incrimination.[118] The privilege "protects against any disclosures which the witness reasonably believes could be used in a criminal prosecution or could lead to other evidence that might be so used."[119] However, *how* a trial judge warns a witness about the privilege against self-incrimination can implicate the Compulsory Process Clause, as discussed later.

An evidentiary rule can implicate the Compulsory Process Clause when its mechanical application sufficiently hinders the jury's determination of guilt.[120] In *Chambers v. Mississippi*, the hearsay rule, coupled with Mississippi's "voucher" rule,[121] precluded the defendant from cross-examining a man who had confessed to the murder Chambers was charged with after that man later repudiated his confession.[122] Chambers was also prevented, on hearsay grounds, from introducing the testimony of the three witnesses who heard the man's confession on three separate occasions.[123] As a result, the defense was

114. *See* Perry v. Norris, 879 F. Supp. 1503, 1509–10 (E.D. Ark. 1995), *aff'd*, 107 F.3d 665 (8th Cir. 1997) (interpreting Arkansas adoption of the Uniform Act).

115. State v. Wimbish, 995 P.2d 626, 629 (Wash. Ct. App. 2000).

116. *See* Barber v. Page, 390 U.S. 719 (1968) (Oklahoma violated defendant's confrontation right when it did not attempt to secure a subpoena from a Texas court for a material witness imprisoned in Texas.). This case is discussed in more detail in section III of Chapter 6.

117. *Id.* at 724 ("[T]he possibility of a refusal is not the equivalent of asking and receiving a rebuff.").

118. Kastigar v. United States, 406 U.S. 441, 444 (1972).

119. *Id.* at 444–45.

120. Chambers v. Mississippi, 410 U.S. 284, 302 (1974).

121. *Id.* at 295 (The "voucher" rule presumes that a party asserts the credibility of the witnesses it calls, thereby preventing that party from impeaching its own witnesses.).

122. *Id.*

123. *Id.* at 291–92.

hindered and became "far less persuasive than it might have been," given the limited opportunity to cross-examine the witness statement or introduce the confessions.[124] Citing other hearsay rule exceptions that allow introduction of evidence bearing trustworthiness and corroboration, the Court held that "the hearsay rule may not be applied mechanistically to defeat the ends of justice."[125]

Referring to the line of reasoning in the *Chambers* ruling, in *Rock v. Arkansas* the Supreme Court struck down a state evidentiary rule that "permits a witness to take the stand but arbitrarily excludes material portions' of the testimony."[126] *Rock* held that Arkansas's per se exclusion of posthypnosis testimony infringed on the defendant's constitutional right to testify.[127]

> A State's legitimate interest in barring unreliable evidence does not extend to *per se* exclusions that may be reliable in an individual case. Wholesale inadmissibility of a defendant's testimony is an arbitrary restriction on the right to testify in the absence of clear evidence by the State repudiating the validity of all posthypnosis recollections. The State would be well within its powers if it established guidelines to aid trial courts in the evaluation of posthypnosis testimony and it may be able to show that testimony in a particular case is so unreliable that exclusion is justified.[128]

E. Interference with the Right to Compulsory Process

1. Prosecutorial Conduct Cannot Thwart Efforts to Obtain Defense Witnesses

To demonstrate that government agents violated the Compulsory Process Clause by dissuading a witness from testifying for the defense, the defendant must show "some plausible nexus between the challenged governmental conduct and the absence of certain testimony."[129] A causal connection between the improper governmental conduct[130]

---

124. *Id.* at 294.

125. *Id.* at 301.

126. 483 U.S. 44, 55 (1987).

127. *Id.* at 61.

128. *Id.* Intertwined with the issues of compulsory process in the context of evidentiary rules is the jurisprudence surrounding the Confrontation Clause. Confrontation Clause doctrine is discussed at length in Chapter 6 of this book.

129. United States v. Hoffman, 832 F.2d 1299, 1303 (1st Cir. 1987).

130. Such as in *Webb v. Texas*, 409 U.S. 95 (1972) (per curiam), where the witness appeared at trial but declined to testify after hearing the trial judge's intimidating admonition.

and the absence of testimony that is both material and favorable to the accused is necessary to establish a Sixth Amendment violation.[131]

For example, the First Circuit has found that a prosecutor's "intemperate" phone call to counsel representing a witness's father did not violate the defendant's constitutional rights. There the prosecutor threatened to file perjury charges against the witness if she testified for the defense, but there was no evidence that the prosecutor's remarks were communicated to the daughter and the defense made no concerted effort to use her as a witness.[132] The defense had attempted to voluntarily interview the witness, but had not sought a subpoena to compel her to testify or sought a trial continuance to find her.[133] In contrast, the Third Circuit found that a prosecutor's repeated warnings and intimidating personal interviews persuaded a witness not to testify and thus violated defendant's right to due process. "The pressure brought to bear on her by the Assistant United States Attorney interfered with the voluntariness of her choice and infringed defendant's constitutional right to have her freely-given testimony."[134]

In addition to constitutional restrictions on the conduct of prosecutors that might inhibit a defendant's right to compulsory process, prosecutors are bound by federal and state law and the relevant ethical rules. For example, 18 U.S.C. § 1512 makes it a federal crime, punishable by a maximum of twenty years' imprisonment, to intimidate, threaten, or "corruptly persuade" a witness to withhold or delay testimony in a federal case. State law is similar.[135] Rule 3.4(a) of the Model Rules of Professional Conduct further restricts the behavior of prosecutors toward witnesses by prohibiting any lawyer from obstructing the ability of an opposing party to access evidence of potential value.[136]

2. Court's Obligation Not to Deter Witness

The defendant's right to obtain testimony from witnesses can also be infringed by a judicial admonition to a witness about the consequences

---

131. *Hoffman*, 832 F.2d at 1303.

132. *Id.*

133. *Id.* at 1305.

134. United States v. Morrison, 535 F.2d 223, 228 (3d Cir. 1976). This court also noted that the good faith of the prosecutor is not "relevant to an inquiry into whether a defendant was denied his constitutional right." *Id.* at 227.

135. *See, e.g.*, CAL. PENAL CODE § 137; IDAHO CODE § 18-2604; N.C. GEN. STAT. ANN. § 14-226; N.Y. PENAL LAW § 215.15.

136. MODEL RULES OF PROF'L CONDUCT R. 3.4 (2021).

of perjury that is so threatening and lengthy that it effectively "[drives] a witness off the stand."[137] The defense's sole witness in *Webb v. Texas* received an admonition that was markedly different from the other witness in the trial. It included the warning "[y]ou don't owe anybody anything to testify and it must be done freely and voluntarily and with the thorough understanding that you know the hazard you are taking."[138] The judge also repeatedly cautioned the defense witness about perjury and its consequences and said that if the witness lied under oath, the court would "personally see that your case goes to the grand jury and you will be indicted."[139] After hearing these comments from the bench, the witness refused to testify and was excused by the judge.[140] The Supreme Court found that the judge had "gratuitously singled out" the defendant's lone witness with his "lengthy admonition" about the dangers of perjury.[141] The judge implied not only that he "expected" the witness to lie but also that he would ensure that the witness was convicted of perjury and served additional prison time.[142] "The unnecessarily strong terms used by the judge could well have exerted such duress on the witness' mind as to preclude him from making a free and voluntary choice whether or not to testify."[143] The Supreme Court summarily reversed Webb's conviction even though, according to the dissent, the weight of the evidence was strong.[144] Most courts, however, have applied a harmless error analysis to compulsory process violations.[145]

United States v. Arthur[146] provides another example of a judge who improperly deterred a defense witness. In this case, the district court erred when it "induced a material witness to exercise his Fifth Amendment right to remain silent and . . . excluded material, exculpatory evidence."[147] While the district court's colloquy to the witness did not

137. Webb v. Texas, 409 U.S. 95, 98 (1972) (per curiam).

138. *Id.* at 96.

139. *Id.*

140. *Id.*

141. *Id.* at 97.

142. *Id.*

143. *Id.* at 98.

144. *Id.* at 98–99.

145. State v. Herbert, 767 S.E.2d 471, 483 (W. Va.) (*citing* Sixth Amendment at Trial, 40 Geo. L.J. Ann. Rev. Crim. Proc. 663, 691 (2011)). Absent a definitive Supreme Court pronouncement, there remains some question on the subject, especially in the area of intimidation of witnesses. *See* Goldblatt, *Disentangling Webb: Governmental Intimidation of Defense Witnesses and Harmless Error Analysis*, 59 U. Chi. L. Rev. 1239, 1251 (1992).

146. United States v. Arthur, 949 F.2d 211 (6th Cir. 1991).

147. *Id.* at 213.

rise to the threatening level of the court in *Webb*, here the judge strongly encouraged the witness to assert his Fifth Amendment privilege.[148]

In contrast, even strong and specific language from the judge may be distinguishable from the improper admonition in *Webb*, if the judge emphasizes the fact that the witness could testify "*if she wished*" and refrains from exerting duress on the witness.[149] One court has held that an admonition to an "uncounseled witness" of her privilege against self-incrimination and "provid[ing] the witness with counsel with whom she conferred privately before making her decision whether to testify" did not raise constitutional concerns.[150]

3. Limitation on Privilege and Confidential Informants

A government informant's identity and testimony are not absolutely privileged at trial, especially when the informant played a prominent role in the criminal event.[151] For over half a century, the Supreme Court has utilized a balancing test between the public interest in affording informants protection from disclosure and the individual's right to prepare a defense.[152] Relevant factors include, but are not limited to "the crime charged, the possible defenses, [and] the possible significance of the informer's testimony. . . ."[153] In *Roviaro v. United States*, the opportunity to cross-examine the law enforcement officers overseeing the sting was not an adequate substitute for cross-examining the informant who had facilitated the deal.[154]

> Where the disclosure of an informer's identity, or of the contents of his communication, is relevant and helpful to the defense of an accused, or is essential to a fair determination of a cause, the

---

148. *Id.* at 216. The judge stated, "I think it's not to your best interest to testify because anything you say may be held against you in another prosecution against you for bank robbery, could and would be used against you. Knowing that, do you still want to testify or do you want to not testify?" *Id.* at 214.

149. United States v. Santiago-Becerril, 130 F.3d 11, 23–26 (1st Cir. 1997).

150. *Id.* at 25. Federal law requires that anyone "in custody as a material witness" and financially unable to maintain legal representation shall be provided counsel. 18 U.S.C. § 3006A(a)(1)(G).

151. Roviaro v. United States, 353 U.S. 53, 63–65 (1957).

152. *Id.* at 62.

153. *Id.*

154. *Id.* at 64 ("The desirability of calling John Doe as a witness, or at least interviewing him in preparation for trial, was a matter for the accused rather than the Government to decide.").

privilege must give way. In these situations the trial court may require disclosure and, if the Government withholds the information, dismiss the action.[155]

4. Whether Courts May Compel the Application of Use Immunity to Further the Right of Compulsory Process

Despite differing outcomes in the lower courts, the Supreme Court has not yet ruled on whether the prosecution must grant immunity to material defense witnesses claiming a Fifth Amendment privilege.[156] The Court has had several opportunities to settle this issue and has denied certiorari in every case, despite multiple dissents by Justice Thurgood Marshall during his time on the bench.[157] Generally, lower courts have found no constitutional requirement for forced immunity so long as there is no prosecutorial misconduct.[158] The Ninth Circuit has held that the trial court's failure to compel the government to grant use immunity does not violate the defendant's right to a fair trial where the defendant has not shown a "direct contradiction" between the testimony the non-immunized witness would offer and that of the government's immunized witness.[159]

---

155. *Id.* at 60–61. *But see* United States v. Tarango, 760 F. Supp. 2d 1163 (D.N.M. 2009) (denying the defendant's request for pretrial discovery of confidential witnesses because the government was still determining the value of the testimony and whether it would use it). "In this case, Tarango will learn the identities of these witnesses and will have the chance to question them. If the United States decides not to call one of its confidential witnesses, and Tarango has a good-faith basis for suggesting that this witness not called has exculpatory evidence, Tarango can ask the Court to revisit this issue." *Id.* at 1169.

156. *See* Justice Marshall's dissent from denial of certiorari in Autry v. McKaskle, 727 F.2d 358 (5th Cir. 1984), *cert. denied*, 465 U.S. 1085, 1087 (1984).

157. *See* Ebbers v. United States, 458 F.3d 110 (2nd Cir. 2006), *cert. denied*, 549 U.S. 1274 (2007); Hunter v. California, 782 P.2d 608 (Cal.), *cert. denied*, 498 U.S. 887 (1990) (Justice Marshall dissenting).

158. *See* United States v. Thevis, 665 F.2d 616, 640 (5th Cir. 1982) (immunity decisions require a "balancing of public interests" and are better "left to the executive branch"); United States v. Turkish, 623 F.2d 769 (2d Cir. 1980), *cert. denied*, 449 U.S. 1077 (1981). *See also* United States v. Robaina, 39 F.3d 858, 862 (8th Cir. 1994) (upholding district court's decision that it did not have the authority to grant a defense witness immunity after the prosecutor declined to offer immunity); United States v. Heffington, 682 F.2d 1075, 1081 (5th Cir. 1982), *cert. denied*, 459 U.S. 1108 (1983); United States v. Fricke, 684 F.2d 1126, 1130 (5th Cir. 1982), *cert. denied*, 460 U.S. 1011 (1983).

159. United States v. Wilkes, 744 F.3d 1101, 1109 (9th Cir. 2014). This opinion further notes that the government's offer of a favorable plea deal to its witness may also compel the grant of use immunity to a defendant's witness. *Id.* at 1105 n.1.

5. Jury Instructions

As noted previously, the trial judge cannot give the jury an instruction that requires the testimony of an accomplice witness for the defendant to be "true beyond a reasonable doubt," because this reduces the burden of proof for the government and effectively requires the defendant to establish innocence beyond a reasonable doubt.[160] This type of instruction has been found to place an improper burden on the defense by allowing the jury "to convict despite its failure to find guilt beyond a reasonable doubt."[161]

However, judges must tread carefully here because it may be reversible error *not* to instruct the jury to weigh accomplice testimony with care and caution.[162] Examples of proper accomplice instructions may be found in model or pattern federal and state jury instruction books. The instruction in the Eleventh Circuit Pattern Jury Instructions is typical:

> You must consider some witnesses' testimony with more caution than others.
>
> For example, paid informants, witnesses who have been promised immunity from prosecution, or witnesses who hope to gain more favorable treatment in their own cases, may have a reason to make a false statement in order to strike a good bargain with the Government.
>
> So while a witness of this kind may be entirely truthful when testifying, you should consider that testimony with more caution than the testimony of other witnesses.[163]

Whether an accomplice instruction should be given often depends on which side calls the witness.[164] The federal circuit or state law must be examined prior to presenting the accomplice as a witness.[165]

---

160. Cool v. United States, 409 U.S. 100, 102 (1972).

161. *Id.* at 102–03.

162. United States v. Solomon, 856 F.2d 1572, 1578–79 (11th Cir. 1988), *cert. denied*, 489 U.S. 1070 (1989) (a cautionary accomplice instruction should usually be given); United States v. Bernard, 625 F.2d 854, 857–58 (9th Cir. 1980) (failure to give accomplice instruction is reversible error when the testimony is important and when other information indicates the testimony may be unreliable).

163. 11TH CIR. CRIM. JURY SPEC. INSTR. 1.1 (2010).

164. Fishman, *Defense Witness as "Accomplice": Should the Trial Judge Give a "Care and Caution" Instruction?*, 96 J. CRIM. L. & CRIMINOLOGY 1, 2 (2005).

165. *Id.* at 3–8.

TABLE OF CASES

INDEX